Jerusalem and the
Holy Land

Jerusalem and the Holy Land

A Phaidon Cultural Guide

with over 285 colour illustrations
and 9 pages of maps

Phaidon

Editor: Dr Marianne Mehling

Contributors: Franz N. Mehling, Maria Paukert M.A., Bernhard Pollmann, Michael Studemund

Photographs: A. A. M. van der Heyden, Norbert Dallinger, Franz N. Mehling

Maps: Herbert Winkler, Munich

Town-plan: Huber Kartographie, Munich

Ground-plans: Hans-Jürgen Schäfer, Mücke

Phaidon Press Limited, Littlegate House, St Ebbe's Street, Oxford OX1 1SQ

First published in English 1987
Originally published as *Knaurs Kulturführer in Farbe: Heiliges Land*
© Droemersche Verlagsanstalt Th. Knaur Nachf. Munich 1986
Translation © Phaidon Press Limited 1987

British Library Cataloguing in Publication Data

Jerusalem and the Holy Land.—(A Phaidon
   cultural guide)
   1. Jerusalem (Holy Land)—Description and travel—
   Guide-books
   I. Knaurs Kulturführer in Farbe, Heiliges
   Land. *English*
   915.694'0454   DS103

   ISBN 0-7148-2445-3

Translated and edited by Babel Translations, London
Typeset by Hourds Typographica, Stafford
Printed in West Germany by Druckerei Appl, Wemding

Cover illustration: Jerusalem, Church of the Holy Sepulchre at sunrise (photo: © Sonia Halliday Photographs)

Preface

The country of the Bible is largely coextensive with the area of the modern State of Israel (Medinat Yisrael), which was proclaimed on 14 May 1948. Israel borders in the south on Egypt, in the north on Syria and Lebanon, and in the east on the kingdom of Jordan. The country has a length of 420 km. and a width of between 20 and 116 km., and covers an area of 20,700 sq.km., not counting the occupied territories, i.e. the West Bank of the river Jordan (5,572 sq.km.), the Golan Heights (1,176 sq.km.) and the Gaza Strip (202 sq.km.).

The borders of the Holy Land have often been changed over the centuries, but it has always been quite small: bounded by the Mediterranean in the west, by the desert (Negev, Arava) in the south and east, and by mountain chains in the north. A land of transitions, it has served as a bridge between Asia and Africa, and as a link between the Mediterranean and the Red Sea. Above all, it is a focus of the great monotheistic world religions of Islam, Christianity and Judaism. It has also been fought over by most world powers.

Pharaohs, Ptolemies, Egyptians and Frenchmen passed through Palestine from the south-west, Hittites, Aramaeans, Assyrians, Babylonians, Arabs, Crusaders and Turks came from the north. They occupied the country, but political geography was stronger than the political power of the occupiers. More tears have been shed, more prayers have been said, and more blood has been spilt for this country than for any other country in the world. This is the Holy Land, the source of Jewish and Christian culture, and the goal of both peaceable pilgrims and of warlike armies. The ethnic, religious and linguistic variety of the State of Israel is as inexhaustible as the list of its occupiers. Jews from over a hundred countries now live within this confined territory: Ashkenazim from Central and Eastern Europe, Sephardim from North Africa, Turkey and the Balkans, black Jews from Harlem and Ethiopia, and Jews from the Indian State of Kerala. Christians from some forty different churches live here, and so do Muslims, most of them Sunni, from several Middle Eastern countries. The national language is Hebrew, but English is widely understood, and Arabic, Yiddish, Russian, Polish, Romanian, French and German are also spoken.

The Jews live mainly within the pre-1967 borders, while the non-Jewish inhabitants live in Upper and Lower Galilee, in settlements along the former cease-fire line with Jordan, and in East Jerusalem. The Druze, a distinctive group among the Arabic-speaking population, differ from Muslims both ethnically and in their religion. Their sanctuary is in Galilee, where the tomb of Nabi Shu'eib is situated not far from Tiberias. The holy places of the Christians are in Jerusalem, Bethlehem and Nazareth and on the shores of the Sea of Galilee. The Arabs venerate Mohammed in Jerusalem and Abraham in Hebron. The fourth religion in the Holy Land is recent in origin, having been founded a mere hundred years ago: the creed of the Bahai, whose international centre is in Haifa.

The inhabitants of Israel, Jews, Christians and Arabs, live in a young State, which is the fruit of European intolerance, Nazi extermination policies, and fervent expectation of the Messiah. In this modern State, formed and run on Western lines, prayers are said in several languages, life is arranged according to different calendars, and irreconcilable claims militate against peaceful coexistence. Indeed, what was said by the Psalmist in exhortation and prayer may now be fittingly said of the whole of Israel:

'Pray for the peace of Jerusalem: they shall prosper that love thee.
Peace be within thy walls, and prosperity within thy palaces!'

As with other guides in the series, the text is arranged in alphabetical order of place name for easy reference. The link between places which are geographically close but separated in the text because of the alphabetical arrangement is provided by the maps on pages 318–24. They show all the principal towns described in the text and also, in the same colour, those subsidiary places mentioned in the environs section at the end of each entry.

The heading to each entry gives the name of the town and, below, its geographical region and a reference to the map section, giving page number and grid reference. Within each entry the main sights are printed in bold type: less significant objects of interest appear under the heading **Also worth seeing** and places in the vicinity under **Environs.** At the end of the book is an index of places mentioned in the text, a glossary of technical terms, and a glossary of Hebrew and Arabic terms.

Abu Ghosh
District of Jerusalem/Israel   p.320☐D 7

The Arab village of Abu Ghosh—
which in the Old Testament was *Kir-jat-Jearim*, the town of the Ark of the Covenant, and which the Crusaders identified with the New Testament Emmaus—lies some 10 km. W. of Jerusalem, to the N. of the Jerusalem-Tel Aviv road. Its outstanding building is a Crusader church, which is

among the best-preserved in the Holy Land.

The village takes its present name from the Sheikh Abu Ghosh who emigrated here from Hejaz and who was entrusted by the Ottomans with the task of making safe this section of the pilgrims' road running from the sea to Jerusalem. The original name was Qaryat el-Enab (Biblical: Kirjat-Jearim).

Crusader church: A reservoir was built at the spring under the Romans, probably in the 2C AD. A stone beside the portal in the N. wall of the church bears the inscription 'Vexillatio Leg(ionis) X Fre(tensis)'. The Roman Tenth Legion 'Fretensis' was stationed here in the 1/2C.

When the Crusaders captured the town in 1099, they found an Arab caravanserai and they identified it as the town of Emmaus, where Jesus ate supper with some of his disciples after the Resurrection (St.Luke 24, 28 ff.). After 1141, when the Order of Knights Hospitallers had taken possession of the land, the Romanesque church was built over the crypt

Abu Ghosh, Crusader church

which stands above the spring. Along with St.Anne's in Jerusalem, this church is among the best-preserved Crusader churches in the Holy Land. It has a nave, two aisles, and square-ended apses. The church is 65 ft. long and 50 ft. wide, and its walls are from just under 10 to nearly 13 ft. thick. The crypt above the spring is also from the time of the Crusaders, but its outer walls are Roman.

Church of Notre-Dame de l'Arche d'Alliance: In the Old Testament, Kirjat-Jearim ('village of the wood') is a town assigned to the tribe of Judah and situated on the borders with the tribe of Benjamin. It was here, on neutral ground as it were, that the Ark of the Covenant stood for twenty years in 'the house of Abinadab in the hill' (1 Samuel 7, 1), before King David brought it to Jerusalem, the new capital of the kingdom. Today the modern church of Notre-Dame de l'Arche d'Alliance ('Our Lady of the Ark of the Covenant') stands on this site. It was built on the ruins of a 5C church, parts of whose mosaic pavement still survive.

Afula
Northern District/Israel   p.318☐E 4

10 km. S. of Nazareth, this growing town was founded in 1925 and is now the hub of the Yizre'el plain (Emeq Yizre'el).
A small fortress, within whose walls *Roman sarcophagi* were worked on, stands in a small park SW of the central railway station.

Environs: Barqai ('Star of the Orient'; 29 km. SW): A kibbutz (500 inhabitants) founded by the HaShomer-HaZa'ir movement in 1947. There is a *regional archaeological museum.*
En Harod (13 km. SE): Name of two adjoining kibbutzim in the Yizre'el valley. The first was founded by Joseph Trumpeldor's Labour Legion at the foot of Har Gilboa in 1921. The Me'uhad 'En Harod kibbutz has stood on the Quimi ridge since 1927. The second kibbutz, 'En Harod (Ihud), broke away from the first in 1953. These kibbutzim maintain two museums and two study centres.

Abu Ghosh, stone seal of a Roman legion

Hayyim Atar Mishkan Le Omanut (Museum for Jewish Art): founded in 1938 by Hayyim Atar (1902–53), a painter and kibbutz member. The museum was built by S.Bikkels. It has over 1,000 paintings, giving a representative survey of Jewish art in the diaspora (works by J.Israëls, M.Liebermann, M.Gottlieb; the Parisian school, represented by J.Pascin, Mané-Katz; contemporary Israeli artists); a collection of works by artists who fell victim to the Nazis; American Realists; over 300 sculptures and more than 8,000 drawings. The library has over 3,000 books. The *Bet Sturman Museum* was founded in 1941 in memory of Hayyim Sturman (1891–1938), the leader of the Haganah, who was among the first settlers in the Yizre'el plain. The museum is by D.Laskov and a Roman milestone stands at its entrance. This museum documents the history of the Bet Shean valley, including excavation finds from nearby: clay vessels and statuettes; exhibits connected with the valley's natural and economic history; Haganah museum and a zoological collection.

Giv'at HaMore (E.): There are *rock tombs* at the N. base of the volcanic Jebel Dahi (1,690 ft.).

HaZorea (22 km. NW): A kibbutz with 850 inhabitants, founded by German Jews in 1936. *Bet Wilfried Israel* (Wilfried Israel Museum of Far Eastern art): This museum is named after Wilfried Israel (1899–1943), who came from Berlin, and houses his art collection: ancient works of art from the Mediterranean area (Egyptian statuettes and reliefs, Greek Tanagra figures, Roman statuettes); ancient Persian ceramics; head of Buddha from the Khmer period; Chinese scroll pictures. Permanent exhibition of 4,000 years of metal work. Palestinian, Egyptian, Persian and Islamic antiques.

Merhavya (2.5 km. E.): The remains of the *Templars' castle of La Fève* (Faba/Castrum Fabai) are in a small park SW of the central bus station, on the site of the medieval Arab village of al-Fula. The castle was captured and plundered after the battle of Hattim. The square Castrum, with its corner towers, could still be seen in the 19C. There are a few architectural remains

Aqua Bella (Abu Ghosh), ruins of a Crusader building

(Roman sarcophagi) in the territory of the Moshav Merhavya, which was founded in 1922.

Mishmar HaEmeq (17 km. W.): A kibbutz with 870 inhabitants, founded in 1926 by the Polish HaShomer-HaZai'r group. There are *archaeological finds* (buildings and an olive press from the Roman-Byzantine period) within the area of the kibbutz. A *monument* by Zeev Ben Zvi (1904–52), standing beside a path on the hill-ridge, commemorates the victims of the concentration camps.

Nein/Na'im (8 km. NE): This Arab village at the foot of Giv'at HaMore was called Naïm at the time of the second temple. According to Christian tradition, it was here that Jesus raised a young man from the dead (St.Luke 7, 11–17). There was a Jewish community in Nein in the 18C. The Franciscans built a *church* (consecrated 1881) on the foundations of a 12C Crusader church, which the Muslims later converted into a mosque. In the E. apse of this rectangular building (52 × 35 ft.), above the altar with its ciborium, there is a painting by the Spanish artist F.Torrescasana

from Barcelona. The town's entrance gate is depicted in the background of this beautifully framed 19C painting (11 × 7 ft.), and further back still is the town itself. *Graveyard* (W. of the town): *Rock tombs* cut into the mountainside. The sarcophagi were later used as drinking troughs. A sarcophagus (7 ft. 7 in. × 3 ft. × 2 ft. 7 in.) without a lid stands on the S. side of a chapel.

Akko/Acre

Northern District/Israel   p.318☐D 3

Acre, a North Palestinian port on the Mediterranean at the northern end of the bay of Haifa, was founded by the Phoenicians. It was assigned to the tribe of Asher, but the Israelites were unable to conquer it (Judges 1, 31). In the main, it was subject to Tyre or Egypt until it was conquered by the Assyrians in *c*. 700 BC. It was known as *Ptolemais* in the Hellenistic period. Jonathan the Maccabean was murdered here by the Seleucids in 143 BC. Ptolemais is mentioned in the Acts of

Afula, fortress, wall with parts of Roman sarcophagi

the Apostles (21, 7) as being the seat of a small Christian community visited by the Apostle Paul.

In the Byzantine period, Acre was a bishop's seat and the archdiocese of Tyre but it fell to the Arabs in 636. An earthquake caused severe damage in 1067. The Crusaders, led by Baldwin I, captured the town in 1104 with the aid of Genoese ships. In 1187 it fell to Sultan Saladin, but it was retaken by Richard the Lionheart in 1191. From 1191 to 1291 it was the capital of the diminished kingdom of Jerusalem, and was under the king's direct rule. It was conquered in 1291 after being besieged for two months by al-Malik al-Ashraf, and was then completely destroyed.

Acre became an important centre of Jewish learning in the 13C. 300 rabbis (including Jacob ha-Katan from Lunel and Samson ben Abraham from Sens) came here from France and England in 1211. In 1260, ben Jehiel ben Joseph from Paris, assisted by 300 pupils, built the yeshiva called 'Midrash ha-Gadol'. The town was deserted for the next few centuries. The Druze Emir Fakhr ed-Din rebuilt it in the early 17C. It was the capital of the vilayet of Sidon in the 18C, when the Albanian el-Jazzar enlarged the town in splendid style (outer fortifying wall, Grand Mosque, Khan el-Umdan, Hammam el-Basha etc.). Napoleon carried out an unsuccessful siege of Acre in 1799. It was under the British mandate from 1918 to 1948, and was occupied by Israeli troops on 17 May 1948. A modern growing town was built outside the walls after 1948.

Crusader town (opposite the Grand Mosque, below the citadel): The former headquarters and administrative centre of the order of St.John of Jerusalem is in the trapezoidal Frankish town of Acre (the town wall is 1,600 ft. long to the E. and 2,600 ft. long to the N.), which in the 13C was protected to the E. by a defensive line 100 ft. further forward and reinforced by towers standing 160 ft. apart. A few vaults (crypt of St.John) and a tower from the town fortifications (Burj es-Sultan) are all that survive of the Crusaders' 38 churches, monasteries and numerous palaces. The

Nein (Afula), church, Resurrection scene (left), Acre, Crusader tomb (right)

headquarters of the Knights of St.John consisted of two great halls (with later Turkish additions), seven knights' halls (one hall for each of the order's languages: Provençal, Auvergne, Italian, Spanish, English, German and French).

St.John's crypt: Three massive round pillars, some 10 ft. thick, support the early Gothic vault with pointed arches and divide the large hall to form two aisles 40 ft. in height, with four bays. Rib vaults and transverse pointed arches spring from the slab above the capital. Once there were three doors on the S. side, leading to the outside; three fireplaces are still to be seen on the E. wall. Two reliefs of lilies on consoles to the NE and SE commemorate the visit paid by the French King Louis VII in 1148.

El-Jazzar mosque (beside the citadel): In 1781/2, Ahmed el-Jazzar the Albanian, a former slave and captain of the Albanian soldiers, built the largest of the four mosques of Acre in the Turkish rococo style, with a tall and slender minaret, on the site of the Frankish cathedral of the Holy Cross.

The *portico of the mosque* is built of pink granite and porphyry decorated with painted tiles. It leads into an enormous prayer hall whose walls are decorated with painted tiles, inlaid marble and arabesques, the tiles and inlay work being in brown and blue. The mihrab is in the middle of the wall opposite the portico and there are Italian marble columns taken from the ruins of Caesarea. The large Frankish vaulted halls have been converted into cisterns and are now underneath the floors, which are covered with Persian carpets. A damascened shrine containing the hairs of the Prophet's beard stands in the prayer hall. The hairs are displayed on the 27th day of Ramadan. The loggias on both sides of the hall are reserved for women.

Church of St.Andrew: This Greek Catholic church of St.Andrew was built on the foundations of the former Templars' church of St.Anne. In the 13C, the Sultan ordered the portico of the Templars' church to be pulled down and rebuilt outside a mosque in Cairo. The church of St.Anne was

Acre, Crusader knights' hall

Acre, El-Jazzar mosque

regarded as the finest Gothic building in the East. There is a carved head of John the Baptist on the N. wall of the forecourt opposite the church, by a staircase.

Khan el-Umdan: Most of the granite and porphyry columns in the arcadedm courtyard were transported here from the ruins of Caesarea in 1785 by order of Ahmed el-Jazzar in order to build the 'caravanserai of columns'. The former monastery courtyard is now the broad courtyard of the caravenserai. and has double arcades. The courtyard is entered through an arched gateway crowned by a five-storeyed clock tower, which is named after Sultan Abdul Hamid II (1876–1918) and was built in 1906.

Israeli Heroes' Museum (citadel): Baha Ullah the Persian, the founder of the Bahai religion, was imprisoned in this building from 1868–92. From 1920 onwards it was used by the British as a prison for the fighters of the Jewish national movement.

Town museum (Hammam el-Basha): This is housed in a Turkish building which was commissioned by el-Jazzar in *c.* 1780 and modelled on the central bath in Cairo (marble columns from Caesarea and Tyre). Since 1954, finds from the Canaanite period have been displayed here in what were the small bathing cubicles. There also also collections devoted to regional archaeology, Druze folklore, Arab ethnology, and archaeological finds.

Also worth seeing: *Greek Orthodox church of St.George* on medieval foundations. A plaque commemorates Major Oldfield, who fell during Napoleon's siege of Acre. *Sea walls:* The W. and S. of the town are protected by immense sea walls built on Frankish foundations. The *Burj Kurajim* ('tower of the vine') is to the N., and the *Burj es-Sanjak* stands to the S.

Environs: Lohame HaGeta'ot (3 km. N.): The 'Fighters of the Ghettos' kibbutz was founded by concentration camp survivors on 19 April 1949, six years after the uprising in the Warsaw ghetto. The multi-storey

Acre, El-Jazzar mosque

museum (1959) by S.Bickels displays texts and pictures showing life in the mass extermination camps and ghettos, as well as Jewish resistance in Poland and the Soviet Union. Ground floor: History of Vilna (Lithuania) and its Jewish community from 1551 to 1940; documentation of the late-19C Zionist socialist movement in Vilna; small wooden statues. First floor: anti-Semitism under Hitler; pictures of the Theresienstadt camp and the Warsaw uprising; a plan of Anne Frank's house in Amsterdam. Basement: plan of Treblinka; photographs from the life of Janusz Korczak; over 2,000 drawings and paintings by prisoners. Part of a Turkish aqueduct is to be seen in the kibbutz.

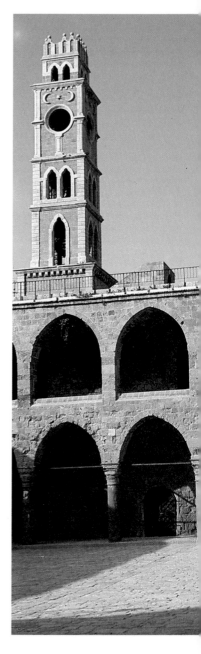

Arad

Southern District/Israel   p.322☐D 10

Arad is situated in an area without any ground water in the NE Negev more or less on the watershed between the Mediterranean and the Dead Sea, being some 15 km. from the W. shore of the latter. Arad has been under construction since 1962, and was planned as a workers' and industrial town of 50,000 inhabitants. Some sources suggested that the Biblical Arad was in Tel Arad, 10 km. to the W. of this new development. Excavations carried out since 1962 have shown that the area was populated continuously from about 3500 BC onwards. It was the main town of the eastern Negev during the Canaanite and Israelite periods and it is regarded as the best example of an early Bronze Age town in the Holy Land. However, owing to the absence of a water source in Tel Arad, the Biblical Arad is now thought to have been 12 km. further to the SW, in Tel Malhata; the so-called Shishak list

Acre, Khan el-Umdan ▷

records two Arads: Greater Arad and an Arad of Bet Jerachem.

Canaanite town: Arad was the seat of a Canaanite king in the NE of the Negev before the Israelites conquered the territory (Numbers 21, 1 and 33, 40). The Israelites conquered the town and called it *Hormah* (21, 3), which means 'they enforced the proscription'. This was intended to indicate the religious character of this conquest. In the list of kings defeated by Israel, Joshua (12, 14) mentions a king of Hormah and a king of Arad.

The town was at its zenith in *c*, 1900 BC, when the fortifying wall was built. This wall, 7 ft. 6 in. thick, encloses the valley in a horseshoe shape. The public buildings were on the lower part of the hill, the private buildings on the upper. The individual blocks of houses were separated by streets and squares. The windowless dwelling houses are in general all built on the same principle: in the middle of the living room there is a wooden support on which the roof rests; a stone bench runs around the four walls of the living room; there are also a kitchen and a courtyard.

Israelite citadel: The citadel with an Israelite shrine was built in the highest part of the town after the 11C BC. The tripartite structure of this temple corresponds to the Temple of Jerusalem (cf. the description of the Temple of Solomon in Jerusalem). Egyptian ceramics which have been discovered indicate that there were trade links between Egypt and Arad, the S. outpost of Israel. King Shishak I of Egypt conquered Arad in *c*. 920 BC, and the town was destroyed by Sanherib of Assur in 701 BC.

Arraba

Northern District/Israel   p.318□E 3

This town in Lower Galilee lies 27 km. E of Acre. Johanan ben Zakkai,

Acre, El-Jazzar mosque, entrance

Hanina ben Dosa and the Petahija priest family all taught in the town known in the Talmud as 'Arav. According to Jewish tradition, the tomb of Rabbi Hanina ben Dosa was revered in Arraba. *Archaeological finds:* Tombs from the 2&3C AD; columns and cisterns; walls of a 1C church. *Hanina ben Dosa:* A restored and fenced-in shrine on the W. side of the hill. There are kokhim (sliding tombs) in the E. wall, with large stones in front of them. A barred iron door on the first floor.

Environs: Deir Hanna (5 km. NE): The Druze Prince Fakhr ed-Din settled in Deir Hanna in the 17C. 100 years later, in 1720, the Beduin Daher el-'Amr built a fortress here, and a small Arab settlement developed around its ruins in the 19C. *Fortification:* Inside the complex there is a small mosque with a mihrab and

lectern. The floor is laid with carpets.
Kaukab (15 km. W.): 7 km. N. of
Ma'agar Netofa. A small Arab village
(1,350 inhabitants) containing the
17C tomb of Sheikh el-Hija lies at the
foot of Har Azmon on the site of the
Jewish Kokhava (?).
Sakhnin/Sihnin (4 km. W.): An
Arab village built on the ruins of the
Jewish town of Sihni or the Roman-
Byzantine Sihnin. It was here, in the
Middle Ages, that the Jews revered
the tomb of Rabbi Joshua of Sihnin
(known to the Arabs as Nabi es-Sid-
diq). Remains of a Roman mausoleum, and Byzantine tombs.
Mausoleum (Maqam es-Saddik):
Inside the almost square shrine (25 ft.
5 in. x 25 ft. 10 in.) there is a fine sarcophagus decorated with Amazon
shields on both sides. Numerous
architectural fragments in the more
recent village houses.

Ashqelon
Southern District/Israel   p.320□B 8

The new town of Ashqelon, the well-
known Mediterranean resort, was
founded in 1948 and lies 50 km. SSW
of Tel-Aviv. The ancient *Askalon* (in
the Bible: Askelon), one of the five
main towns of the Philistines, is 3 km.
to the SW (now a national park).
Askalon was the birthplace of King
Herod the Great, and was a centre of
Greek culture in the Roman-Byzantine period.

History: In *c.* 1200 BC, the so-called
Sea Peoples invaded Syria, Palestine
and Egypt from the Aegean Sea and
the coasts of Asia Minor, and destroyed the Hittite Empire. The origin
of the Sea Peoples is uncertain. Egyptian sources describe them as peoples
coming from the sea or from islands in
the sea. A large group of these Sea
Peoples moved from Northern Syria
through Palestine and was defeated by
the Egyptian king Ramses III. This
group included the Philistines, who
founded the alliance of city states
called Philistia on the coast of Palestine. Askalon, which is documented in
the Egyptian ostracizing texts of the
12th dynasty and in the Amarna
letters (*c.* 1360 BC), became one of the

Arad, Israelite shrine with incense tables

main cities of this alliance of city states.

From the time of their first territorial conquest onwards, the Israelites tried in vain to vanquish Askalon: 'But Judah did not take Gaza with the coast thereof, and Askelon with the coast thereof, and Ekron with the coast thereof. And the Lord was with Judah; and he drave out the inhabitants of the mountain; but could not drive out the inhabitants of the valley, because they had chariots of iron' (Judges 1, 18–19).

Askalon was the main cultic site of Atargatis (Dea Syria), the goddess of fertility and maternity who was worshipped here under the name of Derketo. Herodotus, the Greek historian, describes the shrine of Derketo in Askalon as the oldest shrine of Derketo anywhere: 'Only a few (Scythian soldiers) remained in Askalon and plundered the temple of Aphrodite Urania. I have heard that this is the oldest of all the temples to the goddess. The Cypriots themselves say that the temple in Cyprus was founded from Askalon...The goddess now sent a female disorder to the Scythians who plundered the shrine in Askalon, and also to all their descendants' ('Histories' 1,105).

Askalon came under Assyrian rule in 711 BC, was Tyrian in the Persian period, came under the domination of the Ptolemies in the 3C BC, and was ruled by the Seleucids from the time of Antiochus III onwards. It seems to have paid homage to the Maccabees for diplomatic reasons: 'Then Jonathan left there and encamped opposite Askalon, whose citizens came out to meet him with great ceremony. Jonathan then returned to Jerusalem with his followers, laden with booty.' (1 Maccabees 10, 86–87).

In 104 BC, Askalon became an independent city state with its own calendar, but soon turned into a Roman protectorate and, in the 4–6C AD, was a trading town and artistic centre in the Roman Empire.

The Arabs conquered the town in 638. It was fortified under the Fatimids in the 10C, taken by the Crusaders in 1153 and given further fortifications, but continued to be vio-

Ashqelon, national park, victory goddess Nike (left), goddess Isis with Horus (right)

18 Atlit

lently fought over by Muslims and Christians before finally being destroyed by the Mameluke Sultan Baibars in 1270.

National park: Today the ancient town of Askalon is a national park. Most of the ruins date from the Roman period, when King Herod the Great presented the town with liberal donations of 'baths, splendid fountains and square courtyards which are surrounded by colonnaded passages and are notable for their size and artistry' (Josephus Flavius, on the Jewish War). It is possible to go round the whole town by walking along the semicircle of walls (7 ft. thick and 33 ft. high) which surrounds the Roman and medieval town.

Roman burial chamber: A Roman tomb, discovered in 1931, is to be found some 2 km. to the N. of the ancient town of Askalon. It is a tunnel-vaulted chamber (7 ft. 6 in. × 10 ft.) with space for four sarcophagi (probably 3C AD). The *wall paintings* (restored in places) survive in good condition.

Atlit
Haifa District/Israel   p.318□C 4

The Sebulonite-Levite town of *Kartah* (Joshua 21, 34) was known as *Adarus* when under the rule of Sidon and as *Certha* under the Romans. It lies 14 km. S. of Haifa on a peninsula projecting into the Mediterranean, and occupies the site where the Knights Templar, during the Fifth Crusade, built a Frankish settlement with a castle (Castrum Peregrinorum), a chapel, a palace and several dwelling houses and stables. This settlement remained in the hands of the Crusaders until the Christian kingdom collapsed (1291). The town

Ashqelon, Roman sarcophagus ▷

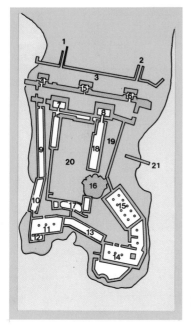

Atlit, Castrum Peregrinorum

Atlit, Castrum Peregrinorum 1 N. portal **2** S. portal **3** Fosse **4** S. gatehouse tower **5** Middle gatehouse tower **6** N. gatehouse tower **7** N. tower **8** S. tower **9** N. vaulted room **10** N. hall **11** NW hall with pillars **12** NW tower **13** W. vaulted rooms **14** SW hall with pillars **15** S. hall with pillars **16** Round church **17** W. crypt **18** S. crypt **19** S. forecourt **20** Courtyard **21** Mole

fell into disrepair over the next few centuries, and was severely damaged by an earthquake in 1837. In 1903, Edmond de Rothschild, who owned the site, founded the Jewish village of Atlit 1 km. to the S. of the Frankish settlement. The town formed a rectangle (1,950 ft. by 500–650 ft.), which has only been excavated in part (bath, church and stables).

Castrum Peregrinorum (Chastel Pèlerin; closed; military area): A new castle was built in 1217–18 by Gautier d'Avesnes, assisted by numerous pil-grims, as a replacement for the older Knights Templar castle of Le Destroit, which stands 1.5 km. distant.

The newer castle is formed by two concentric rings with a deep dividing fosse. It was protected on the landward side by a strong curtain wall which had three towers. Behind this wall, built of massive ashlars, and its inner barbican, there stood a keep, protected by towers projecting at the sides. Rectangular vaulted rooms run around the E., N. and W. sides of the castle. The rectangular *main tower* (El-Karnifeh), 115 ft. tall and built of massive chamfered ashlars, stood by the inner wall. The chapterhouse adjoins this tower. The arches of the vaults were supported by brackets decorated with Saints' heads and some lower sections of the arches have survived. A Gothic octagonal *Templar church* with a central altar stood in the W. part of the castrum, which

measured 650 × 1500 ft. A rib-vaulted hall stands to the W. of this church. *Town church* (near the E. wall): Ruins of an incomplete Gothic church, with a five-sided apse, a transverse bay, and an makeshift W. wall. *Finds:* Stained-glass windows and stone benches. *Bathhouse:* A stone house (rebuilt) in the NE of the town, with a changing room, benches around the sides, and a bathing pool in the middle. Next to this, above the hypocaust, there is a steam bath, converted under the Mamelukes.

Environs: Dor (14 km. S.): A moshav founded in 1949, with 1,500 inhabitants. Ruins of the Biblical Dor and Hellenistic Dora are to be found to the N. of the moshav. The town was first mentioned in 13 BC. Dor, led by Jabin the king of Hazor, fought against Joshua (Joshua 11, 1–2). Dor became the capital of the fourth administrative district under King Solomon, and was strongly fortified in the Hellenistic period. A small Jewish community lived in Dor under Agrippa I (AD 41–4). The town fell into disrepair in the late 4C, and only revived when the Crusaders built their castle of Merle. *Basilica* (near to Kibbutz Nahsolim): A basilica from the 5/6C with a nave and two aisles. On both sides of the building there are colonnades with mosaic pavements. The basilica is surrounded by an atrium. At the E. end of the S. aisle there is a tomb with an opening in the stone lid through which oil was poured: the corpse 'consecrated' the oil, which then flowed into a basin outside. There is a Greek inscription on a tabula ansata on a marble column. *Roman theatre:* This theatre, 200 ft. in diameter and lying to the N. of the hill on which the settlement stood, was partly uncovered in 1950.

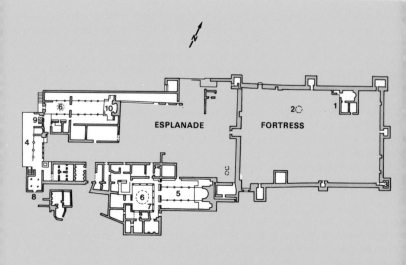

ESPLANADE   FORTRESS

The few finds that have been made date it to the 2/3C AD.

Avdat, acropolis 1 Chapel **2** Cistern **3** Watchtower **4** Nabataean temple portico **5** Church of St.Theodore (S. church) **6** Byzantine monastery rooms **7** Nabataean gate **8** Nabataean colonnaded hall **9** Baptistery **10** N. church

Avdat/Horvat Avedat

Southern District/Israel   p.322□C 11

The Nabataean desert town of Avdat, so named after the Nabataean godking Obodas II (30–9 BC) who was buried here, lies on the old caravan route from Petra to Gaza, some 50 km. S. of Beer Sheva. The remains of dams, canals and cisterns bear witness to the Nabataeans' astonishing skill at irrigating the desert.
The buildings and archaeological finds are mainly from the Byzantine period: two churches, a baptistery and the remains of paintings.

History: Inscriptions, coins, ceramics and architectural finds prove

that Avdat enjoyed its heyday in the 2/1C BC and again in the 3C and 5/6C AD. In the 2C BC, Avdat seems to have occupied a central position on the trade route from Petra, the capital of the Nabataean empire, to the Mediterranean. The finds indicate that there were links with Egypt, Greece and Asia Minor. Avdat was at its zenith under Aretasa IV (9 BC–AD 40), the son of Obodas. He built the retaining walls of the castle hill (2,030 ft. in height), where he levelled a surface for representational and cultic buildings. In AD 106, the Romans incorporated the Nabataean empire into the Imperium Romanum as the province of Arabia. From the 5C onwards, Avdat passed over into the

Avdat, forum

Byzantine sphere and monks settled here. Almost all the buildings on the castle hill date from this period. The Persians conquered the town in 614. Twenty years later it was occupied by the Muslims, and in the 10C it was abandoned for ever.

Byzantine bathhouse: The Byzantine bathhouse is regarded as one of the best-preserved of its kind in the Holy Land. Its design follows the classical Roman model, with a changing room, a cold bath, a hot-air room and a hot-water bath.

Byzantine dwelling house: A peculiarity of these dwellings is that the hollow hewn from the rock forms a single unit with the house itself. The hollows were used as store rooms.

Nabataean burial chambers: The dead were buried in burial chambers cut deep into the rock. The largest and most significant of these Nabataean chambers (31 × 26 ft.) has space for 22 tombs. They were formerly thought to be the burial chamber of Obodas and his family, but today they are dated to the 3C AD.

Acropolis: The Byzantine citadel, with a surface area of 200 × 135 ft., was built in the early 3C on the site of a Nabataean military camp. A chapel and a watchtower. Two churches adjoin the citadel in the W.: the so-called *North church* with a baptistery (early-4C), built on the site of a Nabataean temple, and the *South church* dedicated to St. Theodore: it is a basilica with a nave and two aisles (*c.* 450). Other objects of interest: *Byzantine winepress* on the S. slope of the acropolis; *Nabataean pottery* to the E. of the acropolis; *Roman camp* to the N. of the acropolis.

Avdat, apse of a church

Model farm: In the valley below the acropolis there is a model farm set up by Israeli scientists in 1959. Attempts are being made here to reconstruct the Nabataeans' ancient irrigation system, in order to discover how it was possible to feed the relatively dense population of the Negev desert in Nabataean and Byzantine times.

Environs: En Avdat (5 km. NW): The plain between Avdat and Sede Boqer is traversed by a ravine with a lake. This ravine forms the En Avdat nature reserve.
In prehistoric times, the cliffs of the ravine were settled by tribes who did not live in caves but built themselves huts of twigs and branches and used flint tools. There is a settlement from 80,000–35,000 BC on the N. slope of the ravine.

Banyas
Golan   p.318□F 1

Banyas lies on the ancient trade route from Acre to Damascus, standing on the S. slope of Mount Hermon and possibly occupying the site of the Bib-

Banyas, Sheikh el-Khadr

lical Baal-gad (Joshua 13, 5). The grotto above the source of the Jordan was dedicated to the God Pan (Paneion) by the Greeks, who called the neighbouring town *Paneas*. Antiochus the Great fought several battles here. Herod built a temple in honour of Augustus, and his son Philippus made the town the capital of his tetrarchy, calling it *Caesarea Philippi*. In the New Testament, Jesus and his disciples visited the area of Caesarea Philippi (St.Matthew 16, 13). Agrippa II, who first destroyed the town and then rebuilt it, called it Caesarea-Neronias, in honour of the Emperor Nero. Caesarea-Neronias fell to the province of Syria after Agrippa's death. When Septimus Severus effected the partition of that province in *c*. AD 200, Caesarea Neronias was included in Syrophoenicia. In the 4C it became a bishop's seat. It was fought over by the Arabs and

Christians during the Crusades, and was captured by al-Mu'azzam. Jews lived in the town in the Middle Ages and they knew it as Dan.

Nahal Banyas: This is one of the three great sources of the Jordan, and has been dedicated to local deities since ancient times. A cultic niche flanked by pilasters and Greek dedicatory inscriptions is to be found beside the entrance, which leads to grottoes hewn from the rock. Statues of Pan formerly stood here. Parts of a Herodian building have been uncovered to the N. of the source.

Environs: Subeibe/Qal'at Nimrud (2 km. NE): The *Crusader castle* stands on a hill running from W. to E. The fortification is 1,480 ft. long. The W. side measures 525 ft., the NE side 235 ft. The terrain rises gradually from W. to E. The Frankish castle was originally founded by the Arabs (Qal'at Subeiba). From the parapet there is a view of the associated castles of Beaufort on the cliffs of the Litani to the NW, and Château Neuf at the head of the Huleh valley to the SW. The Arab castle was a Frankish possession from 1129–64. From 1129–32 it was enlarged by Renier Brus, who lost it to the Damascenes in 1132, but recaptured it in 1137. Saladin took the castle in 1164 at the second attempt. The Crusaders attempted to recapture it in 1174 and 1253, but without success. Subeibe was razed during the Fifth Crusade (1217–21), as were some other fortresses. However, inscriptions indicate that Subeibe was rebuilt several times in the 13C. The Mamelukes used it as a prison. Castle: The gentle gradient of the E. slope meant that this end had to be more extensively fortified and it was well guarded by towers and bastions of various shapes and sizes. The W. end, on the other hand, has the natural protection of a steep rocky slope, and was only defended by a simple wall consisting of several polygonal courses. The present entrance is in a gap in the W. wall near the corner tower. Inside there is a large vaulted cistern with an Arabic inscription from 1239/40. The round tower of the W. wall has a fine Arab fan vault.

Beer Sheva

Southern District/Israel   p.322□C 10

Beer Sheva, 80 km. SSW of Jerusalem, is the modern capital of the Southern District of Israel. It is the administrative centre of the Negev, and an important base for tourists. According to the Old Testament,

Subeibe (Banyas), Crusader castle, S. wall with main entrance

Beer Sheva (in the Bible: Beer-sheba) was the dwelling-place of the patriarch Abraham, and also a Canaanite cult site and the southernmost town of the Holy Land.

Well of the seven/well of the oath: According to Genesis 21, 25 ff., Abraham and Abimelech, the Philistine king, swore a pact in Beer-sheba undertaking not to continue opposing one another on account of the well which Abraham had ordered to be dug here. They instructed their shepherds to keep peace with one another. Abraham: 'For these seven ewe lambs shalt thou take of my hand, that they may be a witness unto me, that I have digged this well. Wherefore he called that place Beer-sheba; because there they sware both of them.' The Biblical etymology interprets the name Beer-sheba as meaning 'well of the seven' or 'well of the

oath'. Later, when Abraham moved from Beer-sheba to Hebron, the Philistines filled the well up with earth, and Abraham's son Isaac then had to dig it again.

Isaac and King Abimelech (probably the successor of the other King Abimelech with whom Abraham had sworn the pact in Beer-sheba) undertook upon their oath not to oppose one another. Isaac called the place 'Shiba' ('oath'). 'Therefore the name of the city is Beer-sheba unto this day.' (Genesis 26, 33). A so-called well of Abraham can be viewed in the old part of town.

History: The settlement which developed by the well was allotted to the tribe of Simeon as their inheritance (Joshua 19, 2). This was the most southerly settlement in the whole Holy Land; the expression

Nahal Banyas, rock niches with Roman inscriptions (left), Subeibe (Banyas), Crusader castle (right)

'from Dan to Beer-sheba' was synonymous with 'the whole of Israel' (cf. Judges 20, 1; 1 Samuel 3, 20 and frequently elsewhere). The sons of Samuel, who was a prophet and the last of the ruling Judges, acted as judges in Beer-sheba (1 Samuel 8, 2). The prophet Amos preached against the religious and social abuses in Israel in *c.* 755 BC. He also gave a warning regarding the Canaanite cult in Beer-sheba: 'They that swear by the sin of Samaria, and say, Thy god, O Dan, liveth; and, The manner of Beer-sheba liveth; even they shall fall, and never rise up again' (Amos 8, 14). According to Nehemiah 11, 27/30, Beer-sheba was settled again after the Jews returned from captivity in Babylon.

Owing to repeated destruction, there are very few remains from Roman and Byzantine times in Beer Sheva. From the 7C AD onwards, Beer Sheva degenerated into a caravanserai with a bedouins' market.

Municipal Museum (housed in the rooms of a mosque built in 1915: Ha-Azmaut St.): Archaeological collection with ceramics, ivories and terracottas; a large altar with horns in the courtyard; Byzantine inscriptions (including an edict concerning Beersheba).

Tel Beer Sheva: The remains of settlements dating from the Iron Age onwards have been uncovered at an excavation site some 4 km. NE of the modern town centre: a well (12C BC), a gate (10C BC) with a square with streets leading off it, houses from the 9–8C BC, remains of a Roman fortress (2/3C AD).

Beer Sheva culture: The culture which existed in S. Palestine in the 4th millennium BC made use of copper, and is known as the Beer Sheva culture because of the finds discovered at Beer Sheva. It is characterized by copper objects, pet animals, cultivated plants, ivory statuettes and painted pebblestones.

Environs: Dimona/Dimonä (36 km. SE): The town of Dimona (textile industry, chemical works, nuclear power station) in the N. Negev was laid out in 1955. It is identified with

Beer Sheva, Abraham's fountain

the town of *Dibon* or *Dimon*, which is mentioned in lists of places inhabited by the Israelite tribe of Judah (Joshua 15, 22; Nehemiah 11, 25).

Belvoir/Kokhav HaYarden
Northern District/Israel   p.318☐F 4

This is a Crusader castle 1,800 ft. above the Jordan valley, on the E. edge of the Issachar plateau, 4 km. from the Jordan. In AD 1168, after the Velos family had failed to establish a foothold on the strategically important hill, Ivo Velos sold his small castle to the Hospitallers, who began in the next few years to rebuild the fortress, which stood on Persian and Byzantine foundations. They called their fortress *Belvoir* (Videbellum), because of the magnificent, extensive panorama it offered, or *Coquet* (from the Arabic name *Kaukab el-Hawa*, which preserves the Hebrew name of a small town 800 yards SE of the fortress).

Following the battle of Hattin in 1187, Sultan Saladin did not capture the fortress. However, it did fall into Muslim hands on 5 January 1189. The defenders were freely granted the right to withdraw. It was a Muslim garrison until 1219. Al-Malik al-Mu'azzam, the ruler of Damascus, ordered it to be razed to prevent it from falling into the hands of the Crusaders. However, it passed back to the Crusaders in 1241 as a result of a treaty between the Egyptian ruler Malik es-Salih Ayyub and Richard of Cornwall, although the Crusaders did not manage to rebuild it. The Arab village of Kaukab el-Hawa was built on the ruins of the castle in the early 19C. The fortress was excavated in 1966–7.

Fortress: Belvoir resembles a Roman castrum in some points. Externally it forms a pentagon but inside it is a square. There are 23 ft. high square, basalt towers at the four corners and in the middle of each side and the outer defensive ring of walls is 10 ft. thick (430 ft. from E.-W., 330 ft. from N.-S.). These external defences are

Beer Sheva, beduin market (left), Belvoir, Crusader sculpture from the church (right)

Kokhav H.Y. (Belvoir), stone from synagogue

ture in the second half of the 12C. These include the larger-than-life head of a young man, closely resembling Greek art of the late archaic and early classical periods. This head is probably the work of a Southern French or Northern Spanish artist (1170–5).

The fortress was protected to the N., W. and S. by an 82 ft. wide and 39 ft. deep fosse, the sides of which were sloped to form a glacis. The main entrance is to the SW and was defended by a drawbridge and a complicated system of gateways. Underground passages lead from the fortress far out into the surrounding area. *Finds:* The late-Romanesque capitals discovered in the ruins of the castle are now in the Israel Museum in Jerusalem.

Environs: Kokhav HaYarden (800 yards SE): A Jewish town which existed from the time of the Second Temple until the 4C AD. The Crusaders used the stones from this settlement to build their fortress, including stones from the synagogue with Aramaic and Greek inscriptions.

linked by walls with high battlements and steps lead down from the towers to the fosse. The E. tower, which rises up at the highest point of the pentagon, was a massive fortress in itself. The spacious vaulted rooms running along the connecting walls were able to house a large garrison. These vaults were blown up by Baibars in 1263. There are a bathhouse and a large cistern (5,400 sq.ft.) in the outer courtyard.

The four outer walls and the four towers of the square *inner fortress* (130 x 130 ft.) form a ring within the outer defences and there is another tower by the W. wall. Inside the fortress there were a bakery, a kitchen, vaulted rooms, and, on the upper storey, a church with a tower. The richly furnished *church* (23 × 69 ft.) contained statues and reliefs which are among the few examples of Crusader sculp-

Bet Alfa

Northern District/Israel   p.318□E 4

In 1928 a mosaic pavement was discovered by chance on the territory of the Kibbutz Hefzi Bah (founded in 1922 by members of the Blue-and-White group from Germany and Czechoslovakia) in the Yizre'el valley on the northern slope of Har Gilboa. Together with the mosaic at Hammat Tiberias (q.v.), this mosaic is one of the most important survivals from a Byzantine synagogue. The mosaic and the remains of the synagogue were uncovered by L.E. Sukenik and N.Avigad in 1929.

Synagogue: Two rows of five basalt

Belvoir, fortress, W. gate ▷

pillars each divide the interior of this two-storeyed basilica (35 ft. 6 in. × 40 ft. 6 in.) into a nave and two aisles. The nave is 17 ft. 6 in. wide, the W. aisle measures 9 ft. and the E. aisle 10 ft. An apse 8 ft. deep and 16 ft. 6 in. wide stands at the top of three steps in the S. wall, which is aligned towards Jerusalem. In the centre of the apse, the archaeologists discovered a small shaft, covered with stone slabs, in which the synagogue treasure was probably concealed. There are three entrances in the N. wall and a fourth in the W. wall. A passage which began in a side room on the W. side, in the right aisle, led into a room from which it may have been possible to climb up to a women's gallery. It is possible that this room was used as a Bet ha-midrash (teaching room). Outside the entrances in the N. wall there was a narthex 8 ft. 6 in. long, and outside this again there was an atrium (31 ft. 6 in. × 39 ft.) which was almost as long as the praying area. An open colonnade probably separated the narthex and the atrium. The narthex and atrium had a mosaic pavement, now largely destroyed. There are almost no mosaics in the left aisle, but the nave has a unique mosaic.

Mosaic: This polychrome mosaic, which is in good condition, is divided into three panels and is surrounded by a decorative band with animals, humans and geometric motifs. The band in front of the apse contains a fish, a dove, and a hen with chickens and the frame is filled out with fruits (grapes, a pomegranate, a vine), animals and geometric patterns. Upper panel (in front of the apse): the mosaic depicts a closed Aron ha-kodesh (Torah shrine) with two doors. A conch and a Ner Tamid (Eternal Lamp) are to be seen in the gable of the shrine. On each side of the shrine there is a burning seven-armed menora with three feet, and also a lulav, a shofar, an etrog and a mahta. There is a bird on both sides of the gable, and under each menora a lion. At the edge of this panel there are two open curtains. The left curtain was later destroyed when the bema was installed. Middle panel: signs of the zodiac viewed from the

Bet Alfa, synagogue, mosaic of Helios the sun god (left), Bethany, Lazarus's tomb (right)

front, with inscriptions, are grouped on a quadriga around the Sun God Helios. Behind Helios there are a moon and star. The circle of zodiacal signs (10 ft. 3 in. in diameter) is in a rectangular panel measuring 11 ft. 8 in. × 12 ft. 4 in. The four seasons are arranged in anti-clockwise order in the four corner spandrels but they are not placed by their corresponding months. Each of the seasons is accompanied by its Hebrew name. Lower panel: This mosaic depicts the sacrifice of Isaac and is thus one of the few examples of a Biblical scenes in a synagogue. It is not clear whether the iconography is Jewish or Christian in origin. At the right-hand edge there is a depiction of an altar, and to the left of it is Abraham holding the butcher's knife in one hand and the bound Isaac in the other. In the centre is a ram tied to a tree, and to the left of this are two servants, one of them with an ass. The scene is explained by the beginnings of two quotations from Genesis 22 and by the names of Abraham and Isaac: 'Lay not thine hand' and 'And behold behind him a ram'. Inscriptions: Outside the central N. entrance

there is an Aramaic dedicatory inscription, partly destroyed: 'This mosaic was laid down in the year ... during the rule of King Justinius ... 100 measures of wheat donated by all the town's sons ... Rabbi A ... (and) in good memory of the sons of ... Amen.' In a tabula ansata there is a Greek inscription flanked by a lion and an ox. Both these animals are standing on their heads. 'May Marianos and his son, the craftsmen who performed this work, be held in (good) memory.' The synagogue was built in the late 5C and was destroyed by an earthquake in the second half of the 6C (?). The mosaics escaped the attacks of the iconoclasts, because the synagogue was not rebuilt.

Bethany/El Azariya
District of Jerusalem/Israel   p.320☐E 7

The pilgrims' centre of Bethany lies on the E. slope of the Mount of Olives, 4 km. E of Jerusalem on the road to Jericho. According to the New Testament, Bethany is the place

Bethany, panorama with church of Lazarus

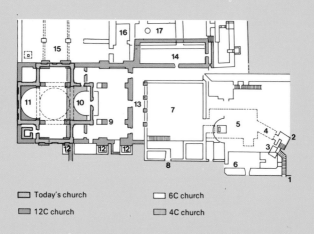

☐ Today's church   ☐ 6C church

▨ 12C church   ☐ 4C church

where Lazarus, the brother of Martha and Mary, lived. This is the Lazarus whom Jesus raised from the dead, and he is not to be confused with the so-called Poor Lazarus who, in the parable of the rich man, is a beggar lying outside the door and hoping to satisfy his hunger with the crumbs falling from the rich man's table. The Arabic name El Azariya is a corruption of the Greek name Lazareion, which was the name of a Christian settlement recorded as having existed in the 4C AD in the area of the village of Bethany. The Hebrew name *Bet-Ani* means 'house of the poor man' or 'house of Ananiah'.

History: Bethany is identical with the Old Testament settlement of *Ananiah** ('house of Ananiah' = Bet Ananiah = Bethany), where Jews from the tribe of Benjamin settled after returning from exile in Babylon (Nehemiah 11, 32). Archaeological

Bethany, church and tomb of Lazarus 1 Present entrance to 17C tomb of Lazarus **2** Anteroom **3** Burial chamber **4** Former entrance to tomb **5** Mosque in crypt **6** Greek chapel **7** Mosque courtyard (former atrium of 4&6C churches) **8** Entrance to El-Ozir mosque **9** Mosaic fragments on middle columns (floor of 6C church) **10** 4C apse of church **11** 6C apse of church **12** Buttresses of Crusader church **13** Portico **14** Byzantine chapel **15** Franciscan abbey **16** Pilgrims' refectory **17** Medieval monastery with mill and oil press

excavations have shown that the place was inhabited even in Persian times (excavation site above the churches on the slope). Jesus often visited this place because his friends Lazarus, Martha and Mary lived here (Jesus and the Apostles are mentioned in St.Matthew 21, 17 and St.Mark 11, 11 as spending the night in Bethany). Before his entry into Jerusalem, and before being betrayed by Judas, Jesus was a guest at the house of Simon the leper in Bethany, where a woman

Bethany, Apostles' fountain ▷

Raising of Lazarus, book illustration

Bethany, church of Lazarus, mosaic

anointed his feet (St.Matthew 26, 6; St.Mark 14, 3; cf. St.John 12, 1–8). Eusebios of Caesarea, the Greek church historian, reported in the 4C that there was a tomb reputed to be that of Lazarus, which was revered in Bethany. Jerome, the Latin Doctor of the Church, stated in 390 that there was a church above this tomb. The Crusaders built a church and a monastery on the site of the house of Martha and Mary. In the 16C the Muslims built a mosque on the ruins of these buildings and barred the Christians from gaining access to the tomb of Lazarus. But in 1613 the custos of the Holy Land obtained permission to build a second entrance to the tomb.

Church of Lazarus: This modern church, built in 1952–4 to plans by Antonio Barluzzi on the foundations of the earlier structures, has no windows. Some remnants of these old churches have survived, an example being the mosaics of the 4C basilica, which had a nave and two aisles. After being damaged in an earthquake, this structure was replaced in the 6C by a basilica which was of equal size and also had a nave and two aisles, but stood 43 ft. further to the E. The Crusaders strengthened the Byzantine basilica and built another church above the tomb of Lazarus. Remains of the N. and S. walls of this church survive. In the 14C, the Arabs converted its crypt into a mosque. A Benedictine convent was built to the S. of the churches in the 12C. The *mosaics* in the church depict Jesus with Mary and Martha, Jesus at the tomb of Lazarus and Jesus in the house of Simon the leper. In the legends and in the visual arts, Mary was identified with Mary Magdalene the sinner, owing to the statement: 'It

QUIA TU ME MISISTI HAEC CUM
A CLAMAVIT LAZARE VENI FORAS

was that Mary which anointed the Lord with ointment, and wiped his feet with her hair' (St.John 11, 2). According to the account which only occurs in St.John (11, 1–45), Lazarus fell ill and his sisters informed Jesus. Jesus answered that the disease would not result in death, remained for two more days in the place where he was, and only then left for Bethany. Lazarus had died in the meantime and had been lying in his tomb for four days when Jesus arrived. When Jesus saw the two sisters weeping, he raised Lazarus from the dead. The Raising of Lazarus has been a popular funerary motif ever since the early Christian period, particularly in paintings in catacombs.

Tomb of Lazarus, by the church of Lazarus. The vault in which the body of Lazarus was laid is a room (8 ft. × 7 ft. 6 in.) which was built of large hewn stones and was originally closed by another stone. The entrance passage, through which the Muslims formerly reached the vault from the crypt, has been walled up. The vault is now entered through a gate only 4 ft. high and 2 ft. 4 in. wide (this is the second entrance built by the Christians in the 17C).

Bet Guvrin (Beit Jibrin)
Southern District/Israel   p.320□C 8

The kibbutz of Bet Guvrin and the hamlet of Beit Jibrin lie almost 40 km. to the E. of Ashqelon. The function of the numerous caves in this area—there are some 2,000 bell-shaped caves and shafts—is still largely obscure.
Bet Guvrin is the ancient *Eleutheropolis* ('free town'), to which Latin rights

were granted by the Roman Emperor Septimus Severus in AD 200. *Mosaic floors* from the 4C (the best of these are now in the Israel Museum, Jerusalem) are witness that the town was wealthy even in Byzantine times ('house of mosaics' at the top of Bet Guvrin hill).

Crusader castle: The remnants of one of the three Crusader castles of Gibelin, Blanche Garde and Ibelin are to be found on the main road leading through Bet Guvrin. They were built in the first half of the 12C by order of Foulques of Anjou in order to secure the route from Jerusalem to Ashqelon. The Mamelukes destroyed Gibelin in 1244, but the castle was rebuilt by the Ottomans in the mid 16C because of its strategic position.

Tell Maresha (Tell Sandahanna): The dominant feature of Bet Guvrin is Tell Maresha, the Biblical *Mareshah,* which is listed in Joshua 15, 44 as a place which was inhabited by the tribe of Judah and was enlarged by King Rehoboam into a fortress along with the neighbouring Lakhish (q.v.):

'And he fortified the strong holds, and put captains in them, and store of victual, and of oil and wine. And in every several city he put shields and spears, and made them exceeding strong, having Judah and Benjamin on his side.' (2 Chronicles 11, 11 ff.). It was at Mareshah that King Asa of Judah defeated the (nomad) Serach, who had invaded the area 'with an host of a thousand thousand, and three hundred chariots' (2 Chronicles 14, 9 ff.). Mareshah is also the native town of the prophet Eliezer (2 Chronicles 20, 37).

Mareshah was devastated by Sanherib of Assur in 701 BC and was settled anew after the period of captivity in Babylon. It subsequently became a centre of the slave trade with Egypt, and had a mixed population. The town declined in importance under Seleucid rule.

The Arabic name *Tell Sandahanna* originates from the 12C Crusader church of St.Anne (now a ruin).

Caves: Extensive fields of caves, some of which are thought to be tombs, are to be found around Tell

Bet Guvrin, Sidonian tomb

Mareshah. These bell-shaped cavities in the limestone date from the 4/5C AD and were hewn out from the top downwards, the radius increasing with depth.

Bethlehem/Beit Lahm

West Bank/Israel p.320□D 8

The town of Bethlehem, 7 km. S. of Jerusalem in the area once occupied by the tribe of Judah, is the ancestral town of the royal family of David and is regarded as the birthplace of Jesus.

Interpretation of the town's name: The original meaning of the name Bethlehem is 'house of (the Canaanite goddess) Lachama', but popular etymology soon interpreted it as 'house of bread' (Hebrew) or 'house of meat' (Arabic). A road leading to Bethlehem is mentioned in Genesis 35, 19 and 48, 7 as the burial place of Rachel, the wife of Jacob the patriarch. Here, and also in Joshua 15, 59, the original name is 'Ephrathah', which the prophet Micah later interpreted as 'fruitful' (Micah

5, 2), an interpretation which the Evangelists understood to be a reference to the Messiah's birthplace. In fact, 'Ephrathah' was originally the name of a tribe which settled in the Bethlehem area. Thus, King David, who was born in Bethlehem, was 'the son of that Ephrathite' (1 Samuel 17, 12); the members of the family of Ruth's father-in-law Elimelech were 'Ephrathites of Beth-lehem-judah' (Ruth 1, 2). The name of the tribe passed into that of the town, which was not called Bethlehem until later: 'in the way to Ephrath, which is Bethlehem' (Genesis 35, 19).

City of David: Bethlehem was mentioned in the Egyptian Armarna letters in the 14C BC, but the spotlight of history did not fall on it until the time of the Biblical Judges, three generations before King David: at that time, Bethlehem and its environs were where David's forefathers acted out their lives. Boaz was a rich landowner here and married Ruth, a poor gleaner of ears of corn, and became the ancestor of David and Joseph (Ruth 2, 1 ff.). David was the youngest of the eight sons of Isai, the

Bethlehem, panorama

Judaean from Bethlehem. After God had rejected King Saul, the prophet Samuel went to Bethlehem and anointed David. This anointment in Bethlehem, reported in 1 Samuel 16, 1 ff., is not mentioned anywhere else in the Old or New Testament; according to 2 Samuel 2, 4, David was anointed in Hebron by the Judaeans and then by the elders of Israel.

David's grandson Rehoboam, who was King of Judah in 926–910 BC, ordered Bethlehem to be enlarged into a fortified town (2 Chronicles 11, 5–6): the area around Bethlehem was re-settled after the return from captivity in Babylon in c. 539 BC (Ezra 2, 21). Bethlehem is also given the name of 'city of David' in the Bible (St.Luke 2, 4) because it is David's birthplace, and the prophet Micah announces: 'But thou, Beth-lehem Ephratah, though thou be little among the thousands of Judah, yet out of thee shall he come forth unto me that is to be ruler in Israel' (5, 2).

Birthplace of Jesus: The Evangelists agree in referring to Bethlehem as Christ's birthplace and this event is clearly foretold in the Old Testament prophecies. St.John 7, 42 reports that there was a dispute regarding Jesus's origin: those who do not believe that Jesus is the Messiah point out that he is from Nazareth in Galilee and ask: 'Hath not the scripture said, That Christ cometh of the seed of David, and out of the town of Bethlehem, where David was?' (St.John 7, 42). The Prophets had described Bethlehem as the birthplace of the Messiah, and Christ must therefore have been born there if he was to be regarded as the Messiah. According to St.Luke, Joseph and Mary lived in Bethlehem, not Nazareth, before Christ was born. The annunciation to Mary took place in Nazareth: 'And in the sixth month the angel Gabriel was sent from God unto a city of Galilee, named Nazareth. To a virgin espoused to a man whose name was Joseph, of the house of David' (St.Luke 1, 26–27). In order to explain why Mary and Joseph were in Bethlehem when Christ was born, Luke refers to a census ordered by Caesar Augustus, for which everyone went to his native town to be registered (St.Luke 2). Joseph and Mary went to Bethlehem, and 'While they were there, the days were accomplished that she should be delivered. And she brought forth her first-born son, and wrapped him in swaddling clothes, and laid him in a manger; because there was no room for them in the inn' (St.Luke 2, 6–7). St.Matthew refers neither to the census nor to the journey to Bethlehem. Bethlehem is stated to be Christ's birthplace in St.Matthew 2. This is after Christ's forefathers, from Joseph through David to Abraham, have been listed in St.Matthew 1. St.Matthew states that after Christ's birth the three wise men from the East called upon King Herod in order to see the new-born King of the Jews. When Herod asked them where this King was supposed to have been born, the wise men answered with a quotation from the Old Testament: 'In Bethlehem of Judaea: for thus it is written by the prophet, And thou Bethlehem, in the land of Juda, are not the least among the princes of Juda: for out of thee shall come a Governor, that shall rule my people Israel' (St.Matthew 2, 5–6). The wise men followed the star, worshipped the child in Bethlehem, presented him with their gifts and returned home. In the meantime, Herod ordered that all male children of the age of two years and less should be killed. The Holy Family had been warned by an angel of these murders, and had fled to Egypt. Joseph, Mary and Jesus returned to Nazareth after Herod's death.

Christian cult site: The church of the Nativity in Bethlehem is regarded as one of the few buildings surviving almost wholly intact from early Christian times. This church, which was built under the Byzantine emperor

Adoration of Christ, by Pinturicchio ▷

Justinian the Great, has survived the passage of time more or less unchanged, despite various conversions, additions and restorations. The essential feature is the cave of the Nativity.

Early cult site: Origenes, a writer on the Christian church, refers in *c.* 215 to Justinus, the pilgrim and martyr who had visited the holy sites in the first half of the 2C: 'They still show the cave in Bethlehem where he was born. It is known all over the region, even to people who do not share our faith. People also know that it was here that he was born who is worshipped by Christians, namely Jesus.' In *c.* 150, Justinus had himself written: 'If anyone should wish other evidence for the birth of Jesus in Bethlehem than Micah's prophecy and the story recorded by his disciples, then let him consider that in Bethlehem, in accordance with the Bible story, a cave is shown, with a manger in which he lay in swaddling clothes.'

The reports by Justinus, Origenes and other pilgrims who visited the holy sites all date from the period after 135, when the Roman emperor Hadrian, after putting down the second Jewish revolt, had built a cult site above the grottoes of Bethlehem. This site consisted of a grove for Adonis, the young lover of Aphrodite, the Greek goddess of love and the Roman Venus. Adonis was originally a Near Eastern vegetation divinity (Semitic: 'adonis' = 'my lord'). He was identified with the Semitic God Tammuz, who was the lover and husband of the goddess Ishtar. Adonis was sent to the underworld (this is the significance of the grotto), as was Ishtar. There were numerous laments on the subject of the disappearance of Tammuz, and the withered vegetation (cf. Ezekiel 8, 14). Thus it was that the myth of Adonis, who spends six months in the underworld and then returns to Aphrodite for another six months, was a symbol of death and rebirth in nature. This myth accorded with the ideas entertained by peasants in the fertile region of Bethlehem. It is possible that Emperor Hadrian's order to build a shrine of Adonis above the grottoes of Bethlehem was also intended to comply with the ideas

Church of the Nativity, 'Gate of Humility', Last Supper icon in Greek choir

of Christians, who regarded these same grottoes as Christ's birthplace. By imperial decree, a Semitic-Greek-Roman cult site was to replace the Christian cult site. This may have been the exact reason why the Christians were induced to emphasize repeatedly their own idea concerning the real significance of the Bethlehem grottoes, namely that they were Christ's birthplace. More credence can therefore be attached to the reports by Justinus, Origenes and other pre-Constantine pilgrims than to later descriptions.

Basilica of Constantine the Great: The first church above Christ's birthplace dates back to the Emperor Constantine the Great and to his mother, St.Helena, who travelled unceasingly about the Holy Land, commissioning many new churches. This one, later pulled down, was consecrated in 339. The octagonal E. section of the basilica was directly above the cave. Steps in the middle of the octagon led to a raised section from which the opening in the closable roof of the cave could be seen.

The octagon and, to the W. of it, the area where the congregation assembled, were joined by another opening which was approached by three steps. The congregation area was in the form of a basilica with a nave and four aisles. The floors were laid with mosaics, and the side walls were decorated with painted stucco, marble blocks and mosaics. The geometric floor mosaics have survived. It is not known where the entrance to the cave was but it was probably outside the church.

Church of Justinian: The church of Constantine was destroyed in the early 6C during a Samaritan rebellion. The Byzantine Emperor Justinian the Great ordered the building to be pulled down, and erected a new church which was oriented on Constantine's basilica and is today in largely the same state as in the 6C. In the 10C, Patriar Eutychios of Constantinople described the role played by Justinian in building the new church: 'The Emperor ordered that the churches destroyed by the Samaritans be rebuilt, and sent to his deputy in Palestine a deputation accompanied by Saba and a large sum of money.

Church of the Nativity, iconostasis

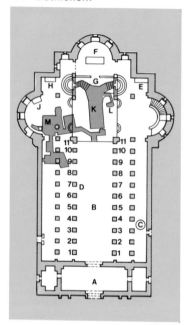

Bethlehem, Church of the Nativity A
Narthex **B** Aisle **C** Byzantine font **D** Floor
mosaics **E** Circumcision altar **F** High altar **G** 17C
iconostasis **H** Altar of the Magi **J** Virgin Mary
altar **K** Nativity grotto **L** Manger altar **M** Grotto of
the Innocents

The Emperor ordered his deputy to
build everything in the manner which
he, the Emperor, had ordered. He also
ordered that the church in Bethlehem
should be torn down because it was
too small, and that it should be rebuilt
in new splendour so that no church in
the Holy City could excel its beauty.
When the delegation arrived in Jerusalem, it built a pilgrims' hospice,
completed the construction of the new
church which had been begun in
Bethlehem, and supervised the reconstruction of the churches destroyed
by the Samaritans.'
Justinian's church was closely
modelled on Constantine's structure.
The nave was extended W. and a
narthex added, and the choir, which

still survives, was built above the cave
on the site of the octagon. Entrances
to the cave were built at the sides of
the altar. The cave itself was given a
marble facing, and the walls of the
church were also covered with marble
slabs and mosaics.
Persian invasion: When the Persians
invaded in 614, they spared the
church of Nativity, supposedly
because a mosaic above the entrance
doors in the W. showed the three
Wise Men from the East wearing Persian costumes and worshipping the
Christ-child.
Arab rule: Caliph Omar visited Bethlehem in 638, after the Persians had
been driven out by the Arabs. He
ordered that the church of the Nativity should not be destroyed, because
he himself revered Jesus as a prophet.
It is said that he prayed in the S. apse
because it was oriented towards
Mecca, and that an agreement was
reached between him and the
patriarch Sophronius to the effect that
Muslims were allowed to pray individually in the S. apse. This meant
that when Caliph al-Hakim decreed
that all Christian sites were to be destroyed, the Muslims were able, in
1099, to prevent the decree from
being applied to the church of the
Nativity in Bethlehem.
Crusaders: Tancred, the Norman
prince, captured Bethlehem in 1099.
In 1101, Baldwin I of Boulogne was
crowned King of Jerusalem in the
church of the Nativity. He refused to
have a golden crown set upon his head
in the city in which Christ was
crowned with thorns. Baldwin's successor, Baldwin II of Le Bourg, was
also crowned in the church of the
Nativity (1118). The church was restored throughout under Baldwin III
(1152–62).
Downfall: After the Latin Kingdom
of Jerusalem collapsed in 1187 and the
Crusaders withdrew, the church fell
into disrepair and was raided by
looters.

Church of the Nativity (Kikar

HaMolad): The courtyard is some 230 ft. long, and is bounded to the E. by the entrance façade of the church, to the S. by the fortress-like outer walls of the Armenian monastery, and to the N. by a fenced-in garden. Three portals originally led from the courtyard into the narthex. Of these three, only the central one, twice reduced in size, survives in the S. half of the richly moulded door lintel. The N. portal was bricked up and disappeared behind the buttress, while the S. portal, after being blocked up, disappeared behind the walls of the Armenian monastery.

Now that three walls have been added, the interior of the narthex is divided into four separate rooms: the S. room leads to the Armenian monastery, the middle one to the basilica, the N. room to the guardroom, and the room in the extreme N. gives on to the tower chapel which can only be entered from the Franciscan monastery. The narthex, which is now vaulted, originally had a timber ceiling. The wooden door leading into the nave retains some remnants of Armenian carving (1227) with two inscriptions (Arabic and Armenian): 'This door was created with the aid of Allah (Praise be to Him) in the days of our ruler al-Malik al-Mu'azzam in the month of Muharram, 624 AH (= AD 1227).' In addition: 'This door was created with the aid of the Holy Mother of God by the hands of Father Abraham and Father Arahel in the time of King Hetum, son of Constantine, in the year 676 (= 1227). May God have mercy upon their work.'

Basilica: The nave and aisles form a rectangular, colonnaded hall, 86 ft. wide, 95 ft. long, with the nave being higher than the aisles. The positions and dimensions of the column bases are the same as those in the nave of Constantine's church, although the earlier church was one bay shorter at the W. wall. Four rows of columns, each consisting of 11 columns 20 ft. high, divide the basilica into a nave

and four aisles of varying widths. The nave is twice as wide as any individual aisle. The clerestory (*c.* 30 ft.) and ceiling of the nave are supported on either side by 10 columns, a semi-column and a pillar. The architrave and ceiling of the side aisles rest on two rows of 11 columns, one row on each side of the building. The columns are 8 ft. 10 in. apart. The clerestory has 11 broad, high round-arched windows without any moulding. The easternmost window on both sides of the nave has been blocked up. The five windows which once pierced the walls of the aisles have today all been walled up on both the N. and S. sides. The E. end has a crossing with four pillars, each with engaged half-columns on two sides, a central, semicircular apse and a transept, each arm of which also ends in a semicircular apse (probably on the model of Roman tombs and Cellae coemeteriales). A Greek Orthodox iconostasis (17C, rebuilt in 1764 and gilded in 1853) blocks the view of the central apse. There are two altars of the Armenian church in the left transept. One altar (N. apse) is dedicated to the Virgin Mary, the other to the Magi (behind the N. entrance to the Nativity grotto). A door leads from the N. apse into the convent of St.Catherine, and from the middle of the S. apse another door leads into the garden of the Greek Orthodox monastery. An octagonal Byzantine font, decorated on four sides with crosses in relief and bearing a Greek inscription, stands in the right aisle. Each of the three apses originally had three large round-arched windows. The windows in the N. apse have been blocked up because of the adjoining convent, and the central window of the S. apse was converted into a door leading into the Greek Orthodox monastery.

Architectural sculpture: The columns in the four colonnades are of red limestone quarried locally. They have finely worked capitals comprising three rows of acanthus leaves nestling around the bowl, the middle leaf of the upper row supporting the small inner volutes, the outer two leaves supporting the outer volutes. The abacus consists of two plinths of unequal size, folding in towards the middle. In the middle of the abacus, on all four sides, there is an ornamental boss with a bud and a cluster of leaves forming a curved relief cross with arms of equal length. Above the capitals there are wooden architraves with rectangular central panels cut out of their under sides. These panels are decorated with lotus blossoms in bas-relief.

Mosaics: Many of the mosaic decorations have survived. In the E. of the church there is a cycle depicting the life of Christ. The Transfiguration, Entry into Jerusalem (E. wall of S. transept), Christ appearing to Doubting Thomas, and parts of the Ascension (E. wall of N. transept), have survived.

The remains of a lavish mosaic floor, probably laid out in the 4/5C for Constantine's basilica, are to be found in the nave, protected by hinged wooden covers. The mosaic pavement, 54 ft. long and 22 ft. 6 in. wide, is now 2 ft.

6 in. below the floor of the Justinian church, the columns of which have obliterated the mosaics in places. In the nave there is a large panel, subdivided into several sections, with geometrical patterns, fruits and acanthus leaves. The W. square-shaped section has an outer geometrical border and an inner one of fruits surrounded by acanthus leaves. The rectangular E. section has two squares to the W., with round slabs and small squares, and to the E. there are four circles with rosettes formed from triangles and ribbon motifs.

Paintings: There are medieval paintings (Italian works?) of Byzantine and Western Saints in the nave and aisles.

Nativity grotto: The system of grottoes known as the Nativity grotto lies underneath today's crossing and the bay which adjoins it to the E. and it is approached by Justinian steps leading down on either side of the choir. The portals are Frankish, while the bronze doors are again Justinian. These doors display a pattern of interpenetrating groined arches whose middle panels are filled with crosses. The long cave (40 ft. 5 in. long and 10 ft. 4

Church of the Nativity

in. wide) runs from W. to E. and has an irregular vault which is partly hewn from the rock and partly built of brick. At the E. end of the cave there is a man-made apse-shaped niche, on the floor of which a star indicates the site of the birth. The star was installed in 1717, stolen in 1847 and replaced by a copy in 1853. It bears the Latin inscription 'Hic de virgine Maria Jesus Christus natus est' ('Jesus Christ was born here of the Virgin Mary'). 32 silver votive lamps—each of them being a symbol for a branch of the Christian church—are suspended above the star.

Fountain of David (N. of the Nativity church): There are three cisterns, one of which has been archaeologically excavated. To the SE there is a well-preserved burial site, now restored, with 18 niche tombs each containing 2–6 individual graves.

House of Joseph (S. of the milk grotto): A small rectangular church (1891). This is said to be the site of the house in which the Holy Family lived in the period between the Nati-

vity and the Flight into Egypt. Traces of an earlier church (mosaic inscription) in the apse and SW section.

Church of St.Catherine: A church consecrated in 1882, with a nave, two aisles and a bell tower. The N. aisle is dedicated to St.Catherine, the S.aisle to the Nativity, and the nave to the Adoration of the Magi. The pavement is of marble, and black and white stones. Three marble altars: the high altar (1860) in the nave is from the previous church, while the side altars are dedicated to St.Francis and St.Anthony (1881).

System of grottoes: A flight of steps in the N. apse of the transept leads to an extensive system of grottoes which has been investigated by archaeologists since 1962 and was given its present form in 1964. The ceramics and pre-Constantine masonry suggest that these caves were in use in the 1&2C AD. The S. section, 16 ft. long and 7 ft. 10 in. wide, of the *Great Grotto* has housed the chapel of St.Joseph since 1621. A painting above the altar depicts the sleeping Joseph being told by the angel to flee into

Nativity grotto, star marking the place of birth

Egypt (St.Matthew 2, 13). A cross with the Greek monogram of Christ is seen on the bare rock ceiling. Four rock tombs, and niche tombs in the E. and N. walls, were discovered in front of the altar in 1962. A triple system of niche tombs with several pits was found in the NE corner of the Great Grotto. In front of this system there is an altar, the so-called *table of St.Jerome*. The massacre of the innocents (St.Matthew 2, 16–18), said to have been killed by Herod, is commemorated in the tombs. The grottoes of St.Jerome are to the W. of the Great Grotto. The new masonry in the W. wall leads to the grotto of St.Eusebius of Cremona, the pupil and follower of St.Jerome, the Doctor of the Church from Strido in Dalmatia, and to the grottoes of two Roman patrician ladies, Paula and her daughter Eustachium. The *grotto of St.Jerome* is in the W. section. St.Jerome (347–419/ 20) founded a monastery in Bethlehem in AD 389, and completed his Latin translation of the Bible here (the Vulgate). An altar and the Saint's cenotaph are to be seen in the grotto. The Crusaders transferred his relics to the church of Santa Maria Maggiore in Rome in the 13C.

Milk grotto: A natural grotto in the limestone rock on the N. slope of Bethlehem. It is said that when the Virgin Mary was suckling the Christ child here, some drops of milk fell on the ground and turned it into white stone. The grotto has been in use since the Iron Age. The inhabitants of Bethlehem built a small chapel (9 ft. 9 in. to the N., 11 ft. 6 in. to the E., 13 ft. to the S., 11. ft. to the W.) outside this grotto on the ruins of a 4C church rebuilt in the 14C. The façade has mother-of-pearl decorations; there is a statue of the Virgin in a niche in the middle of the façade. An entrance in the middle of the church leads to the

◁ *Church of the Nativity, columns with remains of paintings*

Church of St.Catherine, aisle

Crypta lactis B(eatae) M(ariae) V(irginis).

Environs: Artas (4 km. S.): An Arab village with the convent of Hortus Conclusus (founded in 1901), reputedly the site of Solomon's garden (Song of Solomon 4, 12). There is a Mameluke inscription from 1306 on the door of the small village mosque.
Betar (10 km. NW): The scene of the last few hours of the Bar-Kochba rebellion (AD 135). The moat, and remains of the walls and tower, of the *fortress of Khirbet el-Yehud* are to be found on the summit (2,300 ft.). A *Roman inscription* in the valley near the village commemorates the 10th Roman Legion (AD 135). *Finds:* EZ II potsherds from the time of the Kings of Israel.
Beit Sahur/Shepherds' field (1.5 km. E.): The story of the shepherds who were watching over their flocks at

the time of Christ's birth is recorded in two Christian traditions (St.Luke 2, 8–14). *Greek Orthodox shepherds' field* (Keniset er-Ra'wat: E.). The first of the four phases of this building in the valley basin is one of the oldest churches in the Holy Land: the Holy Cave (between AD 350–400), a two-storeyed shrine (5C), a basilica (6C), and a Byzantine monastery with a church (7–10C). Excavation work on these four churches, built between the time of St.Jerome and the Crusaders, has been in progress since 1972, supervised by the Greek patriarchate. The Holy Cave is a crypt, still with the original tunnel vault. The mosaic floor in the bare rock has two crosses, something which was prohibited in the Christian period from 427 onwards. The two-storeyed shrine: 16 steps lead to a room 36 × 49 ft. in area, with an E. apse, a central prayer room and a small W. narthex above the grotto. In the centre of the beautifully framed, apse-shaped mosaic, a delicate network of tendrils and grapes is seen rising from an amphora. In the lower third of the mosaic are two inscriptions, the left one of which survives intact: 'Remember, Lord, thy servant Lazarus and all his donations. Amen!' The basilica: an enclosure (200 × 160 ft.) was built around the shepherds' field under Justinian, who ordered a basilica (50 × 100 ft.), with a large atrium in the W., to be built above the older church in the cave. This basilica was destroyed when the Persians invaded in AD 614. Archaeological finds: mosaic fragments, marble columns, Corinthian capitals and fragments of the marble railings. The monastery church: the basilica was rebuilt to the original plans in the 7C. A stone roof was supported by massive stone pillars. There was a white mosaic pavement on the floor, and the interior walls were painted. A burial site has been uncovered NE of the lower church, with over 100 skeletons, oil lamps, pectoral crosses, and coins. The Byzantine surrounding walls from the 6C have been rebuilt. Orthodox monks were still visiting the crypt in the 15C. *Latin shepherds' field* (Khirbet Siyar el-Ghanam; 2 km. E.): In the 1C AD, the natural caves were inhabited by nomadic shepherds. A small monastery was built above the caves in c. AD 400. A larger monastery stood on the same site from the 6–8C, and was abandoned in the late 8C. Several excavation projects have been carried out in the field which measures 138 xc 262 ft. Three periods can be distinguished. A) poor shepherds' lodging (the finds include cooking pots, lamps, coins, terra sigillata). B) small monastery (coins and architectural remains; substructures of an apse in the NE corner; S. outer wall (this monastery was later covered over by the large monastery)). C) large monastery: a large staircase leads into an irregular forecourt which gives on to the inner courtyards (destroyed). The chapel with its two

hallways was in the NE corner. Materials from the Constantine basilica of the Nativity were used in its construction. Finds: door lintel with crosses, altar fragments, column bases and capitals, coloured mosaic tesserae. There are a stable and old common rooms in the S. section. A bakery, large presses and store rooms are to be found in the W. wing. The numerous grottoes underneath the monastery were used as tombs, reservoirs and cisterns. A ramifying system of grottoes has been discovered N. of the monastery. In the SE corner of the shepherds' field there is a small monastery with a hospice. The church of Sanctorum Angelorum ad Pastores (1953–4) by the Italian architect Barluzzi stands beside the caves in that field. It has a unique dome, which is a mixture of a bedouin tent and a tower.

Bir el-Qutt (2.5 km NE): The 6C Georgian *monastery of St.Theodore*, discovered in 1952/3. A narrow passage leads from the E. of the rectangular monastery (115 × 100 ft.) into a central courtyard surrounded on all sides by columns and decorated with geometrical motifs. There is a Georgian inscription in the courtyard. The monastery church (62 × 25 ft.), with an inner apse, stands to the NE of the courtyard. Underneath the church there is a crypt with four burial places. The mosaic pavement of the nave has been largely obliterated. A door on the SW side led to a chapel, and another door opened on to a corridor covered with white mosaic. This structure survives in good condition, and its roof was supported by six pillars.

Beit Jala (W. suburb of Bethlehem): This is the Biblical Giloh and the birthplace of Ahithophel the Gilonite (2 Samuel 15, 12). *Greek Orthodox church:* A block of stone 5 ft. tall, consisting of a central section and side sections projecting at right angles,

Church of St.Catherine, monastery garden ▷

stands in front of one of the pillars on the left of the nave.

Deir Dosi (7 km. NE): A *monastery of St.Theodosius* built from AD 423–529 and founded in 476. Over 400 coenobites lived in the monastery in the 5/6C. The church (67 ft. 6 in. × 37 ft. 6 in.) is divided by columns into a nave and two aisles, which end in small semicircular recesses in the E. The rectangular main area (37 ft. 6 in. × 25 ft. 6 in.) opens into an internal apsidal transept. The church had three entrances in the W., as well as one in the N. and one in the S. An entrance in the W. led into the narthex (39 ft. long). The archaeological finds include Corinthian and basket-type capitals. The monastery was destroyed by the Persians in 614. The Crusaders rebuilt it, but it was destroyed by the Arabs shortly afterwards. Rebuilt in 1914–52. The modern monastery consists of a rectangular enclosure with corner towers, a large courtyard and a church with a nave and two aisles above the remains of the earlier Byzantine and Frankish churches. St.Theodosius's tomb, along with those of his mother and sister, is in the monastery courtyard. The 'Grotto of the Magi', who—so the Christian legend has it—made a stop here on their way to Bethlehem, is in the crypt of the new church and this also contains the tombs of the monks who were slain in 614 and 808/13.

Deir Kirmizan (SW of Beit Jala): A *Salesian monastery* on the slopes of Har Jala.

Deir Mar Jiryis/Khadr (4 km. SW of Bethlehem): One of the 20 churches in the Holy Land dedicated to St.George. The monastery and church are surrounded by a common wall. There is a courtyard between the monastery and the long wall of the church. *Church:* A Greek inscription states that St.George hid himself in the crypt of the Greek church. Inside the church, by the right long wall, there is an iconostasis with a large image of St.George, and underneath this are numerous tammata (human figures and parts of the human body; a hand holding a pen and writing).

Deir Mar Ilyas (3.5 km. NE): The *monastery*, a 6C Byzantine foundation, was destroyed by an earthquake

Beit Sahur/shepherds' field (Bethlehem), ruins

and rebuilt by the Crusaders in 1160. Elijah is said to have rested here while fleeing from Jezebel (1 Kings 19, 5). However, the likelihood is that the monastery was founded by Elias, the patriarch of Jerusalem (d. 518), and that it was not until the 12C that the Franks dedicated it to the prophet Elijah. Restored in the 18C. The Jordanians used it as a military observation post from 1948–67. It is now a Greek Orthodox monastery.

Tomb of Rachel (1 km. N.): See Ramat Rahel.

Herodion (11 km. SE): See separate entry: Herodion.

Kefar Ezyon (14 km. SW of Bethlehem): A kibbutz founded in 1943, with a *museum* documenting the history of Jewish settlement in the mountains around Hebron.

Khirbet Abu Ghunnein (3 km. NE of Bethlehem): A ruined 5C Byzantine *monastery* uncovered in 1952. An enclosed rectangular monastery (81 ft. 3 in. × 60 ft. 5 in.) arranged around a courtyard. To the N. of the courtyard there is a nave measuring 54 ft. 10 in. × 16 ft. 9 in., with an apse 7 ft. 5 in. in diameter. The main area was divided into three parts in the Islamic period.

Khirbet Bureikut: A *Byzantine church* uncovered in 1976: it is a basilica with a nave and two aisles above a cave converted into a crypt. Fine mosaics in the nave and crypt.

Khirbet el-Hubeila (10 km. SW of Bethlehem): A *basilica* (5/6C) uncovered in 1925. Its dimensions are 52 × 41 ft. Two rows, each of four columns, divided this basilica into a nave and two aisles, with an inner apse. Only three of the columns resting on stylobates are still on their original site. The mosaics are as follows: A polychrome mosaic with geometrical patterns and plant and animal motifs. A flower pattern with 25 leaves is surrounded by a guilloche band. Each of the flowers subdivides a diagonal band, consisting of black leaves, into four zones. In front of the apse there is an octagonal panel with plants and two fish, and a panel with interwoven geometrical lies W. of the nave. The finds include Corinthian capitals with lotus blossoms. The monastery was destroyed by the Persians in AD 614.

Khirbet el-Makhrum (6 km. E. of

Deir Dosi (Bethlehem), monastery of St.Theodosius

Bethlehem): A *monastery of St. Theodosius*, uncovered in 1950. This building (165 × 108 ft.) had entrances in the N. and the E. A narrow corridor to the S. of the courtyard had a mosaic floor and was flanked by two rooms. There was an eight-line Greek inscription in the mosaic.

Khirbet Juhzum (6 km. E. of Bethlehem): A *Marcian monastery* uncovered in 1954. A polychrome mosaic with geometrical patterns, and also a stone monument, are to be found in a small room in the E. There is a six-line Greek inscription on one side, and the other side has a bas-relief of two peacocks facing one another with a cross flanked by two columns. A long room (66 × 20 ft.) has a polychrome mosaic with geometrical patterns; to the N. of this is the dormitory, covered with white mosaic. This monastery was founded in the 6C.

Solomon's pools/Berekhot Shelomo (4 km. S. of Bethlehem): This water system, which was first investigated in 1878, consists of three large basins rising up in a series of steps from the bottom of the valley so that each basin can be emptied into the one below it, each of the three basins being 20 ft. above the next. The top basin is partly hewn from the rock, and partly built of stone; its walls are supported by pillars and stone stairs descend in the SW corner. The basin is 381 ft. long, 228 ft. 6 in. wide at the top, 235 ft. 6 in. wide at the bottom, 25 ft. deep, and has a capacity of some 2,120,000 cu.ft. The middle basin is 423 ft. long, 160 ft. wide at the top, 249 ft. wide at the bottom, and 39 ft. deep, with a capacity of some 3,530,000 cu.ft. This basin is mostly cut from the rock and has rock steps in the NE and NW corners. The E. wall is supported by an embankment. The lower basin is partly hewn from the rock, and has stairs in the SE and NE corners. It is 581 ft. long, 148 ft. wide at the top, 207 ft. wide at the bottom, and 49 ft. deep. It holds 4,590,000 cu.ft. The middle and lower basins have nymphaea which are either built of stone or hewn from the rock. The basins are fed from the S., both by their own springs and by an aqueduct. The three basins, which date from the Herodian period,

Deir Mar Ilyas (Bethlehem), monastery

collected spring and rain water, which was then carried to Jerusalem via an aqueduct. The *Qal'at el-Burak* (NW of the basin area) is a square structure defended by towers which was built as a castle in *c.* 1620 and has since then been used as a caravanserai.

Teqoa (8 km. SE): The Biblical *Tekoah* is mentioned in the Old Testament as being a place south of Bethlehem in the area of the tribe of Judah (Joshua 15, 59). It was the home town of the wise woman who persuaded David to cause his son Absalom to return to Jerusalem after slaying his half-brother Amnon (2 Samuel 14, 2 ff.); it was also the home town of one of David's heroes (2 Samuel 23, 26) and of the prophet Amos (Amos 1, 1). After the division of the kingdom, King Rehoboam ordered Tekoah to be enlarged into a fortress (2 Chronicles 11, 6; cf. Jeremiah 6, 1). Inhabitants of Tekoah are mentioned as working on building the temple in the period following the Exile (Nehemiah 3, 5/27).

Amos is the third of the twelve Minor Prophets and the author of the book of Amos. He is the oldest and most brusque of the Old Testament prophets. He was a herdsman in Tekoah in the southern kingdom of Judah. In *c.* 755 BC, at the end of King Jeroboam II's reign, Amos was active in Beth-el, the temple of the northern kingdom of Israel, before being expelled from Israel at the instigation of Amaziah the priest. His prophecies reflect the foreign political situation (the threat posed by the Assyrians), and also the prevailing social tensions. Amos says that the tyranny practised by the easy-going upper classes will lead to God's judgement manifesting itself in the devastation of the country and the deportation of its inhabitants. The book concludes with two messages of salvation.

Church of St.Nicholas: The ruins of a Byzantine church with a nave and two aisles. The apse in the E. survives in good condition and there is a mosaic pavement of white and pale red tesserae and the remains of column bases. The *Amos Propheteion:* A grotto where the tomb of the prophet Amos is revered. *Font:* 230 ft. from the grotto of Amos there is a font 4 ft. high in the form of an octagonal basin.

Solomon's pools (Bethlehem)

Bet Shean

Northern District/Israel   p.318□F 5

The steeply rising excavation mound of Tel el-husn, on which the old town of Bet Shean stood, is at the E. end of the Yizre'el plain, where it descends into the Jordan valley, 26 km. from the Sea of Galilee. The modern town on the far side of the Wadi el-Melab is now further to the S., in the area of the Hellenistic-Byzantine town. Bet Shean is among the oldest and most important settlements in Israel, and has been inhabited almost without a break from the end of the Neolithic period (3500 BC) until the present day. Bet Shean was first mentioned in documents in the 19C BC. Thutmosis III conquered it in 1479 BC and enlarged it into a powerful fortress, but after his death it was neglected by Ekhnaton. It was an Israelite town from the 11C BC until the downfall of the northern kingdom in 724 BC. Under the name of *Skythopolis,* it gained new life in the Hellenistic period, and became part of the empires of the Diadochi (Seleucids and Ptolomies). It was incorporated into the Hasmonaean empire under John Hyrcanus in 107 BC, and in 63 BC it was the only town W. of the Jordan to be appointed by Pompey to be a member of the dekapolis, the Hellenistic federation of ten cities. Under the Severian emperors (AD 183–235) it was a place of peace and prosperity; the centre of the textile industry, and a large theatre was built. In the 4C, Bet Shean became the capital of the Roman province of Palaestina Secunda, and was also a diocesan seat. In the Byzantine period it was a Christian town with monasteries, churches and a Jewish community which ceased to exist when the town was conquered by the Arabs in AD 636. While it was ruled by the Arabs, it was called *Beisan,* and degenerated into an insignificant provincial town. Adam de Bethune became the Baron of Beisan during the time of the Crusaders and he had a small castle which was destroyed by Saladin in 1183. Saladin's conquest was accompanied by the return of a small Jewish community, which subsequently produced Estori ha-Parhi (1280–1355?), the author of the oldest work in the Hebrew language on the geography of Palestine ('Sefer Kaftor va-Ferah', Venice, 1549). The town fell into disrepair over the next few centuries. The Turks built a serail (government building) here in 1905.

Tel el-husn (= 'hill of strength'; an excavation mound): 18 strata of human settlement were uncovered between 1921 and 1933. Stratum XVIII dates from 3500 BC. Strata XV and XIII are early Bronze Age. The oldest settlement corresponds to the settlement in Megiddo. The early Chalcolite inhabitants (3500 BC) excavated caves in the exposed rock in the lowest stratum of the hill, and built their clay huts above this. There are no signs of permanent settlement during the middle part of the Bronze Age (2000–1900 BC). The period which is a matter of historical record does not begin until stratum X, where there is a Hyksos tomb dated to mid-Bronze Age II. Stratum IX: After Amosis had driven the Hyksos out of Canaan in c. 1500 BC, the Egyptians ruled the town for 300 years. The oldest *temple,* built in a mixture of the Canaanite and Egyptian styles, dates from c. 1350, the so-called Amarna period. The items discovered in the temple include a basalt relief of a fight between a lion and a dog, and a stela which Pa-Ra-em-Heb, in memory of his father Amen-em-Apt, dedicated to the Canaanite god Mekal, the 'Lord of Bet-Shean'. This basalt relief is the only Orthostate stone slab in Palestine. The art of these stone slabs is indigenous to the Syrian-Mesopotamian area. Stratum VII (1300 BC): Two *stele* of Sethos I, in which he recorded hostilities occurring in the

Bet Shean, Roman theatre ▷

first year of his reign (1350 BC). These stele record victories won in various places and give exact topographical details. A *migdol* (fortified tower) and a *residence* of the Egyptian military governor have been excavated. This complex includes provincial *statues* of *Ramses II and III* (13–12C BC). Stratum V (1000 BC): For the first time, the brick walls of the early Iron Age town were given good rubble foundations (1000–850 BC).

Israelite period: Bet Shean fell into Israelite hands at the end of David's rule. It is said that the temples of Dagon and Ashtaroth (1 Samuel 31, 10) survived until the Persian period. Skythopolis: Gentiles settled here after the Babylonian Exile, and the new town was moved into the valley S. of Tel el-husn after the area had been occupied by Alexander. A temple of Dionysus was erected on Tel el-husn, and a theatre was built on the slope beyond the valley in 7 BC.

Temples: Archaeologists have discovered a succession of four temple complexes in the composite Canaa-

nite-Egyptian style. *1st temple:* (temple of Amenophis III, *c.* 1411 BC): This temple, 48 ft. 9 in. long and 46 ft. 7 in. wide, consists of two anterooms and an open courtyard containing two columns supporting the flat roof above the altar room which lies at the end of the building. In the courtyard there are a small altar and some painted stones. Seven steps lead from the courtyard into the upper (roofed) altar room, where there is another altar. *2nd temple* (Seth temple, 1303–1290 BC): An external portico was built on to the 1st temple. *3rd temple:* A new temple (the S. temple) was built under Rameses I (1292–25 BC). This building has a W.-E. orientation. The entrance in the W. leads into a hall with a nave and two aisles. There are six columns, with breast-high walls between them. A wide room which contained the altar adjoins the hall in the E. There were store-rooms N. and S. of the hall. Figures of the gods Seth and Ashtoreth were discovered in this temple. The god most commonly venerated here was Reshef. *4th temple:* The N.

Bet Shean, Roman theatre, entrance (left), Virgin Mary monastery, mosaic (right)

or Ashtaroth temple, which was used for cultic purposes until *c.* 1000 BC, is by Rameses III. The wall is 5 ft. thick, 53 ft. long and 27 ft. wide. Above the four columns inside this rectangular building there are a cornice and a type of clerestory. There is an altar between the two E. columns, and behind these there are stairs leading into the sanctuary. A figure of the goddess Ashtoreth, who was the goddess mainly worshipped here, was discovered inside. The most recent finds are now in the Rockefeller Museum in Jerusalem. They include the Mekal stela, the Pharaoh I stela, an anthropomorphic clay sarcophagus, and the stela of Anat the goddess of war.

Roman theatre (S. of Tel el-husn): This is the largest, best-preserved and probably finest Roman building in Israel. It is an open-air theatre (2C AD) for some 8,000 spectators, built under Emperor Septimius Severus ([AD] 193–211). The lower section of this semicircular complex, with a cavea of basalt, is cut into the ground. The upper section rises above massive substructures, through which nine vomitories (entrances) lead into: the interior, where they open individually on to the passageway (praecinctio). There were small oval rooms, originally domed, at the ends of the short narrow passages which led away from the vomitories. Some of the upper rows of seats have been destroyed, but 14 rows below the passageway survive in good condition. Some fine remnants of the stage wall, built of yellowish marble, can still be seen. It had niches and was decorated with columns of different stones, including Assuan granite. The scenae frons, which is the wall with three doors at the back of the stage, is 295 ft. long. The richly carved beams of the stage wall are preserved in the open air N. of the theatre.

Monastery of the Noble Lady Maria (N. of Tel el-husn): An inscription in the SE corner of the chapel states that 'the Lady Maria', a title assumed by the wives of high-ranking Byzantine officials, founded the monastery. A tombstone in the chapel proves that the monastery

Bet Shean, Roman theatre

cannot have been built much earlier than AD 567. It survived the Persian invasion in AD 614, but was abandoned shortly afterwards. However, the mosaics, many of which have simple geometrical patterns, were not destroyed. The monastery stands in a courtyard whose N. side is adjoined by a single-aisled chapel (38 ft. 6 in. × 20 ft. 6 in.) with an apse 8 ft. 3 in. deep and a portico. Five rooms (possibly monks' cells) are entered from the chapel. Two of the three Greek inscriptions are in the bema, and the third is in the narthex.

Mosaics: The unknown artist used bright colours (sulphur-yellow, golden yellow, orange, brilliant yellowish green, dark green, and various shades of blue, violet and black) for the mosaics, which are today protected by a cover. He used a bright, yellowish and violet pink stone for the human figures. The leaves of the vines, the acanthus calyx, the brilliant plumage of the birds, and the brightly shining goat, are in glass paste, and so too are some of the grapes and fruit baskets. The garments of the figures are partly of glass and two sorts of marble.

Synagogues. *1. Samaritan synagogue* (920 ft. N. of the Byzantine town wall): A basilica (46 ft. 6 in. × 56 ft.) with a nave and two aisles, and an apse in the NW. The nave, aisles and side rooms are decorated with mosaics and the mosaics contain three Greek inscriptions and a Samaritan one. It is unclear why the synagogue faces west-north-west but its massive walls were used for defence. *2nd synagogue:* (in the Jordan valley): Mosaics and inscriptions have been uncovered in various rooms in this larger complex of buildings. A number of rooms are grouped around what might be a courtyard with a peristyle or else the synagogue itself, built in the form of a basilica. This area is almost square (23 × 23 ft.), and its walls are not parallel with one another. The entrances are in the N. and E. The S. wall, which faces Jerusalem, may have contained the niche with the Aron hakodesh (Torah shrine). Stone benches run around the walls. Some of the *mosaics* have been obliterated. A seven-armed menora on a pedestal with three feet (in a medallion) is depicted in the middle of the mosaic

Bet Shean, Roman theatre

floor. To the right of it there is a mahta, and to the left is a shofar (?). The word 'shalom' is to be seen above the menora. Above this medallion, there are seven further medallions (two of them have been obliterated) showing vine tendrils, with vine leaves and grapes, growing out of an amphora. The five surviving medallions depict animals and birds. The medallions are surrounded by a narrow frame with more animals and birds. An ornamental band of birds, fruits and baskets surrounds the frame on three sides. On the W. side there is a partially obliterated panel with a menora (?) flanked by two lions. A panel with two birds and a Greek inscription is to be seen on the N. side, and on the E. side there is an amphora between two birds facing one another. An Aron ha-kodesh, flanked by two menorot on a pedestal with three feet, is to be found in the nave.

Museum (al-Arbain-al-Ghazzawi mosque): This small museum opened in 1958 is in a former 18C mosque. There are only a few finds: tools from

the mid-Stone Age onwards; cult objects from synagogues; mosaic fragments from the Roman and Byzantine periods. The *Leontis mosaic* is an interesting item. Leontis, a rich Hellenized Jew from Alexandria, came to Bet Shean in the 5C AD, and there he built himself a splendid villa with a mosaic (the synagogue [sl]q.v.[sr] is in the NW area of the courtyard). The mosaic consists of three panels: Top panel: the remains of a Greek inscription in a tabula ansata. An image from the Odyssey: Odysseus is bound to the mast of his ship. A man in a boat is fighting a sea monster. Sirens, animals and fabulous beings. Middle panel: a dedicatory inscription in a circle in the middle. Lower panel: a Nilometer, and next to it are a building and the inscription 'Alexandria'. To the right of this, the Nile god sits on a crocodile with a water bird in his hand. A ship, various animals including doves, and plants, are also depicted.

Also worth seeing: The *town park*, with a small *open-air museum*, and a Turkish *serail* (1905) in which ancient

Bet Shean, museum garden

columns were used for the door posts of the portal. *Roman hippodrome* with columns and tympana from old Skythopolis. *Byzantine church* from the 4C AD (W. side of the Roman theatre).

Environs: Nir David/Tel 'Amal (4 km. W.): A kibbutz founded in 1936 and named after David Wolffsohn (1856–1914). *Archaeological museum:* A museum of Mediterranean archaeology, built to plans by the architects S.Powsner, R.Abraham and E.Rogen, and established in 1963 around the Dan Lifshitz collection. The present collection has local finds from the Bronze and Iron Ages (excavated on Tel 'Amal) and a small but choice collection of objects from Rome, Etruria, S. Italy and Greece from the early historical period until the 2C AD: Painted Arab figurines and clay vessels from ancient Athens. Casting moulds for figurines from the archaic to the Hellenistic period. Etruscan clay vessels of the Villanova type. Jewellery of gold and bronze from Etruria. Painted clay vessels from Etruria and S. Italy. Pottery and everyday crockery from Rome. Stone reliefs from Tarentum and figurines from Tanagra and Attica. A woman's head from Phoenicia. A helmet from Lucaniag (5C BC). Medieval Persian ceramics. The museum stands between the kibbutz and the Sakhne Nature Park.
Rehov (4 km. S.): In spring of 1974, a *synagogue* was discovered some 800 yards NW of Tel Rehov, directly to the E. of the road leading from Bet Shean to Jericho. *Finds:* A marble soreg. On its front there is a seven-armed menora on a pedestal with three feet, and its rear has a floral motif (the soreg is now in the Kibbutz En ha-Naziv, 3 km. S. of Bet Shean). The synagogue had a mosaic, three phases of which can be made out. Only a small section of the 1st, lowest mosaic has been uncovered: a black band on a white background. 2nd mosaic: multi-coloured geometric patterns. 3rd mosaic: multi-coloured geometrical patterns and plant motifs. In the mosaic flooring of the narthex there is a 29-line Hebrew inscription, flanked by a black-and-white geometrical pattern. The synagogue (6/7C) seems to have been destroyed in an earthquake in 748/9.
Tel Basul (1 km. W.): A *monastery* from the 4C or early 5C was uncovered by N.Zori on the Tel (hill) in 1961–2. The large monastery courtyard is covered by a fine mosaic containing Greek inscriptions. Seven rooms, including a chapel with an oval mosaic on its floor, are grouped around the courtyard. Each oval contains animal motifs (gazelle, cat, hen, lamb etc.) and plant motifs (olive, pomegranate etc.). At the chapel entrance, peacocks stand opposite one another on either side of a fruit tree. The other six rooms are decorated with geometrical mosaic patterns.

Bet Shearim

Northern District/Israel   p.318☐D 4

Several ancient buildings, probably from the Severian period, stand in a valley on the NE slope of Tel Sheikh Abreiq. Bet Shearim was first mentioned at the end of the Second Temple period as being a fortified town belonging to a large estate owned by Berenice, who was Agrippa I's daughter and Agrippa II's sister. After the failure of the Bar-Kochba rebellion, the patriarch Juda Ha-Nassi (AD 135–220) turned Bet Shearim ('house of the 100 gates') into an important seat of Jewish learning. It was also here that Juda Ha-Nassi, being the head of the Sanhedrin (High Council), drew up the final edition of the Mishna (the record of religious law). In the 3C AD it became fashionable to be buried in Bet Shearim, and leading rabbis from Palmyra, Beirut and Sidon found their last resting place in the burial ground. The town was destroyed by Gallus

Caesar (AD 351–4) during the Jewish revolt of 351, but it continued to be a small Jewish settlement until it was captured by the Arabs.

Burial grounds (W. and N. of Tel Bet Shearim): Spread over a 5 acre area, Catacombs 1–11 were investigated over several digging seasons from 1936–40, catacombs 12–21 were examined in 1953–8, and catacombs 22–27 in 1956–9. The burial mounds from the 2–4C AD consist of individual and family tombs, with 20–400 tombs in each catacomb. Outside the entrance to the shaft there is usually an open forecourt from which a stone door leads into the interior. Some forecourts were covered with coloured mosaics (catacombs 6 and 11).

Catacomb 1 contains 16 corridors cut into the rock, and has 55 burial chambers with 380 tombs, including vaulted burial niches (arcosolia), sliding graves (kokhim), and rectangular graves (loculi) cut into the rock on the ground.

Catacomb 11 has 16 halls with over 400 burial sites. Between the tomb chambers there are a large number of arches cut into the rock. These arcades rest on coarsely carved capitals and squat spiral columns on tall pedestals. Most of the tombs contain coffins of wood, lead, clay or stone. In some tombs there are bodies with no coffins. Stone doors stand at regular intervals to the left and right of a passage. Some of the family tombs (mausoleums) are richly decorated with floor mosaics, walls built of stone, and arcades. The design of the tombs always complies with the Talmudic rules. The earth embankments of catacombs 1–4 have reliefs (some of them decidedly primitive), paintings and inscriptions in the style of Jewish art in the Roman period, influenced by Oriental and Hellenistic tradition. Apart from various seven-armed menorot, there are also numerous human and animal images, often in sgraffito. A unique early-3C mausoleum, built of ashlars and having four façades, stands beside the catacomb. The floor mosaic portrays dolphins, and a vaulted frieze shows an eagle at the apex of the arch. A peaceful procession of animals is seen on one side of this frieze, and on the other

Bet Shearim, sarcophagus with animal ornament

there are wolves tearing each other to pieces. The mausoleum formerly housed a marble sarcophagus whose long sides show the myth of Achilles on Skyros and the myth of Meleager, while the myth of Leda and the swan is seen on the narrow sides (today the sarcophagus is in the Rockefeller Museum in Jerusalem).

Catacomb 14: A portal with three doors, partly restored. Hebrew inscriptions mention the rabbis Simeon, Gamaliel and (H)anina. This tomb vault may have belonged to a family of patriarchs.

Catacomb 20: This underground palace contains 26 halls, 20 of which are open, with over 200 sarcophagi, some of which weigh 3–5 tonnes. The portal with its three doors was rebuilt in 1957 using fragments from the ruins. Three entrances lead into a hall 165 ft. long, with a façade 130 ft. long built of ashlars which rest on three arcades supported by square pillars. There are vaulted halls and burial chambers inside. The limestone and marble sarcophagi are decorated with garlands, tabulae ansatae, eagles, bulls' heads, heraldic lions, menorot,

a Torah shrine, a lulav, an etrog, a shofar and a mahta. The so-called gate sarcophagus (named after the double gate, with four panels, beside the sarcophagus) portrays the Ark of the Covenant. The lid is decorated with carved bands of plants, geometrical patterns, and a two-handled vessel. Hunting sarcophagus: the front is decorated with a rosette and a lion chasing a gazelle. Shell sarcophagus: there is a carved sea shell in the middle of the lid. At the ends of the long side there are two smaller shells, each of which rests on two columns and, on its inside, shows the Ark of the Covenant in the synagogue. Between the shells there are friezes and medallions with depictions of various local animals. Two lions and an ox's head are carved on the upper part of the sarcophagus. On the left, two birds are seen picking at a bunch of grapes. A bird and a lion are seen to the left and right of the Ark of the Covenant. Mask sarcophagus: a bearded man's head resembling that of Zeus is seen on the narrow side. Most of the inscriptions in catacomb 20 are in Hebrew, and on the sarco-

Bet Shearim, burial ground, corridor with sarcophagi

phagi they are all in Hebrew. They mention the rabbis and their relatives: 'This is the son of R.Levi, who made this tomb.' The sarcophagi of local basalt stone are provincial and the reliefs are by local stonemasons. Some, such as the Amazonomachia, are in the Roman style. The sarcophagi were destroyed at the beginning of the Arab invasion, and the marble was sold. The decorative reliefs on the catacombs is a clear witness to the Hellenization of the Jews under the Romans.

Synagogue (above the tombs): The rectangular 3C synagogue (50 × 115 ft.), which is oriented towards Jerusalem, was uncovered in 1938–9. It was probably destroyed by Gallus Caesar in *c*. AD 352/3. One Hebrew inscription and 15 Greek inscriptions, including tombstone inscriptions, have been discovered here.

Oil press (by the synagogue): A large stone with a deep circular channel opening into a small, round collecting vessel in the floor. The wooden posts which supported a horizontal beam were set in two square holes to the left and right of the circular groove. This lower section of the oil press from the 4C is in the second room of a small building.

Equestrian statue (on the hill): This commemorates Alexander Zaid, who discovered the main entrance to the burial ground in 1936. Zaid was killed in a skirmish in 1938.

Museum (next to catacomb 20): This is housed in a former cistern and has a large collection of sarcophagi, sgraffiti, architectural remains of the 2&3C town, a model of the synagogue, depictions of the menora, inscriptions, and a block of reddish glass which weighs eight tonnes and is one of the largest glass blocks in the world.

Bet Shearim, synagogue

Caesarea

District of Haifa/Israel   p.318□C 4

In the early Hellenistic period (4C BC), before Herod built Caesarea Maritima, there was a Phoenician harbour on this site between the modern Jaffa and Acre. This fortified harbour was known as *Stratonas Pyrgos* ('Straton's tower') in Greek, and was probably built by the Sidonian king Abdashtart (Greek: Straton) during the rule of Alexander the Great. In the late 2C BC, Stratonos Pyrgos fell into the hands of Zoilos, the tyrant of Dor, who sold the town to Alexander Jannaeus the Hasmonaean in 90 BC. Herodian Caesarea: When the Romans, led by Pompey, conquered the Hasmonaean state in 63 BC, they separated the coast from Judah and annexed it to Syria. After his victory at Actium, Caesar Augustus gave the area around Stratonos Pyrgos to Herod, who built a splendid Graeco-Roman town on this site. He called it Caesarea in honour of Augustus. This town took 12 years to build (22–10 BC). Two enormous towers flank the harbour entrance, and on an elevated site there was a temple of Augustus with two colossal statues, one depicting Caesar Augustus, the other being a personification of the city of Rome. According to Flavius Josephus, six more larger-than-life statues stood at the harbour entrance.

The pedestal of one of these statues is set in the sea-bed, and was discovered during a diving expedition in 1961. Herod built an amphitheatre, a theatre, a court of justice, as well as a hippodrome outside the town walls. In order to keep the town clean, he constructed a drainage system with underground channels running into the sea. The town wall, stretching for about a mile along the sea shore, extended around the town in a semi-circle. The Jews were a minority even before the town was founded. Tensions increased in the first few decades after Christ's birth until open conflicts arose in c. AD 60 under the procurator Felix (AD 52–60). Some 20,000 Jewish inhabitants were slaughtered under Gessius Florus (AD 66). This was the cause of the subsequent Jewish Wars which led to the destruction of Jerusalem and the temple in AD 70. Titus marched to Caesarea with the booty of war after the destruction of Jerusalem, and 2,500 Jewish prisoners were killed in a fight with wild animals on 4 October 70. The town enjoyed great economic growth in the 2&3C AD, the Jewish community built synagogues and schools, and many leading scholars built their academies in Caesarea.

Christian Caesarea: There was a large Christian community here in the first few centuries AD. It was probably founded by Philip (The Acts 8, 40). Peter baptized the Roman captain Cornelius in Caesarea (Acts 10), Paul passed through the town after his first visit to Jerusalem (Acts 9, 30). It was the residence of the archbishop of Palestine from the late 2C AD onwards. Several councils were held in Caesarea (the first was in AD 195). The town surrendered to the Arabs in 639, and in 1101 it was conquered by the Crusaders. King Baldwin I razed the town and killed its inhabitants. The conquerors, in their looting, plundered the Holy Grail (sacro cantino), which is today preserved in San Lorenzo in Genoa. Sultan Salid captured Caesarea in 1187 and destroyed the fortifications. Richard the Lionheart occupied the deserted town in 1191. In 1218, the Frankish castle was added to and rebuilt by Gautier d'Avesnes and Jean de Brienne. Sultan al-Malik al-Mu'azzam conquered it in 1220. It was recaptured in 1251–2 by King Louis IX of France. The large fosse and the continuous talus date back to him, as does the enlargement of the gates. The town surrendered in 1265 after being besieged by Sultan Baibars for seven days, and was utterly destroyed. Sultan al-Ashraf razed the fortifications in 1291, in order to deny the Franks any permanent sites on the coast. Muslim refugees from Bosnia were settled here by the Turks in 1878. Stones from the abandoned town of Caesarea were used in the rebuilding of Acre in the late 18C.

Excavations: Caesarea was excavated several times between 1873 and 1972. The Roman theatre was uncovered in 1959, the Crusader town in 1960–2, the Jewish quarter in 1956 and 1962, the aqueduct in 1963, and the N. area of the Byzantine road in 1971–2.

Hellenistic period: Potsherds of Aegean and Greek origin. The corner of a house abandoned in the early 1C BC. A massive rampart 310 ft. long and 205 ft. wide ran into the sea. Two enormous round towers.

Roman period: The *Roman theatre,* S. of the town was restored in 1970. It enables us to some extent to determine the history of ancient theatres until Byzantine times. Two semicircular towers were later built above it. The cavea with the original rows of seating running around the orchestra survives from the Herodian theatre, and this proves that the theatre was built in the Hellenistic manner. The euripus (water channel) and the horizontal passageway were modelled on the theatre in Eretria. The floor of the orchestra was covered with painted plaster which has been renovated 14 times and has been decorated with numerous ornamental patterns (geometrical flowers, fish scales). The orchestra wall was decorated in imitation marble (cf. Leptis Magna in Roman Africa). The scenae frons, also

Caesarea, harbour mole with ancient columns

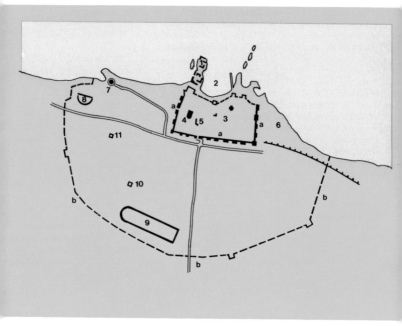

Caesarea a Walls and moat of Crusader town (11-13C) **b** Late Roman- Byzantine town wall (2-6C) **1** Citadel **2** Old harbour **3** Crusader town **4** Crusader cathedral of St.Paul **5** Remains of Augustus temple **6** Jewish quarter in Roman period **7** Roman bath **8** Roman amphitheatre **9** Hippodrome **10** Byzantine business street **11** Theatre

in the Hellenistic style, has a square exedra in the middle with narrow concave niches on both sides of it. The sides towards the podium had delicate plaster work. The painted pulpitum (the front part of the stage, in front of the spectators) was decorated with plaster, like the niches. The cavea and orchestra were rebuilt on the latest Roman lines in the 2&3C AD, reusing materials from the earlier theatre. The central exedra of the scenae frons now became semicircular, and was flanked by deep square niches on both sides. The exedra and the walls facing the public were decorated with rows of columns, and the orchestra (diameter: 100 ft.) was inlaid with marble, while the seats of the auditorium have stone inlay. In the lower part of the auditorium there were either six or seven wedges, each with 13 rows of seats. There was a rectangular platform for the governor in the central wedge. Vomitories led into the auditorium from six entrance arches. A semicircular platform was set up behind the stage in the 3C (cf. the theatre of Dougga in N. Africa). In the 3C or 4C AD, the orchestra was converted into a large water basin (columbetra) for waterworks on the model of Athens and Corinth. The cisterns in the theatre, which were still in use in the Byzantine and Arab periods, date from that time. A stone mentioning 'Pontius Pilatus, Praefectus Judaea' (today it is in the Rockefeller Museum in Jerusalem) was discovered during the excavations.

Caesarea, Roman theatre

Hippodrome (NE of the theatre, some 250 ft. from the harbour): The porta pompae (entrance) of this building oriented towards the NE is in the SW. The arena surrounds an embankment which survives to a length of 2,290 ft. The long side of the arena, which measures 1,480 × 260 ft., is divided by a wall, the spina, with numerous cultic and decorative objects: statues, altars, obelisks and trophies. The spina is still readily discernible. The finds include an obelisk of red porphyry, which has fallen into four pieces. In its present state, it is 34 ft. 6 in. long, 5 ft. 4 in. high and 3 ft. 6 in. wide. The tip found on the W. talus is 3.6 ft. long. There are three conical stumps of red porphyry in the immediate vicinity. Each of these is 7 ft. 9 in. high, with a diameter of 5 ft. 10 in. at the top and of 3 ft. 9 in. at the bottom. These stones were probably the three conical stones (metae) which

stood at each end of the spina. A rectangular block of red granite, 7 ft. 5 in. in length, at the foot of the talus may represent a taraxippos which was intended to frighten horses and induce them to run faster.

Water conduit (1 km. N. of the Crusaders' road): Archaeological evidence shows that the water conduit running above ground to the W. should be dated to the time of Herod, and not the early 2C AD as had been thought until recently. The 2nd, 6th and 10th Roman legions carried out major repairs to it at the time of the Bar-Kokhba rebellion. This conduit carried water to the town from the springs of the lower Carmel some 16 km. away.

Synagogue (N. of the Crusader fortress): Excavated by Avi-Yonah in 1956–62. This synagogue a few yards

Caesarea, aqueduct

above the sea stands on the foundations of older buildings, one of which, from the Herodian period, may itself have been a synagogue. The building (3/4C AD) is of the wide type and is oriented towards the S. The entrance to this building (area: 30 × 60 ft.) was on the narrow E. side. The floor was laid with mosaics. *Finds:* Fragments of a stone panel with a list of priests. Coins.

The synagogue was destroyed in the 4C. Another synagogue, also oriented towards the S., was built on the same site in *c.* AD 450. *Finds:* In the floor mosaic in the portico there is a Greek inscription relating to the founding of the building. Marble columns, capitals with depictions of menorot, a marble panel with a seven-armed menora, parts of a soreg. The Greek inscription on the white mosaic pavement in the narrow portico (area: 36 × 8 ft. in.) reads: 'Beryllus Archisy-

nagogus and Leiter, the son of Justus, made this mosaic with his money.'

Crusaders' town: The citadel on the S. mole of the harbour was excavated in 1960–2, along with the remains of the large keep (62 × 62 ft.) which has collapsed completely. The Crusaders' town, built of grey limestone, occupied a trapezoid area on the harbour. St.Louis built the regularly laid out rectangle of defences in 1254, their long W. side bordering the sea.

The *entrance* is in the E., through a vaulted gate. To the left of this there are ruined houses with a cistern which has a marble outlet leading to a fountain. The Crusaders reused ancient building materials for the foundations of their roads and buildings.

Ramparts: The lower section of the wall is reinforced by a massive embankment inclined at 60°. The E. rampart is 2,150 ft. long, the S. ram-

Caesarea, vaulted passageway

part 900 ft., the N. rampart 900 ft. *Fortifications:* The bank of the ditch survives to a height of 13–20 ft. The ditch is 45 ft. deep, and 23 ft. wide on the rocky side. The rampart above the glacis was 33 ft. high, and the only remains are by the S. gate. In the rampart there are loopholes/firing slits, two of which survive. 16 towers: nine in the E. rampart, four in the S. rampart, three in the N. rampart. These towers, 33 × 56 ft. high, are 25–30 ft. behind the rampart.

Three town gates: The N. gate is in the middle of the N. rampart. A bridge over the ditch stands on a column 5 ft. 6 in. × 14 ft. in height. The rib-vaulted gateway is 27 ft. long. Its columns and capitals are decorated with plant motifs. The gate is reached from the SW corner of the gatehouse. The main entrance of the E. gate is in the E. wall. Access to it is gained via a bridge supported by four columns and four arches. The magnificent hall of this rib-vaulted 13C gatehouse 50 × 15 ft. in area is covered with small rectangular tiles. The gates were reached by drawbridges. In the SW corner were a fountain and a water basin.

Streets: The pointed arches of a street, which was once covered, stand to the left of the E. town gate.

Crusaders' cathedral of St.Paul: The nave of this church which is over 65 ft. long and was never completed was built on the foundations of the large mosque which itself probably stood above a Byzantine church. The church is in the S. part of the Crusaders' town. Ground plan: three apses and a section of the nave whose articulation cannot be made out. The massive apses to the E., and four buttresses of the W. façade, still stand.

Byzantine road with two statues:

Caesarea, rampart

425 ft. long, with some large marble slabs taken from Roman palaces, some of them with white mosaic (to the S. of the road to Or Aqiva). The two *statues,* which are two-and-a-half times life size, were removed by Flavius Strategius from some 2/3C Roman buildings in the 6C. The first statue, which has no head, is of white marble (the upper and lower parts do not belong together), and is draped with a semi-himation. The second statue, which is of red Egyptian porphyry, depicts an Emperor (probably Hadrian). The figure, wearing a red toga and tunic, rests on a pedestal of grey granite.

Environs: Bet Hananya (7 km. NE): The remains of a *Roman aqueduct,* which conveyed water to Caesarea from the springs of Binjamina, are to be found near the moshav founded in 1950. To the N. of Bet Hananya is the *Tel Mevorakh,* with a *Hyksos fortification* from the 15/16C BC. There is a *Roman mausoleum* (3C AD) on the E. slope of the settlement hill: the side sections of the two sarcophagi decorated with reliefs (now in the Rockefeller Museum in Jerusalem) depict the battle between the Greeks and Amazons.

Kerem Maharal (26 km. NE): This is named after 'Maharala' Judah Loew ben Bezalel, the rabbi and Talmudist from Prague (1525–1609). The moshav founded in 1949 has some charming 17C Arab buildings. There is a fine *mosque* in the centre of the village.

Sedot Yam (1 km. S.): A kibbutz which the HaNo'ar-Ha'Oved group founded in 1940 in the immediate vicinity of the ancient Caesarea (Caesarea HaAtiqa).

Zikhron Ya'akov (16 km. NE): This kibbutz, founded by Romanians in

Caesarea, 'Pontius Pilate' stone

1882 on the S. slopes of Mount Carmel, was named after James (Yakov) de Rothschild. *Bet Aaronsohn* (Rehov HaMeyasdim 41): A small natural history museum founded by Aharon Aaronsohn, the botanist (1876–1917). It has a rich collection of plants from Palestine. The memorial site is complemented by a library. The kibbutz of *Ma'ayan Zevi* (600 inhabitants), founded in 1938, is 2 km. N. of Zikhron Ya'akov.

Cana see Kana

Carmel see Karmel

Elat
Southern District/Israel   p.324☐C 16

Elat, where there are no relics of the past, is the southernmost town in Israel and the only Israeli port on the Red Sea. At the same time it is a tourist centre with comfortable hotels and beaches (it only rains one day a month). It lies at the end of the Gulf of Akaba, and the Jordanian town of Akaba is only 5 km. distant. Elat was founded in 1948 as Israel's Red Sea port and rapidly developed into one of the largest in Israel. The main import is mineral oil; Egypt's blockade of the Gulf of Akaba on 22 May 1967 triggered the Six-Day War.

Biblical history: The biblical Elat is often mentioned in combination with the town of Ezion-geber (Deuteronomy 2, 8). Under King Azariah of Judah (773–36 BC), Elat was recaptured from the Edomites and was then enlarged (2 Kings 14, 21–23). The town was mentioned in King Solomon's day (1 Kings 9, 26). In the Roman period it was known as *Aila* or *Aelana*. According to 1 Kings 9, 26, Ezion-geber 'is beside Eloth, on the shore of the Red sea, in the land of Edom'. Solomon used it as a shipyard and trading port, but there is no further mention of it after the 9C BC. Archaeological finds made in 1969 have refuted the theory that the ancient Elat was located in Tell el-Khlefe, between the modern Elat and Akaba. Ezion-geber may have been on the island of Jazirat Firaun, 9 km. to the S. of Elat. Edomite harbour buildings from the early biblical period (12/11 BC) have been discovered here. The Old Testament mentions that trading in gold was carried on with the country of Ofir, which was probably on the W. coast of Arabia, but may have been opposite it, on the coast of Somalia. In the Middle Ages, the Crusaders attempted to revive the gold trade.

Museums: *Maritime museum.* A collection of exhibits recovered from the Red Sea. *Museum of modern art* with a memorial collection of works by Jewish artists who were exterminated. A *marine museum.*

Environs: Coral island (12 km. S.; Egyptian territory, cannot be reached from Elat): Ruins of a *Crusader castle.* The casemate walls, 13 ft. thick, date from the 12C AD.
Nahal-Hakevtovot (SW): Rock walls with drawings and Hebrew,

Aramaic and Greek writing, some up to 2,000 years old.
King Solomon's columns (29 km. NW): Two natural sandstone columns, 165 ft. high, stand side by side. An *Egyptian temple* from the late Bronze Age stands beside these columns.
Timna (25 km. N.): The copper mines of Timna were closed down in 1976 because they had become uneconomic but their ore, which sometimes occurs in the form of malachite, is in popular demand as a semi-precious stone (Elat stone). Nearby are the so-called copper mines of King Solomon, the remnants of ancient copper mines from the third millennium BC, the 13/12C BC, the 10C BC, and the Byzantine period.

Emmaus/Amwas
West Bank   p.320☐D 7

The town of Amwas, which was formerly Arab, was razed to the ground by the Israelis during the Six-Day War. It lies 1.5 km. to the NE of

Coral island (Elat)

the Latrun monastery on the Tel Aviv—Jerusalem motorway. The Arabic name derives from the biblical *Emmaus* (from the Hebrew 'hmm' = 'hot'; it has been interpreted as 'hot well' because there are two hot springs here).

This town was once of strategic significance owing to its location at the point where the coastal plain passes into the Judaean mountains. In 166 BC, Judas Maccabeus defeated the numerically superior and better-equipped army of Nikanor and Gorgias, the Seleucid commanders (1 Maccabees 4, 1–25; 2 Maccabees 8, 23–29). This victory helped pave the way for the recapture of Temple Mount in Jerusalem by Judas Maccabeus in 164 BC. The Seleucid general Bakkhides fortified the town in 160 BC (1 Maccabees 9, 50 ff.). From 47 onwards Emmaus was the capital of the Roman toparchy of the same name. After the death of Herod the Great, Jewish freedom fighters annihilated a Roman cohort at Emmaus, whereupon the Romans destroyed the town. Emmaus was soon settled again, owing to its abundant waters and fertile soil. In 221, the Emperor Elagabalus elevated it to the status of a town named *Nikopolis* ('town of victory'). There was probably already a Christian community here at this time. The central figure of this community was the historian Julius Africanus (d. after 240), who wrote a Greek chronicle of the world which, for the first time, places biblical events side by side with non-biblical events.

El-Keniseh (excavation hill S. of the town): Five structures were uncovered in numerous digging seasons between 1882 and 1927: 1. *Rock caves* and *walls* 2 ft. 7 in. thick (2&1C BC). 2. Remains of a square *Roman villa* (60 × 55 ft.) from the 2/3C AD. 3. *Byzantine church* (3C AD). 4. *Basilica* and *baptistery* (6C AD). 5. *Crusader church* (12C AD).

Roman villa/house of Cleopas: The foundations of a Roman villa from the 2/3C AD are still discernible outside the entrance to the Byzantine church. It has been suggested that this villa was the house of Cleopas,

Emmaus, Byzantine church

The Emmaus disciples, 19C book illustration

one of the two Emmaus disciples, but on the basis of more recent research it is now thought that it was the first shrine in Emmaus—early Christian divine service was frequently held in private houses until the 4C—and dates from the time of Julius Africanus. The lower half of the large church (3C AD) stands directly above the remains of the villa. The few Roman *mosaics* have not been clearly identified but they consist of circles and octagons. The octagons depict a lion devouring an ox, a panther tearing at a gazelle, and birds in lotus blossoms. There is an inscription in a circle.

Byzantine church: This 3C church, 143 × 74 ft. in area, had three entrances in the W. wall, two rows of 13 columns each, seven windows in the N. wall and seven more in the S. wall. There are further entrances between the windows at the E. end, near the side apses which have a N.-S. orientation. The church had three apses. The synthronos and the altar were in the central apse. A Greek inscription was discovered inside a medallion during the excavations of 1882, when a polychrome mosaic floor was also found in the right side aisle.

Basilica (this is the N. church, to the left of the Crusader church): A small building from the 6C AD without any apses. Its side aisles are separated from the nave by two rows of six columns. One entrance to the basilica, in the middle of its W. wall, is part of the narthex. The W. wall has three entrances altogether. **Baptistery** (to the left of the Crusader church): The square baptistery (34 × 34 ft.) is surrounded by walls 3 ft. thick. There are two Greek inscriptions inside a tabula ansata in the E. part of the mosaic, which has geometrical patterns. Another inscription is seen in a tabula

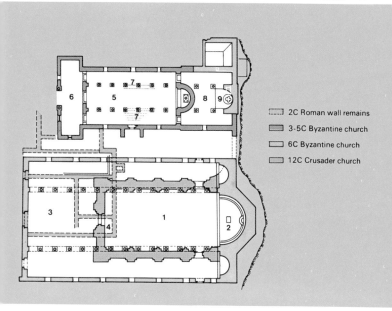

ansata in front of the threshold leading to the S. entrance. A cloverleaf-shaped font from the 5/6C.

Crusader church: This single-aisled 12C Romanesque church was erected on the ruins of two older churches. It was destroyed by Ibrahim Pasha in 1834. The church, 75 × 34 ft. in size, was built inside the much larger Byzantine church, the central apse of which was re-used. The apse is adjoined by walls with ponderous pillars 5 ft. thick which once supported the tunnel vault. The church had three entrances, one in each of the two side walls immediately beside the apse, and a main entrance opposite the choir. The apse of the church is a beautiful piece of masonry, being semicircular inside and polygonal outside, and betrays the influence of Constantinople. Four free-standing columns outside the main entrance of the W. façade formed part of a por-

Emmaus/Amwas 1 12C Crusader church **2** Central apse of oldest church **3** Roman villa (Cleopas' house?) **4** Mosaic remnants **5** 6C Byzantine basilica **6** Narthex **7** Mosaic remnants **8** Baptistery **9** Font

tico. The walls of this single-aisled church survive up to a height of 8 ft.

Environs: Latrun (1.5 km. SW): It was near this Arab village, which is today abandoned, that Joshua fought the Canaanites, and the Hasmonaeans fought the Graeco-Syrians. In the 7C AD it was an important military base used by the Arabs in their conquest of S. Palestine. The Crusaders built their fortress of Le Toron des Chevaliers here in the 12C. The town's name is derived from this fortress (Arabic: el-Torun), but it was interpreted as 'Castrum Boni Latronis' ('house of the good thief') and has been associated with the good thief who was crucified with Christ. *Latrun* *monastery* (Monastery of the Seven Sorrows): This was built by French Trappists in 1927 on the E. side of the Ayyalon valley and its broad façade is visible from afar. The monastery garden has a collection of late classical and early Christian capitals. *Le Toron des Chevaliers:* A Crusader castle built in 1150–70 stands on the hill behind the monastery. Its W. gate (restored by the Ottomans) and three arches from the N. façade still survive.

Sha'alvim (7 km. NW): A Samaritan *synagogue* was uncovered in 1948 on the site of the Biblical Shaalabbin (Joshua 19, 42). There was a mosaic (20 ft. × 10 ft. 6 in.) with geometrical patterns in the middle of this rectangular building. In the centre of this mosaic, a mountain (Har Gerizim) is seen depicted between two seven-armed menorot below a Greek inscription in a circle the upper half of which has been obliterated. There is a Samaritan inscription on the N. edge of the mosaic, and another on the S. edge. The remains of a later mosaic, with geometrical motifs and plants, are to be found some 6 in. above this mosaic. The synagogue, which is 50 ft. 6 in. × 26 ft. 5 in. in area, was destroyed in a Samaritan rebellion in the 5/6C and was later rebuilt.

En Gedi
Southern District/Israel   p.322 □ E 9

The oasis of En Gedi ('fountain of the kid goat' or 'fountain of the he-goat') lies in a subtropical nature park on the W. shore of the Dead Sea, 25 km. NE of Arad. It was a place of abundant fertility even in Old Testament times. The vineyards of En-gedi are extolled in the Song of Solomon (1, 14), and the palms there are used as a symbol of beauty (Sirach 24, 14).

Today the environs of En Gedi are a national park, with tropical species of birds, chamois, gazelles etc. Life in this oasis is made possible by the fresh-water spring, with a cascade of three falls. The way to the spring runs past the kibbutz founded in 1953 and a magnificent view of the oasis and the S. part of the Dead Sea is obtained from the plateau above the waterfall. Great powers of healing are ascribed

Latrun (Emmaus), monastery

to the dark mud which comes to the surface here and originates from the Dead Sea. According to 1 Samuel 24, it was near the spring that the young David hid from King Saul.

The zenith of En Gedi began when Idumaea was conquered by the high priest John Hyrcanus I (d. 104 BC). The inhabitants were converted to the Jewish faith. En Gedi became the administrative centre of Idumaea under Alexander Jannaeus (103–76 BC), who was both king and high priest. It was later conquered by Herod the Great. En Gedi was plundered during the 1st Jewish War in AD 66–70. The Jewish freedom fighter Simon Bar Kokhba and his men sought refuge here during the 2nd Jewish War in 132–135. Bar Kokhba's hiding place is on display in the so-called 'letter cave' some 6 km. SW of En Gedi. Letters (written on papyrus and wooden panels), cultic objects and utensils from the time of the 2nd Jewish War were discovered there in 1960.

Synagogue: The synagogue, a building with pillars, a nave and two aisles, dates from the 5/6C, when En Gedi was a large Jewish town. The *mosaics* in the nave (now in the Rockefeller museum, Jerusalem) were its best feature.

Shulamit spring: The Shulamit spring rises amidst dense weeds to the S. of the En David spring in the nature park. The name 'Shulamit' is interpreted as meaning 'girl from (the town of) Shunema': the spring commemorates Abishag, a beautiful Israelite virgin from Shunem who took care of the old King David and slept by his side: 'Now king David was old and stricken in years; and they covered him with clothes, but he gat no heat. Wherefore his servants said unto him, Let there be sought for my lord the king a young virgin: and let her stand before the king, and let her cherish him, and let her lie in thy bosom, that my lord the king may get

heat. So they sought for a fair damsel throughout all the coasts of Israel, and found Abishag a Shunammite, and brought her to the king. And the damsel was very fair, and cherished the king, and ministered to him: but the king knew her not' (1 Kings 1, 1–4). After David's death, Adonijah, his eldest surviving son, desired to become king instead of Solomon, and asked Queen Bath-sheba for permission to marry Abishag the Shunammite. Solomon realised at once that if Adonijah were to marry Abishag this would cost him the kingdom, and ordered that Adonijah be put to death (1 Kings 2, 17–25).

Abishag the Shunammite has also been identified with the Shulamite who is mentioned in the Song of Solomon as being King Solomon's loved one (Song of Solomon, 6, 13). The Song of Solomon, one of the Books of Wisdom of the Old Testament, is a collection of songs of love and marriage attributed to King Solomon. There is no logical succession in the text, which was probably compiled in the Hellenistic period, not before 300 BC. This does not preclude the possibility that some of the songs, or their original versions, are considerably older. One reason why Solomon is regarded as the author of this book is that he was regarded as especially competent in matters of the heart, since he had 700 wives and 300 concubines. The Song of Solomon sings of the love of a couple who meet and then lose one another, seek for their lost love and find each other again. The male lover is referred to as 'king' (1, 4/12), but the name Solomon is also found here (3, 7/11). The female lover is called Shulamite (6, 13). Metaphors and images are the dominant feature of the dialogue between the lovers (the thighs are marble columns, the breasts are clusters of grapes, the nose is 'as the tower of Lebanon which looketh toward Damascus', etc.). The language always relates to physical objects in a sensual manner, without becoming obscene in its direct and

candid depiction of erotic matters. Only in a few passages is the sphere of metaphorically depicted objects abandoned in favour of purely intellectual formulations, such as in 8, 6–7: 'For love is as strong as death; jealousy is cruel as the grave: the coals thereof are coals of fire, which hath a most vehement flame. Many waters cannot quench love, neither can the floods drown it.'

En Gev

Northern District/Israel   p.318□F 3

This settlement founded in 1937 is on the E. shore of the Sea of Galilee, 10 km. NE of the Zemah crossroads. Finds from the Iron Age and from the post-Babylonian, Hellenistic, Byzantine and Arab periods have been discovered here.

The bronze statue of a *mother and child* by Chana Orloff (1888–1968), the sculptress born in Staro-Konstantinov (Ukraine), commemorates the men who stood fast against the Syrian aggressors at En Gev in 1948.

The En Gev *music festival* is held in the music hall every year.

Environs: Afiq (6 km. E.): A *basalt column*, with an Ionian capital and a seven-armed menora bearing the Aramaic inscription 'I, Judah, the Hazzan', was discovered in the late 19C in the Arab village of Fiq, which has today been abandoned. A large number of *individual finds* have also been made. It is very probable that they originate from a synagogue on the W. edge of the village: a lintel with a seven-armed menora, an etrog and a shofar; a nine-armed menora; a lintel with a five-armed menora; fragments of a frieze with decorations depicting vine tendrils and grapes; parts of a soreg. The column was transferred to the museum of Quneitra in 1967.

◁ *En Gedi, Shulamit waterfall*

Hammat Gader (En Gev), entrance gate to complex

During the war of October 1973 it was taken from there to Meron Golan.

Bet Yerah/Khirbet al-Karak (13 km. SW: A tel (settlement hill), which was mentioned in the Talmud and is 125 acres in area, stretches along the SW shore of the Sea of Galilee. There are traces of human settlement from the early Bronze Age until the Arab period. The tel is famous for the Khirbet-Karak ceramics, which derive originally from Anatolia. The tel was excavated in 1944–6 and 1949–55. *Synagogue:* A synagogue, which with dimensions of 730 × 120 ft. is the largest so far known, was uncovered in 1950 inside a Roman fort. Two rows of columns divide the 5/6C basilica into a nave and two aisles. The apse was in the S. wall, which was oriented towards Jerusalem. A mosaic, today largely obliterated, covered the floor. It depicts plants and animals, including lions and a tree

with two etrogim, and also a man with a horse. A menora, a lulav, an etrog and a mahta are to be seen on the base of a column. A menora, barely still discernible as such, is to be found on the stump of a column. *Church complex:* This building is oriented to the E. and has often been converted. It consists of an atrium and side rooms, a portico, a church with side rooms to the N. and S., and a rectangular diaconicon. In the early 5C the church had a nave and two aisles, and only one apse, with a semicircular priest's bench. Two horseshoe-shaped side apses, a portico and an atrium with a cistern were later added to this main apse. A diaconicon, the floor of which was laid with mosaics, was added on the N. side of the choir in AD 528–39. The nave of this rectangular diaconicon (22 ft. 6 in. × 17 ft. in area) has a polychrome geometrical mosaic in the apse in front of the E. wall. There is a three-line Greek dedicatory inscription within black tesserae. The church was in use until the late 6C/early 7C. *Baths:* A late Roman structure uncovered in 1944–6. The caldarium and tepidarium are located above a hypocaust. The square frigidarium, 35 × 36 ft., is laid with coloured marble slabs. Only the foundations still survive from the bath, which was 6 ft. 6 in. wide and 2 ft. 6 in. deep. In the middle there was a type of canopy, the dome of which was decorated with mosaics. The water came from a conduit leading from Wadi Fayyon to Tiberias. *Roman fort:* A fortress with corner towers and covering an area of 650 sq.ft. Built in the 3C AD, it was abandoned in the late 4C.

Hammat Gader/El Hamma (18 km. SE): The sulphur springs here were used by spas in antiquity, one of these being the spa of Gadara (now in Jordan), which was a centre of Greek culture in the Hellenistic period. In the Roman period Hammat Gader was a member of the decapolis which existed until the 2C AD. A Roman theatre, a Roman bath, and a 5C synagogue, have all been uncovered in Hammat Gader. *Synagogue:* A synagogue excavated in 1932 on the Tell Bani, which is the highest point in Hammat Gader. Three rows of four columns each divide this basilica (43 × 46 ft.) into three aisles. There was another row of two columns facing the S. wall. At the point where the rows of columns intersected, there were L-shaped pillars rather than corner columns. A large apse, and in front of it a bema reached by ascending two steps, were situated on the narrow S. side, which does not run at right angles to the rest of the building but is angled slightly towards the S. There was a soreg on each side of the steps leading to the bema. *Finds:* A seven-armed menora in a cross, and flowers (?) on the rear; parts of a Greek inscription. The remains of benches survive along the walls. *Mosaics:* These consist of simple geometrical patterns in the side aisles, and in the nave (outside the apse) there are two lions, one of which survives only in part. Between the two lions, in a ring with a Heracles cycle, there is an Aramaic inscription relat-

Hammat Gader (En Gev), Roman bath

ing to the building's foundation. Only a few letters at the left edge, and the title in Greek, survive. Underneath this, extending across almost the entire width of the nave, is a band with a four-line Aramaic foundation inscription in a tabula ansata. This is adjoined by two panels with various patterns. There is another foundation inscription in a tabula ansata in the 2nd panel. The remains of another tabula ansata survive in the W. aisle, but the inscription has been entirely obliterated. The synagogue is adjoined by side rooms to the W., S., and E. The whole complex is surrounded by a wall with the main entrance to the E. The synagogue was destroyed by a fire. *Roman theatre:* 350 yards E. of Tell Bani, there is a theatre for some 2,000 spectators. The cavea had 15 rows of basalt seats 2–2 ft. 4 in. in height. The topmost row of seats was 21 ft. 6 in. above the orchestra (diameter: 45 ft.). The paradoi were 11 ft. 9 in. wide. The stage, 19 ft. deep and 97 ft. long, was 5 ft. higher than the orchestra. *Roman bath:* This structure excavated near Hammat Selin consists of a hall (the caldarium) 39 ft. wide,

with a niche to the E. of the entrance. There was a hot spring in front of the niche. To the W., a passage led to another large hall 60 ft. wide, which was probably the entrance hall and the apodyterium.

Kursi (6 km. N.): This has been a pilgrimage site since the 5C AD. The monastery was destroyed in the early 7C. *Byzantine monastery:* This is surrounded by a rectangular wall measuring 475 × 405 ft with the remains of wall paintings on the inside. A single, heavily fortified gate gives access and a paved pathway 165 ft. wide and 165 ft. long leads from it to the church in the middle of the complex. This church (75 × 150 ft.) has a fine mosaic of simple geometrical patterns covering the sanctuary. The medallions in the side aisles which depicted the regions's flora and fauna were destroyed by the iconoclasts. A small room was converted into a baptistery in AD 586. A stone slab by the entrance to an external S. chapel covers the opening of the crypt. The monks' living quarters were N. of the church. Traces of a Roman village, with a small harbour and a mole 110

Kursi (En Gev), Byzantine monastery, water system

yards to the N. of the small tel, are to be found between the monastery precinct and the Sea of Galilee. Jaqov of Kursi, who taught the patriarch Juda Ha-Nassi, was born here.

Sha'ar/HaGolan (2 km. SE of the Zemah crossroads): A kibbutz founded in 1937 by the 'En HaQore group from Poland and Czechoslovakia. *Museum of prehistory and early history:* A collection of exhibits from the neolithic Yarmuk culture of the surrounding area. The finds illustrate the life and work of the first peasants to live in the Holy Land. Finds: Tools, beginnings of pottery, fertility cults and their figurines.

Susita/Qal'at- el-husn (2 km. E. of En Gev): A Seleucid foundation from the Hellenistic period, lying above an earlier settlement. Before being conquered by the Arabs, it was inhabited, and was known by its Greek name of Antiochia Hippos. It was conquered by Alexander Jannaeus, and then by Pompey (63 BC), who made it part of his decapolis. Augustus granted Susita to Herod in 30 BC, and after Augustus' death it fell to the province of Syria (4 BC). The town formerly extended to the Sea of Galilee and Fiq (Aphek) and Umm el-Qanatir were within its boundaries. It was a bishop's seat in the Byzantine period, being one of the seats of Palaestina Secunda. Numerous churches and public buildings testify to the town's prosperity. After the Arabs' victory in the battle on the Yarmuk (AD 636), the town was abandoned. Four *churches* have been uncovered in the course excavation work. The first church (6C) was to the N. of the cardo (the N.-S. axis) and is a basilica measuring 119 ft. 6 in. × 57 ft. 6 in. Two rows of four columns each divide it into a nave and two aisles. Some remains of the synthronos have been discovered in an apse. Second church: a 6C church N. of the cardo and E. of the first one. Third church (6C): N. of the cardo and E. of the second church. The base of the limestone choir is all that survives of the bema. A synthronos has been discovered in the apse. There is a polychrome mosaic with geometrical figures and plant motifs. The fourth church, a cathedral (65 × 130 ft.), dates from the 5C and is to the S. of the cardo and to the E. of

Kursi (En Gev), Byzantine monastery, church, apse

the public baths. There is a large apse at the E. end and behind this is the synthronos with four steps. The bema is raised above the rest of the church and is separated from it by a choir. There are two rows, each of nine columns, between the nave and the aisles. The columns, 16 ft. tall and made of marble and granite, derive from earlier buildings. The church is dedicated to St.Cosmas and St.Damian. *Mosaic:* In the apse there is a mosaic floor for a marble screen. The baptistery on the N. side has three Greek inscriptions. *Roman nymphaeum:* (W. of the cathedral): A bath and a large underground cistern with a vaulted roof. The water, coming from the basalt aqueduct, flowed through a large stone pipe below the cardo. Another conduit carried water from the 'Afiq spring. The pipe built by the Romans was rebuilt by the Byzantines. The remains of a *town wall* are to be found at the S. edge of the town.

Gaza

Gaza Strip   p.320☐A 8

The Egyptian town of Gaza, lying on the SE coast of the Mediterranean 20 km. SW of Ashqelon, has been under Israeli administration since the Six-Day War of 1967 and is the administrative centre of the Gaza Strip. The area around Gaza (the Gaza Strip) is not merely a political creation of Egyptian-Israeli conflict. It has a tradition dating back 4,000 years. The episodic way in which Gaza was sometimes part of King David's kingdom (1004–965 BC), and sometimes belonged to the area of the Jewish State under King Alexander Jannaeus and King Herod the Great in the 1C BC, meant that Gaza was never regarded as belonging to the area of the Holy Land proper.

History: Gaza was probably an important port from as long ago as the beginning of the 2nd millennium BC. Owing to its favourable position on the caravan route from Syria to Egypt, it was often fought over by foreign powers. Gaza first came to prominence under the Egyptian king Thutmosis III (1490–1436 BC), and it remained Egyptian for the following 350 years. From the 12C onwards it was the southernmost and most important of the five Philistine towns on the Mediterranean. It is mentioned in Joshua 15, 47 in the list of towns belonging to the tribe of Judah. According to Judges 1, 19, however, Judah was unable to capture the town, because the inhabitants 'had iron chariots'. In the 8C the area came under the rule of Assur, and in the 7C it was once again dominated by Egypt, but at the same time it always retained a certain independence.

Alexander Jannaeus, the Jewish high priest and king, destroyed the town in 96 BC, after which it was deserted. It was rebuilt by the Romans as a free town on another site after 61 BC and it enjoyed an unprecedented cultural and economic resurgence under them, receiving considerable favours from the Emperor Hadrian (AD 117–138). Almost all the temples built in this period (to Marnas, Helios, Aphrodite, Apollo and others) were destroyed shortly after the town was converted to Christianity under Bishop Porphyrius (396–420). During the Christian period, Gaza was among the most highly cultured towns in the Byzantine Empire; Prokopios of Gaza, who was a Christian sophist and exegete (d. c. 530), his pupil Khorikios, and the neo-Platonic philosopher Aeneas of Gaza (d. later than 486), were among those who taught at the Platonic school of rhetoric in Gaza.

The Arabs captured the town in 635 and converted its inhabitants to Islam: Gaza has been Muslim ever since. It remained a centre of Islamic tradition because it was the burial site of Hashim ibn Abd Manaf, who was the great-grandfather of the Prophet Mohammed, and the birthplace of Abu Abd Allah Ash Shafii (767–820), the founder of the Shafiites who are named after him.

Gaza declined in importance in the confusion caused by the Crusades. During World War 1 it was defended by the Ottomans before being captured by the British in 1917. After the war it became part of the British Palestine Mandate conferred by the League of Nations. According to the UN partition plan of 1947, Gaza was intended to become part of an Arab State of Palestine but when this State was not established, Egypt occupied the town in 1948. The Gaza Strip, an area of 78 square miles stretching from Gaza to the Egyptian border, was created by the Israeli-Egyptian peace treaty of 1949. It was placed under Egyptian administration but more than half of its population were Arab refugees. The Gaza Strip was occupied by Israel in 1956 during the Suez crisis. A UN security force then took control in 1957 and was withdrawn in 1967 at Egypt's request, shortly before the Six-Day War broke out. During that war the Israelis once again occupied the Gaza Strip.

Jami' el-kebir (Grand Mosque):

This building, oriented E.-W., is on the site a 12C crusader church of St.John—a minaret rises from where the central apse once stood.

King David mosaic: A mosaic floor from a Jewish synagogue dating from the 5C (Byzantine period) was discovered near the harbour in 1965. The unusual image depicts King David playing a harp and wearing the attire of the Greek singer Orpheus.

Tell al-Ayyul: During his excavations of 1929–31, the British archaeologist William Matthew Flinders-Petrie discovered the ancient town of Gaza some 7 km. SW of the modern Gaza. Tombs and fortifications from the Hyksos period (c. 1750 BC) have been discovered. Some of the tombs are richly furnished (gold, silver, precious stones).

Golan

p.318□F 2-3

The basalt plateau to the E. of the river Jordan and the Sea of Galilee consists of an area between the spurs of Mount Hermon to the N. and the river Yarmuk to the S., and extends some 20 km. E. of the Jordan. The plateau reaches a height of 3,950 ft. in Har Avital to the W. of Quneitra. The oldest traces of human settlement date from the early part of the Stone Age (500,000–120,000 BC). There were Jewish settlements in Golan in the 2C BC. But the area was not densely populated until the Roman and Byzantine periods, when the roads were excellent and there was a good water system.

At the beginning of the Greek occupation in the 3C BC, Golan became the independent administrative district of Gaulatinus, holding the rank of a hyparchy. The N. part of Golan was part of Phoenicia, and the S. part belonged to Galaaditis. The Seleucids placed the whole of Golan

Arabs won their victory on the Yarmuk (20 August 636). In the 19C, Golan became involved in the conflict of interests arising between the colonial powers. It fell to Syria after World War 1. Since 1981 it has been annexed to Israel.

Most of the archaeological finds date from between the late 2C AD and the first half of the 4C.

For further details, see Banyas, En Gev, Qasrin.

Golan, Gamla mountain

under the rule of the eparchy of Gilead. Alexander Jannaeus the Hasmonaean conquered Golan in 83–80 BC and converted its inhabitants to Judaism by force. In 20 BC, the Roman Emperor Augustus presented the province to King Herod, who greatly developed the region. From 4 BC to AD 34 it was governed by his son Philippus (except for the towns of Hippos [sl] = Susita[sr] and Gadara). He made Caesarea Philippi (the Greek Paneas) his capital. It was under him that Golan became a major Greek cultural centre. Golan fell to the province of Syria after his death, and when Gamla (= Deirt Kruk) fell in AD 67, the Jewish settlement of the Golan came to an end for a long period.

During the 3&4C, Golan became a centre of Jewish teaching and learning. Numerous synagogues were built. This heyday continued until the

Hai Bar Arava, Wild Life Reserve
Southern District/Israel   p.324☐D 15

The Biblical Wild Life Reserve, established in 1968, lies some 50 km. to the N. of Elat. A savannah landscape, with flora and fauna such as may have existed in Biblical times, is set against a background of Sinai to the W. and the massifs of Jordan to the E.

Haifa
District of Haifa/Israel   p.318☐C 3

Haifa, the third largest town and main port of Israel, lies in the S. part of the broadest bay on the coast of Palestine. Its site is dominated by Mount Carmel, which slopes steeply on all sides and is cut into by deep valleys.

In ancient times there were two settlements on the site of modern Haifa, *Shiqmona* to the W. and *Zalmona* to the E, and the area has been inhabited for over 100,000 years. It was first mentioned in the Talmud (3C AD). The name of Haifa may be derived from 'Hof Yafe' ('beautiful coast'). In the 14C BC a small port was built on the mouth of the Qishon and this survived until the 10C BC. The Hellenistic-Roman town of Shiqmona (Sycaminium) did not have a harbour but the Jewish settlement of Haifa, which is mentioned in the Talmud, lay on the seashore on a rocky slab about a mile in length which forms an eastwards extension to the N. end of the cape.

Although this flourishing town of fishermen and glass-blowers was burned down by the Arabs in the 7C by the early 11C Haifa was once again a trading town, with a shipbuilding industry and a Talmudic school. In July 1100, Haifa was trapped between a Venetian fleet and an army of Crusaders led by Tancred. After its fall, all the Jewish and Arab inhabitants were slain but it became the most important port in the Latin kingdom until Acre was taken in 1104. No Jews were allowed to live in the Frankish *Cayphe/Caife* (wrongly derived from the name of Caiaphas the high priest). The Carmelite order, which played an important part in the town's development, was founded in Haifa by Berthold of Calabria in 1155. After the Crusaders' defeat at Hittim, Sultan Saladin destroyed the town (1187), which was recaptured by Richard the Lionheart in 1191. Although the fortifications were extended by Louis IX in 1252, the town was finally captured and destroyed by the Mameluke Sultan Baibars in 1265. The site of modern Haifa was selected by the Bedouin Sheikh Daher el-'Amr, under whom the town enjoyed an economic boom in the 18C through the export of wheat. In 1761, after wresting Haifa from the Turks in 1752/3, Daher el-'Amr ordered that the old part of the town be torn down and that a new town be built on the slope between the terrace and the coast. This town was defended by a wall nearly 700 yards long and forming a trapezium with two equal sides.

Haifa, Elijah grotto, Jewish sanctuary

The Carmelites were allowed to return to Haifa during the rule of Ahmed el-Jazzar (1775–1804), the Pasha of Acre. They built a church and a monastery above the *Elijah grotto*. The monastery was destroyed by Jazzar after Napoleon's troops withdrew in 1799, but was rebuilt in 1827. According to Jewish, Christian and Muslim tradition, Haifa and Mount Carmel were the centres from which the prophet Elijah operated in his struggle against the prophets of Baal (1 Kings 18). The grotto at the foot of Mount Carmel (known to Christians as 'the prophet's school', to Jews as 'Elijah's grotto' and to Muslims as 'al-Hadir'), and the shrine known as 'Altar of the Prophet Elijah' on the mountain (al-muhraqa), both attract numerous Jewish, Christian and Muslim pilgrims. The 'German colony' was founded in 1868 in a marshy area 1.5 km. N. of the town. It was an agricultural settlement belonging to the German Templergesellschaft, a religious reform movement. The Templars built the first paved road from Haifa to Nazareth and the Sea of Galilee. After the Haifa-

Damascus railway line was built in 1905 and the technical college (Technion) was founded in 1912, the town developed rapidly and became the most modern town in Palestine: its population rose from about 2,500 (1854) through 8,000 (1891) to 15,000 (1913), including some 3,000 Jews. A deep-water harbour was built during the period of the British mandate (1929–33); between 1936 and 1939, Haifa was connected to the oil pipeline coming from Iraq. Over 100,000 Jews were already living in Haifa when the State of Israel was proclaimed. The new immigrants built their homes in the Hadar-Hakarmel district of the town behind the fortress.

Today Haifa, the 'town of the future' (Theodor Herzl) has 225,000 inhabitants, including 10,000 Christians, 2,000 Maronites, 3,000 Druze and Bahai, and 7,000 Muslims.

Excavations: *Tel Shiqmona* (Arabic: Tell el-Shemaq): The small hill between the coastal plain and the bay of Haifa has so far only been investigated as far as the stratum which has

Haifa, Bahai archives

yielded Hellenistic remains. Eight Byzantine *floor mosaics*, which belong to a large 6/7C synagogue about 160 ft. long, have been uncovered.

Bahai shrine (Sderot HaZiyyonut): Haifa is the centre of the Bahai religion, and houses the Bahai temple, mausoleums and the Bab shrine. Baha Ullah, the founder of the religion, came to Acre in 1868 after spending some time in Turkish prisons. He remained in prison in Acre until his death in 1892. His son Abas founded a world palace of justice in Haifa, laid out gardens at the foot of Mount Carmel, and built the Bab mausoleum and the temple of the Bahai archives (1909). The new shrine was, however, not completed until 1953. *Bab shrine:* This gleaming white building in European-Oriental style is crowned by a golden dome whose 12,000 scale-like ceramic tiles were hot-gilded in Holland. The walls are of Italian ciampo stone, while the monolithic columns are of pink Baveno granite. The temple has two rooms. The first room is lit by sumptuous crystal chandeliers and contains silver candelabras and Chinese vases with bunches of exotic flowers. A gauze curtain conceals the view into the second room which contains the mortal frame of the man known as 'Bab' (his real name was Mirza Ali Muhammed), who broke away from Islam in Persia in 1844 and was publicly executed in Tabriz in 1850. His bones were transferred to Haifa in 1909.

Carmelite monastery (Stella Maris): In 1828, Italian monks built a new church complex (completed in 1867) on the site of a monastery which was destroyed by Ahmed el-Jazzar in 1821 and which dated from 1767. The monastery is dedicated to the prophets Elijah and Elishah (Elijah is said to have lived in the grotto underneath the high altar). A scroll above the entrance portal commemorates Elijah's mission: 'Zelo zelatus sum

pro Domino Deo Exercituum'. ('I have been very jealous for the Lord God of hosts'; 1 Kings 19, 10). The basilica is crowned by a dome and faced in marble. The ceilings are decorated with events from the lives of the Prophets. A double staircase leads from the choir to a high altar on which there stands a cedar *figure of the Virgin Mary* with a porcelain head (the so-called 'Madonna of Carmel', the work of J.B. Caraventa, 1836). Only the head, hands and feet survive from the original statue which, after being severely damaged, was re-carved in Lebanese cedar. There is a small *museum* beside the monastery entrance.

Haifa museum (26 Rehov Shabtai Levi): Since 1977 this has been the central museum for art ancient and modern and folklore. *Ground floor:* A lecture hall, with stained-glass windows and a painting of the signs of the zodiac in the style of the Byzantine floor mosaics in the synagogues of Galilee. *1st floor:* Folklore and customs: Jewish cult objects from Islamic countries; Asian, African and South American folklore; ancient jewellery. *2nd floor* (museum of modern art): Paintings by Israeli, European and American artists; works by Gustave Bollin, André Cottavoz, Tshuta Kimura, Roni Ben Zvi, Menahem Shemi etc. *3rd floor* (museum of ancient art): Mosaic floor from Shiqmona (at the top of the stairs); finds from Tel Shiqmona and Caesarea (statues of Hercules, Zeus, Bacchus and Pan); Coptic works of art, fragments of paintings from Egypt (2/3C); amphorae from the Persian period; statuettes and decorative objects of carved bone; burial objects (necklaces, gems, medallions and bronze objects).

Mané-Katz museum (89 Rehov Yefe Nof): This French painter (1894–1962) who was born in the Ukraine, where he was known as Emanuel Katz, presented many of his works, and numerous Judaic objects, to the town of Haifa.

Museum of prehistory (124 Rehov Hatishbi): Archaeological finds from the grottoes of Mount Carmel and Galilee, and a natural history department with dioramas of Palestinian flora and fauna.

Museum of music (23 Rehov Arlosoroff): A worldwide collection of musical instruments from all periods of history; a specialist library (the Amly Library) and recordings of Jewish music.

Museum of seafaring (198 Rehov Allenby): Models, maps, nautical instruments, and finds relating to the history of Mediterranean seafaring from antiquity to the present. *Ground floor:* Charts; copper etchings and 16C maps. *1st floor:* Navigational instruments from the Renaissance to the 19C; collection of ancient charts; Roman coastal patrol boats, Jewish warship (1C BC), Egyptian ship (*c.* 1500 BC) and three Egyptian burial ships.

Haifa, Bahai temple

Tikotin museum of Japanese art (89 Rehov HaNassi): 4,000 paintings and drawings from the private collection of the Dutch collector F.Tikotin, including works by Hokusai (1760–1849), Maruyama Okyo (1733–95) and Ando Kaigetsudo (1671–1743).

Also worth seeing: *Grand synagogue* (60 Rehov Herzl): There is a bas-relief on the façade showing Elijah in the chariot blowing the shofar, and the children of Israel following with the golden menora which they are bringing to Jerusalem. *Istiklal mosque* (Gan Faisal): The largest of the three mosques in Haifa stands at one end of the former Islamic graveyard. *Garden of sculptures:* (Sderot HaZijjonut): A park with 17 bronze statues of children by the sculptress Ursula Malbin. *Modern architecture: University of Haifa:* The tall and slender

tower by the Brazilian architect Oskar Niemeyer stands at a height of 1,650 ft. on the ridge of Mount Carmel. *Haifa Technion Forum:* Three main buildings on different levels. The upper piazzetta forms the entrance to the Churchill lecture hall. The main piazza, which is at a lower level, and the sunken garden, lead to the library and the senate house respectively.

Environs: Allone Abba (25 km. SE): German Templars founded the Waldheim colony here in 1908 and after the State of Israel was founded the moshav shitufi (270 inhabitants) was established. The Israeli settlers named it after Abba Berdiczev, the Haganah hero who fell in Czechoslovakia in World War 2. There are good columns in the *Templars' church,* which is today the cultural centre of the moshav.

Hammat Tiberias
Northern District/Israel   p.318□F 3

The ruins of the ancient Hammat Tiberias extend from the hot springs (al-Hammam) to the S. edge of the ancient Tiberias (q.v.). Hammat and Tiberias were orignally two towns which coalesced in the 1C AD. Hammat fell into decline when the Sanhedrin was abolished in 425, but still had a Jewish population from Arab times until the Middle Ages. Legend has it that the hot springs were built by King Solomon and the thermal baths were extensively rebuilt by Ibrahim Pasha in 1833. The 18 radioactive sulphur springs produce up to 55,000 gallons of water every day at a temperature of 60C.

Severus synagogue: A synagogue complex discovered S. of the hot springs in 1947 and excavated in 1961–3. It was named after Severus, son of the leader of the Sanhedrin. A synagogue (49 × 43 ft.) in the Roman-Hellenistic style was built in the second half of the 3C above the ruins of several older buildings. Three rows, each of three columns, divide the building into a broad central and three side aisles, and the stone columns stand directly on the mosaic pavement which covers three of the four aisles. The rectangular building has three entrances in the NW wall. The Torah shrine was on the SE wall, opposite the entrances.

A step leads from the nave to the rectangular sanctuary, which is divided into three parts. The synagogue was destroyed in the late 4C. A basilican reconstruction, with a nave, two aisles and a central apse, was destroyed in 630. The late-7C reconstruction was destroyed in the mid-8C. A Greek foundation inscription at the entrance commemorates Severus, the founder of the synagogue.

Mosaics: Geometrical mosaics in the side aisles, symbols in the mosaics of the nave. The main mosaic in the nave has three panels (S. panel, central panel, N. panel).

S. panel: This rectangular panel (11 ft. 4 in. × 7 ft. 2 in.) is bordered by a guilloche (9.5 in. wide) with five bands, consisting of blue, red and

Hammat Tiberias, Severus synagogue

white tesserae on a black background. The mosaic depicts an Aron ha-kodesh (Torah shrine) flanked by two seven-armed candlesticks (menorot). Between them are the usual cultic objects such as the shofar (ram's horn), lulav (palm twig), etrog (citrus fruit), mahta (incense scoop), hadas (myrtle twigs) etc. Dianthus flowers are scattered over the white background of the mosaic. Each flower has four white petals with red tips. Aron ha-kodesh: an aedicule with a triangular pediment is framed by two small, thin columns which rest on tall cuboid plinths. The torus is marked by two horizontal black lines. Ionic capitals with a pseudo-abacus support a denticulated architrave. There is a ten-pointed shell-shape in the centre of the pediment. The closed, coffered door of the Torah shrine is partly covered by a knotted white curtain (parokhet). This knotted curtain has no parallel in Jewish art.

Central mosaic: This square mosaic (10 ft. 9 in. × 10 ft. 8 in.) contains two concentric circles, 10 ft. 6 in. and 4 ft. 7 in. in diameter respectively. The area between the two circles is divided into twelve segments, each of which contains a sign of the zodiac. In each corner of the square the bust of a woman personifies the seasons of the year. Inner circle: at the centre there is a front-on image of Helios the sun god as a young man driving the chariot of the sun. In his left hand he holds the celestial globe and a whip. Helios is wearing a white tunic with long sleeves and long sleeve facings. A purple cloak hangs from his shoulders. The chariot was obliterated by later masonry and only the horse's red mane survives. Outer circle: the twelve segments are each about 1 ft. 10 in. high and each zodiacal sign bears a Hebrew name. Two of the signs were obliterated in the 8C, and three more were damaged. The heads point towards the sun god, as do the heads depicting the seasons. Signs of the zodiac (reading clockwise, starting at top centre): Dagim (Pisces), Deli (Aquarius), Gedi (Capricorn, partly obliterated), Kashat (Sagittarius, obliterated), Akrav (Scorpio, partly obliterated), Moznaim (Libra), Betulah (Virgo), Arieh (Leo), Sartan (Cancer, obliterated),

Hammat Tiberias, Rabbi Meir's burial site

Te'omim (Gemini, partly obliterated), Shor (Taurus), Taleh (Aries). The word 'Deli' (Aquarius), which is written in reverse, and the uncircumcised young men, both suggest that the artists were not Jewish. Seasons of the year (reading counter-clockwise): Nisan (Spring), Tammuz (Summer), Tishre (Autumn) and Tevet (Winter). The names of the seasons and of their attributes are to be found to the left and right of the head below the outer ring. The iconography of the pictorial motifs indicates that the Greek images have been adapted for the usual zodiacal signs, e.g. Kore with torch = Virgo = Persephone.

N. panel: This tripartite panel (10 ft. 9 in. × 4 ft. 11 in.) is surrounded by a guilloche of five red, brown, yellow, grey and blue bands on a black background. The mosaic panel consists of three parts: two lions flank a Greek inscription in a square of nine panels of equal size.

Domed grave of Rabbi Meir: Rabbi Meir Ba'al Ha-Nes (the miracle-worker) came from Cappadocia in Asia Minor and lived in the 2C AD. In co-operation with Yehuda Ha-Nassi, he wrote the Mishna. Two schoolhouses (battei midrash) stand above the tomb in which, according to another tradition, Rabbi Meir Kazin, Rabbi Meir ben Jakob or Rabbi Meir ben Isaak are said to be buried. In the courtyard outside the mausoleum there is a pillar in the form of a torchholder, into which a burning torch is inserted every year on Lag BaOmer. Two iron doors lead into the mausoleum where there is a large marble sarcophagus. The area is divided by a wall into a Sephardic and an Ashkenazic section, so that each community owns one half of the sarcophagus.

The sarcophagus probably dates from the 13C, the mausoleum from the 19C.

Hazor

Northern District/Israel   p.318□F 2

The settlement hill (130 ft. high, 2,000 ft. long and 650 ft. wide) of the

Hammat Tiberias, synagogue, mosaic

Hammat Tiberias, synagogue, mosaic with two zodiacal signs

Canaanite town of Hazor was discovered in 1875 on the Tell el-Qedeh (Tell Waqqas), 8 km. S. of Lake Hule. The British archaeologist John Garstang began its excavation in 1938, and in 1955–60 further sections of it were excavated by Yigael Yadin in a spectacular series of digs (most of the finds are now in the Israel Museum in Jerusalem). The excavation site, on a plateau measuring 3,300 × 2,300 ft., consists of two parts: the lower town to the N. and the bottle-shaped acropolis to the S.

Hazor is first mentioned in Egyptian execration texts from the 19&18C BC. The Old Testament mentions Hazor in connection with Joshua's conquests (Joshuah 11, 10–13). King Solomon enlarged Hazor, as well as Megiddo and Gezer (1 Kings 9, 15).

Tel Hazor: This excavation hill, 188 acres in area, has 21 strata (layers of human settlement). The most recent of these (stratum I) is dated from the Hellenistic period in the 3/2 BC, and the oldest (stratum XXI) is assigned to the early Bronze Age (c. 2600 BC). The Canaanite town enjoyed its first heyday in the 18&17C BC (stratum XVII). The first Israelite settlement was built in the first millennium on the site of this town, which by then had been destroyed. It was enlarged by Solomon in the 10C BC (gates and casemate walls), and also by King Ahab, who ruled in Samaria in the 9C BC and built the citadel and the large storehouse with rows of pillars (stratum VIII).

Lower town: The first town walls date from the 18C BC. They were destroyed in the 17C and rebuilt in the 15C BC.

Stele shrine: A rectangular room which measures 15 ft. 7 in. × 11 ft. 3 in. and is surrounded by low benches. On one wall there is a somewhat higher niche in which there were ten stele and a seated basalt figure some 16 in. high (the basalt stele are between 8.5 and 9.8 in. in height). The stele (Hebrew: mazzeboth) are a miniature version of a holy site. The seated figure represents a man sitting on a low stool and holding a dish-shaped object in one hand, while the other hand rests on his knee. He is wearing a long tunic, the projecting

hem of which covers his knees. The upper part of the tunic has a round neck-line, at the edge of which a reverse crescent moon (symbol of the moon god) hangs above the breast. The figure has a round, squat head with a low forehead. The nose (slightly damaged) is long and thick, and the eyes are relatively large. This basalt figure is a god. Only the central stela bears a relief. This relief depicts two hands raised in a gesture of supplication, and above them is a symbol of a god made up of three elements: a crescent moon, a disc in the crescent, and two small knot-like crosses hanging in the middle. These depict the crescent moon and the full moon. The stele do not have any heads, the heads probably having been cut off by the Israelites (cf. Deuteronomy 12, 2–3).

Upright temple: Built on the foundations of other temples in the 17/16C BC and rebuilt in the 15/14C. The ground plan is in the form of a rectangle with a SE-NW orientation, in compliance with Mesopotamian architectural tradition. The entrance hall on the SE side has three chambers. and the entrances all lie along the central axis. A doorway, the sockets of which survive, leads into a rectangular room (44 × 29 ft.) with a rectangular exedra on the NW side. The wall is 7 ft. 6 in. thick. This part dates from the 14C. The temple was still in use as a cult site in the 13C BC. Its division into three parts, and the two pillars in the entrance hall, are a structural form which is also to be found in the Temple of Solomon in Jerusalem.

Upright lion (copy in the museum): A basalt slab, with a relief of a king couchant on one side, and the lion's head and front legs on the front. The other side is unworked. This slab, 17 in. wide, 13 in. high and 5 in. thick, is probably an upright which may once have stood on another site.

Finds: A large angular basalt pillar with a carved symbol on the head section. An incense altar 5 ft. 7 in. in height. A square panel in the upper third of the altar's front bears a disc in relief in the middle of which there is a symbol with four rays. Below this there are two long, carved grooves

Hazor, upright temple

Hazor, king Ahab's palace, colonnaded hall

which give the front of the altar the appearance of three columns in relief. The rear is similar in design, but the recessed square panel does not have a relief. At the sides there is an oblong recess which looks like a column. The symbol refers to Hadad, the Semitic weather-god; the temple of the shrine was dedicated to the weather- or storm-god.

Town wall and town gate: The town gate consists of six chambers, three on each side of the 14 ft. wide passageway, and a square tower on either side of the entrance. Similar town gates from the time of Solomon have been discovered in Gezer and Megiddo. The casemate wall is from the 17/16C BC. The overall outer length of the gatehouse is 66 ft. 6 in., and it is 59 ft. 6 in. wide. The bulk of the gatehouse was on the town side, and the two towers projected beyond the casemate. Its chambers had a double function: they were used as guard rooms, and at the same time they supported the ceiling, and possibly also the second storey with its walls and battlements. All that survives of the gate itself are the founda-

tions up to the level of the lime floor of the passage. King Solomon's town occupied only the W. half of the tel; the E. half was not inhabited.

Upper town: This occupies an area measuring 700 × 1,600 ft. Buildings from the Iron Age have been uncovered on two sites. The so-called pillar building, which may have been used as a royal storehouse, is in the central part of the upper town. It dates from the time of King Ahab (871–852 BC).

Citadel (10/9C): This is in the SW part of the upper town and consists of a square room, with a number of other square rooms on the N. and S. sides, and two long narrow halls. The entrance to the citadel was decorated by two proto-Aeolic capitals. An ivory pyx which is very similar to the ivories of Samaria has been discovered in the citadel. It represents a cherub and a kneeling figure before a tree of life (today it is in the Israel Museum in Jerusalem).

Canal system: This system dating from the time of Ahab consists of a shaft which was driven through older layers of settlement and then through the

rock. It measures 62 × 82 ft. at the top and is 98 ft. deep. Staircases 10 ft. wide lead down the four walls of the shaft; the fifth and lowest staircase occupies the whole shaft and leads into a tunnel 82 ft. long which ends in a water basin 33 ft. lower down and 16 ft. wide. This lower rock chamber can be reached by a modern flight of 150 stairs.

Environs: Ayyelet HaShahar (1 km. S.): A *museum* founded by Ayala and Sam Sachs in 1966 to plans by D.Reznik the architect. It has finds from Hazor dating from the mid-Bronze Age to the Israelite period. Clay vessels, weapons, seals, scarabs, cultic objects, figurines and ivory reliefs, and also copies of the finds from Hazor which are exhibited in the Israel Museum in Jerusalem.
Hazor HaGelilit (4 km. S.): *Burial site* of Honi Ha Ma'agel, the rain-maker and miracle healer (d. 67 BC), and his grandchildren. The large burial cave is illuminated by the many candles in the niches.
Tel Qedesh (about 16 km. N.): Only a few traces of the Biblical *Kedesh-*

naphtali (Judges 4, 6; Joshua 20, 7), the Roman Cadassa, the Islamic Qadas and the Frankish Kade have survived. The ruins of the Roman town are in the N. of the settlement hill, and those from the Biblical town are in the S. A temple of Apollo dating from the period of the Second Temple has been uncovered.

Hebron
West Bank   p.320□D 8

Hebron, some 30 km. SW of Jerusalem, has been under Israeli administration since 1967. It is a place of pilgrimage for Christians, Jews and Muslims alike. Tradition has it that Abraham and Sara, Isaac and Rebecca, and Jacob and Lea, are all buried in the Machpelah cave.
Foundation: Hebron was probably founded in the early 17C BC by the Hyksos. Numbers 13, 22 states that 'Hebron was built seven years before Zoan'. Zoan (= Tanis = Auaris in the Nile delta) was the capital of the Hyksos. Further evidence that Hebron was founded in the 17C is

Hazor, lower town

provided by an Egyptian inscription from *c.* 1290 BC, which is dated 400 years after the foundation of Tanis. Hyksos (Graecized form of the Egyptian 'ruler of foreign countries') is the term applied to the kings, possibly Hurrite, who came from Asia during the Egyptian 15th and 16th dynasties.

Pre-Israelite period: The original name of Hebron was *Kiriath-arba* ('four-town' or 'town of Arba'), and for this reason it is more frquently referred to in the Old Testament as 'Kiriath-arba, which is now Hebron' than as 'Hebron' (Genesis 23, 2; 35, 27; Joshua 15, 54; 20, 7; Judges 1, 10). Nehemiah 11, 25 speaks only of 'Kiriath-arba'. Joshua 14, 15 derives the name from the founder Arba, the father of Anak, the ancestor of the Anakim tribe: 'The name of Hebron in earlier times was Kiriath-arba. Arba had been the greatest man of the Anakim' (cf. Joshua 15, 13; 21, 11). In the pre-Israelite period, Hebron was inhabited by the Anakim (Joshua 11, 21; 14, 12–15; 15, 13–14). In relation to the patriarchs, however, reference is made to Hittites (cf. Machpelah cave, below).

Conquest by the Israelites: At the time when Canaan was conquered, Hebron was the residence of Hoham, the Amorite king (Joshua 10, 3; 12, 10) and seems to have had several dependent towns (10, 37). The Israelites, led by Joshua, destroyed Hebron and exterminated its inhabitants: 'And Joshua went up from Eglon, and all Israel with him, unto Hebron; and they fought against it: And they took it, and smote it with the edge of the sword, and the king thereof, and all the cities thereof, and all the souls that were therein; he left none remaining, according to all that he had done to Eglon; but destroyed it utterly, and all the souls that were therein' (Joshua 10, 36–37). After it had been conquered by the Israelites, the tribe of Caleb was given the area around Hebron as an inheritance (Joshua 14, 13; 15, 13), and the town itself became one of the six privileged towns used for refuge and asylum (Joshua 20, 7) and was a town of priests and Levites (Joshua 21, 11). The tribe of Caleb probably belonged to an alliance of six towns under the leadership of Judah (cf. Numbers 34, 19).

Hebron, panorama

Town of David's residence: After Saul, the first king of all the Israelites, committed suicide in 1004, King David moved to Hebron at God's command, and here he was anointed king of the house of Judah by the men of Judah (2 Samuel 2, 1–4) and resided in Hebron for seven years and six months (2 Samuel 2, 11). That is to say, he waged war against the other tribes for seven years and six months, until the way to overall dominion was clear.

After David moved his residence from Hebron to Jerusalem, Hebron declined in importance. However, David's unfaithful son Absalom had himself proclaimed king there (2 Samuel 15, 10). After the division of the kingdom, the town's fortifications were reinforced (2 Chronicles 11, 10) under King Rehoboam of Judah (926–10 BC). After the Jews returned from captivity in Babylon (after 539 BC), the town was once again settled by Jews, but it had already been lost to the Edomites in 597 BC. Judas Maccabaeus, the leader of the Jewish revolt against Antiochus IV Epiphanes the Seleucid, captured Hebron in 164 BC and ordered the fortifications to be razed. The town was destroyed by the Romans in AD 68 during the First Jewish War.

Arab rule: After capturing Hebron in the 7C, the Arabs converted the church, built above the Machpelah cave in Byzantine times, into a mosque and gave it the name of Khalil al-Rahman ('Friend of the Merciful'). From the 10C onwards they called the town *Mashad Ibrahim el-Khalil* ('place of Abraham, the friend of Allah') because, according to the Muslim faith, Abraham is the ancestor of Mohammed.

The Crusades: The Crusaders took Hebron, renaming it *Castel St.Abraham,* in 1100 and converted the mosque back into a church, which they combined with a synagogue to form a large monastery. Next to the Machpelah cave, they built the 'Praesidium ad sanctum Abraham', headed by Gérard d'Avesnes. Jews were not allowed to live in Hebron at this time (1100–1260). The town became a bishop's seat in 1168. It fell to the Muslims after the battle of Qarne Hittim in 1187, and under Mameluke rule

Haram el-Khalil

(1260–1517) it became capital of the district.

Development in the 16C: In the 16C, Hebron, which was now Ottoman, enjoyed a resurgence, which was partly due to the immigration of the Megorashim, the Jews expelled from Spain and Portugal, who brought the art of glass-blowing to Hebron. Matkiel Ashkenazi founded the Avraham-le-Avinu synagogue, and Abraham Pereira founded the Yeshiva Hesed-le-Avraham. Leading Cabbalists came to Hebron from Safed in the late 16C and early 17C.

Hebron in the 19&20C: Some 1,500 Jews lived in Hebron in the late 19C, after the arrival of large numbers of immigrants from E. Europe. Tensions between the Jewish and Arab populations intensified after World War 1. In 1929 there was a pogrom in which 77 Jews were killed. Synagogues and schools were destroyed and Torah scrolls were burned. The pogrom ended when the Jewish inhabitants, of whom there were about 500, were evacuated by British troops.

From 1948 onwards Hebron was part of the Kingdom of Jordan and in 1960 the Jordanians opened the sacred sites to non-Muslims as well as Muslims. The town was captured by the Israeli army in 1967 and the West Bank was occupied. Since then the new Jewish settlement of Qiryat Arba has been under construction on a ridge on the NE outskirts of the town.

Jebel er-Rumede ('Mountain of ruins'): Here there are dwelling-caves dating from the end of the Chalcolithic period and the beginning of the early Bronze Age (in the middle Bronze Age II they were used as burial caves). The history of Hebron begins no earlier than the middle Bronze Age II (possibly not until IIb). The remnants of a *town wall,* 31 ft. thick in parts, survive from this period. Numerous Hellenistic, Roman and Byzantine finds (columbaria).

Der el-Arba'in (Monastery of the forty): This ruined monastery, 92 ft. 6 in. long and 80 ft. wide, still rises to a height of 20–23 ft. in places. The tomb of Jesse, the father of David, has been on display in Der el-Arba'in since the 13C. Massive embossed ash-

Haram el-Khalil, Isaac's cenotaph

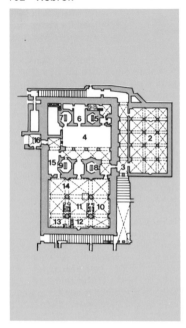

Haram el-Khalil, entrance to Abraham's tomb

Hebron, Haram el-Khalil 1 Entrance **2** Yawu-liya mosque **3** Entrance to Haram **4** Courtyard **5** Leah's cenotaph **6** Jacob's cenotaph **7** Synago-gue **8** Sara's cenotaph **9** Abraham's cenotaph **10** Ibrahim mosque (Crusader church of Castellum ad Sanctum Abraham) **11** Rebecca's cenotaph **12** Isaac's cenotaph **13** Mihrab and minbar **14** Open-ing of Machpela cave **15** Women's mosque **16** Joseph's cenotaph

lars in the walls which are 5–7 ft. thick alternate with badly-fitting boulders. The stumps of columns 1 ft. 8 in. in diameter have been incorporated into the walls both lengthwise and cross-wise. In the SE part of the ruin are the remains of a basilica with an E. facing apse, part of which projects into the outer S. wall of the ruined complex. The nave to the W. of the apse is covered by an Arab wall built diago-nally across it. The cistern on the far side of this wall may have belonged to the atrium of the basilica.

The Islamic shrine *Mashad el-arba'in* (Martyrdom of the Forty) is in the middle of the irregular courtyard with its three cisterns which have been almost entirely filled with earth. The entrance, which has no door, is reached through an arch 12 ft. wide and some 16 ft. high. The ruined interior, 21 ft. long and 10 ft. wide, has a pointed-arched vault. For the Jews, the shrine is the tomb of Ruth (wife of Boaz) and of Jesse (father of David), or the tomb of Caleb who captured Hebron under Joshua.

Haram el-Khalil: This massive building above the Machpelah cave is visible from afar and dominates the Hebron of today. A large irregular rectangle, 205 ft. long and 120 ft. wide, forms the sacred precinct. It is a complex of various buildings (mos-que, basilica, synagogue and cave)

Haram el-Khalil, Jacob's cenotaph

from the Herodian, Frankish and Islamic periods. Around the sacred precinct, Herod built a massive windowless *surrounding wall* 60–65 ft. high with a substructure 40 ft. high and some more recent superstructures (the battlemented top of the wall is from the Mameluke period). Two of what were originally four square *minarets* 40 ft. high still survive. They stand diagonally opposite one another in the NW and the SE.

Four mausoleums with the *cenotaphs* of Abraham, Sara, Jacob and Leah stand in the courtyard of the Haram el-Khalil, which is reached by climbing a flight of stairs and passing through a portal with a flat roof (built under the Caliph Al-Mahdi). The polygonal mausoleums of Abraham and Sara were built in the early Islamic period underneath the roofed section of the courtyard. The polychrome marble cenotaphs are 14C. Tradition

has it that the tombs of the patriarchs and their wives are exactly below the cenotaphs. In 1215, the Crusaders opened the tombs and later bricked up the entrance to the Machpelah cave, which has never been entered since 1266. The *women's mosque* is between the SW outer wall of the haram and the Abraham mausoleum.

Machpelah cave: Israelite tradition associates Hebron with the patriarch Abraham, and thus with the period around 1850 BC. According to Genesis 23, Abraham—the oldest of the Israelite pariarchs and the ancestor of the Jewish people— bought the Machpelah cave from the Hittites, who were the local residents, in order to bury his wife Sara: 'And Sara was an hundred and seven and twenty years old: these were the years of the life of Sara. And Sara died in Kiriath-arba; the same is Hebron in the land of Canaan ... And Abraham hearkened unto Ephron (the Hittite); and Abraham weighed to Ephron the silver, which he had named in the audience of the sons of Heth, four hundred shekels of silver, current money with the merchant ... And after this, Abraham buried Sara his wife in the cave of the field of Machpelah before Mamre: the same is Hebron in the land of Canaan.' Mamre, the town where Abraham lived, is 3 km. N. of Hebron (see under Environs). When Abraham died at the age of 175 years, he too was buried in the Machpelah cave (Genesis 25, 9–10). The patriarchs Isaac (son of Abraham) and his wife Rebecca, as well as Jacob (son of Isaac) and his wife Leah, were also buried in the cave (Genesis 49, 29–32).

Ibrahim mosque: The courtyard of the Haram el-Khalil leads into the mosque (Castellum ad Sanctum Abraham) which was built by the Emperor Justinian as a basilica and was taken over by the Ommayads in AD 638. It owes its present form to the Crusaders (groin vaults in the side aisles). It occupies the S. section of the Haram el-Khalil and is surrounded by the old wall on three sides. Four columns with Byzantine capitals support the ceiling and divide the basilica into a nave and two aisles, all of equal width but the nave is much taller. The walls of the mosque are faced with marble up to a height of 6 ft., and above this a band inscribed with Koranic texts runs round the building. There are three windows on each side of the clerestory. By the rear left-hand pillar there is a dikkah: a high tribune, supported by marble columns, used for recitations from the Koran reciters and leading prayers.

In the middle of the SE side there is a mihrab flanked by columns. Its half-dome is surrounded by an intertwining band of sumptuous inlaid work. Next to this is an old and beautifully worked cedar *pulpit* (minbar) which

Sammu (Hebron), synagogue ▷

Sultan Saladin is reputed to have built here in 1191. It is richly decorated with carvings, and is one of the rare examples of Ayyubidic wood-carving. The *cenotaphs* of Isaac and Rebecca, donated by Tankiz in 1332, are in the mosque.

The structure of the Ibrahim mosque is Frankish, with pointed arches supported by double pillars faced with half-columns. The side aisles have rib vaults. Before 1967 the floor of the mosque was laid with splendid carpets. Since 1967 these have been limited to the area around the mihrab and minbar.

Joseph mausoleum: A small dome at the outer NW corner of the Haram el-Khalil, connected to the Haram by a special entrance. The mausoleum contains the cenotaph of Joseph who, according to Jewish tradition, is buried in Sichem/Shekhem.

Environs: Balut es-Sebat/Eshel Avraham (2 km. NW): Abraham's abode has been venerated here since the 16C. The *Abraham oak* with the surrounding plot of land was acquired by the Russian archimandrite Antonin Krapustin in 1871. A Greek-Orthodox monastery with a hostel has stood here since then.

Bani Na'im (6 km. E.): A monumental system of over 50 *cisterns* stands at the E. edge of the Judaean mountain range, 3,125 ft. above the Mediterranean and 4,415 ft. above the Dead Sea, on the site where the Byzantine village of Kefar Barukh formerly stood. A courtyard with living quarters and colonnaded halls is enclosed by a surrounding wall in the manner of a khan. The surrounding wall is some 26 ft. high and is only broken by a door and some small arrow slits. Its lower courses are of embossed Roman ashlars, the middle ones have flat Byzantine ashlars and above these there is a crowning Arab wall. The *Nebi Lut shrine*, with the tomb of Lot, is in the NW part of the courtyard. There are two Kufic inscriptions above the entrance. Inside

Abraham as host, Byzantine

the *village mosque* is the cenotaph, shrouded in tapestries. Above it is a gold-embroidered inscription on red silk: 'This is the tomb of the prophet Lot. Peace.' Byzantine relief crosses are still readily discernible on some of the ashlars. An ancient door lintel, with rosettes on either side of where there used to be a cross, is built into the outside of the N. surrounding wall.

Bet-Zur (6 km. N.): The 'house of the rock' was sporadically inhabited during the early Bronze Age, and in the middle Bronze Age II (late 17C or early 16C BC) it was a fortified structure with cyclopean walls some 8 ft. thick. *Finds:* Almsgiving spoon (Hyksos period), Egyptian ivory carving (recumbent sphinx), Ptolemaic and Seleucid coins. Two digging seasons were mounted here in 1931 and 1957.

Halhul (5 km. N.): A town 3,300 ft. above the Mediterranean, mentioned

Hebron, Ibrahim mosque, pulpit

Hurbat Suseya (Hebron), synagogue

in Joshua 15, 58. *Jami'a nebi Junes:*
The cenotaph of the prophet Jonah
(Nebi Junes) is inside the basilica
which has a minaret and was converted by the Muslims in 1226. Next
to this cenotaph are the cenotaphs of
the prophets Nathan and Gad (1
Chronicles 29, 29). The *church of
Jonah* built by the Crusaders looked,
to E. Robinson the traveller, like a
'village church in New England'.
Hurbat Aristobulya (7 km. SE):
Ruins of a town founded in the 2C BC
by Aristobul, the Maccabaean king. A
capital taken from a church (or synagogue ?) is today in the Rockefeller
Museum in Jerusalem.
Hurbat Suseya (17 km. S.): A
devastated Arab village with ruins of a
synagogue from the Byzantine-Arab
period. This 4&5C building (30 × 52
ft.) was uncovered in 1971/2 and has
been partly restored. Its entrance is in
the NE, giving on to the courtyard.

The floor of the building was
originally covered with a plain white
mosaic, later replaced by a polychrome one which has been repaired
several times. The mosaic in the NE
corner (between the bema on the E.
wall and the side bema) consists of a
geometrical pattern. The mosaic in
front of the side bema, between the E.
wall and the central bema, depicts a
closed Torah shrine with a conch, and
menorot of differing designs on both
sides of a tripod pedestal. Just to the
right of the right-hand menora there
is a shofar, and a lulav to the left. To
the left of the left-hand menora is a
mahta (?). The mosaic has been obliterated on the right-hand side. The
two menorot and the Torah shrine are
separated by four columns which
support a roof with a pointed gable
over the conch. Next to the outer columns there are flowers, a ram on the
left and another on the right. To the

left of the central bema is a mosaic with a geometrical pattern. The rest of the room is filled by a tripartite mosaic with geometrical patterns, birds, a zodiac, hunting scenes, Daniel in the lions' den, and a rosette. This mosaic is bounded by a broad band with meandering patterns and bird and animal motifs. Inscriptions: A Hebrew foundation inscription in the main entrance, another such inscription in the middle of the narthex, and a tabula ansata with a third foundation inscription in the S. part of the ambulatory. The courtyard of the synagogue was converted into a mosque no earlier than the 10C.

Khirbet Anun (2 km. SE of Halhul): The ruins of a *Byzantine church* dedicated to John the Baptist are to be found in the Biblical Bet Anot (Joshua 15, 59). Ruins of Byzantine buildings (monolithic columns 10 ft. long and 1 ft. 6 in. in diameter; capitals with Ionic volutes and carved Byzantine crosses) lie scattered about the field of ruins where the 'house of the fountain' stood.

Khirbet Asida (10 km. N. of Hebron): Ruins of a 5/6C *Byzantine church* discovered in 1932. Two rows, each of four columns, divide the basilica into a nave and two aisles (49 × 30 ft.). The *mosaic* in the nave shows a trellis of vines rising out of an amphora and forming small, round medallions in which grapes, pomegranates, a cage with a bird, and a flamingo, are all depicted. The animal images in the mosaic were obliterated by iconoclasts in the 8C and replaced by plant ones. The mosaics in the side aisles have geometrical patterns.

Khirbet ed-Dir (16 km. SW of Hebron): The ruins of a *Byzantine monastery* on a steep rock. This building measures 41 × 34 ft. 6 in. and is almost square in shape. Beside the monastery there is a chapel (22 × 10 ft. 6 in.), part of whose walls survive. The door lintel is decorated with a tabula ansata in the middle of which there is a cross with the Greek letters Alpha and Omega. On one side of the cross there are circles surrounding leaves. A Greek inscription consisting of three parts is to be found below these. The lintel may have belonged to the adjoining monastery.

Khirbet el-Kirmil (10 km. SE of

Sammu (Hebron), synagogue, Byzantine crossbeam

Hebron): This town referred to in the Bible as Carmel (Joshua 15, 55) contains two *Crusader churches* and a *Frankish fort*. The Crusaders added a tower to the W. side of the Byzantine basilica. The tower (62 × 48 ft.) had walls up to 9 ft. thick. In 1874, it was still standing up to a height of 23 ft. 6 in. The remains of a round tower 28 ft. in diameter are to be seen on the N. side of the rectangular tower. A ruined basilica, 129 × 66 ft. in area, stands on the E. side of the valley.

Mamre/Ramet el-Khalil (3 km. N. of Hebron): A shrine with an altar stood here in the Israelite period. The Old Testament Trinity appeared to Abraham by the oaks of Mamre and promised that a son, Isaac, would be born to him (Genesis 18, 1 ff.).

After the Romans had destroyed Mamre following the first Jewish uprising (AD 66–70), the Emperor Hadrian built a temple to Hermes-Mercury in the market square in c. AD 130. Large numbers of Jews were sold as slaves in Mamre after the second Jewish uprising (AD 132–5). In the Byzantine period, the Emperor Constantine built a basilica which was destroyed in the Persian invasion of 614. The remains of the basilica are inside a temenos (sacred precinct) around which Herod and Hadrian built a massive wall. The enormous blocks of shell limestone are reminiscent of the Herodian walls in Hebron and Jerusalem. The ashlars stand upright; the stretchers, whose long sides run parallel to the wall, alternate with headers which are perpendicular to the line of the wall.

In the SW corner of the temenos is the *well of Abraham* (bir el-haram), which the patriarch is said to have dug with his own hands. Its Roman outer walls were restored in the time of the Crusaders. This well by a spring has a circular shaft which is 22 ft. 6 in. deep and Byzantine in design. A vault arch 2 ft. thick, the W. end of which rests on an old, shaped stone from a gateway, extends across the opening of the shaft.

Constantine basilica: This church (c. AD 330) was partly built with materials from the temenos. Two rows, each of three columns on stylobates, divide the basilica, which measures 54 × 66 ft., into a nave, two

Hurbat Suseya (Hebron), synagogue, mosaic with menora

aisles and an apse. There are two interconnected rectangular rooms in the NE (prothesis) and in the SE (diaconicon). The semicircular apse, 10 ft. 6 in. in diameter, is to the E. and to the W. is the nave, 29 ft. wide and 43 ft. long, flanked on either side by an aisle 13 ft. wide. The foundation walls survive to a height of 5 ft. 10 in. and a thickness of 5 ft. 3 in. The remains of the foundations of the large *outdoor altar*, said to have been built by Abraham, are in the middle of the temenos. *Finds:* Small metal bells, ear-rings, finger rings, stele for Hermes-Mercury, a head of Dionysos, a head of a lion from an alabaster statuette of Hercules, and numerous coins dating from the Hasmonaeans to the Crusaders.

Maon (20 km. SE of Hebron): In the W. part of the field of ruins are the scant remains of a Byzantine fort (30 ft. 6 in. × 34 ft.), whose walls survive to a height of 4 ft. 6 in.

Nebi Yaqin (2 km. NW of Bani Na'im): A rectangular wall (100 × 65 ft.) wide surrounds a courtyard with a system of cisterns, some ruins, and a mosque in the SW corner. *Mosque:*

Above the door of this mosque (30 × 16 ft.) is a Kufic inscription dating from AD 963. The 'footprints and knee-prints of Abraham' are to be seen on a waxed rock enclosed by a railing inside the mosque, along with numerous votive gifts (scraps of clothing, hair from beards, camel hair).

Samma/Eshtemoa (23 km. S. of Hebron): The history of Eshtemoa is recorded (1 Samuel 30, 28) as far back as the time of King David: after his victorious campaign against the Amalekites, he distributed the booty among the towns and villages to the S. of Hebron where he and his men had been given food and shelter.

Today's village of es-Sammu contains numerous stones with images indicating that there was a synagogue here. A *synagogue* (43 ft. 6 in. × 70 ft.) was discovered at the highest point of the village in 1934. Three niches at a level of about 6 ft. 6 in., the largest of which was in the centre and served as a Torah shrine, are to be found in the N. wall which is oriented towards Jerusalem. Two stone benches, one above the other, run along the N. and

Herodion, courtyard with tower

S. walls. In the W. wall they are interrupted by a bema. In the narrow E. side there are three entrances preceded by a narthex. The narthex contains the remains of a mosaic depicting a date palm (on the right) and an Aramaic inscription relating to the building's foundation. In the early Islamic period the synagogue was converted into a mosque and the S. wall was given a mihrab. A forecourt paved with slabs leads to the narthex via two flights of stairs. *Individual finds:* A stone with a seven-armed menora without a pedestal; a conch with a band of garlands etc. A large *silver treasure* was discovered beside the synagogue: it consists of five clay jugs with 26 kg. of silverware (today the finds are in the Rockefeller Museum in Jerusalem).

Hefer plain/Emeq Hefer/Wadi el-Hawarith

Central District/District of Haifa/Israel

p.320□C 5

The Hefer plain is part of the plain of Sharon and extends along the Mediterranean coast between Hadera and Netanya. It was here that Joshua smote the king of the Canaanite town of Hepher when the Israelites were taking possession of the land (Joshua 12, 17).

Kefar Monash: A moshav with 320 inhabitants, founded in 1946 and named after the Australian general John Monash. *Midreshet Ruppin Institute* (founded in 1948) with a biological research laboratory; a large butterfly collection. *Finds:* Tools from the Neolithic (today they are in the Israel Museum in Jerusalem). *Emeq Hefer regional museum* (1958): A nature museum with a small archaeological department.

Ma'barot: A kibbutz (670 inhabitants) founded in 1933 by the HaS-

Herodion 1 Access ramp 2-4 Semicircular towers 5 Round tower 6 Passages between the surrounding walls (later used as storerooms) 7 Courtyard with peristyle (colonnaded hall) 8 Synagogue (former triclinium) 9 Synagogue (built by the Zealots, later converted into a church) 10 Baths 11 Former triclinium

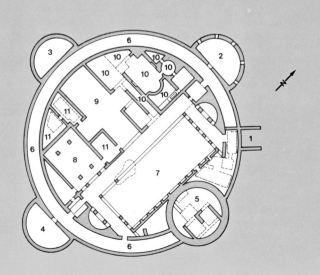

homer-HaZa'ir group from Romania, Bulgaria and Poland. A small *museum:* Finds from the Hefer plain (pottery, hunting weapons, coins). Small library.

Herodion

West Bank   p.320☐E 8

The Herodian mountain fortress of Herodion (Jebel Fureidis/Mountain of the Franks) rises 'like a bosom' (Flavius Josephus) at the edge of the desert 11 km. SE of Bethlehem. From the palace there is an unobstructed view of Jerusalem which is 12 km. to the S., and also of the deep Wadi Khareitum with its prehistoric caves, and the Dead Sea. The conical upper part of the fortress becomes more and more uniformly round the higher it rises, but the top of it is cut off. It stands some 350 ft. higher than its surroundings on a base that is partly man-made. The fortified palace, and the town-like complex around it, were founded by King Herod and are without parallel in the Hellenistic-Roman world, although the Antonia fortress may be regarded as a forerunner.

The splendour of this palace is described by the Jewish historian Flavius Josephus: 'He built round towers around the mountain peak and filled the area, which was surrounded by walls, with a very splendid castle, so that not only did the rooms present a magnificent view from the inside, but the walls, battlements and roofs were fitted out with extravagant opulence on the outside. He conducted an abundant amount of water into the castle from far away at tremendous expense.'

Some basic historical information concerning the fortress has been added following the excavations carried out by Corbo (1962–7), Foers-

Nabi Shu'eib (Hittim), tomb of Jitro ▷

ter (1967–70) and E.Netzer (since 1972). The fort, 32,000 sq.ft. in area, was built by Herod between 24 and 15 BC. He was buried here with great pomp (but his tomb has not been discovered), and the palace became a mausoleum. In the First Jewish War the Zealots used it as a fortress, and in the Second Jewish War it served them as Bar Cochba's centre of resistance and administration (AD 130–5).

Many structural changes were made under Bar Cochba: more living quarters and storehouses were added, and a synagogue with benches around the walls was built in the former triclinium. There is a miqveh (ritual bath) to the S. of the garden area.

In the Byzantine period, heretical monks moved into the baths, which still had a roof at that time, and built a small monastery there. An eastwards-oriented chapel was built on to the SW side of the Herodian cruciform courtyard, and the baths became cells. The monks built a bakery in the caldarium. There are many Christian symbols and monograms on the walls. The monastery was Monophysite and was probably Egyptian in origin. It was abandoned and fell into disrepair after the Persian and Arab invasions of the 7C AD.

Palace: Surrounded by a double concentric wall (the outer wall is 205 ft. in diameter, the inner wall 165 ft.) with four towers, the palace consisted of seven separate structures. 1. a five-storeyed E. tower (diameter: 60 ft.), still standing up to a height of 52 ft. The E. tower straddles the double ring of walls and has a peristyle facing the garden; 2. surrounding walls; 3. semicircular towers (diameter: 53 ft. 6 in.); 4. inner buildings; 5. filling; 6. main stairs; 7. cisterns.

This circular complex is divided into two halves by its N.-S.: the garden in the E. (108 × 41 ft.) with entrances to the N., S. and W., and the multi-storeyed palace in the W. The W. half contains a cruciform courtyard flanked by colonnades on three sides. There is

an apse with engaged columns in the N., and another such apse in the S. A spacious rectangular room (the triclinium) measuring 34 ft. 9 in. × 49 ft. 8 in., with four piers in the corners of the room, is to be found in the W. of the courtyard which is flanked by two apses. The triclinium is partly covered over by a wide entrance staircase for visitors, and has been much altered by the Zealots' additions and the Byzantine chapel.

Fragments of jewellery and plaster, remnants of paintings and mosaics, and gilded capitals and columns, are all witness to the former splendour of this complex. Herod favoured the Pompeian style (the incrustation style), where the painting and stuccoes mimic the structure of an ashlar wall.

To the left of the W. tower are the baths with a square caldarium (14 ft. × 13 ft. 6 in.), of which some columns from the hypocaust still stand. The apodyterium, the tepidarium, and the frigidarium which is 12 ft. × 6 ft. 6 in. in area and 6 ft. 6 in. deep, are reached from the front room. The tepidarium, with its dome 13 ft. 9 in. in diameter, is still in good condition. It was once frescoed and painted in imitation of marble. The capitals of the columns in the portico are a modified version of Hellenistic acanthus capitals.

Below the palace is the *lower town*, with the *Lower Palace* which is 75,500 sq.ft. in area (427 × 177 ft.) and consists of long, vaulted halls and a loggia.

The loggia is in the middle of an artificial terrace 82 ft. wide at an altitude of 2,115–2,200 ft. Archaeologists believe that there was once a hippodrome here measuring 1,150 × 82 ft. To the W. of this is a square building (49 × 46 ft.) which is similar in style and design to the temple of Diana in Nîmes and may have been a nymphaeum, a temple or a pavilion. However, it is also possible that the tomb of Herod lies below the tunnel vault of the nefesh. A pool 227 × 149

ft. in area (it may have been an artificial lake or a reservoir) is to be found
in a large garden. It was later used as a
columbarium, with niches, pilasters
and a vaulted ceiling. A round pavilion 43 ft. 6 in. in diameter, which
may well have been a tholos (circular
religious building), stands in the
middle of this columbarium. A hall 24
ft. 6 in. in diameter, with a ring of columns, occupied the centre of this tholos. Further palace rooms and
buildings for servants and stores were
located in the N. wing of the park.

Herzliyya
District of Tel Aviv/Israel   p.320☐C 6

This, the largest town in the S. of the
plain of Sharon, was founded as an
agricultural settlement in 1924. It is
named after Theodor Herzl (1860–
1904), the founder of Zionism.

Tel Arshaf (NW border of Herzliyya): The ruins of the Canaanite
town of Arshaf, the Assyrian Rish-
pona, the Greek Apollonia, the
Byzantine Sozusa (Redeemer's town),
the Arab Arsuf, and the Frankish
Arsur, are to be found on the edge of
the steep coast. Excavation work was
begun in 1950. So far, an *amphitheatre*
and the Crusader *fortifications* have
been uncovered.

Mosque of Sidna Ali (on rising
ground at the NW edge of Herzliyya):
This shrine harbours the tomb of
Sidna Ali ('Our master Ali'), an Islamic saint who fell in the struggle
against the Crusaders.

Hittim, Horns of/Qarne Hittim
Northern District/Israel   p.318☐F 3

A long mountain with horn-shaped
peaks at both ends (Qarne Hittim =
'horns of wheat') stands 6 km. to the
W. of Tiberias amidst the Lower

Galilean mountains, W. of the Sea of
Galilee and above the modern road to
Nazareth. The fate of the Christian
kingdom of Jerusalem was decided
here in 1187 when the Franks were
defeated by Saladin. This area was
already inhabited by the Palaeolithic.

Environs: Nabi Su'eib (7 km. NW
of Tiberias): A *weli* (shrine) of the
Druze, with the sarcophagus of Jitro
(= Shu'eib), who was their first and
greatest prophet and was Moses's
father-in-law, stands at the NW foot
of the mountain, on the edge of the
Arbel valley. This shrine, decorated
with sumptuous multi-coloured
tapestries, is beneath the dome of a
small *mosque*. The sarcophagus of
Zippora (Sephora), who was Jitro's
daughter and Moses's wife, is in a side
room. The Israeli Druze make a pilgrimage here every spring (26–28
April) in order to celebrate their most
important festival.

Hule plain/Emeq Hula
Northern District/Israel   p.318☐F 2

The attractive Hule valley (68 sq.
miles), 15 miles long and 4–5 miles
wide, is flanked by mountains whose
shoulders rise steeply to a height of
2,300 ft. above the valley floor. The
Via Maris, the main arterial road in
Palestine, ran along the N. edge of the
Hule valley, and in the early Biblical
period almost all the important towns
in N. Palestine lay along this route:
the Hyksos fortress in the S. (see
Hazor), and the town of Dan in the N.
(see Tel Dan) which lies on the main
source of the Jordan. At the time of
the Crusaders, the Hule valley was the
border district between the Muslims
and the Christians; the Franks fortified the crossing points by building
mighty castles (Subeibe, Hunin).
Negro slaves from the army of Ibrahim Pasha of Egypt settled here in the
mid 19C. The first Jewish settlements
were built in the N. and S. of the

valley in the early 20C: in the period between 1939 and 1947 there were already 12 such settlements, including 10 kibbutzim. After the State of Israel was founded, the marshes were drained (1951–8) with the help of the Dutch.

Kiryat Shemona: This growing town is the regional centre of the Hule valley. *Finds:* 100 skeletons around a monumental chieftain's tomb from the Natufa culture, with chains of seashells, and headbands of animals' teeth and gazelles' hooves. The tomb chambers were painted the colour of blood.

HaGosherim (5 km. E. of Kiryat Shemona): A kibbutz with 530 inhabitants, founded by Turkish immigrants in 1948. *Excavations:* Tombs from the mid Bronze Age, some with Hellenistic pottery which was probably introduced by Macedonian soldiers in the 4&3C BC. A fine plough (versoio) from the 4/6C AD.

Hunin (2 km. N. of Kiryat Shemona): 1,650 ft. above the Tel Hay valley are the scant ruins of the *Crusader castle of Chastel Neuf* (Castrum Novum), standing on walls which are Phoenician in origin. Between 1105 and 1107, Hugo of St.-Omer, the prince of Galilee, built a castle which dominated the entire region. It stood on the site of the Biblical Janoah (2 Kings 15, 29). After being destroyed by Saladin it was rebuilt by Onfroi in 1178. It was in the possession of Baldwin IV in 1180, and in 1186 it was held by Joscelin de Courtenay. After the defeat at Hittim in 1187, Hunin was one of the last Galilean castles to remain in Crusader hands. Al-Adil, a brother of Saladin, captured it in 1187. In 1266 the castle fell under the sway of the Mamelukes, who enlarged its defences and built a small mosque. This castle (130 × 130 ft.), with its corner towers, was destroyed by an earthquake in 1837. The few remains are mainly of the Mameluke additions.

Kefar Gil'adi (5 km. N. of Kiryat Shemona): A kibbutz founded in 1916 and named after Israel Giladi (1886–1918), one of the founders of the HaS-

Hunin (Hule plain), Crusader castle of Chastel Neuf

homer movement. In 1926 it was merged with the Tel Hay kibbutz. Near the kibbutz are the ruins of a *mausoleum*, with two tombs from the 2&3C. A *stone statue* of a roaring lion (1926), which is 20 ft. high and is the work of Aharon Melnikov, stands to the S. of the kibbutz, on the site where Josef Trumpeldor and his seven comrades died on 20 February 1920 when defending Tel Hay. *Bet HaShomer museum:* A small museum in the courtyard of a farmhouse, with exhibits relating to the Jewish settlement of Galilee.

Ma'yan Barukh (5 km. NE of Kiryat Shemona): A kibbutz with 400 inhabitants, founded in 1947 by immigrants from South Africa. It was named after Baruch Gordon, the South African Zionist. In 1955, members of the kibbutz founded a small *prehistoric museum of the Hule valley*. Exhibits: Celts from the Palaeolithic; flint tools from the Neolithic and the Copper Age; clay vessels from the early Bronze Age; Roman lamps and glasses; hand mills of stone, and oil presses.

Jericho/Yeriho
West Bank   p.320□E 7

The oldest known settlement resembling a town was built by prehistoric nomads on the Tell es-Sultan between the Elisa spring (Arabic: Ain es-Sultan) with its abundant waters and modern Jericho. In *c.* 7000 BC, Jericho already had the character of a fortified town, with walls, towers and a ditch around the ramparts. There was a mixed proto-urban culture here in the chalcolithic period (5th millen-

Jericho, Tell es-Sultan

Monastery of St.George (Jericho)

nium), and between 2400 and 2000 the area was only sparsely populated. A new town wall was built in the Hyksos period (18–16C BC). After Jericho had been captured by the Israelites under Joshua in *c.* 1200 BC (Joshua 5, 13 ff.), human settlement of the Tell es-Sultan came to an end at the time of the Babylonian Exile (586 BC). In the 6C the town became part of the Persian administrative centre of Yehud. The Hellenistic-Roman Jericho was built to the S., at the entrance to the Wadi Quilt. It was destroyed by Vespasian during the Jewish revolts in AD 66–70. Emperor Hadrian rebuilt it in AD 135 after the Bar Cochba revolt. Numerous monasteries, convents, hospices for monks and pilgrims, and caves and lavras inhabited by hermits, were built in the 2C AD. Jericho was destroyed by the Arabs in 634; there were numerous Ummayad buildings. The Crusaders captured

the town in 1099, and a brief economic boom began as a result of the stream of pilgrims visiting the place of Jesus's baptism (El-Maghtas) on the Jordan. The town was destroyed by Saladin in 1187. Under the Mamelukes and Turks it was an insignificant village. Jericho had 4,000 inhabitants during the period of the British mandate. Since 1967 it has been occupied by Israel.

Tell es-Sultan (2 km. NW of the centre of modern Jericho): The settlement hill known as Tell es-Sultan (Arabic: 'the ruler's hill of ruins'), 71 ft. high, 165 ft. wide and 1,150 ft. long, stands at an elevation of 820 ft. just to the W. of the spring. In 1952–8, K.Kenyon discovered a large settlement from the Neolithic period (7000–6000 BC). The round *Neolithic tower*, built of massive rubble stones (about 56,000 cu.ft.), is 27 ft. high and

Hisham palace (Jericho), stone window

its diameter is 26–33 ft. at the base and 23 ft. at the top. Inside the tower, 22 steps built of stone slabs 2 ft. 6 in. long lead from the E. side to the platform. The remains of the sloping Hyksos wall, which is 20 ft. high and built of crushed earth, are in a large ditch at the N. end of the Tell.

Tutul Abu al-'Alayiq (in the SW corner of the oasis, at the outlet of the Wadi Quilt): A settlement hill in Hellenistic and Roman Jericho. A Hasmonaean (?) *winter palace,* with splendid houses, pools and gardens, was excavated to the N. of Wadi Quilt in 1973–4. The remains of Herodian buildings which have been excavated in the Wadi Quilt include a *double palace* (built in the Roman opus reticulatum manner), the *Kypros castle* on the Tell el-Aqabe, and the *hippodrome* with room for 3,000 spectators to the S. of the Tell es-Samrat.

Synagogue (1 km. N. of Tell es-Sultan): The remains of a 6/7C basilica (33 x 43 ft.) with a nave and two aisles are to be found underneath a house built in 1936. The S. wall, in which there is an apse, is oriented towards Jerusalem. A polychrome mosaic floor with geometrical patterns. The nave has a tripartite *mosaic:* in the centre there is a geometrical pattern with a stylized Torah shrine standing on four feet and a conch. Underneath this, in a circle, there is a seven-armed menora on a pedestal having three feet; on the left there is a lulav, and to the right there are a shofar and the Aramaic inscription 'Shalom al Yisrael' ('Peace over Israel'). Two striking features are the complete absence of any depictions of figures, and the anonymous inscription relating to the foundation.

Environs: Monastery of St.George

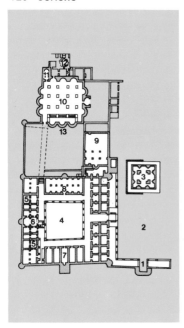

Khirbet al-Mafjar, Hisham palace 1 Main gate **2** Forecourt **3** Embellished basin **4** Palace courtyard **5** Guests' and servants' quarters **6** Audience room with bath **7** Small mosque **8** Two-aisled majlis (state room) **9** Mosque **10** Bath hall with mosaic **11** Diwan (rest room/reception room) with tapestry-like mosaic **12** Calidarium **13** Frigidarium

(5 km. SW of Jericho): A Greek Orthodox monastery on three levels in the desert on the N. rocky slope of the Wadi Quilt. Syrian anchorites built a lavra here in 420–30, and John of Thebes founded a monastery in 480. The monastery was at the height of its fortunes in the 6C thanks to the work of Georgios of Choziba, was destroyed by the Persians in 614, restored by Manuel I Comnenus in 1173, and rebuilt by the Greek monk Kallinikos in 1878. Since 1901, monks have once again lived in the monastery.
Church of the Virgin Mary (the

Hisham palace (Jericho) ▷

monastery church): Numerous *icons* and fine *paintings:* the double-headed Byzantine eagle commemorates the 12C restoration. The iconostasis is of more recent origin.

Church of St.John and St.George: A rectangular church which has a dome and is joined by a narthex to the church of the Virgin Mary. The skull of St.George is in a wooden vessel in the S. niche. On the N. wall is a long reliquary containing the skulls of the 14 monks martyred by the Persians. Fine 6C *mosaics*. The royal doors in the middle are attributed to Alexis Comnenus.

Above the church of the Virgin Mary is the *Elijah grotto,* which is 36 ft. long and decorated with paintings. It is said that the prophet lived here for three years and six months and was fed by ravens. The cave of St.John of Thebes, decorated with 11/12C *frescos,* is 395 ft. E. of the monastery and 230 ft. above the floor of the wadi.

Monastery of St.John (8 km. SE; not open to the public; restricted area): A single-aisled church built in 1882 on the remains of Byzantine and Crusader buildings. Ornaments in the crypt and by the monastery porch bear witness to the medieval buildings. Syrian and Coptic monasteries stand near to this castle-like monastery. A hexagonal Russian Orthodox chapel, an Ethiopian monastery, and a Romanian Orthodox church, all commemorate the baptism of Jesus.

Hisham Palace/Khirbet al-Maf-jar (2 km. NW of the Tell es-Sultan): Ruins of an Ummayad palace (the *Hisham Palace*) excavated in 1935–48. Work on it was begun by Caliph Hisham (724–743). His successor, Caliph al-Walid II (743–4), continued the work. The two-storeyed winter palace, the bath-house and the mosque are among the finest examples of early Islamic architecture. This complex, which was left incomplete because of the murder of Caliph al-Walid, was destroyed by an earthquake in *c.* 746. The forecourt, which is decorated with architectural fragments, leads into the square inner courtyard where there was a domed water basin. In the NW corner of the bath-house, which measures 130 × 130 ft., there is a small *reception hall* with delicate stuccoed elements and a splendid mosaic on the elevated floor of the exedra. The coloured *mosaic* depicts a tree with fruits, and underneath it are three gazelles and a lion: two gazelles grazing on the left, and a lion attacking a gazelle on the right. The floor of the largest room in the *bath-house* is decorated by an abstract geometrical mosaic. This is the largest ancient mosaic to have survived intact anywhere. The palace follows in the tradition of late classical and early Byzantine fortress architecture.

Khirbet en-Nitla (3 km. E.): A 4/5C Byzantine church excavated in 1950. It was destroyed in the 6C, and four chapels were built on its ruins between then and the 9C.

Mons Quarantana/Qarantal (3 km. NW): The *Sarandarion monastery* is one of the three inhabited monasteries in the mountains of the Judaean desert where, as tradition has it, Jesus was first tempted by the devil. The monastery stands 560 ft. above the Jordan plain, on the E. slope of Jebel Qarantal below the Maccabaean fortress of Dok. In 340, St.Chariton built a church and a chapel on the plateau; these were destroyed in the 7C. The *church of the Temptation* (1874) is decorated with over 100 *icons* from the 18&19C. Today it stands between the rock and the 25 monks' cells, above the ruins of a structure built by the Crusaders. In the S. section, 13 steps lead to the chapel of the First Temptation (13 × 13 ft.), where the stone is on display on which Jesus is said to have sat during the first temptation. Ruins and ornamental remains (Ionic capitals, cornices, railing pillars) from Byzantine, medieval and modern times are

Prophet Elijah, Byzantine museum, Athens, 17C ▷

Hisham palace (Jericho), mosaic

Nabi Musa (Jericho)

to be found within a modern monastery on the plateau. The *cave church of St.Elijah*, located 130 ft. below the monastery, includes the monks' premises and was restored in 1949–65.

Na'aran (5.5 km. NW): The remains of a 6C *synagogue* excavated in 1919–21 stand on the rocky spur above the Wadi Nuweime. There are fine polychrome *floor mosaics* with geometrical patterns and depictions of figures.

Nabi Musa (15 km. S.): According to Muslim tradition, the immense *desert monastery* contains the *tomb of Moses* (Arabic: Nabi Musa = 'prophet Moses'). In 1269, the Mameluke sultan Baibars built a dome above the tomb which is 20 ft. long, 7 ft. high and 10 ft. wide and can be reached from inside the mosque through a small gate. The cenotaph is wrapped in a green cloth. In 1490–1500, a large, two-storeyed hospice was built for the numerous pilgrims and a minaret was erected. There was an annual pilgrimage which had an anti-Christian character and proceeded from the Temple Square in Jerusalem to the Nabi Musa. The building, which had fallen into disrepair over the centuries, was rebuilt by the Turks in *c.* 1820. The *maqam* of a pious woman called Aisha stands on a hill some 650 ft. to the E. 2 km. to the SW is the *shrine of the shepherd Hasan*, a rectangular building surrounded by a stone wall. It is said that Moses's body rests in the tomb, which is 7 ft. wide, 20 ft. long and 5 ft. high.

Pharan (15 km. NW): St.Chariton founded the *lavra* of Pharan in the 4C. This was surrounded by a rampart 7–10 ft. high and consisted of three levels built into the S. slope of the wadi. The garden is at the bottom,

Mons Quarantana (Jericho), stone on which Jesus is said to have sat

the 19C common rooms are above it, and above these again is the cave of St.Chariton which has been converted into a self-contained church.

The small chapel of St.Chariton and St.Kyriakos, hung with icons, was at the foot of the lavra. Pharan was completely destroyed in 1978.

Jerusalem

Jerusalem/Yerushalayim

District of Jerusalem/Israel   p.320☐D 7

Jerusalem has been the capital of Israel since 1949. In 1953, the Knesset (the Israeli parliament) declared that Jerusalem 'was, is and remains' the capital of Israel. In the same year, King Husain of Jordan proclaimed that Jerusalem was the second capital of the Hashemite kingdom and an integral part of his kingdom. Israel annexed East Jerusalem during the Six-Day War of 1967. In 1980, one day after the UN General Assembly had, by way of an ultimatum, called upon Israel to evacuate the occupied territories including East Jerusalem, the Knesset declared that the whole of Jerusalem was the capital of Israel.

Holy City: Jerusalem is the Holy City of three world religions: Judaism, because the Temple of Solomon stood there; Christianity, because Jerusalem was the last place where Jesus Christ

View of Jerusalem from Mount of Olives

was active; Islam, because the Prophet Mohammed rode to Heaven from the rock on Temple Mount. The Arabic name of Jerusalem is 'El-Quds' = 'The Holy Place'.

According to Jewish tradition, and in the view of Christian Doctors of the Church, Jerusalem was first mentioned in the Old Testament in the passage from Genesis 14, 17–20: Abraham, the oldest Israelite patriarch and the ancestor of the Jewish people, meets Melchizedek, the priest king of Salem (= shalom = 'peace': 'Jeru-salem' (Hebrew) = 'city of peace'). Here, Melchizedek is described not only as the king of Salem, but as 'the priest of the most high God'. This priest king leaves Salem, goes to Abraham, brings bread and wine and blesses Abraham. As in Psalm 76, 2 and 110, 4 ('In Salem also is his tabernacle, and his dwelling place in Zion', 'Thou art a priest for ever after the order of Melchizedek') and other passages in the Psalms, Melchizedek was interpreted as a model of the Messiah who chooses Jerusalem as his dwelling-place. The Early Fathers interpreted the bread and wine of Melchizedek as a prefiguration of the Eucharist sacrifice, and some Early Fathers went so far as to suppose that Melchizedek was the Son of God in person.

History

C. 1800 BC: Archaeological finds have shown that, to the S. of the later site of the Temple, there was a settlement which may go back to the early Bronze Age (mid 3rd millennium BC), but certainly dates back to about 1800 BC. Jerusalem is probably also mentioned in the 19/18C BC on some Egyptian execratory tablets and in a Sumerian catalogue of gods (if the Sumerian word 'aldima' means Jerusalem).

C. 1360 BC: The oldest definite mention of Jerusalem ('Urusalimmu') is in the Amarna tablets, a collection of ancient oriental clay tablets which were found in Tell el-Amarna, a ruined site in central Egypt. The tablets mainly contain letters from the archive of the foreign ministry of the Egyptian kings Amenophis III (1402–1364 BC) and Amenophis IV = Akh-

Dome of the Rock with Mount of Olives in background

Alphabetical list of interesting sites in Jerusalem

naton (1364–1347 BC). These works are composed by writers at the contemporary courts of the kings. Just under three-quarters of the texts derive from Palestine, Phoenicia and Syria and are the most important source for the history of Palestine and Syria. Jerusalem appears as the residence of one of the numerous hereditary rulers of Palestine who were dependent on the Egyptian king. In one of these letters, Abdi-Cheba, the ruler of the city of Jerusalem, turns to Akhnaton with a request for assistance against the Chapiru, who have been variously identified with the early Israelites.

C. 1220–00 BC: The Israelites conquered Palestine. They fought under Joshua, who succeeded Moses as leader of the Israelites. However, they did not succeed in capturing the Jebusite town of Jebu or Jerusalem: 'As for the Jebusites the inhabitants of Jerusalem, the children of Judah could not drive them out: but the Jebusites dwell with the children of Judah at Jerusalem until this day.'

C. 1000 BC: King David of Israel and Judah conquered the Jebusite fortress of Jerusalem, which was thought to be impregnable: 'The Jebusites said to David, 'You will not get in here. The blind and the lame will hold you off (= the town is so well fortified that sick people are sufficient to defend it)' (2 Samuel 5, 6). 'Nevertheless David took the castle of Zion, which is the city of David. And David said, Whosoever smiteth the Jebusites first shall be chief and captain. So Joab the son of Zeruiah went first up, and was chief. And David dwelt in the castle; therefore they called it the city of David. And he built the city round about, even from Millo round about: and Joab repaired the rest of the city' (1 Chronicles 11, 5–8). After the death of Saul, the first king of all the tribes of Israel, David was appointed king of the tribe of Judah and other southern tribes. This was the beginning of the Kingdom of Judah.

David made Jerusalem the capital of the kingdoms of Israel and Judah. These two kingdoms were united in him in a personal union. When the Ark of the Covenant was transferred

Samuel anointing Saul as king (left), Samuel anointing David as king (right), 14C book illustration

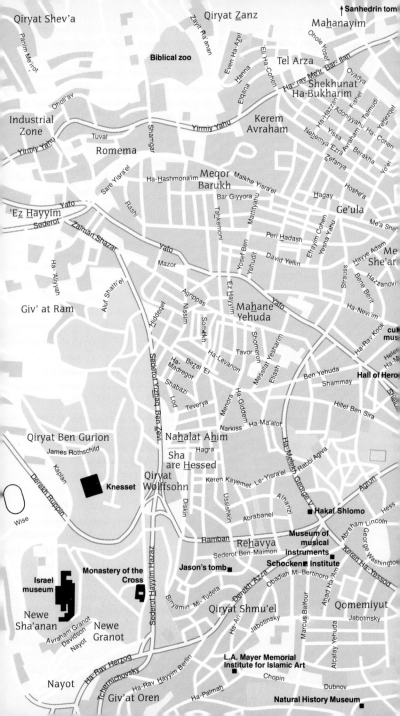

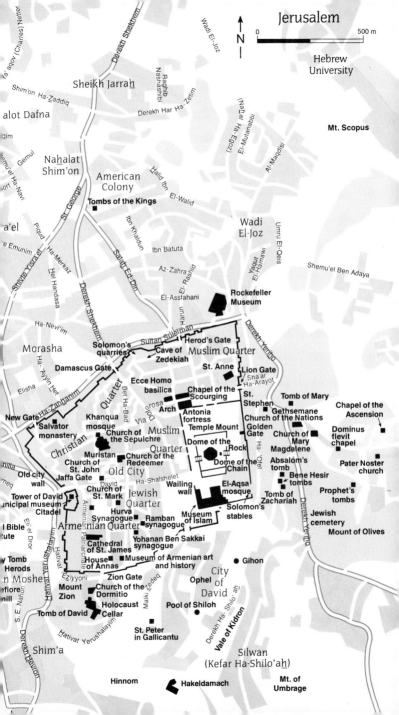

Jerusalem

N

0   500 m

Hebrew
University

Mt. Scopus

Wadi El-Joz

Sheikh Jarra<u>h</u>

Shim'on Ha-Zaddiq

alot Dafna

qim

Na<u>h</u>alat
Shim'on

American
Colony

Tombs of the Kings

a'el

Wadi
El-Joz

Shemu'el Ben Adaya

Az-Zahra

El-Assfahani

Rockefeller
Museum

Morasha

Solomon's
quarries

Cave of
Zedekiah

Sultan Suleiman

Herod's Gate

Muslim Quarter

St. Anne

Lion Gate

Tomb of Mary

Damascus Gate

Ecce Homo
basilica

Chapel of the
Scourging

St.
Stephen

Church of the Nations

Gethsemane

Chapel of the
Ascension

New Gate

Salvator
monastery

Khanqua
mosque

Christian
Quarter

Church of
the Sepulchre

Arch

Via
Dolorosa

Antonia
fortress

Temple Mount

Dome of the
Rock

Golden
Gate

Church of
Mary
Magdalene

Dominus
flevit
chapel

Muslim
Quarter

Pater Noster
church

Muristan

Church of
St. John

Old City

Church of
the Redeemer

Dome of the
Chain

Absalom's
tomb

Old city
wall

Jaffa Gate

Church of
St. Mark

Jewish
Quarter

Wailing
wall

El-Aqsa
mosque

Bene Hesir
tombs

Prophet's
tombs

Tower of David
unicipal museum
Citadel

Hurva
Synagogue

Ramban
synagogue

Museum
of Islam

Solomon's
stables

Tomb of
Zachariah

l Bible
tute

Armenian Quarter

Yohanan Ben Sakkai
synagogue

Jewish
cemetery

y Tomb
Herods

n Moshe
efiore
ill

Cathedral
of St. James

House
of Annas

Museum of Armenian art
and history

Gihon

Mount of Olives

Mount
Zion

Church of the
Dormitio

Zion Gate

City
of
David

Ophel

Tomb of David

Holocaust
Cellar

Pool of Shiloh

Shim'a

St. Peter
in Gallicantu

Silwan
(Kefar Ha-Shilo'a<u>h</u>)

Hinnom

Hakeldamach

Mt. of
Umbrage

Vale of Kidron

to Jerusalem, the city thereby also became the cultic centre and the religious capital of Israel and Judah. It was enlarged under the rule of David and his successor Solomon. Solomon built his royal palace and the Temple in the city of David, and also reinforced the walls of Jerusalem.

926 BC: The joint kingdom of Israel and Judah fell apart after the death of Solomon. Jerusalem continued to be the capital of the smaller southern kingdom of Judah. The city was probably not enlarged any further in the period after Solomon's death, apart from the steps taken to protect the pools to the south.

The post-Solomon period was characterized by frequent sieges and pillages by foreign powers. In 922/1, the Egyptian king Sheshonk I captured the city, 'and he took away the treasures of the house of the Lord, and the treasures of the king's house; he even took away all: and he took away all the shields of gold which Solomon had made' (1 Kings 14, 26). In *c.* 845 BC, Philistines and Arabs captured Jerusalem 'and carried away all the substance that was found in the king's house, and his sons also, and his wives' (2 Chronicles 21, 17). When the city was under the rulership of King Joash (840–801), it was plundered by the Aramaeans (2 Chronicles 24, 23 f.). Shortly after 800, King Joash of Israel tore down a large part of the walls, 'and he took all the gold and silver, and all the vessels that were found in the house of the Lord, and in the treasures of the king's house, and hostages, and returned to Samaria' (2 Kings 14, 14). In 701 BC, Sennacherib of Assyria had to call off a siege after an epidemic broke out (2 Kings 18–19). The Assyrians led King Manasseh into captivity in *c.* 648 (2 Chronicles 33, 11 ff.), in 609 the Egyptian king Necho deposed king Joahas and appointed Joachim king, and in 605 and 597 BC the city was conquered by the Babylonian king Nebuchadnezzar II.

587 BC: The most critical point in the pre-Christian history of Jerusalem occurred in 587 BC, when the Babylonian king Nebuchadnezzar II captured and destroyed the city and led the inhabitants of the kingdom of Judah away into their Babylonian

King Solomon the Wise, 14C

King Ahaziah on his sickbed, 14C

Captivity: 'And in the fifth month, on the seventh day of the month, which is the nineteenth year of king Nebuchadnezzar king of Babylon, came Nebuzar-adan, captain of the guard, a servant of the king of Babylon, unto Jerusalem; And he burnt the house of the Lord, and the king's house, and all the houses of Jerusalem, and every great man's house burnt he with fire. And all the army of the Chaldees, that were with the captain of the guard, brake down the walls of Jerusalem round about. Now the rest of the people that were left in the city, and the fugitives that fell away to the king of Babylon, with the remnant of the multitude, did Nebuzar-adan the captain of the guard carry away. But the captain of the guard left of the poor of the land to be vinedressers and husbandmen. And the pillars of brass that were in the house of the Lord, and the bases, and the brasen sea that was in the house of the Lord, did the Chaldees break in pieces, and carried the brass of them to Babylon' (2 Kings 25, 8–13).

Jerusalem remained a religious centre during the Babylonian Exile. Those Jews who had not been taken into captivity habitually made a pilgrimage to the devastated Temple 'having their beards shaven, and their clothes rent, and having cut themselves' (Jeremiah 41, 5); the sayings of Deutero-Isaiah, the prophet in exile (Isaiah 40–55), proclaim God's saving intervention and his people's return to Jerusalem.

539 BC: The Persian king Cyrus the Great conquered the neo-Babylonian kingdom, and Nabonid, the last neo-Babylonian king, was taken prisoner. His son Belshazzar, who conducted the affairs of government from 550 onwards, died, probably in battle. After Babylon had once again been conquered by the Persians, the Jews began to return. An edict issued by Cyrus the Great had permitted them to rebuild the Temple under Serubbabel, who had been installed by the Persians as governor of the Persian province of Yehud (Judaea).

After the homecomers had built an altar on the site of the destroyed Temple of Solomon, work on rebuilding the Temple began under the governor Serubbabel (a grandson of king

Ark of the Covenant on a relief from Kafarnaum

Joachim of Judah, who was exiled to Babylon in 597). After some difficulties had been encountered during construction owing to resistance by the Samaritans, the Temple was consecrated in 515 BC. This Temple, known as the Second Temple, was later converted under Herod the Great and stood for 585 years until it was destroyed under Titus in AD 70.

C. 450 BC: The city walls were rebuilt under the Persian governor Nehemiah around the middle of the 5C BC (Nehemiah 2 ff.). The report on the building work in Nehemiah 3 gives the first description of the fortifications and other prominent buildings, although it is not always possible to locate these.

332 BC: Jerusalem came under the rule of the Macedonians, but was granted certain privileges because it had surrendered without a struggle. After the death of Alexander the Great in 323 it belonged to the area ruled by the Ptolomeys and fell to the Seleucids in 198 BC. Under the Seleucid Antiochus IV Epiphanes (175–164), who aimed at complete Hellenization in the territory which he controlled, Jerusalem was renamed 'Antiochia', the Temple was pillaged, and the religious rights of the Jews were abolished.

165 BC: The Seleucids' regime of terror led to the Maccabean revolt in 168, a religious struggle waged by the Jews for their liberation. The Maccabeans captured Temple Mount and repaired the sanctuary (this was the origin of the feast of the Temple's consecration). After religious freedom had been attained—the Syrian occupying forces remained in Jerusalem—, the Maccabees began to fight for their political freedom from the Seleucids. In 142, Simon, the last of the five Maccabee brothers, succeeded in gaining Syrian recognition as high priest and an independent ruler. In 141 he forced the Syrian occupiers to abandon Jerusalem. In reward for this the people conferred upon him the hereditary honour of a ruler, military leader and high priest. The dynasty of the Maccabees is known as the Hasmonaeans.

63 BC: Delegates of the Jewish people requested the Roman general Pompey to restrict the rulership of the Hasmonaean kings to the religious and cultic spheres and to transfer political rule to another power, the Romans. The party of Hyrcanus the high priest agreed to this, and Jerusalem was handed over to Pompey. Aristobulus, the brother of Hyrcanus, entrenched himself on Temple Mount and Pompey had to lay siege to it for three months before it fell. The independent kingdom of the Hasmonaeans came to an end when Temple Mount was captured. Hyrcanus continued as high priest and became an ethnarch (governor).

37 BC: In the year 40, the Roman senate appointed Herod the Great to be king of the Jews. Herod captured Jerusalem and began his period of rule. Despite the splendour of his outward power—temple, palace, amphitheatre, agora, senate, citadel—Herod was unpopular with the people: the Jewish upper classes mistrusted him because he was regarded as a Gentile ruler appointed by the grace of Rome. He attempted to legitimize his rulership in the eyes of the Jews by allying himself by marriage with the Hasmonaean royal house, but this relationship by marriage was the source of bitter family intrigues and numerous executions. After his death, the territory which he ruled was divided among his sons. The largest section, which included Jerusalem, went to his son Archelaus, who was deposed by the Emperor Augustus in AD 6. The country was placed under direct Roman administration and was ruled by a procurator.

AD 48/9: The council of the Apostles, which was a meeting of the twelve Apostles and elders, and also Paul and Barnabas who were missionaries among the heathen, was held in Jeru-

Ecce Homo arch ▷

salem, probably in c. AD 48/9, in order to consider the dispute regarding whether heathens who had become Christians must be circumcised in accordance with Mosaic law (The Acts 15, 1–5; Galatians 2, 1–10). The apostolic decree was passed by which heathens who had been converted to Christianity no longer had to be circumcised and, with few exceptions, were not bound by Mosaic law. Thus the council of the Apostles marks the change from the Jewish Christian mission of the Apostles to the heathen Christian mission under Paul; the resolutions passed at the council of the Apostles were also a necessary precondition for the establishment of the universal Christian church.

AD 66–70: The tensions between the Jews and the direct Roman administration led in AD 66–70 to a revolt (the First Jewish War). In 70, during the final phase of this war, the Temple in Jerusalem was destroyed by the Roman general Titus, who later became Emperor.

132–5: After the First Jewish War, the area was declared an imperial province, cultic practices were discontinued in Jerusalem, and the tax which until then had been paid to the Temple in Jerusalem was assigned to the Temple of Jupiter at the Capitol in Rome. The Emperor Hadrian's plans to rebuild Jerusalem as a Roman colony in 132, led to the Second Jewish War, in which Simon Bar-Cochba led an uprising and some 850,000 people died; the Jewish population was exterminated or enslaved.

After the revolt had been put down, the Jews were forbidden to enter Jerusalem, and the city itself was rebuilt as a Roman colony by the name of Aelia Capitolina.

326: Helena, the mother of Emperor Constantine the Great, undertook a pilgrimage to the Holy Land, found the 'True Cross', and began building numerous churches (including the Church of the Holy Sepulchre in Jerusalem). Jerusalem became a Christian holy City as a result of Helena's pilgrimage and her extensive building activities. After the Roman Empire was divided in 395, Jerusalem came under Byzantine rule.

638: Caliph Omar I captured Jerusalem and declared the Temple square to be a sacred precinct of Islam, because the Prophet Mohammed is said to have risen into heaven from the peak of Temple Mount. Jerusalem was now in the hands of the third great religion which considers Jerusalem to be a Holy City. The Ummayad dynasty of Caliphs regarded Jerusalem as in some respects more sacred than Mecca and Medina.

1099: Owing to the cruelty of the Turkish Seljuks, Pope Urban II declared that the First Crusade should be waged. In this Crusade, Jerusalem was captured by an army led by Duke Godfrey of Bouillon (Lower Lorraine), and some 70,000 Jews and Muslims were brutally killed. Godfrey took the title of 'Defender of the Holy Sepulchre'. After his death in 1100, his brother Baldwin I, Count of Boulogne, had himself crowned king of Jerusalem, and the city became the royal seat of a Latin kingdom.

Herodian Jerusalem, model

1187: Saladin, the sultan of Syria and Egypt and founder of the Ayyub dynasty, captured Jerusalem which remained in the hands of the Muslims even after the Third Crusade in 1189–92. In 1228, Frederick II, the German king and Roman Emperor, undertook a Crusade despite being excommunicated by the Pope, and played on internal disputes amongst the Ayyubids to achieve the cession of Jerusalem, Bethlehem and other places revered by the Christians. However, Temple Mount remained Muslim.

1244: The Christians were finally driven out of Jerusalem when the Khwarizm Turks (Tartars) captured Jerusalem and pillaged it.

1260: Jerusalem fell to the Mamelukes.

1517: Jerusalem came under Ottoman rule. The city fell into disrepair after the death of Sultan Sulaiman the Magnificent in 1560.

1917: The British, led by General Edmund Allenby, conquered Palestine during World War 1. Jerusalem was the capital of the British mandate of Palestine until *1948,* after which it was the capital of the newly founded State of Israel.

1963: The city of Jerusalem established the 'Jerusalem prize', an international prize for literature, which is awarded every two years at the International Jerusalem Book Fair to writers, as a reward for their work in support of the freedom of the individual. Well-known winners of the prize include Bertrand Russell, Max Frisch, Jorge Luis Borges, Eugène Ionesco, Simone de Beauvoir, Octavio Paz, Graham Greene and others.

1964: Ahmed Shukeiry founded the Palestine Liberation Organization (PLO) in Jerusalem.

1967: During the Six-Day War, Israel annexed East Jerusalem, which had belonged to Jordan.

1980: The Knesset proclaimed that the whole of Jerusalem was the capital of Israel.

Heavenly Jerusalem (Zion)

Heavenly Jerusalem is the eschatological equivalent of the earthly Jerusalem: as the earthly Jerusalem, being

City of David

Model of the Antonia fortress, Holyland Hotel

the Holy City, is the place where the name of God shall live (1 Kings 8, 29), the heavenly Jerusalem is the place where the people of God will live in an eternal community with God and Christ, without death, sorrow, crying or pain (Revelation 21, 2–4). Thus the heavenly Jerusalem is an image for the completion of the history of salvation. The idea of the eschatological heavenly Jerusalem is based on the idea that the earthly Jerusalem is the Holy City.

City of God: When King David, in *c.* 1000 BC, captured the Jebusite fortress of Jerusalem, which was thought to be impregnable, the city became the residence of a dynasty which God had promised would endure for ever (2 Samuel 7, 16). After the Ark of the Covenant had been transferred to Jerusalem (2 Samuel 6), the highest secular and religious power of Israel and Judah had its seat in Jerusalem, and

God's requirement that there should be a single cultic site for Israel had been fulfilled in Jerusalem. This requirement was formulated in the collection of laws in Deuteronomy (Deuteronomy 12, 4–7). The city accordingly underwent a religious and ideological elevation: God had installed his priestly king in Jerusalem, and this king crushed the other peoples (Psalm 132, 2, 5). Jerusalem was regarded as 'the city of our God: God will establish it for ever' (Psalm 48, 8). There were to be no sanctuaries apart from the Temple in Jerusalem, and for this reason all the tribes made a pilgrimage to Jerusalem (Psalm 122, 4), to the 'city of God' (Psalm 87, 3), the 'house of the Lord' (Psalm 122, 1).

Renegation, judgement and renewal: Isaiah, who lived before the Exile, was the first prophet in whose works God's judgement on Jerusalem,

Via Dolorosa, Station I, beginning of Way of the Cross procession

passed because of the sinfulness of its inhabitants, is made the dominant theme. He accused Jerusalem and the people of Israel, and called woe upon the 'sinful nation, a people laden with iniquity, a seed of evildoers, children that are corrupters' (Isaiah 1, 4); the kings have become perverted into 'rulers of Sodom', the population is the 'people of Gomorrah' (Isaiah 1, 10). In Ezekiel, the catalogue of sins committed by the inhabitants comprises idolatry, murder, disrespect for father and mother, exploitation of the weak, the poor and foreigners, oppression of orphans and widows, desecration of the Sabbath, fornication, bribery, taking of increase, usury, greed for booty, covetousness of officials, blackmail and robbery (Ezekiel 22). 'How is the faithful city become an harlot! it was full of judgement; righteousness lodged in it; but now murderers reign. Thy silver is become dross, thy wine mixed with water: Thy princes are rebellious, and companions of thieves: every one loveth gifts, and followeth after rewards: they judge not the fatherless, neither doth the cause of the widow come unto them' (Isaiah 1, 21–23). God will pass his judgement over Jerusalem by reason of these abuses, and also by reason of the idolatry (Isaiah 2, 8), the exploitation of the lower classes (Isaiah 3, 14), the haughtiness of the women (Isaiah 3, 16–4, 1), the rigorous methods used in the economy (Isaiah 5, 8), and the dissoluteness (Isaiah 5, 11 ff.). However, the judgement will not destroy the city and its population, but is understood as a purification and is a precondition for re-establishing Jerusalem as a holy city: 'In that day shall the branch of the Lord be beautiful and glorious, and the fruit of the earth shall be excellent and comely for them that are escaped of Israel. And it shall come to pass, that he that is left in Zion, and he that remaineth in Jerusalem, shall be called holy, even every one that is written among the living in Jerusalem: When the Lord shall have washed away the filth of the daughters of Zion, and shall have purged the blood of Jerusalem from the midst thereof by the spirit of judgement, and by the spirit of burning. And the Lord will create upon every dwelling place of mount Zion, and upon her assemblies, a cloud of a flaming fire by night: for upon all the glory shall be a defence. And there shall be a tabernacle for a shadow in the daytime from the heat, and for a place of refuge, and for a covert from storm and from rain' (Isaiah 4, 2–6).

Centre of the Messianic kingdom: When Jerusalem, after being purified by the judgement, will once again be called the 'city of righteousness' (Isaiah 1, 26), it will become the centre of the Messianic kingdom. All the peoples will then flock to Mount Zion in Jerusalem, 'for out of Zion shall go forth the law, and the word of the Lord from Jerusalem' (Isaiah 2, 3 = Micah 4), Jerusalem will one again be the seat of a king (Micah 4, 8) whose name will be 'The Lord our righteousness' (Jeremiah 33, 16). 'At that time they shall call Jerusalem the throne of the Lord; and all the nations shall be gathered unto it, to the name of the Lord, to Jerusalem: neither shall they walk any more after the imagination of their evil heart' (Jeremiah 3, 17).

The prophecies regarding God's judgement upon Jerusalem appeared to many to be harbingers of the city's destruction by the Chaldeans in 587 BC, and the population's deportation into Babylonian Captivity. This interpretation which equated the destruction by the Chaldeans with God's judgement upon the city had to give rise to the expectation that the second part of the prophecies would now also be fulfilled, namely the city's elevation to the seat of a God who was

King and to the centre of the Messianic kingdom. Here it is Deutero-Isaiah, the prophet in exile, who announces to those who have been banished to Babylon that they will return home to Jerusalem (Isaiah 40, 1–11). He relates this homecoming not only to the city's rebuilding, but also to the beginning of God's reign as king over the nations (Isaiah 52, 7–9): 'Thus saith the Lord God, Behold, I will lift up mine hand to the Gentiles, and set up my standard to the people: and they shall bring thy sons in their arms, and thy daughters shall be carried upon their shoulders. And kings shall be thy nursing fathers, and their queens thy nursing mothers: they shall bow down to thee with their face toward the earth, and lick up the dust of thy feet; and thou shalt know that I am the Lord: for they shall not be ashamed that wait for me' (Isaiah 49, 22–23). From 539 BC, when the Jews, afer returning from exile, were confronted with the real state of affairs in Palestine, the belief that the real city of Jerusalem would be the centre of the Messianic kingdom only existed for a short while, an example being the prophet Haggai who, in his speeches made in 520 BC, attributed the present wretchedness of Jerusalem to the fact that the Jews had not yet built a new Temple (Haggai 1, 1–11); Haggai prophesied that God's blessing would once again rest upon the people of Israel from that day onwards on which work on building the Temple was begun (Haggai 2, 10–19): 'For thus saith the Lord of hosts; Yet once, it is a little while, and I will shake the heavens, and the earth, and the sea, and the dry land; And I will shake nations, and the desire of all nations shall come: and I will fill this house with glory, saith the Lord of hosts' (Haggai 2, 6–7). Haggai hoped that Serubbabel, the grandson of the penultimate king of Judah, would provide the historic turning-point, namely the city's definitive renewal

Dome of the Rock, part of façade ▷

(Haggai 2, 21–23). When these expectations were dashed, the post-Exile prophet Trito-Isaiah still hoped for divine intervention in his description of the future glory of Zion (especially Isaiah 60 and 62: pilgrimage of the nations to the blessed Jerusalem, and the glorified city of God): 'A voice of noise from the city, a voice from the temple' (Isaiah 66, 6).

Projection to the end of time: It was hoped that Jerusalem, after the return of the Jews from Babylonian Exile, would become the Holy City and the centre of the Messianic kingdom. When this hope did not reach fulfilment, the idea of Jerusalem as the renewed Holy City was projected to the end of time, and the 'Holy City' became the 'Heavenly City' projected to the end of days. This becomes particularly clear in the book of Zechariah. The prophet Zechariah, in the chapters written in *c.* 520–518 BC, describes in his nocturnal visions the beginning of a (historical) time of salvation, which is related to the renewal under Serubbabel of the House of David. However, Deutero- or Trito-Zechariah, in chapters 12–14 which

were written in the 4/3C, describes the purification and salvation of the city in a (non-historical) end of time. The elevation of Jerusalem to the Heavenly City will be preceded by the invasion of the nations from the north, who will be driven out by God. 'And it shall be in that day, that living waters shall go out from Jerusalem; half of them toward the former sea, and half of them toward the hinder sea: in summer and in winter shall it be. And the Lord shall be king over all the earth: in that day shall there be one Lord, and his name one. All the land shall be turned as a plain from Geba to Rimmon south of Jerusalem: and it shall be lifted up, and inhabited in her place, from Benjamin's gate unto the place of the first gate, unto the corner gate, and from the tower of Hananeel unto the king's winepresses. And men shall dwell in it, and there shall be no more utter destruction; but Jerusalem shall be safely inhabited (Zechariah 14, 8–11).

Christ as the redeemer of Jerusalem: Whereas the post-Exile prophets projected the renewal of Jerusalem to the end of time, a time which was not his-

Via Dolorosa, relief at Station IV

torically defined, the renewal of this city becomes tangible again in the New Testament through the person of Jesus. The prophetess Hanna, who had seen the Christ child in the Temple, spoke 'to all them that looked for redemption in Jerusalem' (St.Luke 2, 38). In St.Luke's Gospel, Jerusalem is the predetermined centre of the work of salvation because, according to the prophets' predictions, Messianic liberation of the chosen people refers mainly to the Holy City of Jerusalem: Moses and Elijah 'appeared in glory, and spake of his decease which he should accomplish at Jerusalem' (St.Luke 9, 31 = Christ's Transfiguration): 'And it came to pass, when the time was come that he should be received up, he steadfastly set his face to go to Jerusalem' St.Luke 9, 51). 'And he went through the cities and villages, teaching, and journeying toward Jerusalem. Then said one unto him, Lord, are there few that be saved?' (St.Luke 13, 22–23). 'And as they heard these things, he added and spake a parable, because he was nigh to Jerusalem, and because they thought that the kingdom of God should immediately appear' (St.Luke 19, 11). When he entered Jerusalem, Jesus was really celebrated as a king, 'and a very great multitude spread their garments in the way; others cut down branches from the trees, and strawed them in the way' (St.Matthew 21, 8). Christ was deliberately applying to himself Zecharaiah's prophecy and its teaching 'that it might be fulfilled, which was spoken by the prophet, saying, Tell ye the daughter of Sion, Behold, thy King cometh unto thee, meek, and sitting upon an ass, and a colt the foal of an ass' (St.Matthew 21, 4–5; cf. St.John 12, 15). The simple mount in the prophecy in Zechariah 9, 9 was intended to indicate the peaceful manner of his reign. But Jesus was also rejected by the inhabitants, and the punishment of Jerusalem was prophesied: 'O Jerusalem, Jerusalem, thou that killest the prophets, and sto-

nest them which are sent unto thee, how often would I have gathered thy children together, even as a hen gathereth her chickens under her wings, and ye would not! Behold, your house is deserted (by God). For I say unto you, Ye shall not see me henceforth, till ye shall say, Blessed is he that cometh in the name of the Lord' (St.Matthew 23, 37–39). The destruction of Jerusalem, the coming of the Son of man, and the Last Judgement, are described in juxtaposition in Christ's speech which is reproduced in St.Matthew 24–25 and concerns the end of time (cf. St.Luke 21, 5–36). *Jerusalem after the death of Christ:* Jerusalem, as seen in the light of the prophets' predictions, had to be assessed anew after the death of Christ, who had been expected to put into effect the kingship of God in Holy Jerusalem. St.Luke places, between the city's destruction and the end of time, an intermediate period of uncertain duration, the 'age of the pagans' (St.Luke 21, 24) which, according to St.Paul, will end when all Israel is saved (Romans 11). In the

Ethiopian chapel attached to Church of the Holy Sepulchre

Acts of the Apostles, Jerusalem, which is the point where the Gospels end, becomes the point from which Christianity begins (The Acts, 1), and the miracle of Pentecost took place in Jerusalem in accordance with the Old Testament prophecies (The Acts, 2). That miracles include the glossolalia: The Apostles spoke the languages of all the peoples (The Acts 2, 6), and the confusion of tongues in Babel was thereby eliminated (Genesis 11, 9)—a symbol of the Apostles' universal mission, proceeding from Jerusalem.

Revelation: The Revelation of St.John the Divine concludes with the vision of God's new world after the Thousand Years' Reign and the final victory over Satan. Then, at the end of time, the heavenly Jerusalem will descend from heaven to earth, 'prepared as a bride adorned for her husband' (Revelation 21, 2). It is a city of pure gold, designed as a square (= perfection), surrounded by a wall of jasper with twelve foundation stones (= the twelve Apostles) and twelve gates (= the twelve tribes of Israel). There is no temple 'for the Lord God

Almighty and the Lamb are the temple of it' (Revelation 21, 22); that is, the destruction of the temple of earthly Jerusalem marked the end of the Old Covenant, and then the body of Christ symbolized the New Covenant).

Via Dolorosa

The Via Dolorosa (Latin: 'way of suffering') begins in the old Muslim quarter of the city and ends in the Church of the Holy Sepulchre. It passes through the Stations of the Cross, at which Christ's Passion is remembered. The Gospels mention only eight of the fourteen Stations which are passed through. The route has been frequently altered over the centuries. Processions take place every Friday at 3 p.m. (Stations X to XIV are in the Church of the Holy Sepulchre):

I.   Pontius Pilate condemns Jesus to death (St.Matthew 27, 22–26).
II. Jesus takes up the Cross (St.John 19, 16–17).
III. Jesus falls under the weight of the Cross for the first time.
IV. Jesus meets his Mother.
V.   Simon of Cyrene helps Jesus to bear the Cross (St.Matthew 27, 32).
VI. Veronica hands her sudarium to Jesus.
VII. Jesus falls under the weight of the Cross for the second time.
VIII. Jesus comforts the weeping women.
IX. Jesus falls under the weight of the Cross for the third time.
X.   Jesus is stripped of His raiment (St.Matthew 27, 35).
XI. Jesus is nailed to the Cross (St.John 19, 18).
XII. Jesus dies on the Cross (St.John 19, 30).
XIII. Descent from the Cross.
XIV. Entombment (St.Matthew 27, 60).

Crucifixion as a death penalty originated in the Orient (Persia) and was

Greek patriarch outside Church of the Holy Sepulchre

mainly practised by the Carthaginians, the Greeks and the Romans. It was regarded as a degrading and contemptuous means of execution. Roman soldiers led Jesus to his Crucifixion (St.Mark 15, 16/20). According to St.John 19, 17, He himself carried His Cross to the place of execution, but it is more likely that He—following Roman custom—only carried the cross beam, because the whole Cross would have been too heavy. According to the Synoptists, Simon of Cyrene was compelled to carry Jesus's Cross or its cross beam (St.Matthew 27, 32). Jesus was handed an anaesthetic drink before the Crucifixion (St.Mark 15, 23), and after this He was stripped of His raiment (St.Matthew 27, 35) and nailed to the Cross (St.John 20, 25). Jesus was the first of the three crucified men to die, so that it was no longer necessary to break His legs in order to bring about His death (St.John 19, 31–33), but one of the soldiers pierced His side with a spear to determine whether He was really dead (St.John 19, 34).

Christ's Cross may have been either the Latin cross with arms of unequal length (Latin: 'crux imissa oblonga'), the Greek cross with arms of equal length ('crux imissa quadrata'). It cannot, however, have been the T-shaped Egyptian cross ('crux comissa') because the superscription on the Cross was attached over Christ's head.

It is widely assumed that the Crucified Christ sat on a stake (Latin: 'sedile'), which was intended to prolong His agony. The fact that one of the bystanders put a sponge full of vinegar on a reed and intended to give it to Jesus to drink (St.Matthew 27, 48) suggests that His feet were about a yard above the ground. At His Crucifixion, the reason why He had been condemned was, in accordance with Roman custom, written on a panel which was borne before the condemned Christ on His way to execution and was attached to the Cross above His head. 'And set up over his head his accusation written, This is Jesus the King of the Jews' (St.Matthew 27, 37).

1st Station: The Via Dolorosa

Church of the Holy Sepulchre, dome and tower

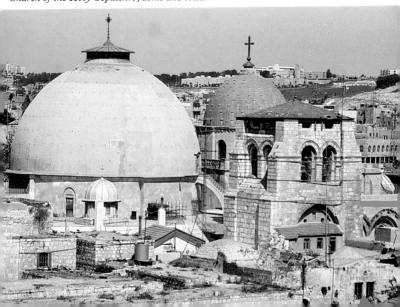

begins in the school yard of the Omariye Upper School for Boys, where there is a good view of the Temple esplanade. This building was once a Turkish military barracks on the site of the Herodian Antonia fortress. According to St.John 19, 13, Gabbatha (Hebrew: 'rising ground, elevation'), in Greek 'Lithostrotos' = 'stone pavement', was the place of Pilate's judgement seat where Christ was sentenced to death on the Cross. It was either in the Antonia fortress or in Herod's palace; tradition locates it in the Antonia fortress.

Antonia fortress: The Antonia castle occupied a strategically strong site to the N. of the Temple. It is first mentioned after the return from Babylonian Captivity (Nehemiah 2, 8: 'citadel of the temple' and Nehemiah 7, 2: 'citadel'; cf. also 2 Maccabees 4, 12/28; 5, 5). Christian tradition regards it as the place where Jesus was condemned to death on the Cross. The original building was destroyed in 167 BC by the Seleucids who built the Baris (= 'castle') in its stead. King Herod the Great enlarged the Baris into a splendid fortified palace with gorgeous rooms, colonnaded halls, bath-houses and barracks. He called this palace Antonia in honour of his benefactor Marcus Antonius, the Roman triumvir. This rectangular building (330 × 490 ft.) was on a rocky plateau 80 ft. in height and falling away steeply on all sides and dominating the Temple. The largest of the four towers in this fortified palace was 115 ft. high; steps led down to Temple Square at two points. It was suggested that Herod designed this building as a 'tyrant's stronghold to oppress the people'. The palace not only dominated the Temple precinct but made it impregnable: anyone wishing to capture the Temple precinct first had to capture the Antonia fortress, which was itself virtually impregnable. During the period of the Roman procurators after the death of Herod, there was always a Roman cohort in the Antonia fortress. One of its functions was to watch over Temple Square (The Acts 21, 31–40). It is uncertain whether the Antonia fortress was also the seat of the Roman governor (praetorium): 'They then led Jesus from the house of Caiaphas to the Praetorium' (St.John 18, 28). Christian tradition affirms this and regards one part of the fortress as the place where Pontius Pilate, the Roman procurator, sentenced Christ to death on the Cross. During the First Jewish War, the Jewish rebels seized the fortress (AD 66) and put up a heroic resistance, but were starved out and forced to surrender. Titus, the Roman general who later became Emperor, ordered the fortress to be razed (AD 70).

2nd Station: A point opposite the Omariye school, marked by a board, is the Second Station, where Jesus took up the Cross.

Chapel of the Flagellation: This Franciscan chapel is to the right of Station II. It was originally built by the Crusaders, fell into disrepair during Ottoman rule, and was rebuilt in 12C style in 1929. Scourging, that is to say whipping with a cat-o'-nine-tails or a knotted whip or with rods, was introduced into Judaism under Roman-Hellenistic influence: it is first mentioned in 2 Maccabees 7, 1 as having occurred in the period of the Seleucid ruler Antiochus IV Epiphanes (160's BC). In the area occupied by the Jews, scourging probably replaced flogging with a stick, the punishment known from the Old Testament. St.Paul reports the following: 'Five times I had the thirty-nine lashes from the Jews; three times I have been beaten with sticks' (2 Corinthians 11, 24–25; another translation: 'Of the Jews five times received I forty stripes save one. Thrice was I beaten with rods'.)

Condemnation Chapel: The Condemnation Chapel, which is also Franciscan, was built by Wendelin

Tomb of Zachariah ▷

Hinterkeuser in 1903. It stands on the foundations of a chapel in Byzantine style.

Ecce Homo arch: After Christ had been scourged and crowned with the Crown of Thorns, Pilate ordered Him to be brought forth to the Jews with the words 'Ecce homo' = 'Behold the man!' (St.John 19, 5). The arch is part of a gate from Hadrian's time (2C AD). Tradition has it that it spans the place where Pilate ordered Christ to be brought forth to the Jews.

Ecce Homo basilica: The N. arch of the Ecce Homo arch is part of the Ecce Homo basilica (2nd half of 19C) which belongs to the French Sisters of Zion and adjoins the Notre-Dame de Sion monastery.

3rd Station: The chapel by the 3rd Station was built by the Polish community in 1947. The arch above the door lintel shows Jesus falling under the weight of the Cross.

4th Station: The 'Chapel of the Swooning Virgin' (mid 20C) and the Armenian Catholic 'Church of the Virgin Mary's Sorrows' (1881) stand by the 4th Station, which commemorates Jesus encountering His mother, an event not recorded in the New Testament.

5th Station: A Franciscan chapel dating from 1881 commemorates the site where Simon of Cyrene helped Jesus carry the Cross. In classical times the town of Cyrene was rich and powerful and lay in the fertile district of Cyrenaica on the N. coast of Africa (today it is in Libya). It came under Roman rule in 96 BC.

6th Station: Tradition has it that the chapel cared for by the Little Sisters of Jesus stands on the site where a woman wiped Jesus's face with her napkin (Latin: 'sudarium'). The monastery associated with the chapel is said to have been built where her house stood. Neither Veronica's sudarium nor Veronica herself is

mentioned in the Bible. However, in the Roman Catholic church the sudarium is revered as a valuable relic. Legend has it that the pious Veronica handed it to Jesus while on his way to His execution so that He might wipe His face with it, thus leaving the imprint of His features on the cloth. The cloth was folded three times, and three identical imprints are thus supposed to have been created. It is said that one of these remained in Jerusalem, while the other two went to Rome (St.Peter's basilica) and Jaén in Spain. However, some ten other towns claim to possess such imprints. Vera Icon ('true image', i.e. an image not painted by human hand) is the name given to these authentic images of the face of the suffering Christ. Hence it is often thought that the name Veronica is a corruption of Vera Icon, although according to another tradition the name Veronica derives from Berenike who, in the Jewish-Christian legend of the Clementines, was the Canaanite woman's daughter healed by Jesus. In the Acts of Pilate, and also in the works of Rufinus, Cassiodorus and Malalas, Veronica is the name of the woman who suffered from haemorrhages, was cured by Jesus and, according to Eusebius, dedicated a metal statue in Paneas to Jesus. The Veronica legend only dates back to *c*. AD 500, and is a Western variant of the Oriental legend of Abgar from Edessa: Abgar, king of Edessa, suffered from an incurable disease and wrote to Jesus asking to be healed; Jesus sent a letter containing an imprint of His face on a linen cloth and thus restored Abgar's health. This so-called Edessa image was taken to Constantinople in 944 and is alleged to have arrived in Rome in 1204 after the Crusaders captured Constantinople. In Rome it was first kept in S.Silvestro in Capite and then in the sacristy of St.Peter's from 1870 onwards. The problem of the Veronica image is that according to the legend it ought to show the face of the suffering Christ bearing the Cross, whereas it actually gives a shadowy, pale imprint of Christ after His death on the Cross. The name 'Our Lord's napkin' or 'veronica' is documented in Rome only from the late 13C onwards. Miraculous napkins are also mentioned in Acts 19, 12, where those of the Apostle Paul were taken from him in Ephesus and used to cure the sick.

7th Station: A Franciscan chapel (1875) commemorates the second occasion when Jesus fell under the weight of the Cross.

8th Station: A stone with a cross and the inscription IC XC NIKA ('Jesus Christ is victorious') marks the point outside Jerusalem's walls where Jesus said to the lamenting women: 'Weep not for me, but weep for yourselves, and for your children. For, behold, the days are coming, in the which they shall say, Blessed are the barren, and the wombs that never bare, and the paps which never gave suck. Then shall they begin to say to the mountains: Fall on us; and to the hills, cover us.' (St.Luke 23, 28–30).

9th Station: A pillar marks the point where Jesus fell for the third time under the weight of the Cross.
The remaining Stations of the Cross are in the Church of the Holy Sepulchre.

Church of the Holy Sepulchre

The Church of the Holy Sepulchre stands above the place where Christ was crucified, died, was entombed and rose again, and hence is one of the most sacred Christian sites. The last five Stations of the Via Dolorosa are inside this church.
Status quo: Every Christian community tried to gain as much terrain as possible for itself inside the Church of the Holy Sepulchre. In 1852, the

Omar mosque (El Omariye), minaret ▷

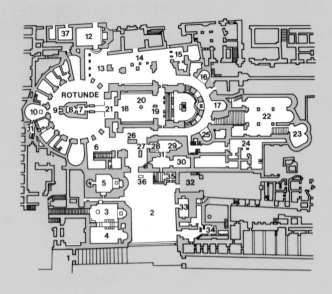

Jerusalem, Church of the Holy Sepulchre 1
Entrance **2** 12C atrium **3** Chapel of St.John and
baptistery **4** Jacob chapel **5** Chapel of the Forty
Martyrs and belfry **6** Place of the Three Women **7**
Angel chapel **8** Burial chapel with Holy Sepulchre
9 Copts' chapel **10** Jacobites' chapel **11** Joseph
of Arimathaea's tomb **12** Franciscan chapel **13**
Mary Magdalene altar **14** Virgin Mary arch **15**
Chapel of Christ's prison **16** Longinus chapel **17**
Chapel of the parting of the raiment **18-20** Catholicon **19** Greek choir **20** Navel of the world
(marble dish) **21** Latin choir **22** Helena crypt **23**
Crypt of the Finding of the Cross **24** Medieval
cloister **25** Mocking chapel **26** Anointment stone
27 Adam chapel **28** Former tombs of Godfrey of
Bouillon and Baldwin I **29** Crucifixion altar, Sta-
bat Mater altar and half-statue of the Virgin Mary
30 Chapel of the Nailing to the Cross **31** Golgotha **32** Michaelis chapel **33** Armenian chapel of
St.John **34** Abraham chapel **35** Chapel of the
Black Virgin/Chapel of Egyptian Virgin (underneath) **36** Epitaph of Philippe d'Aubigny **37** Franciscan monastery

also the rotunda with the chapel of the
Holy Sepulchre and the anointment
stone, belong jointly to the Greek
Orthodox (patriarchates of Constantinople, Alexandria, Antioch and Jerusalem), to the Armenians and to the
Latins (Roman Catholics); only individual chapels belong to the Copts,
Syrians and Ethiopians.

Architectural history: The area
around the Golgotha rock was a place
of reverence for Christians as early as
the 1C AD. When the Roman Emperor
Hadrian, after the Bar Kochba revolt
in 135, expelled all Jews from the city
and built the town of Aelia Capitolina
on the site of the devastated Jerusalem, he also attempted to destroy the
Christian sites in order to blot out the
memory of them. The ground of the
sites of the Crucifixion and Resurrection was levelled and a temple to
Venus the goddess of love was
erected.

Ottoman government therefore
passed the 'Law of the Status Quo'
which determined their interests and
is still in force today. The whole
Church of the Holy Sepulchre and

Via Dolorosa, Station XI

Helena, mother of Emperor Constantine the Great, visited the Holy Land in 326. Makarios, Bishop of Jerusalem, informed her that the sites of Jesus's death and resurrection were underneath Hadrian's temple of Venus. At Constantine's command, the temple was pulled down and a basilica was built above the holy sites. It was consecrated in 335 as 'Anastasis', meaning church of the Resurrection. The basilica was destroyed by the Persians in 614 and later rebuilt. The Caliph al-Hakim systematically destroyed it again in 1009, when even the sepulchre was almost completely torn down. The new structure built by the Crusaders was dedicated in 1149.

Entrance: A paved 12C forecourt, with a colonnaded portico dividing it from the street, stands outside the late Romanesque main portal, which is itself 12C from the time of the Cru-

saders (originals of the lintels decorated with reliefs are in the Rockefeller Museum) of the Church of the Holy Sepulchre. The three Greek chapels of St.James, St.John and St.Mary Magdalene and also that of the forty martyrs are on the W. side. The belfry, which dates from the time of the Crusaders and was originally three storeys higher, stands above the chapel of the forty martyrs. The E. side of the forecourt is formed by the Greek monastery of Abraham, the Armenian chapel of St.John, and the Coptic chapel of St.Michael. To the right of the portal, stairs lead to the chapel of the Franks, which was walled up in the 12C.

Anointment stone: The first holy site after the entrance is the anointment stone, a reddish limestone slab (1810) which is regarded as the place where the body of Jesus was anointed before His Entombment.

Chapel of Adam: Underneath the Golgotha chapel is the Greek Orthodox chapel of Adam, in which a skull said to be that of Adam, the first man, was found. The fact that the chapel containing Adam's skull is directly underneath Golgotha, the site of the Crucifixion, accords with the medieval typologies. These typologies are interpretations of New Testament persons and events, arrived at through extrapolation from the Old Testament. Thus, Paul describes Christ as 'the last Adam': 'The first man Adam was made a living soul: the last Adam was made a quickening spirit' (1 Corinthians 15, 45). Adam in Genesis, who transgressed God's commandment, is the countertype pointing to the 'coming' Adam, that is to say Christ, who obediently fulfils God's will: 'Adam is the figure of him that was to come' (Romans 5, 14). In St.Luke—in contrast to St.Matthew—Jesus's family tree begins with Adam. In the medieval typologies, Adam was assigned to Christ, Eve to the Virgin Mary, and the Fall of Man to the Redemption on the Cross. This is why, in depictions of the triumphal Cross, the risen Adam, redeemed by Christ's blood flowing down, is often to be found at the foot of the Cross. The same applies in the Adam chapel: under a pane of glass in the apse, a crack in the rock can be seen and through this Christ's blood is said to have run down from the Cross to fall on Adam's skull and thus purge him of the original sin.

Golgotha: The Golgotha rock above the Adam chapel contains Stations X to XIII of the Via Dolorosa: Jesus is stripped of His raiment; Jesus is nailed to the Cross; Jesus dies on the Cross; Jesus's body is laid in His mother's lap. The name Golgotha (probably from the Aramaic gulgulta = 'skull') is interpreted by the Evangelists as meaning 'place of a skull' (St.Matthew 27, 33; St.Mark 15, 22; St.Luke 23, 33; St.John 19, 17). This is the place where Jesus died on the Cross. The name 'Mount Calvary' derives from the Latin calvaria = 'brain case, skull'). The explanation which the Greek writer Origenes (3C AD) and a Jewish tradition give for the name is that Adam's skull was found here and Adam was buried here (cf.

Church of the Holy Sepulchre, anointing stone

Adam chapel, above). But Jerome, the Latin Father of the Church (4/5C), derives the name from the skulls of the persons buried there. The most probable interpretation is that Golgotha was a skull-shaped hill outside the city walls of Jerusalem and was used as a place of execution and burial.

The mosaics and paintings at the individual altars of Golgotha (including a 16C altar table, donated by Fernando de'Medici, the Tuscan Grand Duke) depict events recorded in the Gospels and Apocrypha. The Crucifixion, being the central event in the life of Christ, developed into the main theme of Christian iconography. On the altars, the Crucifixion occupies a central position and is proportionately larger than the scenes which surround it on either side - the Passion (on the left) and the scenes after the Crucifixion, from the Deposition to the appearances of the Risen Christ (on the right). Death by crucifixion was regarded as the most disgraceful form of execution, and for this reason reference to it was avoided in early Chris-

tian painting; neither was Christ depicted as suffering, but as living after death and triumphing on the Cross. This image of God who, through the Cross, overcame death and triumphed prevailed up until the Romanesque period.

In Gothic art, the suffering or dead Christ was emphasized. He wore the Crown of Thorns instead of the ruler's crown, and the four nails were replaced by three nails with the feet penetrated by a single nail. The head, previously raised in majesty, appears inclined to one side and distorted with pain. This suffering was still more drastically depicted in the 14C, under the influence of mysticism. At the same time, narrative elements filled the picture. The 'Crucifixion' became 'Mount Calvary', and the place of execution was crowded with curious onlookers.

Rotunda: Leaving Golgotha, the visitor passes the anointment stone and enters the rotunda. Its dome, some 165 ft. high, spans Christ's sepulchre. The masonry of the rotunda is Constantine up to a height

Church of the Holy Sepulchre, Greek Orthodox divine service (left), tomb of Joseph of Arimathaea (right)

of about 35 ft. (4C); the section above is 11C.

Christ's sepulchre: St.Matthew 27, 59–60 relates that, after the Crucifixion, Jesus was laid in a rock tomb, which had yet to be used and which belonged to Joseph, a rich man of Arimathaea. A stone was rolled in front of the tomb after Jesus had been interred. The tomb was in a garden near the place of Crucifixion (St.John 19, 41). The 'very great' stone closing the tomb entrance must have been round, because it was possible to roll it (St.Mark 16, 3[nd4]). It was necessary to lean forwards in order to look into the burial chamber (St.Luke 24, 12; St.John 20, 5/11), which means that the opening to the tomb must have been low. When the women discovered the empty tomb after the Resurrection, two angels were sitting in the burial chamber 'the one at the head, and the other at the feet, where the body of Jesus had lain' (St.John 24, 12; cf. St.Mark 16, 5–6), thus implying it was a bench-type tomb. According to St.John 19, 17/20, Jesus was crucified outside the city wall. The present Church of the Holy Sepulchre is inside the city wall, as in AD 41, Herod Agrippa ordered a wall to be built around the N. of Jerusalem, taking in Golgotha and Joseph of Arimathaea's tomb.

The sepulchre of Christ shown in the Church of the Holy Sepulchre is not regarded as authentic by Anglicans, who consider that Christ's real burial site is the so-called garden tomb, which is located not far from the Damascus gate, outside the present city wall. This structure hewn from the rock has two chambers and was built at about the beginning of the Christian era.

Above Christ's sepulchre rises a kiosk (1810) in Turkish rococo style, 27.2 ft. long, 19.4 ft. wide and 19.4 ft. high. The lamps hanging in front of the portal belong to the Latins (top row), Greeks (middle rows) and Armenians (lower row). The portico of the burial chamber is called the angel chapel because tradition has it that the angels who announced to the women that Christ had risen were sitting here. The body of Christ lay in the burial chamber proper, on the bench which is now faced in marble.

Garden tomb

Chapel of the Copts: A part of the rock tomb is to be seen at the altar of the chapel on the rear side of the Holy Sepulchre.

Chapel of the Jacobites: The 4C Constantine wall can be seen in the chapel of the Jacobites (members of the Syrian Orthodox church) between two pillars opposite the chapel of the Copts.

Tomb of Joseph of Arimathaea: A small passage leads to the tomb of Joseph of Arimathaea. This is a Jewish burial chamber from the 1C AD (the only items surviving in their entirety are two sliding posts) next to the chapel of the Jacobites. Joseph, a rich man from Arimathaea (St.Matthew 27, 57) was a highly regarded member of the Jewish High Council (St.Mark 15, 43) and is described in the New Testament as a good and just man (St.Luke 23, 50). He was a disciple of Christ, but only secretly, for fear of the Jews (St.John 19, 38). After the Crucifixion, he requested Christ's body from Pilate and ordered it to be buried in the rock tomb which he had enlarged for himself and which lay outside Jerusalem (St.Matthew 27, 57–60; St.Mark 15, 42–47; St.Luke 23, 50–56; St.John 19, 38–42).

Altar of Mary Magdalene: The painting by the Cuban artist del Rio (1855) above the Mary Magdalene altar, which belongs to the Roman Catholics, depicts the appearance of the Risen Christ, whom Mary Magdalene first thought was a gardener. Magdalene was one of Jesus's most loyal disciples. She came from the town of Magdala on the W. shore of the Sea of Galilee. According to St.Luke 8, 2–3 and St.Mark 16, 9, she assisted Jesus with her possessions after He had cast seven devils out of her. The Gospels report that she was present at the Crucifixion (St.Matthew 27, 55–56, St.Mark 15, 40) and the Entombment (St.Matthew 27, 61) and that, along with two other women, she discovered the empty tomb on Easter morning (St.Mark 16, 1 ff.). In addition, she is regarded as the first witness of the Risen Christ ('Noli me tangere', St.John 20, 11 ff.).

Chapel of the Appearance: The Franciscan Chapel of the Appearance (Christ appearing to His mother)

Church of the Holy Sepulchre, catholicon with 'navel of the world'

Church of the Holy Sepulchre, Christ's prison

stands to the left of the Mary Magdalene altar and was originally the sacristy of the Constantine basilica. The chapel adjoins the Franciscan monastery which stands beside the Church of the Holy Sepulchre.

Arches of the Virgin Mary: There are seven arches of the Virgin Mary. Some are Byzantine, and others were assembled or rebuilt from different parts in the 11C.

Catholicon: The visitor passes through the so-called Emperor's arch and enters the Catholicon, which is the main Greek Orthodox church and also the nave of the Crusaders' church. The marble dish directly below the dome is known as the 'navel of the world'.

Prison of Christ: The Greek Orthodox 'Prison of Christ' chapel from the Byzantine period stands at the E. end of the N. aisle.

E. ambulatory: There are three chapels in the E. ambulatory: the chapel of Longinus (the soldier who pierced Jesus's side with his spear; St.John 19, 34), the chapel of the Division of the Raiment (St.John 19, 23 ff.), and the chapel of the Mocking.

Chapel of Helena: Between the chapel of the Division of the Raiment and the chapel of the Mocking of Christ, steps lead down to the Armenian chapel of Helena, the former crypt of the Constantine martyry (a nave, two aisles, and 12C dome). St.Helena, the mother of Emperor Constantine the Great, founded almost all the church buildings in and around Jerusalem.

Crypt of the Invention of the Cross: 13 steps lead from the S. aisle of the Helena chapel into a former cistern where St.Helena is said to have found Christ's Cross. In 348, Cyrillus of Jerusalem attributed the Invention of the Holy Cross to Constantine the

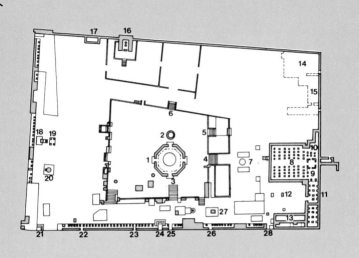

Jerusalem, Temple Mount 1 Dome of the Rock 2 Chain cupola (Qubbet es-.Silsileh) 3-6 Arcades 7 El-Kas (fountain) 8 El-Aqsa mosque 9 Minbar Nur ed-Din 10 Omar mosque 11 Women's mosque 12 Qubbat Yusef Agha 13 Islamic museum 14 Solomon's stables (Christ's cradle) 15 Mihrab Daud/Omar 16 Golden gate (walled up) 17 Solomon's throne 18 Sabil es-Sultan Suleiman 19 Qubbat Suleiman Pasha 20 Qubbat Suleiman 21 Bab el-Ghawanima 22 Bab en-Nadhir 23 Bab el-Hadid 24 Bab el-Qattanin 25 Bab el-Mathara 26 Bab es-Salam 27 Qubbat Musa 28 Moors' gate

Great, but St.Ambrose assigned this honourable act to St.Helena.

Temple Mount
Haram esh-Sharif

Temple Mount, a sacred precinct of the Islamic religion, occupies about one sixth of the old city's area. The Dome of the Rock, which is among the best-preserved monuments of early Islamic architecture, stands here. This landmark of the city has been the source of much dispute. The Dome itself is Islamic, but the Temples of Solomon and Herod also stood here. The Prophet Mohammed rode to Heaven from the rock which gives the Dome its name.

Abraham's sacrifice: According to Jewish, Christian and Islamic tradition, the history of Temple Mount begins with an event from the earliest Biblical times. In order to test the patriarch Abraham, God called on him to sacrifice his only son Isaac as a burnt offering. 'Take now thy son, thine only son Isaac, whom thou lovest, and get thee into the land of Moriah; and offer him there for a burnt offering upon one of the mountains which I will tell thee of' (Genesis 22, 2). Abraham set out with Isaac, 'and they came to the place which God had told him of; and Abraham built an altar there, and laid the wood in order, and bound Isaac his son, and laid him on the altar upon the wood. And Abraham stretched forth his hand, and took the knife to slay his son' (22, 9–10). At this moment, an angel called on Abraham to stop, and Abraham saw a ram which had caught itself in a thicket, and took the ram and offered it up as a burnt offering instead of his son. 2 Chronicles 3, 1 identifies this mountain in the land of Moriah with the Temple Mount in Jerusalem, where Solomon built his temple 'where the Lord appeared unto David his father, in the place that David had prepared on the threshing floor of Araunah the Jebusite'. Later tradition accepted this description of the place.

Shrine of the Ark of the Covenant: It was only at a relatively late date that the Israelites built a temple. While they were wandering nomads, they always took a travelling shrine with them. This was the Tabernacle (tent of the Covenant or the 'tent of meeting'), a portable shrine which Moses ordered to be made during the Israelites' march through the wilderness and which served as the centre of Israelite divine service. The sacrificial

cult was practised in it until the Temple was built in Jerusalem. The Tabernacle was set up in various places in Canaan, the last being in Jerusalem under David. According to the priestly writings, the Tabernacle is the central dwelling shrine, of God's constant presence (Holy of Holies). The name 'tent of meeting' derives from the fact that God indicated to Moses that the tent was the place 'where I will meet you, to speak there unto thee' (Exodus 29, 42). On Sinai, God called on Moses to build him a 'sanctuary', and then God would dwell amidst the Israelites: God showed Moses a 'pattern' of how to build and furnish this dwelling place (Exodus 25, 8 ff.). A tax was levied on the Israelites so that the Tabernacle could be built (Exodus 25, 2–7, cf. Exodus 38, 24 ff.). The Israelites donated so much that Moses had to call a halt (Exodus 36, 5–6). The Tabernacle was divided into the Holy of Holies containing the Ark of the Covenant, and the Holy Place with the table for the shewbread, the seven-branched candlestick, and the altar of incense. These two rooms

Temple square, N. section

were separated by a curtain (for detailed descriptions see Exodus 25, 10–27, 21; 36, 8–38, 31). The furnishings corresponded to those in the Temple in Jerusalem. The tribes invaded Palestine in the 13C BC and gradually settled there. It was only at this time that the question of a permanent site for the Ark of the Covenant arose, so that the idea of a temple as a religious and political centre also developed. Jewish temple buildings outside Jerusalem: Before there was a definite governed territory, the first stationary temple here—in contrast to the Ark of the Covenant which, although mobile, had also had several permanent sites—was the 'house of the Lord' in Shiloh, on the mountain range where the Ark of the Covenant was set up (Joshuah 18, 1; 1 Samuel 1, 3). After the Philistines had carried off the Ark of the Covenant as their booty at the battle of Eben-ezer (1 Samuel 4, 1–11), they also destroyed the shrine of Shiloh (Psalm 78, 60–62; Jeremiah 7, 12/14; 26, 6). Excavation works searching for the temple of Shiloh have not yet met with success. King Jereboam I elevated Bet-El and

Dan to the status of public shrines with a temple and a cult of bulls. His aim in this was to prevent the inhabitants of Israel, after the division of the kingdom, from continuing to make the pilgrimage to the temple in Jerusalem. The temple of Bet-El, in comparison with which Dan was always only of secondary importance, was destroyed by King Josiah of Judah (2 Kings 23, 15). Another Jewish temple has been excavated in Arad in the NE of the Negev. The Samaritans built their own temple on Mount Garizim after they had been barred from building the Second Temple in Jerusalem following the return of the Jews from Babylonian Exile.

Refusal to build a temple in David's reign: The question of a permanent site for the Ark of the Covenant did not become acute until the reign of King David, when Jerusalem became the capital and a royal palace was built there. David, who had ordered the Ark of the Covenant to be transferred to Jerusalem, wanted to build a temple here, but he was promised that Solomon, David's son and successor, would build this temple. The reason

Temple square, W. section

Dome of the Rock, S. entrance

given for this refusal to build a temple in David's reign was that it would mean a break with tradition. In the later books of the Chronicles, another reason is given: 'Thou hast shed blood abundantly, and hast made great wars: thou shalt not build an house unto my name, because thou hast shed much blood upon the earth in my sight' (1 Chronicles 22, 8). On both occasions, the refusal to build the temple is related to the promise that David's son Solomon will construct this temple. However, David began to obtain building materials.

The temple of Solomon: Solomon began his reign in 964 BC, and work on building the temple began 'in the second day of the second month, in the fourth year of his reign' (2 Chronicles 3, 2) and continued for seven years (1 Kings 6, 37–38).

Chronological table:
*c.*1000 BC King David
*c.*950 BC Temple of Solomon completed
587 BC Temple of Solomon destroyed by the Chaldeans

	under Nebuchadnezzar
538 BC	Cyrus, the Persian king, issues an edict that the Temple in Jerusalem be rebuilt
515 BC	Second Temple consecrated (Temple of Zerubabbel)
from 19 BC	Temple converted and rebuilt throughout by Herod the Great
AD 64	Building work completed
AD 70	Destroyed by the Roman general Titus
AD 135	Finally destroyed by the Roman Emperor Hadrian

The Temple of Solomon was some 100 ft. long, 35 ft. wide and 50 ft. high, and the entire temple complex with its annexes was about 170 ft. in length and 90 ft. in width. A three-storeyed ambulatory, with chambers and rooms housing Temple utensils, Temple treasures and provisions, ran along three sides of the Temple. The Temple proper projected above this ambulatory and had small barred windows. The flat roof was lined with cedar on the inside.

The Temple complex proper con-

Dome of the Rock (left), medrese and silver dome of El-Aqsa mosque (right)

sisted of the portico, the Holy Place and the Holy of Holies. The Holy Place contained the incense altar and the Golden Altar, and on each of the two sides there were five seven-armed golden candlesticks and five shewbread tables. The Holy of Holies contained the Ark of the Covenant between two gilded olive-wood cherubs facing the Holy Place. The cherubs' wings met in the middle above the Ark of the Covenant.

In front of this splendidly decorated temple complex (described in 1 Kings 6 and 2 Chronicles 3–4) there were two forecourts. Everyone could enter the outer forecourt, while the inner forecourt, which was probably at a slightly higher level, was intended for the priests. The inner forecourt contained the brazen altar for burnt offerings, the brazen bath (for the priests' purificatory ablutions), ten portable water pots, and two brass columns to the left and right of the entrance.

In King Solomon's reign, this Temple was the central shrine of all Israel and Judah. When this overall kingdom was divided after Solomon's death, separate shrines were set up in Bet-El and Dan in the northern kingdom of Israel (1 Kings 12, 26 ff.). After the Temple of Solomon had been plundered and desecrated several times, it was destroyed under Nebuchadnezzar in 587 BC.

The Temple of Herod the Great: According to Josephus Flavius ('Jewish Antiquities' XV, 11), King Herod the Great made a speech to the Jews in which he prepared them for the immense project of tearing down the Temple of Zerubbabel and building a new temple in its stead.

The Jews were sceptically disposed towards this costly project, mainly because they believed that the king would no longer be able to finance the building of such an enormous temple as soon as the old Temple had been torn down. But Herod assured the Jews that he would not order the old Temple to be torn down before everything necessary to complete the new Temple had been procured: 'He was as good as his word in this. He obtained 1000 waggons to bring up the stones, chose 10,000 experienced

Temple square, prayer niche

foremen, bought priestly vestments for 1000 priests, had them trained them partly in stone carving and partly in carpentry, and prepared everything most carefully. Only then did he start work on the Temple' (Josephus Flavius). It can be seen from this report that Herod, in building the new Temple, respected the customs and usages of the Jews (according to Christian reports, he did not do this), because he did not use laymen to build this Temple, which no layman was allowed to enter, but employed priests instead. By taking these steps, Herod seems not only to have been attempting to win over the Jewish people for himself and his policies. It appears that another object was to present himself as a religious and law-abiding Jew.

In order to put his project into effect, Herod caused the area of Temple Mount to be almost doubled by means of demolition, banking up, and building enormous retaining walls. The outline of the present Temple esplanade accords with the ground plan of the Herodian Temple complex. The entire area was surrounded with walls like a fortress, with the Antonia fort in the N. The Temple precinct proper was at an elevated level, with panels in Greek and Latin warning every Jew that he should not enter it (one panel is now in the Rockefeller Museum, see under Museums).

Reconstructions of the Herodian Temple, which was consecrated in 18 BC and destroyed in AD 70 (see a reconstruction in the garden of the Holyland Hotel), are mostly based on descriptions by the historian Josephus Flavius. But in his 'Jewish War', Josephus gives a description differing from that in his 'Jewish Antiquities'. From the 'Jewish Antiquities': 'The enclosing wall had four gates on its western side. One of these led to the royal castle through a valley which lay in between, two others led to the outer city, and the fourth gate led to the city proper. A large number of steps enabled the walker to descend into the valley and climb out of it again. For the city lay directly opposite the Temple and, being surrounded by a deep gorge in the south, gave the impression of a theatre. In the middle of the fourth side of the enclosing wall, which faced the south, there were more gates and and a triple royal colonnaded hall which extended longitudinally from the eastern to the western side of the valley where it could no longer be continued. The whole stucture was one of the strangest upon which the sun has ever shone. The valley was so deep that when one looked down into it one began to feel dizzy. An immeasurably high hall was built above the valley so that anyone on the roof of this hall who wished to measure both elevations by eye was seized by dizziness before his gaze had reached the bottom of the immense depths. Four rows of columns had been set up opposite one another, reaching from one end of the hall to the other; the fourth of these rows of columns was let into a stone wall. Each column was so thick that three people holding each other by the hands could just span it with their arms. The length was 27 feet, and each column rested on a double bulge. There were 162 columns altogether. Their capitals were in the Corinthian style, and were magnificent and wonderful works . . . The roofs were decorated with images which were carved deep into the wood and displayed various forms; the middle roof was higher than the other two. At the front of the capitals there was a stone wall which was decorated with inserted columns and was very exactly faced, so that anyone who has not seen it cannot imagine its beauty, and anyone who did see it was filled with amazed delight.'

Post-Herodian temple buildings: The Herodian Temple was destroyed by fire in AD 70, at the end of the First Jewish War. The Romans penetrated

Citadel, tower of David ▷

through the Antonia fort into the Temple precinct after the Jews had themselves set the halls on fire. All that survived of the Temple was today's Wailing Wall. After the Jewish revolt had been put down in 132–135, Emperor Hadrian ordered a Temple of Jupiter to be built on Temple Mount. This Temple was destroyed under Emperor Constantine the Great in the third decade of the 3C. Constantine permitted the Jews to pray in the city every year on 10 August, the day on which the Temple was devastated. Emperor Julian the Apostate, who was opposed to the Christians, organized the rebuilding of the Jewish Temple in 361; Jews were permitted to continue travelling to Jerusalem, but work on the Temple was stopped again after an earthquake and the early death of the Emperor in 363.

Muslim shrine: After the conquest of Jerusalem in 638, Caliph Omar prayed at the rock of Temple Mount and remembered Abraham's sacrifice. The Dome of the Rock was built in the 7C above the Rock of Abraham, from which the Prophet Mohammed is said to have ridden into heaven on his miraculous horse el-Buraq. The El-Aqsa mosque, oriented towards Mecca, was built on the S. side of the esplanade. The Dome of the Rock was granted the same rights as the Kaaba in Mecca, and Jerusalem became a destination for Muslim pilgrims. After the Crusaders captured Temple Mount, the El-Aqsa mosque became the headquarters of the religious Order of the Knights Templar (Fratres militiae Templi) who were named after Temple Mount and gave themselves the task of protecting the Jerusalem pilgrims.

Temple Mount has remained in the possession of the Muslims from 1187, when Jerusalem was conquered by Sultan Saladin (1137–93), until the present day.

Dome of the Rock (Qubbet es-Sakhra): The Dome of the Rock, with its gilded dome on an octagonal base, is the real landmark of modern Jerusalem. It is at the same time the best-preserved and most significant early Islamic architectural work, and the third holiest Islamic site, coming after the Kaaba in Mecca which—so tradition has it—was consecrated by Abraham and his son Ismael, and the Prophet's tomb in Medina. According to Islamic tradition, the rock from which the building takes its name was the starting point for the Prophet Mohammed's journey into heaven on his miraculous horse el-Buraq.

Political and religious background to the building: If—as Islamic tradition relates—the function of the Dome of the Rock, built in 688–91 under the Ommiad Caliph Abd al-Malik, was to preserve the memory of the Prophet Mohammed's nocturnal journey into heaven, then it would not have been necessary to build the so-called Dome of the Heavenly Journey (which is also associated with Mohammed's nocturnal ride) immediately next to the Dome of the Rock. The motives for building the Dome of the Rock are far more complicated and, as is usually the case with such magnificent buildings, were political in nature. Rebellions, separatist endeavours, and disputes regarding the caliphate, dominated political affairs during the rule of Abd al-Malik, the ninth Caliph (= 'successor') after Mohammed and the fifth ruler from the Ommiad dynasty. The inhabitants of the holy sites of Mecca and Medina also rebelled against Abd al-Malik and appointed Abdallah Ibn es-Sobair as their religious and secular leader. Abdallah Ibn es-Sobair had made Mecca the seat of his government, and the annual stream of pilgrims to Mecca and Medina meant that increasingly large sections of the Muslim world were coming under the usurper's political and religious influence. Abd al-Malik therefore decided to build a third shrine in Jerusalem. Here the shrine lay within his own, secure sovereign territory. Two centuries later, in *c.* 875, the Arab historian Yakubi reported on this political maneouvre, which was doomed to failure: 'Abd el-Malik forbade the population of Syria to go on pilgrimages to Mecca, because Abdallah Ibn es-Sobair was able to secure the population for himself and subject them to his rule. Abd al-Malik knew this very well, and therefore issued this ban. But the people grumbled and said: 'How can you forbid us to go on the pilgrimage to Mecca when Allah himself ordered us to make the pilgrimage?' But the Caliph replied: 'Did not Ibn Shihab as-Suri tell you that Allah's messenger said: The people are to travel to three houses of prayer, the Haram house of prayer in Mecca, my house of prayer in Medina, and the house of prayer in the Holy City of Jerusalem? This last holy site has now been selected for you. And this rock, upon which Allah's messenger placed his foot when he ascended into heaven, shall be deemed by you to be Allah's house!' Then Abd al-Malik built a dome above the rock, hung brocade curtains inside the building, and appointed doorkeepers for the shrine. The people adopted the custom of organizing processions around the rock in the manner in which they were in the habit of walking around the Kaaba in Mecca. This custom was preserved during the epoch of the Ommiad dynasty.' Another reason for building the Dome of the Rock was given in c. 985 by Mukaddasi, the Arab historian: 'In the opinion of Abd al-Malik, Syria was a country which had long been ruled by the Christians. He saw the many splendid churches which the Christians still possessed, such as the Church of the Holy Sepulchre in Jerusalem and the churches in Lydda and Edessa. To prevent the Muslims from being blinded by the splendour of the Christian buildings, Abd al-Malik wanted them to have a fine building of their own, which was to be unique and a wonder of the world. Gaining his inspiration from the splendour and size of the Church of the Holy Sepulchre, he therefore decided to build the dome above the rock, which can still be admired there today.'

Architectural history: Caliph Abd al-Malik ordered Byzantine architects and Arab artists to build the Dome of the Rock in 688–91. The dedicatory inscription reads as follows: 'This Dome was built by Allah's servant Abdallah, the Imam al-Mamun, the lord of all the faithful, al-Malik in the year 72, and Allah took the Dome out of his hand and deigned to bless it.' The year 72 of the Hijra is the same year as AD 691, but al-Mamun did not hold the caliphate until 813–33; by substituting his own name for the name of Abd al-Malik, he wished to claim for himself the credit for building the Dome of the Rock; however, the falsifiers forgot to alter the year. The inscription was probably 'corrected' in this way in the course of repair work in 831. The dome collapsed for the first time in 1016, but was rebuilt in its former splendour shortly thereafter; damage resulting from an earthquake in 1033 was also quickly repaired. The Crusaders converted the Dome of the Rock into a church bearing the name 'Templum Domini' ('Temple of the Lord'), covered the rock with marble and built an altar on it. In 1187, the Dome once again fell into the hands of the Muslims led by Sultan Saladin. The building was last subjected to an overall restoration in 1958–64.

Architecture: The Dome of the Rock is a centrally planned structure with an octagonal base and a dome. The exterior of the base is faced in marble up to a height of 18 ft. The upper zone of the base, and the drum, are decorated with ornaments and Koranic verses on several tens of thousands of faience tiles. The dimensions are as follows:

Height:	177 ft.
Diameter:	180 ft.
Length of sides:	67 ft. 6 in. (outside)
	63 ft. (inside)

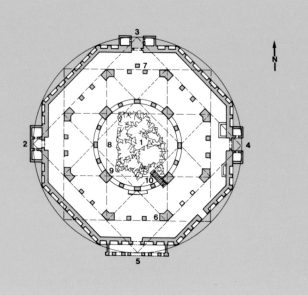

Jerusalem, Dome of the Rock 1 Holy Rock
(es-Sakhra) **2** W. gate (Bab el-Gharb) **3** Paradise
gate (Bab el-Jenneh) **4** Chain gate (Bab es-Silsileh) **5** S. gate (Bab el-Qibleh) **6** Mihrab **7** Slab
which is said to have covered Solomon's tomb
and into which Mohammed is said to have ham-
mered 12 golden nails **8** Fingerprints of the
Archangel Gabriel **9** Prophets' footprints **10** Stairs
to 'souls' fountain' (Bir el-Arouah)

Dome diameter: 78 ft. (outside)
                66 ft. 6 in. (inside)
Crescent on
dome: 12 ft. high
Rock: 58 ft. 10 in. long
                43 ft. 3 in. wide
                4–6 ft. 6 in. high

Four gates, arranged at the points of
the compass, lead into the Dome's
interior:
– W. gate (Bab el-Gharb),
– Paradise gate (Bab el-Jenneh) in the
  N.,
– Chain gate (Bab es-Silsileh) in the
  E.,

– S. gate (Bab el-Qibleh).

When the Byzantine architects were
planning the building, which is
radially symmetrical, they described
around the Holy Rock a circle inside
which they drew a square whose sides
face towards the four points of the
compass. Pillars supporting drum and
dome were placed at each corner of
this square. The architects then drew
a second square at 45 degrees to the
first, so that a regular eight-cornered
figure was formed. A second such
figure was then drawn around the
rock by halving the lengths of the
sides, and the pillars stand at the
points where the squares intersect and
along the lines drawn between these
points.

Interior: Except for three columns
which were replaced by replicas
during the last restoration, all the columns and capitals come from 2–6C
Byzantine and late Roman buildings.

Dome of the Rock

Some of them still have crosses, a clear indication that they came from churches. The dome is decorated with stuccoed arabesques.

Holy Rock: The Holy Rock is associated not only with Abraham and his son Isaac, but also with the altars used for burnt offerings in the two Temples built after the time of Solomon. The cavity at the N. end of the rock may have been used to collect the sacrificial blood. Items to be seen include footprints of prophets and fingerprints of the Angel Gabriel who held the rock steady when Mohammed rode into heaven. A reliquary houses a hair from the Prophet's beard.

The Muslims venerate Elijah, Abraham, David and Solomon in the square cave below the Rock. According to Islamic tradition, the souls of the dead meet for prayer twice weekly in the 'souls' well' (Bir el-Arouah) underneath.

Qait-Bey fountain: Many of the numerous cisterns in the area of the Temple Mount were formerly access routes which led right into the Temple and were reserved for priests and the people organizing cultic observances. Only later were they converted into water reservoirs. According to Jewish tradition, the Holy of Holies in the Temple occupied the site where the Qait-Bey fountain, built in the form of a monument, now stands. This fountain (1487) was donated by the Egyptian sultan Qait Bey.

Dome of the Chain (Qubbet es-Silsileh): A pavilion which is open on all sides and resembles a smaller version of the Dome of the Rock stands to the E. of the Dome of the Rock proper. The Jews refer to it as David's place of judgement, and the Muslims regard it as the place where, on the

Day of the Last Judgement, good men will be separated from evil men by a chain. The Dome of the Chain is of particular significance because it stands in the very middle of the Temple esplanade. It was probably built under the Caliph Abd al-Malik (685–705), who is said to have used the drum of the dome as a treasure chamber. The Crusaders converted the dome into a chapel and dedicated it to Jacobus, the first Bishop of Jerusalem. The ceramic facing was donated by Sultan Suleiman the Magnificent (1494–1566).

El-Aqsa mosque: El-Aqsa, which has seven aisles and faces towards Mecca, is the largest mosque in Jerusalem, being almost 295 ft. long and nearly 200 ft. wide. The contrast between its silver dome (58 ft. high) and the golden dome of the Dome of the Rock sets the tone for the overall appearance of Temple Mount. The name El-Aqsa means 'the farthest' and refers to the Koranic verse 17, 1 concerning the Prophet Mohammed's nocturnal journey (cf. above: Dome of the Rock): It was here that Mohammed, on his miraculous horse el-Buraq, reached the farthest point of his journey as measured from Mecca, in order then to ascend into heaven from the Holy Rock of the Dome of the Rock.

History: Relatively detailed reports, including some early ones, exist regarding the architectural history of the Dome of the Rock, but not for the El-Aqsa mosque. This is all the more surprising because the mosque is the central shrine of the Muslims on Temple Mount, whereas the Dome of the Rock is to some extent only an appendage. However, pilgrims in the 7–9C seem to have been attracted by the splendour of the Dome much more than by the mosque.

It was immediately after the conquest of Jerusalem in 638 that Caliph Omar I ordered the first structure, probably in wood, to be built here, probably above the ruins of a devastated Byzan-

tine church. Rebuilt several times over the following centuries, it was not until 1033, during the rule of the Fatimid Caliph az-Zahir, that the mosque was given what, in essentials, is its present form. After being captured by the Crusaders in 1099, the Temple precinct was handed over in 1119 to the Order of the Knights Templar, who derived their name from the Dome of the Rock, which they referred to as 'Templum Domini' ('Lord's Temple') because they considered it to be the place where Christ taught. The Dome of the Rock was therefore left unaltered. However, the Knights Templar converted the mosque into a house of their Order and had extensions built in the W. and E. on the site of the present Islamic museum and the women's mosque. After being captured by Sultan Saladin, the entire complex once again resumed its original Islamic function. The last overall restoration was in 1938–42.

Interior: The central aisle, 55 ft. in height, is adjoined by three aisles, each of them 39 ft. in height, on the left, and by three more of the same height on the right. A threefold succession of arcades rises above the columns of the central aisle, which were donated by the Italian dictator Benito Mussolini. The 11C triumphal arch before the area of the dome is decorated with mosaics, and there are late-12C mosaics on the inside of the dome.

Stables of Solomon (Christ's cradle): The so-called stables of Solomon, in the SE corner of the Temple precinct beside the El-Aqsa mosque, are an enormous subterranean complex some 54,000 sq.ft. in area and consisting of 13 aisles with 88 pillars supporting the vaults. Some of the structural components date from the time of King Herod the Great. Its name derives from the belief that the stables for the sacrificial animals were housed here in King Solomon's day. A shell-shaped recess from the

Roman period is referred to as 'Christ's cradle'. The Virgin Mary is said to have stood here when presenting the Christ-child in the Temple. The best view of the Kidron Valley and the Mount of Olives is obtained from the SE corner of the Temple precinct.

Golden Gate: The walled-up Golden Gate on the E. side of Temple Mount is identified with the Beautiful Gate in the New Testament, i.e. that gate in the Temple of Jerusalem which led from the forecourt of the heathens into the women's forecourt. It was here that St.Paul healed a man lame from birth (Acts 3, 1–10). The Golden Gate is among the most significant sites not only iconographically (it is a symbol of the Virgin Mary), but also because, in both Jewish and Muslim traditions, it is the place to which the Messiah is to return.

The Golden Gate is further thought to be that through which Jesus entered Jerusalem on a donkey on the Sunday preceding His death (Palm Sunday) and also the gate where Joachim and Anne, parents of the Virgin Mary, met after an angel had promised her birth. Thus the Golden Gate (in Latin 'porta aurea') was interpreted as a symbol for the Immaculate Conception of the Virgin Mary.

Walled up centuries ago, the Golden Gate is Byzantine in origin. There are two versions as to its construction: Eudokia, wife of the Byzantine emperor Theodosius II, settled in Jerusalem in 444 and gave orders for the city fortifications to be rebuilt. The E. wall of Temple Mount, which also served as the city wall, was reconstructed too, and here Eudokia ordered that the Golden Gate be built in memory of St.Peter's healing the lame man. According to the second version, the Golden Gate was built after the Persians had captured Jerusalem in 614. It is said that when the Byzantine Emperor Herakleios II visited Jerusalem in 629 after the Persians had withdrawn, the Golden Gate was built so that the Emperor who had recovered the 'True Cross' from the Persians might pass through it and enter Jerusalem. The walling-up of this gate is also said to be asso-

Dome of the Rock, cupola

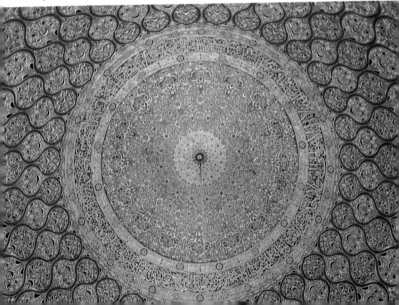

ciated with the Emperor's entry, for when Herakleios, with the 'True Cross', was about to ride through the Golden Gate, 'the stones of the gate suddenly fell down and joined together as if the gate was walled up. The Angel of the Lord appeared above the gate so that everyone took fright. He held the sign of the Cross in his hands and spoke: When the King of all Heaven passed through this gate to go to His Passion, He rode humbly on a donkey, and not in regal splendour. He thereby gave an example of humility to all those who adore him. With these words the Angel vanished. Then the Emperor wept bitterly, took off his shoes, removed all his garments except his shirt, took the Lord's Cross and bore it humbly as far as the gate. And lo, the hard stones heard the word of the Lord, and the walls rose up to where they had been before, and it became an open entrance for all men.' This depiction in the medieval collection of legends entitled 'Legenda aurea' was based on the idea that Christ rode through this gate when He, coming from the Mount of Olives, entered

Jerusalem to the jubilation of people waving palm branches (St.Matthew 21, 1–11) and then, according to St.Matthew, immediately went into the Temple and drove out the dealers and moneychangers (St.Matthew 21, 12–17). It was thought that the vision in Ezekiel 44, 1–2 foretells the fact that Jesus was to enter Jerusalem through this gate and that the gate must be walled up: 'Then he brought me back the way of the gate of the outward sanctuary which looketh toward the east; and it was shut. Then said the Lord unto me; this gate shall be shut, it shall not be opened, and no man shall enter in by it; because the Lord, the God of Israel, hath entered in by it, therefore it shall be shut.' According to Jewish tradition, this gate will remain shut until the 'end of days'. Then the Messiah will enter here. It is for this reason that the Jews call this gate the 'gate of mercy'. When walking around the city hall, they stop here and implore God to grant them mercy. After Caliph Omar captured Jerusalem in 638, the gate was closed to all 'unbelievers'. During the time of the Crusaders, one of the

Chain dome

entrances was opened on Palm Sunday and at the feast of the Exaltation of the Cross (14 September). It is said to have been finally walled up after the Crusaders departed. The Muslims also associate this gate with the time of the end, because it is near the valley of Jehoshaphat, the 'place of the Last Judgement': good men will enter through the N. entrance ('Gate of Grace'); the S. part is called 'Gate of Mercy'.

Wailing Wall (known officially as the Western Wall; in Hebrew: Kotel haMa'aravi): The Wailing Wall, which is part of the Herodian wall surrounding the Temple esplanade, is all that remains of the Second (Herodian) Temple. It is at the same time a symbol of the Temple and a memorial its destruction and is thus the holiest site for Jews. The name 'Wailing Wall' derives from the fact that, for a period of several centuries, Jews from the Diaspora came to Jerusalem to pray here. After E.Jerusalem was annexed by Israel, the official designation 'Western Wall' was introduced, because it was part of the former W. wall of the Temple. The Holy of Holies of the devastated Temple was also in the W., so that a particular connection was established in Jewish mysticism (Kabbala) between the surviving section of the W. surrounding wall and the Holy of Holies, which has not survived: the presence of Yahweh had passed from the devastated Holy of Holies and moved to the W. wall.

The wall is almost 60 ft. high. Its lower layers have ashlars from the Herodian period, above this there are layers from Roman and Muslim times. The upmost layers date from the 19C. The enormous Herodian ashlars continue for 19 layers under the ground, the lowest layer being built on rock.

Excavation site: Considerable finds have been made in excavation work to the N. and SW of the Wailing Wall. The so-called Wilson arch, which spans 42 ft. and is 51 ft. wide, was part of a water-supply system in the Maccabean period. The excavation site in the SW (Archaeological Garden) includes a burial site from the 10–8C BC and some finds from the time of

El-Aqsa mosque

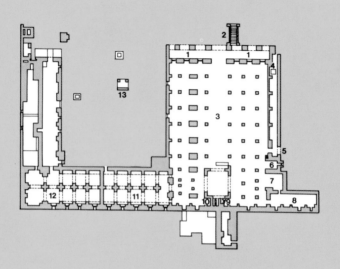

Jerusalem, El-Aqsa mosque **1** Portico **2** Stairs to underground room **3** Prayer room **4** Fountain **5** Elijah's gate **6** Prayer niche of Zacharias **7** Mosque of the 40 martyrs **8** Omar mosque **9** Mihrab **10** Pulpit **11** White mosque **12** Islamic museum **12** Yussef dome

Herod the Great and the Ommiad caliphs: Herodian road, parts of the Herodian Temple wall, remains of Byzantine houses, parts of palaces (Abd al-Malik, Queen Helena of Adiabene), etc.

Mount Zion

Zion was originally the name of the Jebusite fortress occupied by David on the E. hill of Jerusalem: the SW hill has borne this name since Byzantine times, because it was believed that David's city stood here. In addition, prophetic literature and the Psalms give the name of Zion for Jerusalem as the spiritual centre of God's people and the seat of God (see: Heavenly Jerusalem).

The central building on Mount Zion is the *Dormitio church,* which was built by order of the German Kaiser Wilhelm II and the archbishopric of Cologne. According to tradition, it stands on the site where the Virgin Mary died; the 'Crypt of the Dormition' is the religious centre. The church stands on the site of the Byzantine Hagia Sion (late 4C), an enormous building with a nave and four aisles which was destroyed in 996 and described as the 'mother of all churches' because it was regarded as the place where Jesus washed the disciples' feet, where the Last Supper began, where Peter denied Jesus, where Judas betrayed Him, and where the disciples, after Christ's Ascension, experienced the outpouring of the Holy Ghost in an Upper

Solomon's stables

Room. The rooms of the two-storeyed building standing beside the Dormitio church, which contains the (empty) tomb of King David (16C, Muslim) commemorate these holy sites today.

Holocaust Cellar: The Holocaust Cellar (Martyrs' Chamber), not far from the tomb of David, commemorates the victims of the Nazi reign of terror.

St.Peter in Gallicantu: The church of St.Peter in Gallicantu (St.Peter of the Cock-crow), consecrated in 1931, stands on the E. slope of Mount Zion on foundations dating from the Herodian and early Christian periods, and commemorates Peter's threefold denial of Christ (St.Matthew 26, 75). A grotto which can be seen from the lower church is identified as the place where Jesus was held prisoner by the High Priest Caiaphas.

Kidron Valley

The Kidron ('the dark one') is a valley with a stream of water until early summer. It lies between Temple Mount and the Mount of Olives (St.John 18, 1). The Kidron formed the E. city boundary of Jerusalem in the time of the Israelite kings (1 Kings 2, 36–37). It does not have a source, but collects the rainwater descending from the slopes of Mount Scopus, the Mount of Olives and Temple Mount. Flowing through the Arab village of Silwan, it winds through the Judean wilderness and runs out into the Dead Sea S. of Qumran. The Kidron valley was used as a burial site for the common people at the time of the Kings of Judah (2 Kings 23, 6; cf. Jeremiah 2, 23). The kings Asa and Josiah burned heathen idols here (1 Kings 15, 13; 2 Kings 23, 4/6).

Valley of Jehoshaphat: Christian, Jewish and Muslim traditions identify the Kidron Valley with the place where the 'nations' (heathens) will be judged in the time of the end. The prophet Joel (3, 2/12) gave this place the symbolic name of 'Jehoshaphat' ('the Lord judges'). From the fact that God would sit here in judgement upon the heathen, it was deduced that God would also waken the dead here and judge all people. The Kidron Valley has therefore become a favoured burial site. The *tombs* to the left of the road (2/1C BC) are among the best tomb monuments in Jerusalem.

Tomb of Absalom: The so-called tomb of Absalom, son of David, dates from the 1C BC. It is a free-standing monument with a square pedestal (Ionic columns, Doric frieze), hewn entirely from the rock, with two burial chambers, an attic and a conical superstructure.

Absalom, who was king of Jerusalem for a while during his rebellion against David, was the third son of David to be born in Hebron. His mother was Maacah, the daughter of king Talmai of Geshur (2 Samuel 3, 3). His appearance accorded with the ideal of a prince or king: 'But in all Israel there was none to be so much praised as Absalom for his beauty: from the sole of his foot even to the crown of his head there was no blemish in him. And when he polled his head, (for it was at every year's end that he polled it; because the hair was heavy on him, therefore he polled it:) he weighed the hair of his head at two hundred shekels after the king's weight' (2 Samuel 14, 25–26). He won over all the Israelites' hearts by his sympathetic nature.

Amnon, David's first-born son, fell in love with Tamar, Absalom's sister. By means of a ruse, he brought it about that he was alone with her and raped her. David was angered by this occurrence, but did not take any steps against Amnon; from that time on the ravished Tamar led a secluded life in Absalom's house (2 Samuel 13, 1–22). Two years later, Absalom invited David's other sons to the feast of the sheep-shearing, ordered Amnon to be slain there and fled to Geshur, his

Golden Gate

mother's home town (2 Samuel 13, 23–37). It was not until three years later, when David's wrath had cooled, that Absalom returned to Jerusalem, but was excluded from the court for a further two years (2 Samuel 14). When he had been reinstated in the king's favour, Absalom acquired a bodyguard of fity men and began to stir up the Israelites against David by complaining to them of deficiencies in the administration of justice and holding out to them the prospect of obtaining more justice if he became judge. In this way he 'stole the hearts of the men of Israel'. After stirring up the people for four years, he went to Hebron with 200 men on the pretext of being obliged to fulfil a vow. When in Hebron, he sent messengers to the tribes of Israel with the following announcement: 'As soon as ye hear the sound of the trumpet, then ye shall say, Absalom reigneth in Hebron' (2 Samuel 15, 10). More and more people joined Absalom in Hebron, including David's adviser Ahithophel, and when David heard the news: 'The hearts of the men of Israel are after Absalom', he left Jeru-salem with the troops still remaining to him, and fled (2 Samuel 15).

In order to make it clear to all the people that he was king and that his father David was no longer king, Absalom, following the advice of Ahithophel, ordered a tent to be built on the roof of the palace and lay with David's ten concubines 'in the sight of all Israel' (2 Samuel 16, 15–23). This was at the same time the fulfilment of the judgement passed on David because of his behaviour in the matter of Bath-sheba and Uriah: 'Behold, I will raise up evil against thee out of thine own house, and I will take thy wives before thine eyes, and give them unto thy neighbour, and he shall lie with thy wives in the sight of this sun' (2 Samuel 12, 11).

In aiming to deal David the final blow, Absalom followed a tactically incorrect piece of advice given him by Hushai the Archite (2 Samuel 17, 1–23). David was warned and himself made preparations for battle (2 Samuel 17, 24 ff.). The two armies joined battle in the wood of Ephraim, and Absalom's troops suffered a severe defeat. When Absalom, on his

Wailing Wall

mule, was riding under a large oak tree, his hair became caught in the branches. David's general Joab saw him there and—against David's express orders—seized the opportunity to slay the rebel. He thrust three darts into Absalom's heart. Joab's ten armour-bearers smote Absalom dead. They threw his body into a pit in the wood and heaped stones on top of it. King David was inconsolable when he heard of his son's death (2 Samuel 18, 1–19).

Absalom, during his lifetime, had ordered a memorial stone to be set up for him in the 'king's dale', saying: 'I have no son to keep my name in remembrance: and he called the pillar after his own name: and it is called, unto this day, Absalom's place' (2 Samuel 18, 18). Tradition associates this memorial stone with the so-called Tomb of Absalom.

Bene Hesir tombs (tomb of St.James): The tomb of the Hesir family of priests dates from the second half of the 2C BC. It consists of several burial chambers behind a loggia-like façade with a richly decorated architrave (ancient Hebrew inscription). According to Christian tradition, James the brother of the Lord (James the Just) was buried here after his martyrdom. James the brother of the Lord was one of the so-called brothers of Jesus (St.Matthew 13, 55; St.Mark 6, 3; Galatians 1, 19) and is said to have written the Epistle of James. Christ apeared to him after His Resurrection (1 Corinthians 15, 7), and he was probably thereby converted. He subsequently played a central role in the Judaeo-Christian community in Jerusalem and was regarded as one of its 'pillars' (Galatians 2, 9).

Tomb of Zechariah: The tomb of Zechariah (1C BC), 30 ft. in height, is hewn entirely from the rock (Ionic columns) and has a pyramidal roof. Tradition associates it with the prophet Zechariah, one of the twelve Minor Prophets. He appeared in Jerusalem in the second and fourth years of the reign of Darius the Great, the Persian king (520–518 BC; Zechariah 1, 1&7; 7, 1), that is to say shortly after the return of the first Jews from

Wailing Wall, slips in the joints of the wall bearing the requests of the faithful

Babylonian Captivity, and in the same period as the prophet Haggai. Like the latter, Zechariah advocated the rebuilding of the Temple in Jerusalem.

Gihon: Gihon ('pouring forth') is the only spring in Jerusalem from which water flows all the year round. It rises in a grotto at the foot of Mount Ofel. Today the Christians call it the 'Virgin Mary spring', while the Muslims refer to it as the 'spring of the mother of steps' (because there are 32 steps leading up to it) or 'spring of the Virgin Mary'. The name is thought to derive from the former unusual nature of the water which would bubble up for several minutes and then remain calm for hours, almost like a fountain. The walls of Jebus, the town which preceded Jerusalem on this site and was inhabited by the Jebusites, could not be built as far as Kidron Valley or around the spring of Gihon. For this reason the Jebusites built a tunnel from the spring to a point underneath the town. This tunnel could be reached from inside the town through a shaft which was 43 ft. deep and had no steps. Water was drawn through this shaft in buckets hanging on ropes.

Tunnel leading to the pool of Shiloh: During the Assyrian onslaught in the late 8C BC, King Hezekiah (725–697 BC) ordered the upper watercourse of Gihon to be blocked, and routed the water westwards into the city of David (2 Chronicles 32, 30; cf. 2 Kings 20, 20 and Ecclesiasticus 48, 17) in order to secure the city's water supply in the event of its being besieged by an enemy. The tunnel, which is some 1740 ft. long and ends in the city at the pool called Shiloh, was built at the point where, in the time of Hezekiah's predecessor Ahaz (736–725 BC), an open watercourse ran along the SE hill (Isaiah 7, 3; cf. Isaiah 8, 6). The S-shaped tunnel, hewn from the rock, descends by a little more than 6 ft., its height varies between 3 and over 16 ft., and its width between 1 ft. 10 in. and 2 ft. 2 in. The tunnel building was begun on two sides, and a six-line contemporary Hebrew inscription (discovered in 1880 and now in Istanbul) celebrates the meeting of the workers: 'See the

Wailing Wall, the faithful with prayer shawls and prayer thongs

tunnel. This is the story of how it was built. When the miners were swinging their axes, one miner towards another, and when there were only three more cubits to dig, a voice of one miner was heard calling to his comrades, for there was an echo in the rock, both from the north and from the south. On the day when the miners broke through, they struck one against the other, axe against axe, and the water flowed from the spring into the pool, 1200 cubits wide. The rock above the miners' heads was 100 cubits in height.' Approximately in the middle of the tunnel, along which it is possible to walk, dead-end galleries can be seen. They are witness to the miners' efforts to tunnel in the correct direction.

Pool of Shiloh: The water was routed from the Gihon spring through the tunnel to the pool of Shiloh inside the city. The word 'shiloh' comes from the root slh = 'send, send off', and the most likely meaning is 'transmitter, pipe, canal'. That is, 'shiloh' first referred to the canal, and only later to the pool (cf. St.John 9, 7: 'Siloam (Shiloh), which is, by interpretation, Sent.) It has been supposed that Shiloh was not originally an open pool, but an underground cistern, whose ceiling later collapsed (before the time of Christ). It is not known what the pool looked like in the time of Christ; according to St.Luke 13, 4, there was a tower near it ('tower of Siloam (Shiloh)'). Jesus healed a blind man here by anointing his eyes and telling him to wash himself in the pool of Shiloh (St.John 9). As a result of this miracle, the water of the pool, to which healing properties had already been assigned by rabbinical tradition, was considered by Christians too to have curative powers. The Roman emperor Hadrian built a shrine by the pool in AD 135. The so-called pilgrim of Bordeaux described this shrine in 333. In the 5C, the Byzantine empress Eudokia ordered a church to be built by the pool of Shiloh to commemorate the healing of the man born blind. The Persians destroyed this church in 614. But the Muslims also adopted the tradition relating to the water's healing powers, and built a mosque. At Rosh Hashana (in September/October), the Jews

Orthodox Jew at the Wailing Wall

Wailing Wall, Bar Mitsvah ceremony

hold the Tashlih ceremony here, at which the sins are symbolically thrown into the water.

Ophel: Ophel ('hump') is the steep hill to the SE of Temple Mount between the Kidron Valley and the Tyropoeon Valley; the Gihon spring rises on its E. slope. The city of the Jebusites and later of David is thought to have stood on Ophel. The Old Testament mentions building works which King Jotham (756–741) ordered to be carried out on the wall of Ophel (2 Chronicles 27, 3).

Hinnom: Hinnom, properly Ge-Hinnom ('valley of Hinnom') or Ge-Ben-Hinnom ('valley of Hinnom's son'), is the valley which runs out into Kidron Valley in the S. of the old quarter of Jerusalem (Joshua 15, 8; 18, 16). 'Gehenna', the Greek and Latin name for Hell, derives from the Hebrew word Hinnom, as does 'Gahannam' (Jahannam), the Muslim name for one of the hells.

Topheth and Molokh cult: The cultic site of Topheth, where children were sacrificed to the Ammonite god Moloch, is in the valley of Hinnom. The form and appearance of Topheth are unknown. The word itself is interpreted as 'place of fire' or 'hearth' (and was a name for hell in the Middle Ages in Europe). Ahaz (736–725 BC) was the first king of Judah who, so it is reported, sacrificed in the valley of Ben-Hinnom and 'burnt his children in the fire' (2 Chronicles 28, 3; 2 Kings 16, 3), but this cultic site seems to have been here in pre-Israelite times.

Gehenna: After King Josiah (639–609) had ordered the cultic sites to be destroyed in all Judah (2 Chronicles 34, 1–7), the memory of the sacrifices offered up in the valley of Hinnom remained alive. The name of Hinnom became a general designation for Hell. This change in the name's meaning dates from the prophet Jeremiah, who predicted that the valley of Hinnom would one day be called the 'valley of slaughter'.

Hakeldamach: The Greek Orthodox monastery of St.Onuprius (the Aceldama monastery), and the so-called field of blood or potter's field

Mount Zion with Church of the Dormitio

('Hakeldamach'), are on the S. slope of the valley of Hinnom. According to The Acts 1, 18, Judas, after betraying Jesus, purchased a field with the thirty pieces of silver, 'and falling headlong, he burst asunder in the midst, and all his bowels gushed out.' The field was later given the name Hakeldamach.

Mount of Olives

The Mount of Olives, a hill 2655 ft. high to the E. of the city beyond the Kidron Valley, is one of the most sacred sites for Christians and Jews. Christ ascended into heaven from the peak of the Ascension Hill. Jesus and his disciples often went to the Garden of Gethsemane at the W. foot of the mountain, which was also the place where Jesus was taken prisoner. It is the oldest and largest Jewish burial site and its W. slope is the place where the Messiah is expected to appear at the end. The name Mount of Olives dates from the abundance of olive trees which stood here in Biblical times (only scanty bushes today).

Physically the Mount of Olives is part of a chain of hills which begins with Mount Scopus in the N. of Jerusalem and continues at varying heights across the el-Medbase (2715 ft.) where the old Hebrew University stands; at the place called 'Viri Gali-laei', comes to the first of the three hills of the Mount of Olives. The middle one of the three is Ascension Hill (2655 ft.). The 'Mountain of Umbrage' (in Arabic: Baten el-Hawa; 2435 ft.) adjoins this in the S.

Israelite shrine: During the rebellion of his son Absalom (cf. Kidron Valley: Tomb of Absalom), King David fled from Jerusalem and 'went up by the ascent of Mount Olivet, and wept as he went up, and had his head covered'. In this context, the peak of the Mount of Olives is described as a place 'where God is worshipped' (2 Samuel 15, 32). From this it was deduced that there was an Israelite shrine on the peak of the mountain at the time of David in *c.* 1000 BC.

Tomb of the Virgin Mary: The tomb of the Virgin Mary, who is also

Church of the Dormitio, crypt

revered by the Muslims, is to be seen in a Byzantine crypt of a church dating from the time of the Crusaders (1130). A church stood above the Virgin Mary's alleged tomb as early as the 4C. Existing narratives, reports and legends of the death of the Virgin Mary date from no earlier than the 5C. In the Apocrypha, the year of the Virgin's death is calculated as follows: she was 14 years old when she conceived by the Holy Ghost, and 15 when she gave birth to Christ, who lived for 33 years. The Virgin lived for at least another 12 years after the death of Christ, because the Apostles preached for 12 years in Judea and the surrounding areas. According to this calculation, the Virgin died at the age of 59. When an angel announced to the Virgin that she would go to heaven and be united with her Son in three days' time, she requested that all the Apostles should be present at her death. The apostles were then raised up on clouds and led to her. At the third hour of the night, Jesus came with the heavenly host of angels, patriarchs, martyrs, confessors and virgins, who all stood around the Virgin's bed. Christ took Mary's soul up to heaven in His arms.

Getsemani (Gethsemane): Getsemani (Aramaic: 'oil-press'), the garden at the foot of the Mount of Olives in the E. of Jerusalem, is the place of Christ's Agony and subsequent capture (St.Matthew 26, 36 ff.; St.Mark 14, 32 ff.; St.John 18, 1 ff.). The garden may have belonged to a disciple, because the place was well known to Judas Iscariot the traitor, 'for Jesus ofttimes resorted thither with his disciples' (St.John 18, 2). The place revered in Jerusalem today as the Garden of Gethsemane accords with the references in the Gospels and also with tradition.
Grotto: The disciples are said to have been asleep in the Getsemani grotto, a cave some 62 ft. long, 33 ft. wide and up to 11 ft. high, when Jesus, in despair of dying, was asking His Father to remove the cup from Him (St.Luke 22, 41). During the night of Thursday to Friday preceding the Passover feast, no pilgrim was allowed

Church of the Dormitio, Last Supper room (left), archaeological finds near St.Peter in Gallicantu (right)

Tomb of Absalom

Tunnel to pool of Shiloh

to leave either Jerusalem or the districts which belonged to the city of Jerusalem, and for this reason Jesus wanted to spend the night with his disciples in the cave of Getsemani, instead of going to Bethany as He otherwise did (Getsemani is on the way to Bethany). Tradition has it that it was in this cave that Judas betrayed Jesus and Jesus was arrested (hence its other name 'Betrayal Grotto'. The floor of the grotto was decorated with mosaics in the early Byzantine period, and tombs were later built here. The grotto has been in the possession of the Franciscans since 1392.

Garden: Some of the ancient olive trees in the present garden of Getsemani are said to date from the 1C AD and remind the visitor of the garden's Aramaic name of 'oil-press'. A church with splendid mosaics stood here in the 4C. Aetheria, also known as Egeria or Silvia, who was probably a nun from S. France or NW Spain, visited and described the holy sites in *c.* 400. In her description of the journey she refers to the church as 'ecclesia elegans'. This church was destroyed in the Persian invasion of 614, and in the 12C the Crusaders built a 'Church of the Redeemer' in its stead, but this fell into complete disrepair by the 14C. Today's *Church of the Nations* (1919–24) was built with donations from twelve nations. Construction work was supervised by the Italian architect Antonio Barluzzi. The three rocky elevations in the apses are the church's pièce de résistance. This is said to be the place where Jesus prayed three times before being taken prisoner (St.Matthew 26, 39 ff.).

Church of Mary Magdalene: The Russian Orthodox church of Mary Magdalene, with its seven onion towers gleaming with gold, stands halfway up the Mount of Olives, above the Church of the Nations. In 1885, Tsar Alexander III ordered this church to be built in 16C Russian baroque style in memory of his mother

Kidron Valley with tombs and Mount of Olives

Bene Hesir tombs

Maria Aleksandrovna. Inside there are good *paintings* by Vasily Vereshchagin and Aleksandr Ivanov. The Grand Duchess Elizaveta Fyodorovna, who was the sister of the last Tsarina and was murdered during the Russian Revolution, is buried in the crypt.

Dominus flevit: Tradition has it that the dome of the Franciscan chapel of Dominus flevit ('the Lord wept'), consecrated in 1955, stands above the site where Jesus, when entering Jerusalem, wept and predicted the destruction of the Temple (St.Luke 19, 41–44; cf. 19, 37: 'at the descent of the mount of Olives'). The present church stands on the foundations of a 6C Byzantinet structure (some floor mosaics survive).

Prophets' tombs: According to tradition, the Minor Prophets Haggai, Zechariah and Malachi (6–5C BC) are buried in the so-called prophets' tombs. However, the tombs, which consist of 36 niches hewn from the rock in two semicircular passages, actually date from the 4/5C AD (for Zechariah, see: Kidron Valley, tomb of Zechariah). Haggai, a post-Exile prophet, is the tenth of the twelve Minor Prophets. The Old Testament book of Haggai is a collection of five prophetic speeches given in the second half of 520 BC and dealing with the rebuilding of the Temple in Jerusalem after the return of the Jews from Babylonian captivity. The dating is deduced from the editor's marginal notes (e.g. 'in the second year of Darius' referring to the Persian king Darius the Great). According to Ezra 6, 14, work on building the Temple made good progress 'inspired by Haggai the prophet'. It was consecrated in 515 BC. Nothing more is known of Haggai as a person. Malachi ('my messenger') is the twelfth and last of the Minor Prophets. The Old Testament book of Malachi was written in the post-Exile period, probably in the 5C BC.

Jewish burial site: According to Zechariah's prophecy, the Messiah's feet will stand on the Mount of Olives on the Lord's day, while according to Ezekiel he will enter Jerusalem from

Rock tombs at monastery of St.Onuphrius

the east. In the Jewish tradition, the east of Jerusalem is equated with the Mount of Olives. 'And his feet shall stand in that day upon the Mount of Olives, which is before Jerusalem on the east, and the Mount of Olives shall cleave in the midst thereof toward the east and toward the west, and there shall be a very great valley; and half of the mountain shall remove toward the north, and half of it toward the south' (Zechariah 14, 4). 'Afterward he brought me to the gate, even the gate that looketh toward the east; and, behold, the glory of the God of Israel came from the way of the east: and his voice was like a noise of many waters: and the earth shined with his glory ... And the glory of the Lord came into the house by the way of the gate whose prospect is toward the east' (Ezekiel 43, 1–4; cf.: Golden Gate on Temple Mount). On the Day of Judgement, the Messiah will enter his sanctuary from the east (= Mount of Olives); before he enters there, he will be on the Mount of Olives: 'And the glory of the Lord went up from the midst of the city, and stood upon the mountain which is on the east side of the city' (Ezekiel 11, 23). It is due to these prophecies that the W. slope of the Mount of Olives is a favoured burial site for Jews. Many Jews came to Jerusalem to die here and be buried on the mountain where, according to tradition, the Messiah will appear on the Day of Judgement in order to enter the Holy City. At the same time, the W. slope of the Mount of Olives, lying outside the city, accords with regulations regarding the purity of burial sites.

Pater Noster church: Tradition has it that Christ taught the Lord's Prayer ('Pater noster') on the Mount of Olives (St.Luke 11, 1–4; St.Matthew 6, 9–13). The first church to commemorate this was built by the Crusaders. The present structure was founded by the French Princess Aurelie de la Tour d'Auvergne. This building, completed in 1875, displays the Lord's Prayer in over 64 languages on majolica tiles.

Eleona: The first significant Christian building on the Mount of Olives was Eleona ('Mount of Olives basi-

Monastery of St.Onuphrius

Pool of Shiloh

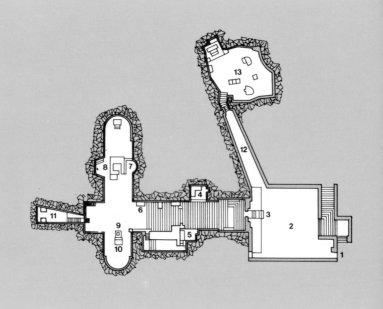

Jerusalem, tomb of Virgin Mary 1 Access **2** Anteroom **3** Entrance **4** Chapel with the tombs of Anne and Joachim, the Virgin Mary's parents **5** Chapel with St.Joseph's tomb **6** Greek Orthodox altar **7** Mihrab (Islamic prayer niche) **8** Armenian altar **9** Cistern **10** Abyssinian altar **11** Vaulting **12** Passage **13** Grotto of Jesus's death struggle

lica'), which was rediscovered in 1910 in the course of excavation work. It was built in the Constantine period in the 4C and consisted of a crypt, an atrium, a portico and a monumental staircase to the Kidron Valley. Eleona was destroyed by the Persians in 614, and its crypt ('Grotto of Instruction'), which was restored and consecrated anew in 1927, was regarded as the place where Jesus made his speech concerning the time of the end (St.Matthew 24–25).

Ascension chapel: The small octagonal mosque on the peak of the Mount of Olives stands on the spot where Christ, according to tradition, ascended into Heaven. A footprint of the Risen Christ is displayed under a pane of glass inside the building. This originally open building was erected by the Crusaders in *c.* 1150 and was later given a dome. A chapel dedicated to the memory of Christ's Ascension stood here in the late 4C.

According to St.Luke 24, 51, St.Mark 16, 19, and The Acts 1, 9–11, Christ ascended into heaven before the Apostles' eyes. The time and place have been exactly delimited, and the authors are referring to a concrete historical event 40 days after Christ's Resurrection (Acts 1, 3), on the Mount of Olives (Acts 1, 12) and near Bethany (St.Luke 24, 50). After the Risen Christ had given the Apostles some final instructions and advice, 'he was taken up; and a cloud received

Tomb of the Virgin Mary ▷

him out of their sight' (Acts 1, 9). While they were still looking up into heaven, two angels suddenly stood beside them and promised that Christ would return. Christ had Himself foretold His Ascension: 'What and if ye shall see the Son of man ascend up where he was before?' (St.John 6, 62). Matthew and John do not mention Christ's Ascension; the passage in St.Mark 16, 19 belongs to a section of text which is not to be found in the oldest texts, and is part of a 2C compilation of the reports contained in other Gospels concerning the appearances of the Risen Christ and His instructions. Thus St.Luke is the only New Testament author to describe Christ's Ascension as a visible historical event. Other authors state that the Risen Christ is in Heaven where he sits on the right hand of His Father and although this presupposes an Ascension into Heaven, the Ascension is not described. Christ Himself had foretold that He would sit at the right hand of God in Heaven (St.Matthew 26, 64). When St.Stephen was being stoned, he saw Heaven open and Jesus standng on the right hand of God (Acts 7, 55). Reports and comments concerning where Christ will be after the Ascension, and referring to His return at the end of time, are to be found throughout the New Testament, but there are few passages which refer to the Ascension direct, and these give the impression of being confessions of faith: 'He that descended is the same also that ascended up far above all hevens, that he might fill all things' (Ephesians 4, 10). 'For Christ is not entered into the holy places made with hands, which are the figures of the true; but into heaven itself, now to appear in the presence of God for us' (Hebrews 9, 24). 'Jesus Christ: who is gone into heaven' (1 Peter 3, 21–22).

The Christians originally remembered the Ascension at Whitsuntide. The festival of the Ascension, celebrated on the 40th day after Easter, began to be celebrated in the 4C. Muslim belief also holds that Christ ascended into Heaven (in order to see the Prophet Mohammed).

Mountain of Umbrage: To the S. of the Mountain of Umbrage (also

Getsemani, church of nations

known as the Mountain of Perdition), King Solomon built shrines for his foreign wives 'for Ashtore the abomination of the Zidonians, and for Chemosh the abomination of the Moabites, and for Milcom the abomination of the children of Ammon' (2 Kings 23, 13). Solomon's wives burnt incense and sacrificed to their gods here (1 Kings 11, 7–8). King Josiah ordered the shrines built by Solomon to be destroyed (2 Kings 23, 13–14).

Viri Galilaei ('men of Galilee'): Tradition identifies the N. peak of the Mount of Olives as the place called Galilee where the Risen Christ gave the eleven Apostles instructions for their world-wide mission (St.Matthew 28, 7/16–20; Acts 1, 11).

Russian convent: Only rarely are visitors permitted to enter the White Russian convent with a belfry ('Russian tower'), from which there is a view as far as the Dead Sea.

Betfage: The former village of Betfage ('house of the green figs'), now a Franciscan complex, with domestic buildings, church, cisterns, tombs (one of these is closed by a stone) and a wine press decorated with mosaic tiles, was formerly the place where Jesus borrowed a colt from two disciples on Palm Sunday (St.Mark 11, 1; St.Luke 19, 29; St.Matthew 21, 1). The annual Palm Sunday procession begins in Betfage on the Sunday before Easter. The name 'Palm Sunday' derives from the procession of palms which was held in Jerusalem as early as the 4C in order to commemorate Jesus's entry. In the 8C the procession began in Bethany. After the ban pronounced under the Fatimid caliph al-Hakim had come to an end, during the time of the Franks, the procession started from Bethany once again. The Turks then banned the procession in 1563, and today the Palm Sunday procession of the Latin patriarchate begins in Betfage and ends at the church of St.Anne in Jerusalem. *Franciscan church:* Byzantine chapel built in the 4C to commemorate Jesus's ride on the colt. The Crusaders later built two defensive towers above the ruins of the chapel, and one of these towers was later used as a

Ascension chapel

church. In 1876, a peasant found a painted stone cube which the Franks had cut from the rock from which Jesus is said to have mounted the colt. The Franciscans acquired the site and built a new church in 1883. Inside the church there are fine monochromatic frescos by C.Vagarini on the side walls, depicting Christ's entry into Jerusalem. The painting in the apse shows Jesus riding through the jubilant multitude. *Cube:* On the S. side of the rock restored by C.Vagarini in 1950, Christ is shown with Lazarus and Martha and Mary, who were brother and sisters (St.John 10, 20–30). On the N. side, the village inhabitants are seen watching the colt being untied. The multitude is depicted waving palms on the E. side, and on the W. side the rock bears the name of Betfage and a mutilated inscription. According to an old tradition, the prophetess Huldah is said to be buried in Betfage (2 Kings 22, 14–20). Today the Biblical Betfage is associated with the village of al-Tur on the S. hill of the Mount of Olives.

Tombs of the Kings

The so-called tombs of the kings were long regarded as the burial site of the kings of Judah and they are among the most interesting burial sites in Israel. In 1863 the French archaeologist F.de Saulcy discovered that Queen Helene of Adiabene in Mesopotamia, who had converted to Judaism, built them as family tombs in the 1C AD. In 1863, the richly decorated queen's sarcophagus—today in the Louvre in Paris—had not yet fallen prey to the looters of tombs.

Kings were buried in the town where they had their residence. Thus, David was buried in the city of David (1 Kings 2, 10), and Solomon was also interred in the city of David (1 Kings 11, 43). The Old Testament text regarding the burial of the subsequent kings of Judah goes as follows: 'And he slept with his fathers' (Jereboam: 1 Kings 14, 20), and 'slept with his fathers, and was buried with his fathers in the city of David' (Rehoboam: 1 Kings 14, 31; Abijam: 1 Kings 15, 8; Asa: 1 Kings 15, 24).

Dominus flevit and Mary Magdalene church

Jehoiada, the High Priest of Jerusalem, was also interred here 'because he had done good in Israel, both toward God, and toward his house' (2 Chronicles 24, 15–16). Although the kings Jehora, Joash and Ahaz were interred in the city of David, they were, owing to their godlessness, 'not (buried) in the sepulchres of the kings' (2 Chronicles 21, 20; 24, 25; cf. 28, 27). King Uzziah was buried as a leper 'in the field of the burial which belonged to the kings' (2 Chronicles 26, 23). An Aramaic inscription indicates that Uzziah was buried again in another grave in the New Testament period: 'The bones of King Uzziah of Judah have been brought here, do not open!' King Hezekiah was only buried 'on the slope going up to the tombs of the sons of David' (2 Chronicles 32, 33). This may mean that the burial site was already full in the time of Hezekiah, for Hezekiah's successors were also buried elsewhere: Manasseh and his son Amon were interred in the garden of Uzza, the garden of their own house (2 Kings 21, 18/26; 2 Chronicles 33, 20).

A knowledge of the siting of the kings' tombs is assumed in Nehemiah 3, 16 and The Acts 2, 29: 'Men and brethren, let me freely speak unto you of the patriarch David, that he is both dead and buried, and his sepulchre is with us unto this day.' The location of the kings' tombs in present-day Jerusalem is not known. The so-called *tomb of David* is to be seen on Mount Zion in the basement of a building which is crowned by a minaret and stands beside the Dormitio church. This is actually a cenotaph rather than a tomb proper and has crowns and cultic objects. The Christians were the first to revere this site as David's tomb in the 12C. It was later also venerated by the Muslims and, from 1948 onwards, by the Jews as well. It may well be that this site is revered as David's tomb as a result of confusing the Christian Mount Zion and David's Zion.

The usual type of tomb in the oldest Biblical times was the family tomb in which the dead person was intended to be united with his forefathers. That is to say, the solidarity of the family group continued to be recorded even

Mary Magdalene church with Jewish burial sites

Betfage, Franciscan church, fresco

after death. The tombs were usually outside a village or town. The family tomb of the patriarch Abraham and his successors was the cave of Machpelah near Mamre/Hebron (Genesis 23, 19). Deborah, Rebekah's nurse, was buried under an oak near Beth-el (Genesis 35, 8). Saul and his sons were interred under a tamarisk (1 Samuel 31, 13). However, Joseph's bones, which had been brought from Israel, were buried on his hereditary possession in Sichem. It was regarded as a punishment for anyone not to be buried in his fathers' tomb (1 Kings 13, 22). Abraham bought the cave of Machpelah from Ephron the Hittite 'that I may bury my dead out of my sight' (Genesis 23, 4). Abraham's wife Sarah (Genesis 23, 19), and later Abraham himself (Genesis 25, 9–10), were buried here. The patriarchs Isaac (Abraham's son) and his wife Rebekah, and Jacob (Isaac's son) and

his wife Leah, were interred in this tomb too. 'I am to be gathered unto my people: bury me with my fathers in the cave that is the field of Ephron the Hittite, in the cave that is in the field of Machpelah, which is before Mamre, in the land of Canaan ... there they buried Abraham and Sarah his wife; there they buried Isaac and Rebekah his wife; and there I buried Leah' (Genesis 49, 29–31). Jacob's last wish was that he be buried in his father's burial place (Genesis 47, 30). Others to be buried in their father's house were Simson the judge (Judges 16, 31) and Asahel the hero (2 Samuel 2, 32). King David ordered that the bones of Saul, of his son Jonathan and of the seven relatives who had been executed, be transferred to the tomb of Saul's fathers.

However, only the well-to-do could afford a family tomb, while poorer people were buried in a particular place outside the town. In Jerusalem, the 'graves of the common people' were in the Kidron Valley (2 Kings 23, 6; cf. Jeremiah 26, 23). Joseph of Arimathaea, in whose family tomb Jesus was buried, was also a rich man (St.Matthew 27, 57).

The oldest form of tomb recorded in the Bible is the cave tomb, which as a rule was accessible by a slope from above. A further development of this is the shaft tomb, in which the entrance was dug downwards as a shaft as far as the level of the horizontally adjoining burial chamber; a stone might divide the shaft from the chamber. In the bench tomb, the dead were laid on benches hewn from the rock at the sides of the cave. In the Hellenistic period the bodies were laid in individual tunnels which were dug horizontally into the rock.

Sanhedrin Tombs

The Sanhedrin tombs, where members of the Jewish Supreme Council were buried, are in Sanhedria, the N. part of the city. Within these caves hewn from the rock and much used in the 1C AD, there are vaulted tombs, sliding gallery tombs, closing stones etc.

The Supreme Council (in Greek 'synhedrion' meaning 'community of persons sitting together', which was Hebraized into 'sanhedrin') was the highest religious, judicial and political authority of the Jews after their return from Babylonian Exile in 538 BC. Other names for it in the Bible apart from 'Supreme Council' include 'Council of Elders' (Judith 11, 14; 15, 8; 1 Maccabees 12, 6; The Acts 22, 5) or 'the senate' (2 Maccabees 11, 27). The origins of this authority date back to the time of Persian rule after the Babylonian Captivity, when the Persians granted the Jews their own jurisdiction (Ezra 7, 25–26; cf. 5, 8; 6, 7; 10, 8). The Romans took away from the Jews the right to put any man to death (St.John 18, 31). After Jesus had been questioned by the Supreme Council, He therefore had to be brought before the Roman governor Pontius Pilate before He could be executed. The Supreme Council, including the High Priest, consisted of 71 members. The Council was headed by the officiating High Priest. The number of 70 plus 1 derives from Exodus 24, 1/9 and Numbers 11, 16–17: 'And the Lord said unto Moses, Gather unto me seventy men of the elders of Israel, whom thou knowest to be the elders of the people, and officers over them; and bring them unto the tabernacle of the congregation, that they may stand there with thee. And I will come down and talk with thee there: and I will take of the spirit which is upon thee, and will put it upon them; and they shall bear the burden of the people with thee, that thou bear it not thyself alone.' Apart from the High Priest, the members were the former High Priests and the members of the families from which the High Priests usually came (Acts 4, 6), and also the Pharisees and Saddu-

'Russian tower' at Russian convent ▷

cees, who were opposed to one another (Acts 23, 6).

Other Tombs

Garden tomb See: Christ's sepulchre.

Herod's Family Tomb: Near the King David Hotel there is a rock tomb from the 1C AD, with four burial chambers facing the four points of the compass. Discovered in 1892, it is identified as the family tomb of Herod's dynasty, although there is no relevant inscription or any other evidence of this.

Mount Herzl: The *tomb of Theodor Herzl* (the founder of political Zionism), together with a Herzl museum, is in a park on the edge of the suburb of Bayit Ve-Gan. Other leading Zionist personalities are also buried in the park. The *Jewish Military Cemetery* is in the N. of the park.

Jason's Tomb: A pyramidal tomb dating from the Maccabean period in the Alfasi Road.

Old City Wall

The old city wall is some 40 ft. high and can be walked along. Built in 1534–40 under Sultan Suleiman the Magnificent, it accords approximately with the city fortifications as they were at the time of Emperor Hadrian. Many of the foundations are Byzantine. Of the six gates built by Suleiman, only the Jaffa, Zion and Damascus gates survive in their original form.

Damascus Gate: The Damascus Gate, nearly 46 ft. high and decorated by battlements and turrets, is the largest and most beautiful of the gates in the old city and lies on the border of the Christian and Muslim quarters. In the town of Aelia Capitolina built by Emperor Hadrian, the cardo maximus (main street) began at the Damascus Gate. Parts of what is known as the third city wall (1C AD) have been found under the bridge in the course of excavation work. The Roman column behind the Damascus Gate is at the assumed centre of the Province of Judea.

Sanhedrin tomb

Solomon's Quarries/Cave of Zedekiah: An extensive man-made system of caves (discovered as late as the 19C) is to be found outside the city wall, some 500 ft. E. of the Damascus Gate. Traces of ancient quarrying have given rise to the assumption that the columns for the Temple of Solomon were quarried here (hence the name 'Solomon's Quarries'). Another tradition regards this cave as the place where Zedekiah, last king of Judah, hid from the Chaldees before being captured and blinded (cf. 2 Kings 25, 1–25; 2 Chronicles 36, 11–21).

Herod's Gate: An undecorated building, so called because Jesus was led to Herod's palace along the street which passes through the gate; He was subsequently mocked by Herod (St.Luke 23, 6–12). A sheep market is held here every Friday.

Lions' Gate: Legend relates that the only gate still open in the E. of the city wall was built by Suleiman after he had been instructed in a dream to construct a wall surrounding Jerusalem, or be torn to pieces by lions. The two Mameluke lions on each of the two sides of the gate date from the time of Sultan Baibar (1260–77). Christians call this gate Stephen's gate, because tradition has it that St.Stephen was led through this gate to be stoned. The Muslims refer to the gate as Bab Sitti Maryam (Mary's gate), because the birthplace of Mary is revered in the nearby church of St.Anne, while her tomb is venerated in the Kidron Valley. The Jewish name of Jehoshaphat Gate derives from the Kidron Valley's other name, the Valley of Jehoshaphat. The modern monument in front of the Kidron bridge commemorates how Israeli paratroopers gained access to the old city from the Lions' Gate in 1967.

Golden Gate: The Golden Gate, which is wreathed in legend although it has been walled up for centuries, is part of the wall surrounding Temple Mount (see Temple Mount).

Single, Double and Threefold Gate: The Herodian Threefold Gate

Herodian family tomb

and the Double Gate on the S. side of the wall surrounding Temple Mount were also walled up centuries ago. The Single Gate probably led to what are known as Solomon's stables. The stairs leading up to the Double Gate, above which the El-Aqsa mosque stands, were originally 460 ft. wide.

Dung Gate: The name of this gate appears in the Old Testament (Nehemiah 2, 13; 3, 13–14; 12, 31) and it was here that the inhabitants of Jerusalem threw their refuse out of the city into the Tyropoon Valley and the Kidron Valley.

The present structure dates from the 1950s, but was much altered in 1985. A small arch above the lintel shows how small this gate was originally.

Zion Gate: This gate, which leads from the SW part of the old city to Mount Zion (the Muslims also call it Bab en-Nebi Daud or David's gate, because they passed through this gate to reach David's supposed tomb on Mount Zion) was built in 1540 and was the last one to be constructed in the old city. Its design, however,

dates back to the Mamelukes. Originally the wall was intended to include Mount Zion but there were insufficient funds for this.

Jaffa Gate: Dating from 1538, it opens into the Christian and Armenian quarters of the city and stands at the beginning of the former trade route to the port of Jaffa. When Kaiser Wilhelm II came to attend the consecration of the Lutheran Redeemer's Church, part of the city wall between the Jaffa Gate and the citadel was torn down to enable the distinguished guest to enter.

Citadel with David's Tower: The citadel, which has been destroyed and rebuilt several times, stands to the right of Jaffa Gate. Today it is an excavation site and a city museum. Originally a fortress of the Maccabees, it may even have been their royal castle. Later on it was the palace of Herod the Great (parts of which survive, e.g. David's Tower) and a garrison in Roman times (which burned down in AD 66). During the Byzantine period it was a monastery

Royal tomb

for a time and later a Crusaders' castle (Frankish defensive moat). The present structure is mainly early 14C.

New Gate: Built as late as 1889, this gate gave the patriarchs direct access to their residences in the Christian quarter.

Other Religious Buildings

St.Anne's Church: St.Anne's church, which stands not far from the Lions' Gate, is one of the best-preserved Crusaders' churches in the Holy Land. Tradition has it that it occupies the site of the house of St.Anne, mother of the Virgin Mary. The basilica, which has a nave and two aisles and resembles a castle, was built in *c.* 1140 on the ruins of previous buildings (5C). It was used as a mosque for 700 years after Saladin occupied Jerusalem.
Pool of Bethesda: Beside the church of St.Anne there is an archaeological excavation site with the remains of a pool from the early Roman imperial period. Here Jesus healed a crippled man (St.John 5, 1 ff.).

St.Stephen: The Dominican church of St.Stephen (1883–1900) is in the new part of the city, not far from the Damascus Gate. It stands on the (still surviving) foundations of a 5C basilica which had a nave and two aisles and was dedicated to St.Stephen the protomartyr *(Byzantine floor mosaics)*.

Monastery of the Cross: This 11C monastery was built by Georgian monks on the foundations of a 5C building with surviving *Byzantine floor mosaics*. The massive, windowless walls surrounding the monastery give the impression of a fortress. 11–16C *frescos* illustrate the history of the Holy Cross after which the monastery is named. According to tradition, the building stands on the site where Lot planted the tree from which the wood of Christ's Cross was later carved.

Hadassah synagogue (in the Hadassah medicine centre outside the city): A rectangular building designed by the American architect Joseph Neufeld in 1962. Steps lead down to the interior which has 12 *stained-glass*

Damascus Gate

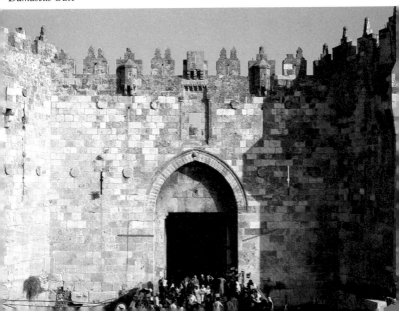

windows by Marc Chagall (1887–1985) with subjects taken from Jacob's blessing (Genesis 49) and Moses's blessing (Deuteronomy 33). On the N. wall: thet tribes of Naphtali, Joseph and Benjamin. E. wall: tribes of Reuben, Simeon and Levi. S. wall: tribes of Judah, Zebulun and Issachar. W. wall: tribes of Dan, Gad and Asher. In Jewish mysticism, the numbers 3 and 4 signify wisdom, reason and knowledge, manifested in the patriarchs Abraham, Isaac and Jacob, and the division of the universe into Aziluth (the world of emanation), Beriah (world of creation), Jezira (world of formation) and Asiya (world of the visible). 3 and 4 added together produce the mystical number 7 (7 days of the week, 7 arms of the menora, the words of Yahweh are seven times purified) (Psalm 12). Multiplication of 4 by 3 results in the mystical number 12 (12 tribes of Israel, 12 signs of the zodiac, 12 gates of ancient Jerusalem, 12 patriarchs, 12 Minor Prophets).

Christian quarter

The central sanctuary in the Christian quarter, which also contains the various patriarchates (Latin, Greek Orthodox, Greek Catholic, Coptic, Ethiopian), is the Church of the Holy Sepulchre. The two mosques next to the Church of the Holy Sepulchre are the *Khanqa mosque*, to the N., and the *Omar mosque* to the S., both of which date from the late 12C and have 15C minarets.

Muristan with the Church of the Redeemer and the Church of John the Baptist: The area some 430 ft. square lying to the E. of the Christian Quarter is known as Muristan (meaning 'hospice' in Persian) after a hospice built here in the early 9C by Charlemagne. In 1896, Sultan Abdulhamid II presented the E. section of Muristan to the German state, and the W. section to the Greek Orthodox church (today the Greek bazaar is at the centre of the area). Kaiser Wilhelm II had the Lutheran *Redeemer's church* built. This basilica has three apses in 12C Crusader style; the oldest sections are the medieval door with signs of the zodiac, the Frankish columns and capitals, and the cloister (11&13C) under the provost's house.

Herod's Gate, sheep market

The 11C Greek Orthodox *church of John the Baptist* was built on an earlier Byzantine structure and rebuilt by the Crusaders in the 12C. The lower church (5C) is the oldest surviving church Jerusalem.

Salvator monastery: The administrative centre for the Catholic sites in the Holy Land is housed in this monastery, whose buildings include the Salvator church (1885) and the Franciscan pilgrims' hospice of Casa Nova (1847, enlarged in 1947).

Alexandra hospice with church of the Russian Orthodox community: (Opposite the Redeemer's Church) Parts of Herod the Great's city wall and of a gate belonging to the Hadrian town of Aelia Capitolina were discovered when this 19C church was being built.

Armenian quarter

The traditional residential area of the Armenian community (which has been in Jerusalem since the 5C) stretches from the Jaffa Gate to the Zion Gate (see St.Polyeuctus church under 'Also worth seeing') and covers the N. part of Mount Zion. A Maro-nite monastery, the Anglican church of Christ (with a hospice), and St.Mark's monastery of the Syrian Jacobites with the church of St.Mark, are to the E. of the citadel. The S. section of this quarter was at its zenith under the Armenian patriarch Krikor Baronder (1613–45). Today this section is occupied by the walled complex of the *Armenian monastery,* where the palace of Herod the Great formerly stood. The Armenian monastery complex includes the cathedral of St.James, the monastery of the olive tree, the house of Annas, a theological seminary (since 1843), the residence of the Armenian patriarchate, the Gulbenkian library, and the Edward Mardigian Armenian art and history museum (see Museums), as well as the two- and three-storeyed houses of the Armenians, who number about 3,500, with primary schools, secondary schools, and workshops.

Cathedral of St.James: Dedicated to the two apostles called James: James the Great, brother of the John the apostle and son of Zebedee (St.Mark 1, 19), whom Herod

Lion Gate, detail

Agrippa I had beheaded in AD 44, and James the Less, son of Alphaeus (St.Mark 3, 18), who was either stoned in AD 62 or hurled from a tower by Pharisees in AD 66, and is regarded as the first bishop of the early Christian community. The cathedral stands in the heart of the Armenian quarter, the SW part of which is formed by the walled Armenian patriarchate. After lengthy quarrels with the Greek Orthodox community, Mahmud II handed the cathedral over to the Armenians in 1813. A memorial to St.James was built on this site in *c.* AD 420, and in AD 444 the female patrician Bassa, who came to Jerusalem with the Empress Eudokia, constructed a chapel in honour of St.Manas, an Egyptian martyr (d. 295). Along with the Armenians, who were their only allies in the Holy Land, the Crusaders built the present cathedral on the foundations of an 11C Georgian monastery of St.James. Building materials used inside the cathedral are mainly medieval. The cathedral is entered by a 17C vestibule, which was built when the entrance was moved to its present position. Two synamders or nakuses (Armenian for gong) hang in the church entrance; these are old wooden planks which were struck instead of a bell, when Christians were banned from ringing bells in the 9C. The church has a nave, two aisles, and four columns which support the tall drum of the dome. In the 17C the pillars were made square and decorated with blue tiles from Spain up to a height of 7 ft. (the Spanish and Armenians jointly revere St.James, who is said to have worked as a missionary in Spain and whose bones are preserved in Santiago de Compostela). The church is topped by a hexagonal star-shaped tower.

Nave: The nave, which measures 57 × 82 ft., has a central crossing and is a typical example of Armenian architecture. Gilded wooden carvings, and inlay in mother-of-pearl and tortoiseshell, are to be seen inside the church. The splendid altar appears to the visitor as 'a golden fire of icons and monstrances' (C.Thubron). The altars of John the Baptist (right) and the Virgin Mary (left) occupy the E. apses. The tomb of James the Less is

Triple gate or Hulda gate

below the middle altar. A domed bishop's throne is to be seen on the left; on the right is the throne of the Armenian patriarch. A magnificent iconostasis conceals the choir apse. *Left aisle:* This contains the chapels of St.Makarios (bishop of Jerusalem under Constantine), St.Menas, St.James the Great, and St.Stephen (the latter, dating from the 10C, is today used as a sacristy and baptistery). The chapels of St.Makarios and St.Menas are closed today and contain the patriarchate's treasury, with valuable 13C manuscripts, including gospels by T.Roslin, the Armenian illustrator (guided tours on application). *Right aisle:* A secret entrance in the S. wall leads to the chapels above the side apses. A panel inserted between painted tiles conceals a splendid carved door dated 1356. The narthex of the medieval church is today the chapel of Echmiadzin. The delicate decorations on the door identify it as being the former main entrance. The pilasters in the S. wall were walled up in the 17C by order of the patriarch Eleazar who wanted to become the catholicos

(the highest ecclesiastical dignitary) of the Armenians, and abruptly moved this office, which was associated with the Armenian town of Echmiadzin, to Jerusalem. He ordered an altar to be built in the chapel using stones from Mount Tabor, Mount Sinai, the Holy Sepulchre and the river Jordan. Beautiful tiles, manufactured in Katahia in Turkey in 1729, show Persian and and Chinese influence. The fountain at the entrance was built in 1876 in honour of Sultan Abdul Hamid's (1842–1918) accession to the throne.

Church of St.Mark: Tradition has it that the 12C church of St.Mark, which belongs to the Syrian Jacobites, stands on the site where the 'house of Mary', the mother of St.Mark the Evangelist, stood. It is said that there was a chapel here in the 2C.

House of Annas: The building known as the house of Annas is an early-4C chapel. It stands on the site where Annas, the Jewish High Priest, lived. After the Romans deposed Annas in AD 15, Annas's five sons and his son-in-law Caiaphas were granted the office of High Priest one after the

Bethesda pool, partial view

other. Annas retained his influence even after being deposed. This is why Jesus, after His arrest, was first brought before Annas, and only thereafter before Caiaphas, the officiating High Priest (St.John 18, 13/24). The *Olive Tree monastery* stands beside the house of Annas. It is named after a fenced-in tree to which—so tradition has it—Jesus was bound the night after being taken prisoner.

Jewish Quarter (HaRova HaYehudi): The Jewish quarter, located in the SW of the old city, borders on the Armenian quarter in the W., on the Muslim quarter in the E. and on the bazaars in the N. In the Roman-Byzantine period, the cardo maximus (Rehov Habad) ran through today's Jewish quarter. In the early Islamic period, Jewish life was concentrated in this part of the city, where the Crusaders opened a German pilgrims' hospice in 1140. Ramban (acronym for Rabbi Moses Ben Nahman), a scholar from Spain, founded a community in the time of Baibars, the Mameluke sultan. Many Sephardim came to Jerusalem (see Yohanan ben Zakkai synagogues) after the Jews were expelled from Spain and Portugal. In 1701, Rabbi Yehuda Hassid arrived in the Holy City along with 500 faithful followers from Poland. They built a synagogue (see Hurva synagogue) in the grounds of the former Crusaders' church of St.Martin. The first Jewish hospital (see Misgav Yerushalayim) in the Holy Land was built here in the mid 19C. Some 15,000 Jews lived in this overpopulated quarter in the late 10C, and until 1948 there were about 5,100. The new plan for the city's development, drawn up in 1968, provides that 5,000 people (including 1,000 to 1,500 yeshiva students) will one day live in the rebuilt Jewish quarter. The light-coloured Jerusalem stone is to be used for the houses, which are only

Monastery of the Cross, frescos ▷

Hadassah synagogue, stained-glass window by Marc Chagall

permitted to be from two to four storeys in height.

Hurva synagogue: An early-18C building by Rabbi Yehuda Hassid. It remained incomplete after the Rabbi's death and was therefore called Ha-Hurva (ruin). A splendid reconstruction was carried out in 1864 (until 1948 it was the largest Ashkenazic house of prayer in Jerusalem). In 1949, Hurva became a victim of the Arab-Israeli war. After the reunification, a synagogue was built as a memorial (it is a centrally planned domed structure with a massive arch). Reconstruction work has been in progress since 1977.

Ramban synagogue: The oldest known Jewish house of prayer in Jerusalem was constructed in the late 14C by converting a Frankish church. This synagogue was named after Ramban (Rabbi Moses Ben Nahman), the Spanish scholar and cabalist,

although it has not been demonstrated that the building has any connection with that scholar. A row of two columns divides the main hall into two aisles. The synagogue was closed in 1586 by order of the Turkish governor. Destroyed in the Arab-Israeli war, it was rebuilt after 1967. On the rear wall is a panel bearing the report which Ramban sent to his family in Spain.

Misgav Yerushalayim: Over the last few years, a Spanish-Jewish study centre (architect: Moshe Safdie) has been built on the site of the Misgav Ladakh hospital. The complex is bounded to the N. and E. by the yeshivot of Porat Yoshev and HaKotel, and in the W. and S. by the new residential houses of the Jewish quarter. The study centre comprises a museum, a lecture hall, a library and study rooms. The domes are reminiscent of Mameluke architecture.

Cathedral of St.Jacob, gospel book of the noble lady Keran (1265) by T.Roslin

Yohanan ben Zakkai synagogues
(Rehov Bet El): This complex of four
synagogues (1. Ben Zakkai, 2. Eliya
Hanavi, 3. Stambuli, 4. Emzai synagogue), named after Rabbi Yohanan
ben Zakkai (1C AD), is today subordi-
nate to the Sephardic community.
After the end of the Six-Day War in
1967, and after the reunification of
Jerusalem, work on the historically
exact reconstruction of the synagogues was begun.
Ben Zakkai synagogue: This synagogue was built between 1606 and 1610.
The long room with its groin vaulting
accords with Gothic-style Islamic-
Frankish architecture. The two
Torah shrines (Aron ha-kodesh) are
in the middle of the E. wall. The
bema of the first synagogue had six
steps. Up to 100 believers could sit
around the bema. The restored synagogue was to have room for up to 250
believers, and so the bema was built

with only one step. The Aron ha-
kodesh was rebuilt in accordance with
the original, on the model of the synagogues in Istanbul (the stone is tiled
on the inside). The doors of the Torah
shrines are by the Israeli craftsman
Bezalel Schatz; the wall paintings by
Jean David above the Torah shrines
depict earthly and heavenly Jerusalem. *Eliya Hanavi synagogue:* This
synagogue built between 1615 and
1625 (the Prophet Elijah is said to
have once been present here) was
originally the study room of the Ben
Zakkai synagogue. It was built in the
traditional Byzantine-early Arab
style, and is a square room with four
columns supporting the vault arches.
Above the vault is a dome resting on a
drum. The richly carved 16C Aron
ha-kodesh is from Livorno, and the
prophet's chair is to be seen in the
side niche. The entrance door was
carved by Shraga Weil, an Israeli.

Emzai synagogue: The Emzai or middle synagogue was built between 1702 and 1720. It was originally the courtyard of the Ben Zakkai synagogue, and its style and structure accord with that synagogue. *Stambuli synagogue:* The style and plan of this synagogue (*c.* 1740) accord with the Eliya Hanavi synagogue. The richly decorated 17C Aron ha-kodesh is from Ancona, while the baroque pulpit is from Pesaro. The entrance door was carved by Buki Schwarz, an Israeli.

Sidna Omar mosque: A 15C building.

Cardo: Large parts of the Roman cardo were excavated in 1976–85. There are now some interesting sights in the Jewish quarter.

Also worth seeing: *Yeshiva Porat Yosef. Yeshiva Etz Haim* (architect: Moshe Safdie).

Modern Architecture

Buildings in Byzantine, Islamic, Romanesque, Gothic, neoclassical, Oriental and European styles are to be found in Jerusalem. During Ottoman rule in Palestine, the houses were built either in the traditional style of Arab villages or in the urban architectural style of the Mediterranean. There were also Turkish buildings which were frequently designed by German architects. Jerusalem architecture shows at least four striking elements: domes, arches, cantilevered vaults, and the use of stone, which has been compulsory since 1918. Before World War 2, the modern architecture of Jerusalem was the work of European architects such as Clifford Holliday (Foreign Bible Society, 1930; Scottish Church, 1930), A.St.B. Harrison (see Rockefeller Museum), and Erich Mendelsohn (Israel National Bank, 1937; Mount Scopus Medical Centre, 1937). After the State of Israel was founded, the buildings of the *Hebrew University* were erected (Wise lecture hall: Karmi/Meltzer, 1957; Jewish National Library: S. and M.Nadler, S.Pozner, H.Evron, Z.Armoni, A.Yasky, 1960), and so were the *Jerusalem Municipal Theatre* (S.M. Nadler, S.Bixon, 1971), the *Saltiel Community Centre* (M.Goerits, A.Spector, M.Amisar),

Cathedral of St.Jacob, lectern (left), Hurva synagogue (right)

the *Yad Vashem Memorial Shrine* (A.Elhanani, A.Sharon, B.Idelson, 1957—see Museums), the *Israel Museum* (A.Mansfeld/D.Gad,—see Museums), the *Knesset* (J.Klarwein/D.Karmi,—see Also worth seeing), the *Hebrew Union College* (H.Rau, 1963), the *Kennedy Memorial* (D.Reznik), and the *Shrine of the book* (F.Kiesler,—see Israel Museum). The new satellite towns which surround Jerusalem like a defensive belt are not always of great interest. An example is the satellite town of Gilo (overall planning by A.Yasky, Y.Gil and J.Sivan). 10,000 residential units are being built here.

Museums

Armenian Art and History Museum (in the Armenian quarter): Armenian cultic objects, documents, handicrafts.

Giv'at Ha Tahomshet (Sederot Levi Eshkol, Ramat Eshkol): A museum in memory of the Israeli soldiers who fell in the Six-Day War of 1967.

Hakal Shlomo (Chief Rabbinate; Ha-Melekh George): Seat of the Israeli Chief Rabbinate; musem with Jewish cultic objects; Jewish folk art (Sir Isaac and Lady Wolfson Museum).

Heroes' Hall (Migrash ha Russim): Memorial museum (in the Jerusalem State prison) documenting the work of the Jewish underground movement in the period before the State of Israel was founded.

Herzl museum (Mount Herzl): A museum dedicated to the memory of Theodor Herzl, the founder of political Zionism.

Islamic Museum (Temple Mount; W. transept of the El-Aqsa mosque): Islamic art, manuscripts (mainly religious), handwritten editions of the Koran, etc.

Israel Museum (between the Holy Cross monastery and the Hebrew University): This museum complex designed by the architects A.Mansfeld and Dora Gad comprises six

Israel museum, shrine of the book

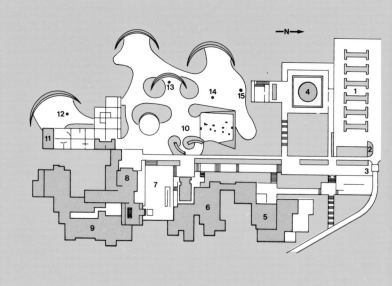

departments: 1. Bezalel museum of
art; 2. Samuel Bronfman museum for
Bible and archaeology; 3. Billy Rose
garden of art; 4. Shrine of the book
(architect: F.Kiesler); 5. D.S. and
J.H. Gottesmann centre for Bible
studies; 6. Department for children
and young people.

The main building is a loosely connected succession of cubes connected
by flat-ceilinged rooms of different
sizes (Departments 1, 2 and 6). One
particular unit is the *Shrine of the
book,*whose gleaming white dome
structure contains the Dead Sea
Scrolls (see Qumran) and other finds
from the caves of the Judean wilder-

ness. To the W. of the main building
is the the *Billy Rose garden of art,*
which Isamo Noguchi, the American-
Japanese landscape gardener and
sculptor, laid out in four and a half
acres of grounds, with sculptures by
Rodin, Maillot, Lipchitz, Picasso,
Smith, Moore, Vasarely, Kadishman,
Calder and Niki de Saint-Phalle. The
Bezalel has outstanding paintings
from all the Western schools, including works by Tintoretto, Bartholo-
meus Bruyn and Flemish and Dutch
artists. The 19&20C painters represented here include Delacroix, Cour-
bet, Cézanne, Gauguin, Redon,
Braque, Picasso and Chagall. Contemporary art (including Israeli
painters) is also well represented:
Joseph Zaritsky, Reuben Rubin,
Egon Schiele and others. The *Samuel
Bronfman Museum* has the terracotta
statue, 1 ft. 3 in. in height, of 'Aphrodite of Carmel' (4/3C BC). The Vit-

torio Veneto synagogue (1701; 23 × 43 ft.;1 23 ft. in height). The Horb synagogue (1735; 26 × 16 ft.), a rare example of a wooden synagogue. Marble railings from Byzantine churches, and the 'Pontius Pilate stone' from Caesarea.

L.A. Mayer Memorial Institute for Islamic Art (2 Rehov HaPalmah): This museum named after the Swiss orientalist Leo Ary Mayer (1895–1959) was donated by Vera Bryce Salomon. *Room 1:* Sassanid and early Islamic art (12C bronze water jug from Nishapur with engraved frieze of animals; 10C ceramic dish with Kufic inscriptions from Iraq or Iran). *Treasure chamber:* Jewellery and metal vessels (collected by Ralph Hararri). Jewellery from Fatimid Egypt and the Persian seljuks. *Room 3:* Mongolian art. Sir David Salomon's collection of clocks is to be seen along with carpets, textiles and musical instruments. The museum has a comprehensive library of Islamic art, and some 17,000 slides and 26,000 photographs of Islamic art and archaeology.

Agricultural museum (13 Heleni Ha-Malka): Agricultural implements, including some from pre-Christian times.

Model of ancient Jerusalem (in the grounds of the Holyland Hotel): A reconstruction of Jerusalem as it was in the 1C AD, on a scale of 1 to 50.

Montefiore windmill (Mishkenot Shaananim): Documents concerning Yemin Moshe, the first Jewish residential quarter outside the old city walls.

Museum of musical instruments (7 Rehov Smolenskin): History of music.

Natural history museum (6 Rehov Mohilever): Birds and mammals. A separate anatomical department.

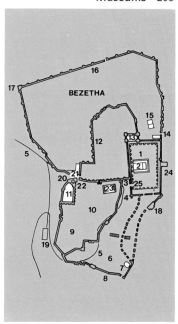

Jerusalem in ancient times 1 Temple Mount **2** Temple **3** Wilson's arch **4** Robinson's arch **5** Aqueduct **6** Lower city **7** Pool of Shiloh **8** First wall **9** High priests' palaces **10** Upper city **11** Palace of Herod **12** Second wall **13** Antonia fortress **14** Israel pool **15** Sheep pools **16** Third wall **17** Psephinus tower **18** Hulda gates **19** Snake pond **20** Phasael tower **21** Mariamne tower **2** Hippicus tower **22** Hasmonaean palace **24** Susa Gate **25** Barclay Gate

Old Yishuv Court Museum (6 Rehov Or Ha-Hayim): This renovated house with a 19C patio has utensils and authentic interiors showing the life of the Jewish old city inhabitants from about 1800 to 1948. The room in which Rabbi Isaak Luria (1534–72) may have been born is on the ground floor. From the 17–20C it was used as a Sephardic house of prayer. The *Or Hayim synagogue* (1742), which was used as an Ashkenazic house of prayer in the 19&20C, is on the upper storey.

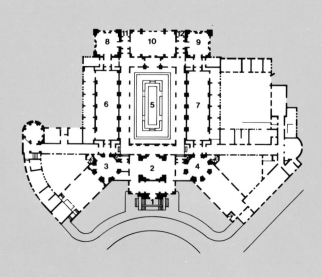

Jerusalem, Rockefeller Museum 1 Entrance
2 Tower room **3** S. octagon **4** N. octagon **5** Courtyard **6** S. gallery **7** N. gallery **8** S. room **9** N. room
10 W. gallery **11** Intermediate room (coin cabinet) **12** Intermediate room (jewel room)

Papal Bible institute (Rehov Paul
Émile Botta): Archaeological museum;
library; archives.

Rockefeller Museum (N. part of
the city, near to Herod Gate): The
Rockefeller Museum (architect: Aus-
ten St.Barbe Harrison), opened in
1938, is among the best archaeological
museums in Israel. The Rockefeller
and Israel Museums have been under
joint administration since 1967.
Southern octagon: Finds from Bet
Shean (q.v.): stele of Pharaoh Sethos
I (1318–1304 BC). The upper part of
the basalt column 8 ft. in height shows
Pharaoh Sethos I bringing gifts to the
Egyptian god Re. Underneath this is a
hieroglyphic inscription reporting the

successful repulsion of an attack on
Beth Shean. Statue of Ramses III
(1196–1166 BC): a basalt statue 5 ft.
high. Basalt flat relief (14C BC): a
basalt upright 2 ft. 11 in. tall. *Southern gallery:* Finds from the palaeolithic, mesolithic, neolithic and
chalcolithic periods and the earlier
and later Bronze Age. Burial objects
and skulls (Galilee skull). Remains of
a man from Mount Carmel. Skeleton
from a crouched burial position.
Bronze" Hittite battleaxe. Cultic
objects and utensils. Mekal stele of
limestone, 11 in. high. *Southern room:*
Islamic wood carvings (wooden
beams and panelling) from the
Ommiad El-Aqsa mosque (8C AD)—
see Jerusalem. *Intermediate room:*
Coin cabinet with Jewish coins from
the 1&2C AD. *Western gallery:* Stuccoes and sculptures from the Hisham
Palace (see Jericho). The windows
and vault sections, with their rich

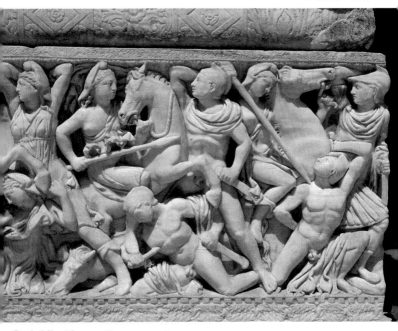

Rockefeller Museum, Roman sarcophagus

ornaments and figures, are from the palace bath-house. *Intermediate room:* Canaanite and Hellenistic gold decorations. Carved elephant's tooth. Finds from Beth Shean and Tell al-Ayyul. *Northern room:* Two Romanesque frieze strips from the S. façade of the Church of the Holy Sepulchre (see Jerusalem). One frieze shows scenes from the life of Jesus, and the other, a marble frieze 12 ft. 4 in. long, shows conventional animal and plant decorations as well as nude humans. Symbols: dragons (Antichrist, heresy, devil); sirens (female lust, temptation); centaur (pride, arrogance and male lust); birds (parsimony); nude men (lechery). *Northern gallery:* Finds from the Iron Age (territory occupied by the Israelites) to the Islamic period. A terracotta 5 in. in height showing a Madonna and Child from the 6C AD (Bet Shean). The image of the suckling mother is paralleled only

by Coptic art in this period, and is influenced by the Egyptian-Hellenistic Isis (Isis suckling Horus). A reconstruction of a central Canaanite burial cave from Jericho, with the original burial objects (*c.* 2000 BC). Anthropomorphic clay sarcophagus (1100 BC). Some clay discs painted with Hebrew letters are the so-called Lakhish epistles from the 6C BC (see Lakhish). Ivory items from the palace of King Ahab of Israel (see Samaria). Bronze statue of Heracles (2C BC). Bust of the Empress Salonina (3C AD). Reconstruction of a Hyksos tomb (*c.* 1800 BC) discovered in Jericho in 1954. *Northern octagon:* Jewish antiquities. Menora depictions from the synagogues (1–6C AD). Mosaic from the synagogue in En Gedi (q.v.). *Courtyard:* Architectural sculptures, sarcophagi, and fragments of buildings from the Roman and Frankish periods, are to be found under the side galleries of the patio. A marble sarcophagus 6 ft. 9.5 in. long depicting Amazons. An (incomplete) sculpture of a woman on the lid. A fight between Amazons and Greeks is shown on the front. This sarcophagus may be from Athens. 10 reliefs by Eric Gill on the patio walls depict the countries and nations which have decisively influenced the culture and history of Palestine.

Schocken Institute for Jewish Research (6 Balfour): Autographs, early printed books, manuscripts.

City museum (in the citadel, next to Jaffa Gate): A municipal historical museum. Documents and excavation finds mostly relating to the grounds of the citadel, which is the former palace of Herod the Great.

Yad Vashem (Har Hazikkaron, near Mount Herzl): A State memorial site to the Jews who met their deaths in the period of Nazi terror, 1933–45.

Also worth seeing: *Biblical zoo* (Kiryaz Zanz): A park in a forest, with animal species that occur in the Bible. *Knesset* (Derekh Ruppin): The Israeli parliament building, designed by the Israeli architects Joseph Klarwein and Dov Karmi, stands on Kiryat Ben Gurion, the Government hill, opposite the Israel Museum. It was opened in August 1966. Entrance hall: A larger-than-life painting of Theodor Herzl (1860–1904), the founder of Zionism. Reception hall: Wall tapestries and floor mosaics by Marc Chagall (1887–1985). The gobelin triptych shows 'Creation' on the right, 'Exodus from Egypt' in the middle, and 'Entry into Jerusalem' on the left. The triptych, which is 15 ft. 9 in. high, 67 ft. long and almost 1100 sq.ft. in area, is one of the largest tapestries produced in recent decades. It was woven in a French gobelin workshop in 80 different shades. Debating hall: The wall (behind the podium) of hewn white stone is a

work by the Israeli sculptor Dani Karavan. Menora: A sculpture, 16 ft. high and 13 ft. wide, of a massive bronze menora, stands opposite the main entrance (the seven-armed candlestick has been the State of Israel's emblem since 1948). The sculpture is by Benno Elkan (1877–1960), an artist born in Dortmund. The menora has 29 reliefs with scenes from Jewish history. From left to right: 1st branch: The prophet Isaiah, surrounded by wild animals, proclaims the word of God. Rabbi Yohanan ben Zakkai leaves the burning city of Jerusalem and founds a new religious centre in Yavne. The Golden Age of the Jews in Spain. The Jews in Babylonian Exile. 2nd branch: Ezra reads the Torah to his people. Job with his friends. Talmud. The Song of Solomon. 3rd branch: David's fight against the Philistines. Jewish refugees landing. Abraham's sacrifice. Middle: 1st branch: Moses raises his arm to bless Israel. The tablets of the law. Rachel mourns for her children. Ruth. The prophet Ezekiel watches the bones being resurrected. The uprising in the Warsaw ghetto. 'Shema Israel' ('Hear, O Israel'). Beginning of the Jewish confession of belief. Halutzim—Jewish settlers in the Promised Land. Right, 1st branch: The prophet Jeremiah weeps at his people's godlessness. The Maccabees. Hassid. Nehemiah rebuilds the walls of devastated Jerusalem. 2nd branch: Rabbi Hillel explains to a stranger the content of the Jewish law in three words: 'Veahavta lere'akha kamokha' ('Thou shalt love thy neighbour as thyself'). Rabbi Hanina teaches the Torah in public despite the ban imposed by the Romans. Kabbala: this is Jewish mysticism based on interpreting the Old Testament in accordance with the numerical value of the Hebrew letters and words. Halakha ('standard, rule'): this legal instruction discusses and interprets questions and rabbinical decisions regarding ethics, law and ritual. 3rd branch: Bar Kochba after

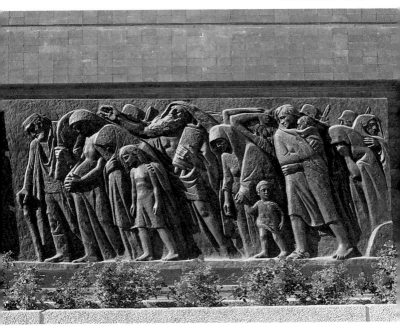

Yad Vashem, memorial tablet: 'The Ghetto Uprising–The Last March'

the failure of the revolt. Messianic hope. Jacob struggling with the angel. On the middle pillar: 'Hear, O Israel'. On the lower two pillars are the words of the prophet Zechariah: 'Not by might, nor by power, but by my spirit, saith the Lord of hosts.' The menora was donated by the British parliament.

Yemin Moshe: Built in 1858, it was the first Jewish quarter outside the ramparts of the old city. Sir Moses Montefiore (1784–1885) ordered the so-called Tura houses (Batei Tura) to be built. They are low, crenellated residential houses which were called Mishkenot Sha'ananim ('dwelling-places of the blissful'). The ruined quarter has been renovated over the past few years. Today the two long, single-storeyed buildings are inhabited mainly by artists. The Jerusalem Music Center is housed in one building. Nearby is the Montefiore windmill, which is today used as a museum (Yad Montefiore) and is dedicated to Montefiore's works and memory.

Western section. Mea Shearim: Meir Ben Isaac Auerbach (1815–78), the 'rabbi of Kalish', came originally from Dobra in Poland. Accompanied by a group of Jewish zealots, he left the protective old city of Jerusalem in 1875 in order to settle outside the city walls in a spot just between Heavenly and Earthly Jerusalem (Yerushalayim shel Mala and Yerushalayim shel Mata). They named this new district Mea Shearim, the hundred gates, because 'Isaac sowed in that land, and received in the same year an hundred-fold' (Genesis 26, 12). Mea Shearim was the second Jewish quarter to be built outside the city walls after Yemin Moshe. Since then, 'Torah, prayer and benificence have not ceased to be practised' (Shmuel Yosef

Agnon) in the narrow, multi-storeyed houses, synagogues and yeshivot (schools where the Talmud is taught). As in the Eastern European shtetl, the inhabitants dress in shtreimel (hat trimmed with fur), peiyot (long locks at the temples), kippah (small cap) and striped caftan. Yiddish is spoken. The inhabitants of Mea Shearim, of whom there are some 3,500, reject the State of Israel. The synagogues, yeshivot, bate midrash (houses of study) and hadarim (religious schools) can be visited with a guide (visitors are asked to dress decently). Items of interest: Yeshiva Talmud Thora Mea Shearim (Rehov Shonei Halakhot), the Beit Yosef synagogue (Rehov Mea Shearim), the Yemenite synagogue and the Cabalists' synagogue (Rehov David). The inscription on the panel above the entrance to a synagogue in a back yard reads: 'This house can be neither sold nor given away until the coming of the True Messiah.'

Russian Compound (Migrash ha-Russim): Russian pilgrims acquired a large piece of land on Jaffa Road in 1860 in order to provide accommodation for the numerous bogomolzy (pilgrims). On this piece of land they built a large complex surrounded by a massive wall and containing the Russian Orthodox cathedral (green dome) and a hospice. A Russian badge bearing the words of the prophet Isaiah 'For Zion's sake will I not hold my peace, and for Jerusalem's sake I will not rest' (Isaiah 62, 1) is to be found at the entrance gate leading into the complex. Near the entrance is an enclosed column, 39 ft. high, which was probably intended for the Herodian temple building but was broken while being transported. This column is popularly known as 'finger of Og', after Og, the giant who was king of the Ammonites and ruled Bashan in the time of Moses (Deuteronomy 3, 11; Joshua 12, 4–5).

St.Polyeuctus church (Rehov Hanev'im): A large Armenian *mosaic* measuring 12 ft. 10 in. × 20 ft. 8 in. was accidentally discovered in 1894 in the cellar of a house N. of Damascus Gate. The main pattern shows an amphora with two peacocks opposite one another. Vine tendrils rise from the amphora, forming animated medallions with drawings of various types of birds. A fruit dish with birds on both sides of it survives from part of an additional mosaic pattern. The Armenian inscription 'In memory and for the soul of all unknown Armenians whose name is known to God alone' is seen in a tabula ansata. This mosaic built in AD 586 is perhaps one of the best in the Holy Land. It doubtless covered the floor of a 6C Armenian burial chapel, because many tombs have been found close to the house. A few years ago the house in Prophet's Street was consecrated and became a church.

YMCA (Rehov HaMelekh David): A building (1933) designed by A.L. Harmon, the architect of the Empire State Building, with an observation tower 150 ft. high. A figure depicting the seraph who appeared to the prophet Isaiah stands on the tower (Isaiah 6, 2). The front bears the Jewish confession of faith in Hebrew 'The Lord our God is one Lord' (Deuteronomy 6, 4), and on the left is Isaiah's prophecy 'And his name shall be called Wonderful, Counsellor, The mighty God, The everlasting Father, The Prince of Peace' (Isaiah 9, 6). An imitation of the 6C Madaba map, showing the map of the Holy Land, is to be seen on the floor of the entrance hall (the original of the map mosaic discovered in 1884 is today in the Jordanian town of Madaba). The *Herbert Clark Museum*, with antiquities from the Middle East ranging from primeval times until the Arab period, is housed in the YMCA next to a room of silence, which serves as a symbol of reconciliation among men, and some prayer rooms.

Bukhara quarter (Rehov HaBukharim): A quarter founded by Turkmenian Jews in the second half of the 19C. They called it Rehovot (Hebrew for 'extension'). 180 Bukhari families lived in Jerusalem in the late 19C, and in 1936 there were over 200. Their synagogue (Rehov HaBukharim) is open to all Oriental Jews, and their houses are decorated with many sumptuous tapestries. They still speak their Jewish Tadjik dialect, a variant of Judaeo-Persian. They wear their picturesque costumes on feast days.

Environs: En Kerem/Ain Karim (4 km. W.): Tradition has it that John the Baptist was born in this town, which is now a suburb of Jerusalem. The scenic beauty of the area has attracted numerous artists. Today En Kerem is a flourishing artists' colony with galleries and restaurants. En Kerem is variously identified with the Old Testament *Beth-haccerem* (En Kerem = vineyard spring', Beth-haccerem = 'house of the vineyard'), a town not specified any further but located in the environs of Jerusalem (Nehemiah 3, 14; Jeremiah 6, 1). *Church of St.John the Baptist:* The Franciscan church of St.John the Baptist was built in 1674 on the ruins of a structure erected by the Crusaders. The Crusader building dates back to a pilgrim named David who, in 1106, located a cave underneath the site where the church was later built, and identified this cave as John the Baptist's birthplace. The so-called Venus Pudica, which was discovered in excavation work carried out in 1942 in what is now the S. chapel, leads one to suppose that a heathen shrine formerly stood where the church now is. *Church of Visitatio Mariae:* The Franciscan church of Visitatio Mariae stands on the opposite side of the valley. It consists of the upper and lower churches, both of which have mainly modern decorations, and there is a crypt by the *Virgin Mary fountain,* where the Virgin Mary and Elizabeth are said to have met. In this crypt, a cave is to be seen in which John the Baptist is reputed to have been kept hidden during King Herod the Great's Massacre of the Innocents. *Russian Laura* (monastery): The Russian convent of Mar Zakariya stands above the church of Visitatio Mariae. Until 1947, the Russian nuns came from Gethsemane garden (see

En Kerem (Jerusalem), Virgin Mary fountain

En Kerem (Jersalem), Visitatio Mariae church, frescos

Jerusalem) at the Feast of the Visitation and met at the Virgin Mary fountain of En Kerem where they brought together the icons of the Virgin Mary and Elizabeth which they had taken with them. *St.John in the Wilderness* (monastery): The Franciscan monastery (1922) of St.John in the Wilderness is some 2 km. from En Kerem. There are traces of 12C monastery buildings. A grotto converted into a chapel is regarded as the place where the Baptist prepared himself in solitude for his mission (St.Luke 1, 80).
Tomb of Rachel (8 m. S.): See under Ramat Rahel.

Jib (Gibeon)

West Bank   p.320□D 7

The Arab village of Jib, where archaeologists believe they have rediscovered the Biblical *Gibeon*, is on a rocky hill 10 km. to the N. of Jerusalem. However, it is a matter of dispute whether this village surrounded by orchards and vineyards can be identified with the Biblical Gibeon. The ancient water supply system of Jib is among the most remarkable in the Holy Land. *Gibeon:* Gibeon—the name means 'hill-place'—was originally inhabited by the Hivites, a Canaanite people (Joshua 11, 19). 'Gibeon was a great city, as one of the royal cities, and ... it was greater than Ai, and all the men thereof were mighty' (Joshua 10, 2). When the Israelites occupied the territory, the Gibeonites concluded a treaty with the Israelites by means of a ruse which enabled them to continue living under the Israelites' (Joshua 9). When the ruse was later discovered, the Gibeonites were not slain but were damned to be 'bondmen, and hewers of wood and drawers of water for the house of my God' (Joshua 9, 23). The Gibeonites who concluded this treaty were not simply the inhabitants of Gibeon the town, but also those of the Canaanite towns of Chephirah, Beeroth and Kirjath-jearim, which formed a federation.

Battle of Gibeon: Under the terms of the treaty, Joshua defended the Gibeonites against five Amorite kings who suffered a severe defeat at Gibeon (Joshua 10, 10). In the Old Testament, this victory is poetically embellished by a text from the lost 'Book of the Upright'; Gibeon attained great fame as the place where the sun stood still during the battle: 'Sun, stand thou still upon Gibeon; and thou, Moon in the valley of Ajalon. And the sun stood still, and the moon stayed, until the people had avenged themselves upon their enemies. Is not this written in the book of Jasher? So the sun stood still in the midst of heaven, and hasted not to go down about a whole day. And there was no day like that before it or after it, that the Lord hearkened unto the voice of a man (Joshua).

Destruction by Saul: King Saul (*c.* 1024–*c.* 1004 BC) attempted to exterminate the Gibeonites despite the treaty between the Israelites and the Gibeonites. After his death, the latter demanded of King David that seven of Saul's descendants should be handed over to them in order to atone for this campaign of destruction. The Gibeonites executed these men in Gibea-Saul (2 Samuel 21, 1–14).

Location of the tabernacle: The tabernacle dating from the Israelites' time in the desert, together with the altar of the burnt offering, stood in the high place of Gibeon, which was a cultic site (1 Chronicles 21, 29; 2 Chronicles 1, 3), and the site is described as 'the great high place' (1 Kings 3, 4). David transferred to Zadok the priest the task of serving at the tabernacle in the high place of Gibeon (1 Chronicles 16, 39). King Solomon sacrificed here

Jib, pool of Gibeon

and, in a dream, asked God for wisdom, which was then granted to him (1 Kings 3, 5 ff.).

Pool of Gibeon and Helkath-hazzurim: During the war between David and Saul's son Ish-botheth, the latter's general Abner met with David's general Joab at the pool of Gibeon. Abner and Joab agreed that twelve men from each of their two sides should stage a battle. 'And they caught every one his fellow by the head, and thrust his sword in his fellow's side; so they fell down together; wherefore that place was called Helkath-Hazzurim (field of the stone knives), which is in Gibeon' (2 Samuel 2, 16). The pool of Gibeon is also mentioned in Jeremiah 41, 12. It is identified with the water reservoir 35 ft. 5 in. deep, which was probably built in the 12/11C BC, still in the Canaanite period. 79 steps lead down to the bottom of this reservoir. Some

3,000 tons of limestone had to be quarried to build it. In the 9/8C, a tunnel nearly 165 ft. long was dug, leading from the bottom of this reservoir to the spring at the foot of the hill. This spring is still in use today, and it is possible to walk along the tunnel.

Stone of Gibeon: It was at the so-called stone of Gibeon that David's general Joab slew Amasa, the general who had failed during a revolt against David (2 Samuel 20, 10).

Jordan

p.318–320□F 1-7

The Jordan, which runs for some 330 km., is the longest river in Israel and the whole of Palestine. It is at the same time the lowest-lying river in the world. It rises from various sources in the Hermon mountains. Nahal Dan, Nahal Hermon and Nahal Senir, the three main source rivers, meet in the northern plain of Hula. Between Lake Hula and the Sea of Galilee, the Jordan descends by some 850 ft. over a distance of only 14 km., and resembles a mountain river. After flowing out of the Sea of Galilee it passes through the deeply cut Jordan rift, enters the Dead Sea and, at its mouth, reaches the lowest-lying depression in the world (1,285 ft. below sea-level). The Yarmuk and the Jabbok are its major tributaries.

The Jordan plain is first mentioned in connection with Abraham and Lot (Genesis 13, 10). The Dead Sea is thought not to have existed at this time. The waters of the Jordan were believed to have healing powers. Thus, the prophet Elisha told Naaman the Aramaean to wash himself seven times in the Jordan in order to cure himself of leprosy (2 Kings 5, 10–14). The four Evangelists all agree that John the Baptist baptized people

Jordan, Christ's baptism, by Jean Colombe ▷

in the Jordan. The synoptics report that Jesus was baptized in the Jordan. This river formed the natural boundary between Canaan and Trans-Jordan in the Biblical period. Today it is the river forming the boundary between Israel and Jordan. Since the Six-Day War of 1967, the Allenby Bridge, 12 km. N. of where the Jordan flows into the Dead Sea, has been the most important of the border crossing-points between Israel and Jordan.

Kafarnaum (Capernaum)/Kefar Nahum

Northern District/Israel   p.318☐F 3

This small, unfortified town, not mentioned in the Old Testament, is on the N. shore of the Sea of Galilee, 4 km. from the Jordan. Probably originally a Herodian foundation, it was not destroyed in the 1&2C AD, because it did not take part in the revolts against Rome.

Kafarnaum (Hebrew: Kefar Nahum: 'village of Nahum') is the place where Jesus preached and worked miracles (St.Mark 1, 21–34: Jesus in the synagogue of Capernaum; healing Simon Peter's mother-in-law; healing the sick and those possessed by devils). This first synagogue no longer survives, but in the 2C or 3C AD a new house of prayer was built beside the first synagogue. The original town stood between the synagogue and the Sea of Galilee. A new district to the E. of the town was built in the mid 4C. One of the dwelling-houses to the S. of the synagogue was venerated by the first Jewish Christians as being the house of Simon Peter. An octagonal sanctuary, of which only a few foundations survive, was built on this site in the mid 5C.

The village fell into disrepair after the Arab conquest. The Franciscans acquired it in 1894. In 1905 the German archaeologists Kohl and Watzinger uncovered the E. and central aisles of the synagogue, which had collapsed in an earthquake. The Franciscans uncovered the rest and also revealed the octagonal church of St.Peter. Excavation work continued after 1968.

Synagogue: Probably built in the mid 3C and rebuilt in the 4C. The façade of this rectangular building has three doors and faces Jerusalem. The synagogue has a N.-S. alignment and is surrounded in the E. by an irregularly formed atrium. The wall was built of hewn blocks of stone, and was decorated with pillars on the outside. Two rows, each of seven columns, divide the basilica into three aisles, which are themselves separated by a stylobate rising 5.5 in. above the floor. Opposite the entrances, a third row of columns runs parallel to the rear wall in the N. There is a Greek inscription on one of the Corinthian columns at the rear: 'Herod son of Monimos, and Justus his son, built this place together with their children.' The monolithic columns stand on a cubical pedestal which connected the plinth and the Attic base. The corner pedestals have half-columns with a section cut out of them, so that they are heart-shaped. This is typical of synagogues in Galilee and Golan. A menora, a shofar and a mahta are engraved on

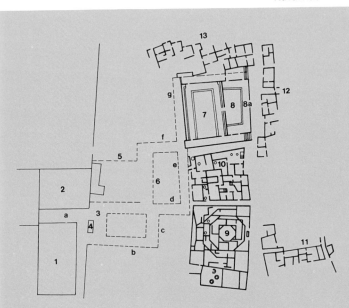

Kafarnaum, ruined site **1** Franciscan monastery **2** Garden **3** Entrance **4** Kiosk **5** Oil press **6** Mill vessels **7** Synagogue **8** Atrium **9** House of Petrus (insula sacra) **10** Dwelling houses (2C BC - 4C AD) **11** Insula III **12** Insula IV **13** Insula V **a** Floor mosaic from Cana **b-g** Architectural fragments from the synagogue (7)

Kafarnaum, Jesus healing the nobleman's son (St.John 4, 46–50), book illustration (1476)

one of the Corinthian capitals. There is a straight architrave above the capitals. The floor is covered with limestone slabs. Stone benches run along the long W. and E. sides. The stairs up to the (women's) gallery were in the W. corner of the N. side. There was a timber roof above the galleries. There is a large semicircular lunette above the *main portal* on the S. façade. On each side of the window in the arch there is another, small window. Two small free-standing columns with Corinthian capitals support a lintel in the form of a gable with a conch in the middle. Twig-like decorations climb above the gable from both sides. There was a double window above the arch, and above the windows was a frieze which had acanthus leaves and lions. The middle of the frieze formed an arch above the double window. Outside the synagogue was a narrow balustrade with stairs leading up to it from its narrow sides. The courtyard, which may have been used as a schoolhouse (bet hamidrash), could be entered from all three sides through several entrances. *Façade:* Four only slightly projecting columns divide the façade into three sections: the middle entrance leads into the middle aisle and the outer entrances into the side aisles. *Architectural sculpture:* The synagogue, which is in the Graeco-Roman style, is richly decorated with architectural sculpture of yellowish limestone. The symbols and iconography are from the Roman-Jewish world: menora, shofar, mahta, hexagrams (Star of David), heptagrams (Star of Solomon), Ark of the Covenant, Roman double eagle (emblem of the Tenth Legion), Roman victor's laurels. The cornices with their acanthus tendrils have a swelling, bulging shape. Palm leaves and sprawling acanthus leaves alternate with one another in covering the moulding; the cornice is formed by egg-and-dart moulding, denticulations and pater-noster. The Corinthian capitals and cornices have isolated medallions on the acanthus tendrils, displaying various motifs: rosettes, hexagrams, heptagrams, pomegranates, grapes, a cantharus, a candlestick and other cultic objects.

House of Simon Peter (S. of the

Kafarnaum, synagogue

synagogue): A 5C octagonal church was built above Simon Peter's house. The central octagon became the sanctuary. On the E. side there was an apse with the baptistery. *Mosaic:* The central mosaic in the sanctuary shows a peacock with a geometrical background and lotus blossoms around the edge. Three entrances (in the W., NW and SW) led into the octagon. Five of the octagon's sides were surrounded by a colonnaded hall. This building was destroyed when the Arabs invaded.

Environs: Khorazin/Khirbet Karazeh (10 km. NW, 890 ft. high, in a wilderness of basalt): The Biblical Chorazin, along with Capernaum and Bethsaida, was among the towns cursed by Christ for their lack of belief (St.Matthew 11, 21 ff.). Shortly after the Bar-Kochba rebellion, the later town was built on the ruins of an earlier settlement. The town grew in the 2C AD along with Jewish settlement in Galilee. The synagogue built in the 2/3C AD was destroyed in the second half of the 4C, along with some other parts of the town, at a time

when Christians were opposing Jews. There are no traces of human settlement from the 8C to the 13C. The Arab village of Karazeh, now abandoned, was built in the 19C.

Synagogue: This building has a N.-S. orientation, with the entrance in the S. wall. The three portals of the synagogue, which was hewn from dark grey basalt and measures 75 x 55 ft., lead into the interior which is divided into three aisles by two rows, each of five columns (the central aisle is 21 ft. 6 in. wide, and the side aisles are each 10 ft. 6 in. in width). There was another row of columns opposite the entrance, parallel to the rear wall. Three entrances, in front of which there is a terrace with two staircases leading up to it, are to be found in the side facing Jerusalem. The stylobates, which project only a little way above the ground, supported rectangular pedestals which are hewn from the same one block of stone as the Attic base of the columns. Above the pedestals there stood monolithic columns, 16 ft. high, with Ionic and Doric capitals, and above these there was an architrave. The three-storeyed *façade*

Kafarnaum, Simon Peter's house

Khorazin (Kafarnaum), synagogue

Khorazin (Kafarnaum), oil press in house near synagogue

Khorazin (Kafarnaum), throne of Moses (now in the Israel Museum, Jerusalem)

measures 54 ft. in height up to the roof. Underneath there are two columns at the corners, and three entrances. A cornice supported by two embellished brackets is to be seen above the lintel of the middle portal. There was an arched window above the cornice. Above, there are three windows decorated with conchs. Two of them have arches, and the third one is topped by a pediment. According to the Israeli archaeologist Yeivin's attempt at reconstruction, there was a menora with seven branches on the lintel of the two side entrances, and to the right and left of this was a wreath with a Heracles loop, and on the other there were probably two menorot, each with seven branches. The friezes of the top storey had various decorations: the head of Medusa, and human figures harvesting and pressing wine-grapes. Pilasters having Attic bases and Corinthian capitals divided the E. wall into five sections. There is a cornice above the columns. *Architectural sculpture:* Medallions showing tendrils with animal protomes; putti with doves; a lion fighting a centaur. *Finds:* Moses' throne, on which Pharisees and scribes used to sit. The artistically constructed basalt seat bears the inscription: 'In good memory of Judan ben Ishmael who built this stoa and this staircase. May he take his place among the righteous' (today this is in the Israel Museum in Jerusalem). Three underground rooms have been uncovered beside the synagogue: a miqveh (ritual immersion bath) measuring $11 \times 7 \times 13$ ft., a cistern 270 sq.ft. in area, and a small storeroom. A necropolis with dolmens has been discovered to the E. and N. of the synagogue. Some 300 dolmens were used as burial chambers in the 6–4 millennia BC.

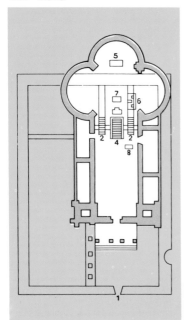

Cana, Franciscan church 1 Church entrance **2** Stairs to choir **3** Hebrew inscription **4** Stairs to crypt **5** Main altar **6** Fountain **7** Old jug

Cana, Marriage at Cana, gospel book

Kana/Kafr Kanna
Northern District/Israel   p.318☐E 4

It was in the Biblical Cana that Jesus performed his first miracle (St.John 2, 1–11), commemorated by two churches. In 1881, the Franciscans built a church above the foundations of a 3/4C synagogue and other church buildings. This was because they considered the miracle to have taken place in Kafr Kanna, a town on the pilgrims' road leading to the Sea of Galilee (modern experts now locate it in the ruined site of Khirbet Kana, 9 km. NW of Kafr Kanna).

Franciscan church (in the centre of the town): When building this church (consecrated in 1883), the Franciscans discovered columns, capitals, friezes and an Aramaic inscription relating to the building's foundation.
There is a curving red dome, visible from afar, above the *crypt*, which is 17 × 16 ft. in area. In the middle of the crypt there is a marble structure adjoined by a piece of living rock. In the crypt are an old cistern, and a reproduction of the 'waterpots of the marriage of Cana', which is intended to call the miracle to the onlooker's mind. The waterpot is surrounded by a railing. At the entrance to the parish church there is an Aramaic inscription concerning the building's foundation. A stone with a cross and a rosette is to be found in the *nave*, above the entrance shortly before the stairs leading to the crypt. The stone bears the following inscription: 'Honourable memory to Yoseph, Tanhum's son, Busta's son, and his sons, who created this mosaic. May it serve as a blessing to them. Amen.' The remains of a geometrical pattern are beside the right-hand inscription. The *altarpiece* displays the Virgin Mary's presence when the miracle was worked.
The *paintings* on the walls of the church are intended to symbolize the holy marriage.

Karmel/Har Karmel
District of Haifa/Israel   p.318□D 3-4

The Carmel ridge, 32 km. long, 8 to 10 km. wide and up to 1,790 ft. in height, gradually rises from the SE to the NW and divides the Yesreel plain from the Sharon plain. Numerous caves with traces of human settlement from the palaeolithic period are to be found on those slopes of Mount Carmel which face the sea.

Mount Carmel (the name means 'orchard') bounded the territory of the tribe of Asher in the N. (Joshua 19, 26). It is not only the name that refers to the abundance of trees on Carmel and to that mountain's fruitfulness; the prophets frequently allude to it (Isaiah 33, 9; 35, 2; Jeremiah 50, 19; Amos 1, 2; Nahum 1, 4; cf. Song of Solomon 7, 5: 'Thine head upon thee is like Carmel'). It was on Mount Carmel, probably on the summit, that the contest between the priests of Baal and the prophet Elijah took place in order to determine whose prayer would be heard by God. Elijah's pupil Elisha was also on Mount Carmel (2 Kings 2, 25; 4, 25). God's judgement upon Carmel (1 Kings 18): In the third year after a famine broke out, God sent the prophet Elijah to King Ahab because Ahab wanted to make the rain fall again. Elijah called on Ahab to order the 450 prophets of Baal to gather on Mount Carmel, called the Israelites thither and arrived, with the people's agreement, at the following arrangment: The idols' prophets, and Elijah as the representative of belief in Yahweh, should each prepare a bull for the sacrifice and lay it on wood, but should not light any fire, but rather each call upon the name of his God. 'The God that answereth by fire, let him be God.' After the prophets had failed to make the wood burn by their rites and evocations, Elijah went up to his sacrificial bull, made some preparations and, at the time of the meal offering, called upon God as follows: 'Lord God of Abraham, Isaac, and of Israel, let it be known this day that thou art God in Israel, and that I am thy servant, and that I have done all these things at thy word. Hear me, O Lord, hear me, that this people may

Cana, Franciscan church (left) and Greek Orthodox church (right)

know that thou art the Lord God, and that thou hast turned their heart back again. Then the fire of the Lord fell, and consumed the burnt sacrifice, and the wood, and the stones, and the dust, and licked up the water that was in the trench. And when all the people saw it, they fell on their faces: and they said, The Lord, he is the God; the Lord, he is the God.' Elijah utilized the people's mood and ordered the prophets of Baal to be led to the brook Kishon and be killed. A little later the rain fell; it had been the third year of no rain.

Environs: Daliyyat HaKarmel (22 km. SE of Haifa): A Druze village (7,400 inhabitants) with a *burial ground* and *cisterns*. At the end of the main street there is a summerhouse by Lawrence Oliphant (1829–97), a pioneer of Zionism.
En Hod/'Ein Hawd (14 km. S. of Haifa): A moshav founded by Algerian immigrants in 1949. Since 1954 it has been an artists' village. Courses in painting and sculpture are held in the community centre. Large exhibition hall and modern amphitheatre.
Isfiya (8 km. SE of Haifa): A district where a Druze settlement became established in the 18C (5,500 inhabitants). In ancient times, the Jewish district of Huseifa was here. It was destroyed by the Byzantines in the 7C. *Synagogue:* A building from the 5/6C AD, excavated in 1933 and oriented towards the E. There is a fine mosaic floor. The *mosaic:* A mosaic strip 3 ft. wide, with various motifs, surrounds the prayer area inside the building. In addition to a depiction of a menora with seven branches and a mahta, a shofar, an etrog and a lulav, the mosaic fragments show remnants of a zodiac, one of the four seasons, a vine ornament with birds, and a tabula ansata with an inscription relating to the synagogue's foundation. This mosaic is at the same stage of iconographical development as those in Bet Alfa, Hammat-Tiberias, Na'aran and Yaphia. The synagogue must have been destroyed before the iconclasts appeared in Palestine, because the mosaic does not show any signs of wilful destruction.
Khirbet Summaq (24.5 km. SE of Haifa): Remains of a *synagogue* from the 3C AD, oriented towards the E. Two lions (?) surrounding a bull's head (or a vase) are to be seen on the door lintel of a side entrance.
Muhraqa (27 km. S. of Haifa): A small *Carmelite monastery* stands at a height of 1,580 ft. on a S. spur of Mount Carmel. Tradition has it that HarMuhraqa is the mountain where the prophet Elijah built his altar in his dispute with the priests of Baal. In 1886, Italian monks built a small *monastery* on the ruins of an older church below the spring of Bir el-Mansur. A statue of the prophet Elijah in plain white stone stands in front of the church.
Nahal ha-Ma'arot/Wadi el-Mughara/Valley of the Tombs (2 km. from the Haifa-Tel Aviv road): These caves formerly inhabited by huntsmen were discovered in 1928 and uncovered by English and American archaeologists in 1929–34 and 1967–8. Items testifying to an independent culture (sickle blades, fishing spears of flint, etc.) were found above the strata of palaeolithic tools. This culture extended as far as Egypt in the S. and up to the middle of Lebanon in the N. It is called Natufium after Wadi en-Natuf, the place where it was first discovered. The Natufis of Mount Carmel lived by hunting. *Finds:* Small stone implements, sickles. The Natufis buried their dead below the dwelling rooms of the living: collective burial in a completely squatting position and individual burial with the knees raised. Burial objects: dentalia (decorative chains made of shells; necklaces of teeth drilled through, gazelles' toe-bones, etc.). The finds are today in the Rockefeller Museum in Jerusalem and in

Kefar Bar'am, synagogue, entrance ▷

the Bet-Pinhas Museum in Haifa. Caves: 1. Me'arat Tannur/Arabic: Mughurat et-Tabun/Cave of the stove; 2. Me'arat ha-Gedi/Arabic: Mughurat es-Sukhul/Cave of the kid; 3. Me'arat HaGamal/Cave of the camel. The 'woman of Tabun' was discovered in the 1st cave. This is a skeleton from the natufium (*c.* 18,000 BC), adorned with a headband of stone beads.

Kefar Bar'am
Northern District/Israel   p.318☐E 2

A kibbutz in Upper Galilee. The abandoned Maronite village of *Bir'am* is located nearby, on the site of a Jewish settlement from the Roman-Byzantine period, 2 km. from the Israel-Lebanon border. Judaeo-Christian architectural fragments are to be found along with remnants from the Jewish period (two synagogues).

Synagogue (3C): This was built in the Syrian-Hellenistic period and is among the oldest buildings in Galilee. It is the only ruined synagogue to

have survived up to the height of the second storey, and as such it provides information on the synagogues in Capernaum/Kefar Nahum and Khorazim. This building measuring 50×66 ft. is almost undamaged up to the second storey.

The *entrance* faces towards Jerusalem. Outside the entrance there was a colonnaded hall 17 ft. 7 in. wide, supported by eight columns. The columns have Attic bases, and the capitals have egg-and-dart moulding, a cavetto and an abacus. The entrance consists of a middle gate 8 ft. 8 in. high and 4 ft. 8 in. wide, and two smaller side entrances. Above the middle entrance is a lintel with a tabula ansata. Above this is a convex frieze showing an amphora with tendrils growing out of it. The cornice is above the frieze. There was a bracket in the form of a double volute to the right and left of the door lintel. The convex frieze above the lintel of the W. side entrance has a rope pattern, while that at the E. side entrance has laurel leaves. Above each lintel of the side entrances there is a rectangular window, crowned by a gable with a

Kefar Bar'am, synagogue

decorated relief and embellished by vine tendrils on both sides. A Hebrew inscription reading 'Built by El'azar bar Yudan' is to be found on the window-sill of the E. window.

Inside the building, two lengthwise rows of columns and one transverse row divide the rectangular hall structure into three aisles. The floor was laid with simple tiles.

Maronite church (on a small hill outside the synagogue): Abandoned 19C village church. The lintel above the door, which is walled up today, shows a cosmic cross with the four points of the compass, depicted by small rosettes. Two quadrupeds on both sides, then two cosmic crosses with five crosses and two tabulations. A large stone with a cosmic cross inside a circle with the four points of the compass in the form of dots is to be found S. of the lintel and at the same level.

Environs: Jish (11 km. S.): This village, which is mainly inhabited today by Maronites and Melchites, was the largest settlement (Gush Halav/Giscala) in Upper Galilee in the first few centuries AD. First mentioned (Josephus Flavius) in the Jewish Wars (AD 66–73), in which the Zealot leader Johanan ben Levi of Giscala defended the last Galilean fortification in AD 68. It surrendered to Vespasian. After the destruction of the Second Temple, Jews lived in Jish until the 13C. The remains of two *synagogues* survive. One of these stood at the town's highest point, and the other was outside the town, on the W. slope of Nahal Gush Halav, 2 km. away. *Maronite church:* A plain church (1886). A painted stone, with a rose window with crosses opposite one another in the middle of it, is to be seen on one wall of this church with its nave and two aisles. The rosette is bordered by a frieze, with a bird on the left and a lamb in front of a cross on the right. The church stands on the foundations of a 3/4C synagogue.

Sasa (7 km. SW): A kibbutz founded by the Ha-Shomer-HaZa'ir movement in 1949, at a height of 2,935 ft. on the top of a hill. The old Sasa is mentioned in the Talmud as a town of

Kefar Bar'am, Maronite church

wise people. *Museum:* Local finds are exhibited in an attractive little old building: columns, architectural fragments from the Roman period, Arab and Druze cultural implements. *Synagogue:* Main entrance in the E., with two doorposts; parts of the interior have stylobates; there is a heart-shaped column. This synagogue has a W. orientation and its position makes it unique in Galilee. The remains of an Ottoman fortress belonging to Emir Daher el-'Amr.

Sifsufa (11 km. SE): A moshav founded in 1949. In the *mosque* is a stone 5 ft. long, and in its middle is a garland whose lower ends form a Heracles knot. A bull's head (?) is depicted on both sides. The stone is probably from a synagogue destroyed

in the Byzantine period. There are some dolmens SW of the village.

Khan el-Ahmar
West Bank/Israel   p.320□E 7

Behind the settlement of Ma'ale Adummin on the road from Jerusalem to Jericho, lie the ruins of the monastery of S. Euthymius, who founded a centre for Christian settlers at the beginning of the 5C. There are the remains of a *mosaic floor* in the Church. In the northernmost section of the Church lie the graves of the saint and his followers. Other buildings include a refectory, sacristy, store room and defence tower.

Lachisch/Lakhish
Southern District/Israel   p.320□C 8

What is now the ruined hill of Tel Lakhish, lying some 25 km. W. of Hebron, was inhabited from the fourth millennium BC onwards (chalcolithic caves).

History: Lakhish, the Biblical *Lachish,* developed into an urban

settlement in the first half of the third millennium BC. In *c.* 1700 BC, the Hyksos fortified it and built a defensive ditch around it. In *c.* 1500, the Canaanites, after driving out the Hyksos, built a temple standing on this defensive ditch, which had been filled in. Thus the temple is referred to as a ditch-type temple. There is a cultic room measuring 33×16 ft., with seating benches along the walls; a cultic site with an altar in front of the S. wall; the temple was twice converted and enlarged, and continued functioning until 1200 BC. A well shaft 130 ft. deep in the NE of the town dates from the Canaanite period. The Canaanite city state of Lachish came under Egyptian hegemony during the reign of Thutmosis III (1490–1436). Lachish was first mentioned by name in the Amarna period, when it rebelled against Egyptian rule and was destroyed on several occasions. *Conquest by Joshua:* Joshua 10, 3–35 relates how Lachish was conquered by the Israelites. Jarmuth, the king of Lachish, had joined the coalition of

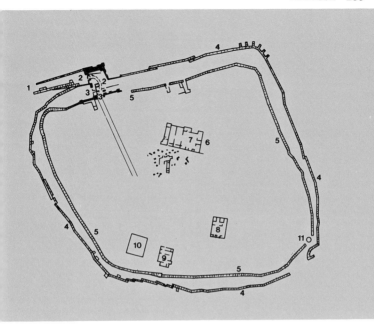

Lachish 1 Ramp **2** Double gate **3** Place where Lachish epistles were found **4** Outer rampart **5** Inner rampart **6** Israelite palace **7** Persian palace **8** Sun temple **9** Hellenistic structure **10** Tunnel shaft **11** Canaanite fountain

five Canaanite kings who wished to prevent the Israelite invasion. They were annihilated in the battle of Gibeon, and Joshua ordered the king of Lachish and the other kings to be beheaded, and Jarmuth's head to be hung on a tree. The Israelites conquered the town of Lachish after only a two-day siege, and Joshua 'slew it with the edge of the sword, and all the souls that were therein'. This town is said to have been captured after only two days. At first sight this appears unlikely as it occupies a strong hilltop site, but excavations have shown that Lachish was not fortified at the time when the Israelites took possession of the territory (c. 1220

BC). Joshua assigned the devastated town to the tribe of Judah (Joshua 15, 39), and over the following centuries it lay in ruins.

Second largest city in Judah: King Rehoboam (926–910 BC), Solomon's son and successor, ordered Lachish to be expanded into a fortress (2 Chronicles 11, 9), and the double *surrounding wall* is also thought to have been his work: its outer wall, of cut stone and dry brick, is 13 ft. thick; the inner wall 20 ft. One of Rehoboam's successors—Abijah or Asa—enlarged Lachish in sumptuous style, and he built a fortified palace on a plateau. The enormous gate—90 ft. wide, with a multi-storeyed outer wall some 23 ft. wide—was used until it was destroyed by Sennacherib of Assur in 701 BC. Excavations have shown that Lachish, after being expanded in c. 900, was not only the strongest fortress in SW Judah, but was also larger

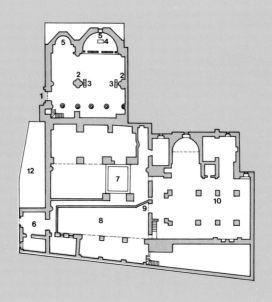

Lod/Lydda, church of St.George (1-5)/El-Khadr mosque (6-12) 1 Church entrance 2 Pillar of Crusader church 3 Stairs to crypt 4 Altar 5 Crusader apses 6 Entrance to mosque 7 Purification fountain 8 Courtyard 9 Gate to mosque 10 Column with Greek inscription 11 Byzantine apse 12 Shops

than Jerusalem, the capital. Lachish was the most important city in the kingdom after Jerusalem. When a revolt against king Amaziah broke out in Jerusalem, Amaziah fled to Lachish 'but they sent after him to Lachish, and slew him there' (2 Kings 14, 19; 773 BC). The city was destroyed by an earthquake in *c.* 760 (cf. Amos 1, 1) and subsequently partly rebuilt.
Destruction: King Sennacherib of Assur captured Lachish during his Palestine campaign in 701 BC, set up his headquarters here, and used the city as a military base for his campaign which led to Jerusalem (2 Kings 18, 14–17). The great import-

ance which the Assyrians attached to conquering Lachish can be deduced from the reliefs in Sennacherib's palace in Nineveh. After Sennacherib withdrew, the town was rebuilt, except for the palace. When Nebuchadnezzar II the Chaldean devastated the kingdom of Judah in 587 BC, Lachish and Azekah were the two towns which withstood the enemy the longest (Jeremiah 34, 7).

Lod/Lydda
Central District/Israel   p.320□C 7

First mentioned in the lists relating to the cities of Thutmosis III (1465 BC). Peopled by the tribe of Benjamin at the time of the Israelite occupation (1 Chronicles 8, 12). Devastated by the Assyrians in the 8C BC, rebuilt in the 5C, and settled in the 4C BC by the

Jisr Jindas (Lod), detail of Baibars' bridge

Greeks who called it *Lydda*. Captured by the Hasmonaeans in 143 BC (1 Maccabees 11, 34). Under Rabbi Eliezer ben Hyrkanus it was the seat of a small sanhedrin and a large yeshiva. Judah ben Pazi, Joshua ben Levi, Hanina bar Hama, Elieza bar Kappara and others all taught here. It was a Christian community in the early Christian period. Peter healed the palsied and bedridden Aeneas in Lod (The Acts 9, 32–35).

Lod was captured by the Romans in 67 BC and became the capital of a toparchy. It was called *Diospolis* under Emperor Septimius Severus (193–211), and as *Georgopolis* ('town of George') under the Byzantines, because legend has it that St.George was born here.

Lod became a Christian town in the Constantine period. The tomb of St.George has been displayed in the church of St.George since the 5C.

Lod was the capital of the province of Filistin after Lod was captured by the Arabs and until the town of Ramla was built. Richard the Lionheart rebuilt the town which had been destroyed by Abd el-Malik, the Ommiad. Jews settled in Lod after it had been recaptured by Saladin in 1191. Estori ha-Parhi, a Jewish traveller, found a Jewish community here in the 14C.

The last Jews left the town in 1921 after some unrest. It was recaptured by the Israeli army on 10 July 1948.

Church of St.George/El-Khadr mosque: A church rebuilt under Kyrillos the patriarch in 1870. The double sanctuary occupies the site of the 6C Byzantine church of St.George and of the 12C Crusader church which replaced it.

The middle apse, the N. apsidiole, and a Gothic arch, all date from the Crusader church. Contrary to tradition, these structures are not oriented towards the E. but towards the N. The arch in the nave rests on a compound pillar and buttresses an engaged arch which rests on a half-column. The cornice is formed by the moulding of the capitals with their foliate ornament. The cornice projects so far from the wall that there is a gallery above it and the clerestory has a window set in an arch. Between the two Frankish columns in front of the iconostasis, two staircases lead down to the crypt containing St.George's sarcophagus. The Saint is depicted on the cover, which was restored in 1871.

Environs: Batn el-Yamani (7 km. E.): *Roman family tomb* with ten niches in the walls, which are decorated with frescos and stucco reliefs.
Jisr Jindas/Baibars bridge (2 km. N.): Stone bridge with pointed arches which the Mameluke sultan Baibars ordered to be built on Roman foundations in 1273 from the stone of a Crusader church. Two lions (Baibars's heraldic animal), which are copies of Lion Gate in the E. wall of Jerusalem, frame an Arab inscription: 'In the

name of dear and gracious Allah. May his blessing rest upon our master Mohammed, his family and all his companions. Our master, who is the great Sultan el Malek ed-Dahar Ruh ed-Din Baibars, ordered that this holy bridge be built ... May God glorify their victories and grant them his grace. Under the leadership of the humble servant Abd ed-Din Ali es-Sawak, who is striving for God's grace, which may God grant to him, his father and his mother. In the year 671.'

Modi'im (Modi'in; 10 km. SE): *Tombs of the Maccabees*: Mattathias and his sons Eleasar, Johanan, Jonathan and Judas. Simon, the fifth son, built the tomb for his father and his brothers. Schoolchildren and youth groups meet at the tombs during the Hanukka festival. Every year, the Maccabean sports organization lights a torch in Modi'im, and relay runners bear it to the presidential palace in Jerusalem. *Midya* is 2 km. E.; the Maccabees are said to have been born in this small Arab village.

Modi'im (Lod), Maccabees tomb

Mamshit/Kurnub
Southern District/Israel   p.322☐D 10

What is today the ruined town of Mamshit (Arabic: Kurnub) in the Negev, 6 km. SE of Dimona, was formerly called Mampsis, being the only town of the Nabataeans to be completely surrounded by a wall. It was founded in the 1C AD, and fell into disrepair after being captured by the Arabs in 634. *Dwelling houses* survive from the Nabataean period (they have two or more storeys, and fortress-like outer walls with window slits). The largest dwelling house is building XII, which is the palace and is 21,500 sq.ft. in area. *Finds:* 10,500 silver coins (tetradrachmas from AD 100–200) in a bronze jug 3 ft. 4 in. tall. Doorposts with ornamented Nabataean capitals (bull's head, human head, amphora); round columns with capitals stood on a surviving L-shaped stylobate. Each stone was subdivided into four panels by incisions. A door lintel shows the sculpture of a male deity. *Frescos:* The wall paintings are in strips measuring 1 ft. 4 in. and 3 ft. 11 in. in width. The lower section has rosettes and patterns resembling tapestries, as well as symbolic mythological patterns (the Greek inscription reads 'agathos daimon'—'a good spirit'). The other section displays Eros and Psyche sitting on a couch. Eros has angels' wings, and Psyche has a butterfly's wings. Both are clearly identified by Greek inscriptions.

Eastern church (martyrium): This mid-4C Byzantine building (martyr-

Mamshit, entrance to building

ium), with a nave and two aisles, was the main church in Mamshit.

Mar Saba
West Bank   p.320□E 8

The monastery of Mar Saba, founded in AD 483 by St.Sabas (439–532), resembles a bulwark on the flanks of foothills on the slope of Kidron Valley, 12 km. E. of Bethlehem. At the age of eighteen, this monk born in Cappadocia joined the monks Euthymius and Theoctistus, separated from them in AD 474, and founded today's monastery at the 'winter brook of Siloam' in AD 483, after first living there for five years as a hermit. The following persons lived here in the 7&8C: John of Damascus (AD 675–749) who was a father of the church, Cosmas and Stephen Melodes who composed songs, and Stephen Thaumaturgus. The monastery was destroyed by the Arabs in AD 614. It flourished during the Crusades, but was then devastated by the Mamelukes. Between 1800 and 1850, the monastery was strongly fortified against the Abediye bedouins. After being destroyed by an earthquake in 1834, it was completely rebuilt in 1840 with the Tsar's assistance.

Monastery: Since 1929, a hexagonal structure has stood in the courtyard on the site of a much smaller aedicule where the tomb of St.Sabas lay from AD 532 until the Crusades. The *chapel of St.Nicholas*, where St.Saba founded the first church, is to the NW of this building. The royal doors of the *iconostasis*, and the five *icons* above the painted strip on the opposite wall, date from the 15C. Reliquaries containing the skulls of the monks martyred by the Persians and Arabs are in a small side room opposite the entrance door. To the E. of the courtyard is the *Theotokos church*, which is dedicated to the Annunciation, with the *tomb of St.Sabas*, whose body was

brought back in 1965 from Venice, where it had been taken by the Crusaders. It rests in a glass coffin lined with green silk.
In front of a cave there is a small chapel where St.John of Damascus wrote many of his works. His tomb disappeared during the Crusades.

Masada/Mezada
Southern District/Israel   p.322□E 9

Masada (Hebrew: 'rock fortress') is a fortress in the Judean wilderness on an isolated mountain plateau rising to 1,440 ft. above the W. shore of the Dead Sea. Herod the Great enlarged the fortress, which was founded by the Maccabees, into a refuge in 36–30 BC. In AD 73, Masada was the last stronghold of the Jewish Zealots and of the Essenes in the battle against Rome. Nearly all the information concerning Masada derives from the historical work 'The Jewish War' by the Jewish historian Josephus Flavius, but is largely confirmed by the excavations. The surviving ruins (including buildings from the later period: synagogue, Byzantine chapel) are an impressive document to the quality of Herodian architecture.

History: In the neolithic period, men lived in the almost inaccessible caves of the rocky massif; the flat summit, some 2,000 ft. long and up to 750 ft. wide, was also inhabited from *c.* 1000–700 BC. Jonathan Maccabaeus, the Jewish high priest who, from 160–143 BC, led the Jews against Graeco-Syrian foreign rule, ordered a castle to be built on the inaccessible plateau. The castle was enlarged by Johanan Hyrkanus I (134–104 BC), the high priest and de facto king.
When Herod was besieged in Jerusalem in AD 40 during his battles with the Parthians and Hasmonaeans, he broke out of the palace at night and

Mar Saba, church, iconostasis ▷

fled with his family to the fortress at Masada, which was not yet in Parthian hands. He left the women there, giving them sufficient food and the protection of his younger brother Joseph with a garrison of 800 men, while he travelled on to Petra to obtain help. While Herod was being appointed king of the Jews in Rome (in opposition to Antigonos, who was anti-Roman and supported the Parthians), Antigonos, with Parthian assistance, began to besiege Masada, but was unable to capture the impregnable rock fortress. Herod returned from Rome, defeated the besiegers and liberated his relatives. After this victory he had practically the whole of Idumaea under his control. In 36–30, he enlarged Masada into the largest fortress in his country (according to Josephus Flavius, Masada was intended as a bulwark against Cleopatra, the queen of Egypt, who was demanding from Mark Antony, the Roman triumvir, that Herod be deposed).

After Herod's death, Masada became a Roman garrison but it was captured by the Jews in AD 66, at the outset of the Jewish War, and continued to hold out against the Romans in the year 70, after the end of the war. In the autumn of 72, the Roman governor Flavius Silva advanced against Masada with the X legion and some auxiliary troops, and began to besiege the fortress which was garrisoned by 1,000 men, women, old people and children. It was not possible to starve the besieged population into submission, because they had enormous supplies of food. The Romans therefore built a ramp made of stone, wood and sand up one side of the fortress. This ramp is still clearly visible. They built a tower on it and kept the castle under fire from there, while at the same time they advanced against the wall with a battering ram. When the besieged inhabitants realized their hopeless position, they decided not to surrender but to go to their deaths together by killing one another. By drawing lots, it was decided who of the 960 men, women and children should die first and who should do the killing. When nearly everyone had been killed, the survivors believed 'that they would be wronging those

Mar Saba, monastery

murdered if they survived the latter even for a short time. So they quickly threw all their possessions on to a heap and set it on fire. They then drew lots and selected ten men who were to be the murderers of all the others. Then each one lay down beside his family members, the women and children, who already lay dead, embraced them with their arms, and readily proffered their throats to the men who had to carry out the unhappy task ... But the lonely last man surveyed the crowd of those who lay dead to see whether anyone had remained alive after all the killing and still required his hand. When he realized that they were all dead he lit fires at several points in the palace. Then, having gathered his strength, he thrust the sword right through his body and collapsed beside his family' (Josephus Flavius).

According to the writings of Josephus Flavius, only two women and five children, who had hidden in a cistern, survived this mass suicide.

Fortress wall: A casemate wall 4,300 ft. long surrounds the rocky plateau of Masada. It is a double wall, and partition walls divide the intervening space into chambers which served as accommodation for the soldiers, storerooms and arsenals. The wall around Masada contains ten such chambers.

Herod's terraced palace: This palace outside the walls was not discovered until 1955. The upper terrace contains the living rooms and a semi-circular balcony, while the middle terrace is formed by a colonnaded pavilion. The hall in the lower terrace contains well-preserved wall paintings.

Dwelling house: The nine apartments in the dwelling house—each with two small rooms and a large courtyard—were probably used by officers as accommodation. A considerable number of Israelite silver coins were discovered in one of the apartments.

Main palace: Herod's main palace extends over an area of almost 43,100 sq.ft., with residential and domestic wings, sections for storage and ad-

Masada, Byzantine gate on W. side

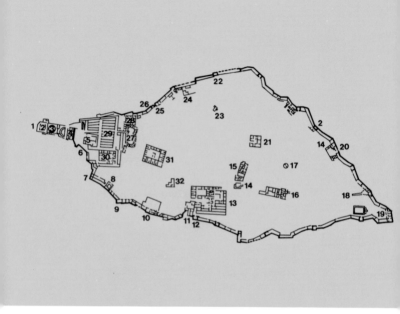

ministration, and the splendid *throne room*.

Megiddo

Northern District/Israel   p.318☐D 4

The settlement hill of Tel Megiddo (Tell el-Mutesellim) to the NE of Kibbutz Megiddo is on the SW edge of the Yesreel plain in the N. of Israel. Its 20 strata of settlement from the neolithic period (7500–4500 BC) until Persian times were uncovered in three series of excavation (1903–5; 1925–39; 1960–7).
Megiddo was devastated so many times that the Revelation of St.John (Revelation 16, 16) describes this city state, under the name of 'Harmagedon' (Har Megiddo = 'Mountain of Megiddo'), as the embodiment of the last battle between good and evil.

Masada 1-4 Palace on terraces (N. palace) **2** Lower terrace **3** Middle terrace **4** Upper terrace **5** Thermal baths **6** Water gate (N. gate) **7** Tower **8** Synagogue **9** Casemate wall **10** Gate **11** W. gate **12** Tower **13** Main palace (W. palace) **14** Miqveh **15** Small palace **16** Small palace **17** Columbarium **18** Cistern **19** S. bastion **20** Cistern gate (S. gate) **21** Small palace **22** Tower **23** Dwelling houses from Byzantine period **24** Zealots' dwelling houses **25** Snake-path gate (E. gate) **26** Casemate wall **27** Quarry **28** Building **29** Magazine **30** Administrative building **31** Byzantine building **32** 5C Byzantine church

Megiddo is mentioned in the annals of Thutmosis III (1490–1436 BC), in the Amarna epistles (14C BC) and in the clay tablets of Taanach.
The oldest layer (stratum XX) was immediately next to the rock: chalcolithic village with rectangular and apsidal buildings of air-dried brick (earlier than 3500 BC). Stratum XIX (3300–3000 BC): Small shrine 40 × 13 ft. in area, with an altar; a town wall of air-dried brick from the older Bronze Age I period. Strata XVIII–XVI

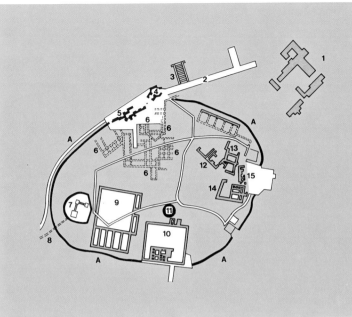

(older Bronze Age II period, 3000–1950 BC): town wall 26 ft. long (surviving up to a height of 13 ft.), and above it was a structure of air-dried brick, no longer present today. High-level shrine, with an altar for burnt offerings. Older Bronze Age III period: three temples, each of 30 × 45 ft., and there is an altar opposite the entrances in the long wall. Stratum XV (1950–1850 BC): Canaanite town which Thutmosis destroyed in 1468 after a six-month siege at Wadi Layyun. Megiddo was rebuilt shortly thereafter. Stratum VIII (late Bronze Age II, 1350–1130 BC): This was one of Megiddo's heydays, when it was an Egyptian provincial capital and a meeting place between the Egyptian south and the Mesopotamian north. There are over 200 sumptuously carved ivory works in the temple treasury. They are among the most magnificent examples of Canaanite

Megiddo 1 Museum **2** Ramp **3** Outer N. gate (Solomon's town gate) **4** Canaanite town gate (15C BC) **5** Canaanite town gate (18C BC) **6** Excavations **7** Water supply system **8** Underground water tunnel **9** Stables **10** Solomon's palace **11** Grain silo **12** Double temple **13** Astarte temple (E. temple) **14** Chariot driver's palace (10C BC) **15** Chalcolithic temple

art. Megiddo was destroyed in c. 1130 BC. Stratum VI (1150–1100): Captured by the Israelites. Stratum IV B (time of Solomon up until the Palestine campaign of Pharaoh Shishak): A new palace, a citadel, an imposing casemate wall, and the pincer-shaped portal, were built under king Solomon (965–928 BC).

Under king Ahab (871–852 BC), the palace was enlarged and the stables built. The casemate wall was replaced by a simple stretch of wall reinforced by projections. The water installations begun under Solomon were completed. After being captured by

Megiddo, Astarte temple

Megiddo, underground water duct

Tiglat-Pileser III (745–727 BC), the town was rebuilt in *c.* 733 BC, with the old town walls being used. Megiddo became the capital of the Assyrian province of Galilee. It was last settled between 450 and 350 BC.

Temple of Astarte (Stratum XV): A temple rebuilt in *c.* 1900 BC and facing the rising sun. It consists of a portico, a main room and a sanctuary, and their rear wall adjoins the altar area. Steps at the sides lead to the square altar. Further cultic rooms, probably consisting of a double temple for a pair of gods, adjoin this at an acute angle towards the W.

Stables: Rectangular, pillared, three-aisled buildings ranged in parallel. They housed some 480 horses. Limestone feeding troughs (today in the Rockefeller Museum in Jerusalem) stand between two upright stone

Megiddo, Solomon's gate

posts for tying up the horses, with openings for the ropes (the posts also did duty as roof supports).

Underground tunnel (9C): The old steps leading to the tunnel can be seen to the right of today's ascent. There is a spiral staircase round the edge. The shaft leads 80 ft. down into the earth, and after its inclination has altered by 40 it passes into a tunnel with pointed roof which runs for 230 ft. In times of war, this tunnel enabled the inhabitants to gain unimpeded access to the springs outside the town.

Town gates (10C): Three gates from three different phases of building are to be found immediately above the N. town gate. They are: a gate of Solomon; a late Bronze Age stone gate (16C BC); and a city gate from the 18C BC. The town gate of Solomon is a so-called 'pincer' gate. Three rectangular

chambers, which open towards the passage and were probably intended for guards, are on both sides of the passage which runs from N. to S.

Palace: A palace (75 × 70 ft.) which is grouped around a rectangular courtyard and stands on the S. side of the town wall from the 2nd half of the 12C (stratum VI). Small cell-like rooms are arranged along the surrounding walls, whereas the larger room, the room of state, is inside the building.

Casemate wall with palace: Parts of a casemate wall from Solomon's times are found to the E. of the palace. The palace (90 × 70 ft.) was also used as an observation post.

Silo (S. side): A large round grain silo dug into the earth and dating from the time of king Jeroboam II (787–747

BC). The inner walls have seven staircases. Behind them there are two
enormous complexes erected by king
Ahab above Solomon's palace
buildings.

Meron

Northern District/Israel   p.318☐E 3

The settlement of Meron lies to the
N. of Wadi Meron, on the E. spurs of
HarMeron (Jebel Jarmuq). According
to Josephus Flavius, the settlement
was fortified. Along with Khirbet
Shema and Jish (Gush Halav/Gis-
cala), Meron was known in the Talmudic period for its olive oil. After
the end of the Second Jewish War (AD
135), numerous learned men (Simeon
bar Yohai, Hillel) settled in Meron.
Meron became a place of pilgrimage
in the Middle Ages, owing to its
significance in the development of
Isaak Luria's mysticism.

Excavations: These were carried out
between 1971 and 1975. Finds in the
Lower Town: a beautifully carved
doorpost; a miqveh from the 1C AD;
barrel-makers' workshop. Finds in
the patricians' houses: massive door
lintel on two monolithic doorposts;
storage room. No remains of any town
fortifications have been discovered.

Synagogue: The style of this synagogue is that of the early form of 3/4C
synagogues. It has two parallel longitudinal rows of columns, and one
transverse row. It is decidedly a long
structure, in contrast to the almost
square ground plans of other synagogues in Galilee. The front side which
faces S., along with the main entrance
and the W. side entrance, is all that
survives of the structure which
measured 89 × 45 ft. The W. wall was
hewn from the living rock. Only a few
remnants of the N. wall still survive.
Two rows, each of eight columns,

Meron, synagogue ▷

divide the building into three aisles. The columns did not stand on the stylobate direct, but on a pedestal. The two rear corner columns were heart-shaped. There was an architrave above the columns, and above that again was a cornice. The interior had coloured lime-wash. The posts of the main portal are monoliths 10 ft. high, and were decorated with fascias and Lesbian cymatium.

A roughcast channel leads from the rock above the synagogue to a small basin in the W. wall. On the W. side, outside the main façade, there was a bench hewn into the stone.

Mausoleum of Simeon bar Yohai: A building with white domes, a small square courtyard, and an enormous room with limestone roughcasting. Two domed tombs mark the point where Simeon bar Yohai and his son Eleasar are said to be buried. Part of Simeon's cenotaph projects into the adjoining prayer room behind an iron grille. The pilgrims lay their petitions on the wooden board above. Stone stairs lead from the courtyard to the roof, on which there are two massive

copper pipe-shaped containers to the left and right of the domes above the tombs. On the day of the feast (Lag ba-Omer), these containers serve as enormous torches.

Environs: Khirbet Shema (1 km. S.): Khirbet Shema was originally part of the neighbouring Meron settlement. In the 3C AD, Khirbet Shema became an independent Jewish village, inhabited until the Arab period. *Synagogue:* A wide building 36 × 49 ft. in area. Its longitudinal axis runs from W. to E. Two rows, each of four columns, divide it into three aisles. None of the eight capitals, or of the four column bases in the S. row, are alike. A menora is depicted on the N. door lintel, and an eagle with extended wings is seen on the S. doorpost of the W. entrance. A passage beside the W. entrance leads from the prayer room into a small room with the remains of wall frescos. Mausoleum of Shammai Ha-Zaken (50 BC–AD 30). The tomb of one of the Sanhedrin leaders has been venerated here since the Middle Ages. The stone tomb is probably from the 3/5C

Meron, mausoleum of Simeon bar Yohai

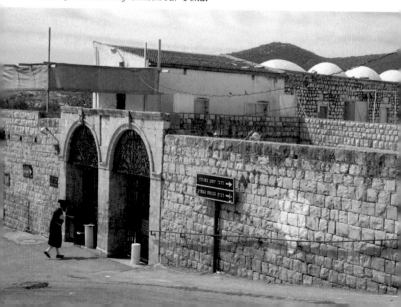

AD. There are recesses for two tombs in the floor. The bones were buried lower down.

Mizpa
West Bank   p.320☐D 7

Tell en-Nasbe, the Biblical Mizpah (?), is 12 km. N. of Jerusalem. Today it is an excavation site where finds have been made dating as far back as the early Bronze Age.

Mizpa ('observation post') is a place in the area peopled by the tribe of Benjamin (Joshua 18, 26) and lies on the road to Sichem. It was the political and religious centre of the Israelites during the time of the Judges. The tribes gathered in Mizpah to hold consultations regarding the disgraceful deeds of the men of Gibeah, and decided to annihilate the tribe of Benjamin (consultation in Mizpah: Judges 20, 1–10). Samuel, the judge and prophet, gathered the Israelites here to pronounce judgement (1 Samuel 7, 5–7/11/16). He assembled the people here and had Saul elected king (1 Samuel 10, 17 ff.). King Asa of Judah enlarged Mizpah into a border fortress opposing the northern kingdom of Israel (1 Kings 15, 22). At the time of the prophet Hosea (c. 750–722 BC), Mizpah was part of Israel (Hosea 5, 1). After the kingdom of Judah was destroyed by the Chaldees in 587 BC, Mizpah became the seat of Gedaliah the governor (2 Kings 25, 23; Jeremiah 40, 6), who was also murdered here (Jeremiah 41, 3). After the Jews returned from Babylonian Exile, Mizpah was settled again (Nehemiah 3, 19) and was the seat of a Jewish district (Nehemiah 3, 7). In the Maccabean period, Mizpah, which was situated 'opposite Jerusalem, since Mizpah was traditionally a place of prayer for Israel', became the place where the rebellion against the Seleucids began (petitionary divine service in Mizpah: 1 Maccabees 3, 46–60).

Montfort
Northern District/Israel   p.318☐D 2

The ruined castle of Montfort, the *Starkenburg* castle of the Teutonic Order, is on the S. bank of the Wadi Qurein, on a narrow rocky spur projecting westwards 590 ft. above the river. A 12C French family of Crusaders built the fortress and sold it to Hermann von Salza in 1228. The Teutonic Order enlarged the castle, and until 1271 it remained the Order's main fortress, archive and treasury. Captured by Baibars in 1271. Montfort was excavated in 1926.

Montfort Castle (Qal'at el-Qurein): The castle is protected by a deep ditch and a tall keep. The remnants include an external wall, a square hall (4,300 sq.ft.) whose pointed arches are borne by octagonal columns, the foundation walls of a chapel (26 × 75 ft.) divided into a nave and two aisles by two rows of four octagonal columns each, and an external tower.

Montfort, castle

Nahariya/Nahariyya
Northern District/Israel   p.318☐D 2

Nahariya was founded in 1934 as an agricultural settlement by German Jews and is today one of the most beautiful lakeside resorts in Israel. It was the first Jewish settlement in West Galilee.

Excavations: During the course of construction work in 1947, an East-facing *Canaanite temple* was discovered here dating from the 15C BC. This was built in three parts and measures 20 × 35 ft. It is thought to have been dedicated to the fertility goddess Ashera. *Finds:* Cult objects and votive offerings together with two metal figurines; a jug whose neck takes the form of a seated monkey; and a stone mould measuring 9 x 3 in. which was used for the casting of bronze figurines of Ashera.

Municipal Museum (Town Hall): This contains exhibits ranging from early historical times to the Byzantine period. These include glass objects found in tombs dating from the 3C BC; wine vessels made of copper (1750–1550 BC); a stone statue, 9 inches high, of the horned goddess Ashera-Yam (Astarte of the sea); and an anthropomorphic stone coffin, 3 ft. 6 in. high, which is fashioned in the Phoenician style with some Egyptian accretions and dates from the 5C BC.

Environs: Evron (1 km. S.): Kibbutz (with 580 inhabitants) established in 1945 by immigrants from Germany, Poland and Romania. The remains of a palaeolithic settlement and a 5C church have been discovered in its grounds. *Church:* This was excavated in 1951 and measures 60 × 33 ft. It has a nave and two aisles, which are separated by two rows each containing five columns. The N. side contains a baptistery and two other rooms. Various stages of construction can be identified. The original building dates from around AD 415 and had an atrium which was flanked by a portico made up of two rows, each containing three columns. A narthex was added in 490. The portico contains mosaics with geometrical patterns. 13 Greek inscriptions, and one Syrian one, are inlaid in the pavement.

Gesher HaZiv (5 km. NE.): Kibbutz (with 500 inhabitants) established in 1949 by immigrants from America. It has a small archaeological *museum* of local history.

Hanita (15 km. NE.): Kibbutz established in 1938 (100 inhabitants). In 1952 its members installed a small *museum* of local history in a house which had previously been built in the Arab style on the ruins of a Byzantine church. The exhibition includes prehistoric flint blades, reconstructions of Copper Age objects, clay vessels, bronze objects, figurines dating from the middle and late Bronze Age, mosaics, and a model of the Byzantine church. There is also a natural history collection.

Rosh HaNiqra (12 km. N.): Armies and caravans have been travelling across this white chalk mountain for more than 5,000 years. During his march towards Egypt, Alexander the Great had steps cut into the cliff here which have since become known as the 'Scala Tyriorum' (in Latin), or 'Sulam Tsur' in Hebrew (meaning "the ladder of Tyros').

Nazareth, panorama

Shave Ziyyon (3 km. S.): A moshav (with 600 inhabitants) established by German immigrants in 1938. *Worth seeing:* a *Byzantine church* (with a narthex) dating from the 5C, which was excavated in 1955–7. The floor mosaic is dated to the year AD 486 by a Greek inscription. The basilica has an inner narthex, a nave and two aisles. The N. aisle is decorated with a circular floor mosaic containing the symbol of the Cross. Other crosses can be seen beneath the altar niches in the nave.

Tel Akhziv (6 km. N.): The old town of Akhziv was settled from the middle Bronze Age until the time of the Crusaders. The old name has been retained by the Arab fishing village of ez-Zib. In Byzantine times, Akhziv was a fortified town and had a Jewish community. it was called 'Casal Lamberti' by the Crusaders. *Excavations:* Two *cemeteries* were uncovered in

1941–4 to the E. and S. of Akhziv. The easterly cemetery of er-Ras contains Bronze Age tombs and numerous rock tombs from the Iron Age, while Phoenician burial chambers were discovered in the cemetery to the S. (Buqbaq).

Nazareth/Nazerat/En-Nasira
Northern District/Israel   p.318□E 4

Nazareth, which was settled by the Bronze Age (there are tombs ranging from the Iron Age to the Hasmonaeans) and was first mentioned in the New Testament (Matthew 2,23; 4,13; 21,11) as a 'town on the mountain', lies on the southern edge of the Galilean mountains, above the Plain of Yesreel, in a slight declivity which is bounded to the South by Jebel esh-Sheikh. Together with Jerusalem and

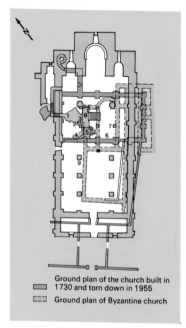

Ground plan of the church built in 1730 and torn down in 1955

Ground plan of Byzantine church

Nazareth, Annunciation church 1 Annunciation grotto **2** Virgin Mary column **3** Archangel Gabriel column **4** Martyrion **5** Konon mosaic **6** Christ monogram **7** Font **8** Angel chapel **9** Pillar of Crusader church

in the first half of the first millennium BC as storerooms. Above these stood small houses.

During the Jewish War, when Galilee was the focus of Jewish resistance to Rome, Nazareth was destroyed (in 67 BC), together with Japhia (Yafa). The priestly family of the Haspises, or Pise, lived here in the 2C AD, and it remained a predominantly Jewish town until Byzantine times. There is no record of any Christians in Nazareth, except for Konon, who died a martyr's death here in the 3C AD. The pilgrim from Piacenza, visiting the town in 570 BC, noted a synagogue and the Church of the Assumption.

Nazareth was captured by the Arabs after their victory over the Byzantines at Yarmuk (20 August 636). In 1099, the Crusaders made it the administrative capital of Galilee, under the rule of Tancred. Tancred built a new church above the cave of the Annunciation and transferred the see of Skythopolis (Beisan) to Nazareth. The town was captured by Saladin in 1187, after his victory at Hittim, was regained by the Christians in 1230 and 1250, and destroyed, together with all its churches and monasteries, by the Mameluke Sultan in 1254. The Franciscans were granted permission to return to Nazareth in the 16C. In 1630, after eight months' work, they finished building a new church immediately above the remains of the old Church of the Annunciation.

The centre of the old town is inhabited by Arabs (here predominantly Christian), while the modern suburb of Illit houses the relatively recent Jewish immigrants from Eastern Europe and North Africa. In 1970, Nazareth possessed 24 churches and monasteries of all denominations, serving 7,000 Greek Catholics (Melchites), 5,000 Greek Orthodox, 3,000 Catholics, 600 Maronites, and a few Protestants and Anglicans. The old town lies in a hollow surrounded by high mountains, while the new town stretches to the N. and E. of Tel Hanuk.

Bethlehem, it is for Christians one of the three most important towns in the Holy Land, for Joseph and Mary lived here and it was the home of Jesus (Luke 4,16) until His baptism by John the Baptist (Mark 1,9).

The town was at first of no importance in pre-Christian times, but its fortunes later improved rapidly due to its proximity to the Via Maris, a trade route between Damascus and Egypt. Excavations since 1956 have shown that the hill on which stand the Church of the Annunciation and the Church of St.Joseph has been settled since the time of the Patriarchs (the second millennium BC). Graves have been discovered dating from the second millennium BC, together with subterranean caves which were used

'Ave Maria' by Julius Schnorr of Carolsfeld

Church of the Annunciation, mosaic

Church of the Annunciation: In 356, the Empress Helena built a small church, based on the design of the 3C synagogue church, on top of the foundations of an earlier and smaller church in the very centre of the Jewish community and just above the spot where the angel Gabriel is supposed to have told Mary of the coming birth of Jesus (Luke 1, 26–38). Excavations beneath the mosaic have revealed the existence of an earlier mosaic incorporating a cross (the use of the cross in floor decorations was banned under the Emperor Theodosius, who ruled from AD 408–50). A third church was built on the site in the 12C, in the Burgundian style, by Tancred, the Crusader king. This basilica was oriented to the E. (250 × 100 ft.), with a nave and two aisles which ended in three apses. Its floor was 4 ft. beneath the level of the present church. The roof was supported by grey granite columns which had been taken from the pagan buildings of antiquity. The grotto was situated beneath the N. aisle, extending not quite as far as the bay beneath the vault in the nave. The grotto's rocky ceiling rose some 10 ft. into the basilica itself, and had the rough shape of a trapezium cut into the surrounding rock. This church was destroyed by an earthquake in 1170, before its building was completed. It was rebuilt, only to be destroyed again in 1263 by the Mameluke Sultan Baibars, who did however spare the grotto. Later, the Franciscans, who had a presence in Nazareth from 1620, won permission from the Emir Fakhr ed-Din to build a small brick chapel. They rapidly built a new church, the fourth, during the reign of the Emir Daher el-'Amr; this one,

◁ Church of the Annunciation, W. façade

however, faced North-South instead of East-West, which is why the choir now stands above the grotto. It originally measured 73 × 40 ft, and was divided by two rows of columns into a nave and two aisles. Then, in 1877, it was extended to the S. with the addition of a vaulted roof. A staircase with 16 steps led down from the nave to the rectangular Chapel of the Archangel, from which another two steps led down to the grotto (23 × 20 × 10 ft). The floor of the present church stands 11 ft. above the grotto. The bare rocky ceiling of the grotto disappeared in 1730. On each side of the nave a flight of twelve steps was built, leading upwards; at the same time, the rock was covered with marble slabs, and the flat surface thus made available was used for the choir and the high altar. Fifth church: this was built by the Italian architect Giovanni Muzio to the design of Antonio Barluzzi. It was consecrated by Cardinal Garrone on 23 March 1969. This modern church was built on top of the lower layers of the stone which had composed the old Crusader church, 25 ft. above the original floor. The church complex, which measures 227 × 97 ft. and is crowned by a dome 123 ft. high, is entered opposite the gabled W. façade, which is flanked by a tower on each side.

W. façade: This is decorated with a large relief and describes the theme of the Incarnation. The themes depicted and inscriptions show the evangelists and the Old Testament prophecies which have referred to Christ (Genesis 3, 15; Isaiah 7, 14). At the top on the left is the Archangel Gabriel, with the Virgin Mary top right, and beneath them the four apostles Matthew, Mark, Luke and John together with their respective symbols of man, lion, bull, and eagle.

◁ Church of the Annunciation, mosaic in choir

The Latin inscription says that 'The angel of the Lord told Mary that the Word has become flesh and lived in us'.

S. façade: The S. door depicts scenes from the life of the Virgin Mary by the American artist Frederick Shrady. The two side doors, decorated by the Italian G. Mucchi, depict the theme of the Song of Songs, here applied to the Virgin Mary. On the S. façade can be read the prayer 'Salve Regina' by the 11C Bishop Aimar of Le Puy (?): 'Hail, Queen, mother of mercy, who art our life, our bliss, and our hope, hail. We, Eve's banished children call to you, we sigh to you, we lament and weep in this vale of tears. You who art our intercessor, turn your merciful eyes towards us, and, after this misery, show us Jesus, the blessed fruit of your womb, kind, sweet, gentle Virgin Mary.' The statue of the Virgin above the door is by the Italian F. Verocco.

The modern church consists of two parts, an upper and a lower church, which are linked by two large spiral staircases to the N. of the two towers in the W. façade.

Upper church: The floor of the upper church is of inlaid marble and depicts the Virgin Mary and the Marian Councils; it is by the Italian Adriano Alessandrini. The scenes are linked by the coats-of-arms of the Popes who expounded the doctrine. The large mosaic (1,600 sq. ft.) on the wall of the choir is by the Sicilian artist Salvatore Fiume and shows Christ in the red robes of the high priest, inviting mankind with outstretched arms to come to Him. Next to Christ is the doubting St.Peter, with the enthroned Virgin in the background. In the foreground on the right are shown the Popes Benedict XV, Pius XI, Pius XII, John XXIII, and Paul VI. On either side of the Holy Spirit, represented as a dove, and the all-seeing eye runs the creed which has been recognized since the second Council

Gabriel church ▷

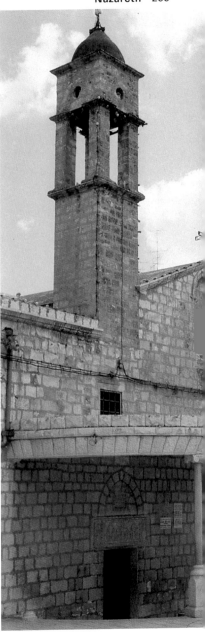

of Constantinople in 381: 'I believe in one holy, Catholic and apostolic Church'. The windows in the choir are by Max Ingrand. The high altar was made by the Belgian C. Colruyt in the form of a small boat on which the tabernacle stands. On each side of the choir there are depictions of the hierarchical and charismatic Church, as well as the Palestinian Church and its most important holy places. The E. side of the sanctuary (50 ft. deep and 63 ft. high) has a mosaic by the Italian artist d'Angelo which represents the Church and the doctrine of the Council in the light of the dogmatic 'Lumen gentium' constitution. In front of this stands a white altar. Roughly in the middle of the upper church, which has a nave and two aisles, there is an octagonal aperture through which the grotto can be seen beneath. Above this aperture is the bright dome, 190 ft. high, which resembles the open bloom of a lily pointing downwards. The lily has long been a symbol of the Virgin Mary. There are 16 petals, each petal having two curved surfaces, and on each of these 32 surfaces the letter M appears (standing for Mary, who gave birth to the Messiah). In Jewish numerology, the number 32 is interpreted as the sum of the 22 letters of the Hebrew alphabet and the Ten Commandments issued by God at the creation of the world. The stained glass windows in the octagonal drum are by Yoki Aerbischler from Switzerland. The 14 ceramic frescos decorating the eight concrete pillars which support the tower are by the Italian Angelo Biancini and depict the Stations of the Cross. The chapel to the right of the choir has frescos by the Spaniard Ubeda Pineiro which depict the teachers and martyrs of the Western and Eastern Churches, and Paul VI embracing the Greek Orthodox Patriarch Athenagoras on the Mount of Olives in 1964. To the left of the choir is the chapel for the saints

◁ *Gabriel church, gilded iconostasis*

of the Franciscan Order. Its wall paintings, by the Italian artist Barluzzi, represent the visions of St.Francis, with a Jerusalem Cross (the symbol of the Francisans and the Crusaders) in the background.

Baptistery: This is almost octagonal and stands on the right side of a courtyard off the N. gate. It contains bronzes by Bernhard Hartmann and ceramics by Irma Rochelle. The large window is by Max Ingrand.

Grotto of the Annunciation: The grotto (23 ft. long, 20 ft. wide, and 10 ft. high) has been roofed over with a copper baldacchino by the Belgian C.Colruyt. The strip of copper is decorated with the scene of the Annunciation and the words :'Hail Mary, full of grace. He became man from the Virigin Mary through the Holy Spirit'. The restored Byzantine apse contains an altar with the inscription 'Verbum hic caro factum est', meaning that 'The Word here became flesh'. Two pillars to the right of the passageway to the Chapel of the Archangel are thought to have belonged to the old synagogue church. The N. pillar is called 'Mary's pillar' and the one to the S. 'the pillar of the Archangel Gabriel'. According to tradition, they mark the exact places where the Archangel and the Virgin stood at the Annunciation. The adjoining *Chapel of the Archangel* contains the altar of Gabriel at its W. end and, at the E. end, the altar of Joachim.

Church of the Archangel Gabriel (over Mary's spring): Also known as the house of Mary (in Arabic, Bait Mariam). The church measures 74 × 48 ft. and is aligned E.-W. On each side there are 17 steps leading up 8 ft. 8 in. to the terrace formed by the courtyard at the back of the church. The N. end of the church, which is approached by 6 steps leading up from the aisle, is built next to rising ground, so that the vault above it is itself at ground level. The Crusaders built their church on the site of an earlier Byzantine church which, according to the Gaulish Bishop Arnulf, had been erected around 670 over Mary's spring and 'in the middle of the town'. This Frankish church was destroyed in 1263. In 1741, permission was given to Greek Orthodox monks to build the present church (which is also called in Greek the Church of the Annunciation) on top of the foundations of its medieval predecessor.

The spring bubbles up at the other end, in a small apse situated in a cave (57 ft. deep) inside the hill.

Church of St.Joseph: This comprises a nave and two aisles and was built around 1914 in such a way as to incorporate the remains of a medieval church with three apses. The latter had in turn been built on top of the foundations of a still earlier Byzantine church whose baptistery can still be seen. The font, which has been carved into the rock in the crypt, measures 7 × 7 ft. and is decorated with a white mosaic which has been carefully inlaid around the black basalt.

Next to the font are some roughly hewn steps leading down to a narrow passage which curves through 180 and then widens into an underground *cave* 7 ft. high. The cave has been recently enlarged to an area of 34 × 17 ft. It contains a row of bell-shaped silos, dating from pre-Byzantine times, which have been sunk a bit below the ground. Since the 17C this cave has been designated as Joseph's workshop. Excavation work has shown it to have been inhabited as early as the Stone Age, so that it forms part of the very oldest, underground, settlement here. A flattened stone is supposed to have been used by the Holy Family as the table on which they took their meals.

Monastery of Our Lady's Terror/ Notre-Dame de l'Effroi (in the S. part of the town): It was here that the Virgin Mary was supposed to have frozen with terror when she saw her son being taken to the top of the hill by the furious Nazarenes (Luke 4, 29).

Mensa Christi: This is a block of stone, 12 ft. long by 10 ft. wide, which is set in the middle of a small domed church standing on a slope which forms part of the chain of hills rising to the W. It was here that the risen Christ sat down for the last time to eat supper with His disciples. The chapel on the L. was built over this block of stone around 1800, and the present church was constructed to incorporate it in 1860–1.

Environs: Ginnegar (10 km. SW.): Kibbutz founded in 1922 at the bottom of Balfour wood, on the site of the Talmudic Nagengar.

Mal'ul (12 km. W.): This is the Nahalal of the Bible and the Mahalul of Roman and Byzantine times. It was once the site of the Qasr ez-Zir Mausoleum (the name means Palace of Zir), which was a square building incorporating an interior and four kokhim. Two churches have been preserved: the *Greek Orthodox church*, which faces W. and comprises a single nave (1884); and the *Greek Catholic Church*, which is a basilica with a nave and two aisles and a dome in the centre supported by four columns. Ornamented doors. There are looping patterns on the N. door.

Mash-had (5 km. NE): According to the Arab and Jewish traditions, this was the birthplace (called Gath-hepher in the Bible) of the Prophet Jonah, known in Arabic as Nabi Yunis (2 Kings 14, 25). In the Middle Ages it drew both Arab and Jewish pilgrims. The *Nabi Yunis Mosque* includes a small courtyard, with a small room to the left containing the cenotaph, and a corridor to the right leading to the mosque itself, which incorporates a mihrab. The chapel has two domes. To the right of the main door there is a Greek inscription measuring 2 ft. 11 in.×1 ft. 2 in. It is likely that a synagogue stood on this site which was then converted into this mosque.

Shefar'am/**Shafa 'Amr** (18 km. NW): After the destruction of Judaea, this was the seat of the Supreme Council. Fortified by the Crusaders.

Museum of the Franciscans, capital from Crusader period

In 1761 its name was changed from Daher el-'Amr to Shafa 'Amr. Jews lived here up until the 19C; in fact, the last one left in 1920. The town is a holy place for Christians, Arabs, and Druze, and contains Roman and Byzantine tombs, Byzantine cisterns, and two fortresses, As-Saraya and Al-Burji, which were erected by Daher el-'Amr on top of earlier structures built by the Crusaders.

Yafa/Yafit en Nasra (2 km. SW.): This was referred to in the Old Testament (Joshua 19, 12) as Japhia, a town belonging to the tribe of Zebulun. It was conquered by Titus in AD 57. *Synagogue:* This dates from the 3C and was excavated by M.L. Sukenik in 1950. It measures 50 x 63 ft. and was in the form of a basilica with a nave and two aisles, separated from each other by two rows of columns, each row containing five columns with Attic bases. Unlike the other synagogues in Galilee, it is aligned E.-W. and faces E. The S. stylobate is decorated with mosaics. These are composed of 13 different colours and end in a section of geometrical patterns. In the middle of the mosaic,

parts of two medallions have been preserved. These belonged to a circle of 12 such medallions which enclosed another, smaller circle in its centre. This was probably a representation of the zodiac rather than the 12 tribes. Some depictions of animals have been preserved, notably a tiger, a dolphin, and an eagle with outstretched wings standing over the head of the Medusa. (This mosaic is now in Jerusalem).

Zippori/Saffouriya (5 km. NW): The ruins of the former capital of the Roman province of Galilee are situated here, on the summit of a hill 807 ft. high and 1 km. to the N. It was known to the Hasmonaeans as Sephoris and was probably used as their administrative centre of Galilee. After the Roman conquest, it was made the Roman administrative capital by Gabinius. During the first Jewish rebellion, the town was surrendered to Vespasian by its inhabitants. Hadrian replaced its Jewish administration with a Gentile one and renamed the town Diocaesarea. It has had a resident bishop since the 5C. The Crusaders held the town, which they called Le Sephorie, and

Zippori (Nazareth), fortress

built a fortress here. There are only some remains left of the Crusader castle of Saphoriesinos, and these have been incorporated into the SW wall of the Turkish fortress (on whose second floor the Turks built a school in 1880). This present *fortress* was built by Daher el-'Amr in 1745 on the site of the Crusader castle. Some portions of the medieval walls have been preserved. *St.Anne's Church:* The Crusaders built a church on this site on top of the ruins of a Byzantine church dating from the 3C. (Sephoris is supposed to be the birthplace of St.Anne, the mother of the Virgin Mary). The Crusader church was destroyed by Baibars. The modern church dates from 1860, and has been discovered to contain a mosaic originally belonging to the Byzantine church. The E. part of the modern church incorporates medieval building materials. *Synagogue:* When the Crusader church was excavated in 1909, the remains of a mosaic containing a commemorative inscription were discovered in front of the outer N. wall. The inscription is set in a circle; parts of the upper four lines are preserved, but the bottom two are missing. It reads: 'To the memory of Rabbi Judas (bar Tan) chum (ba)r Buta, who endowed this tablet. Blessings be on him.' It is now housed in the Crusader church. *Roman theatre:* This was excavated in 1931 and had space for 4,000/5,000 spectators (diameter 123 ft.).

Negev
Southern District/Israel   p.322–4□C/D 12/13

The Negev ('Negeb' in the Bible; the word means 'arid country') is the name given to the region of steppe and desert between Gaza and the Juda mountain range to the N. and the desert area of the Sinai peninsula to the S., extending to Elat on the Red Sea. It constitutes some 60 per cent of the total area of the state of Israel, and

its modern capital and administrative centre is Beer Sheva. Although its scanty rainfall and lack of water-holes during the Israelite period meant that only a few areas could be cultivated, there is evidence, from the numerous hills with ruins and from the prehistoric sites which have been excavated, that in pre-Israelite times, when it belonged to Egypt's sphere of influence, the Negev was more densely settled.

After the Israelites had conquered the Negev (Joshua 11, 16), its N. region formed the S. part of the tribal lands of the tribe of Judah, as well as becoming the home of the tribe of Simeon. The Negev was also settled by the Cenites (to the S. of the Judah desert) and Caleb (to the S. of Hebron. Note also the raids mounted by David into the Negev: I Samuel 27, 10 and 30, 14).

The climate and fauna of the Negev were feared (Isaiah 21, 1 mentions 'whirlwinds', and Isaiah 30, 6 speaks of 'the land of trouble and anguish, from whence come the young and old lion, the viper and fiery flying serpent').

Further details may be found under Beer Sheva, Arad, Avdat, Mamshit, and Shivta.

Netanya
Central District/Israel   p.320□C 5

Netanya was founded in 1928 among the sand dunes of the Plain of Sharon and named after the American philanthropist Nathan Strauss (1848–1931). Towards the end of the 1930s a diamond-cutting industry was established by immigrants from Antwerp and South Africa.

Archaeological finds: There are numerous finds along the coast dating from the Mesolithic and Neolithic periods. A *Roman aqueduct* has been uncovered in the centre of the town. Numerous *rock tombs* in the countryside around N. which date from Byzantine and Roman times.

Khirbet Hannuna: The remains of a Roman-Byzantine settlement, including a mosaic and a winepress.

Also worth seeing: *Khirbet Umm Khalid* (to the S.), which contains the remains of a Crusader castle. *Gan Hamelekh* (Park of the King): Modern amphitheatre facing the sea. *Institute of the blind* (Rehov HaHistradrut 4): This includes the adjacent *museum* and a large *library* with works in braille.

Environs: Avihayil (4 km. N.): Moshav established in 1932 which includes the *Bet HaGedudim Museum* (Jewish Legion Museum). This displays documents, letters, and photographs concerning the Wingate Brigade.

Hadera (18 km. N.): This town, which today numbers 37,000 inhabitants, was founded in 1890 by immigrants from Lithuania. Its quarters include Nahli'el, which was founded by immigrants from the Yemen in 1912; Newe Hayyim (1936), which is named after the Zionist Hayyim Arlosoroff; Giv'at Olga (1950), which was named after the wife of Yehoshua Hamkin; and Hetzi Bah (1914). *Worth seeing:* Graves dating from the period of the Second Temple; a Roman mausoleum; remains of a Byzantine building and the remains of an Arab khan, now the community centre for the synagogue, which has been restored.

Kefar Glickson (35 km. NE): Kibbutz founded in 1939 and built in the Bauhaus style. The dining-room and common rooms are on the hill, and form the nucleus of the kibbutz, around which the houses and children's creches spread out along the slope. The cowsheds, storage rooms, and workshops are laid out geometrically in the plain.

Tulkarm (16 km. E.): Arab town between the Samarian Hills and the Plain of Sharon. It has been settled since Roman times. *Worth seeing:* Graves dating from the early Bronze Age and *Roman buildings* including cisterns, wine presses, a mausoleum, and a stone altar with a Greek inscription.

Rock formation in S. Negev

Peqi'in/Buqei'a

Northern District/Israel   p.318□E 3

There is said to have been a Jewish community here continuously since the destruction of the Second Temple. The Arabs arrived here around AD 1000, then came the Crusaders, and finally the Druze settled here in the 18C.

Synagogue: The new synagogue was built in 1873 and is said by local

tradition to have been constructed with stones from the Second Temple. It contains two engraved stone tablets (to the left of the entrance, in the wall). One shows a seven-armed candelabra, or menora, which has been chiselled out of the stone, with Lulav and Etrog on the left and Shofar and Mahta on the right. The other depicts the Ark of the Covenant (also chiselled out of the stone).

Cave of Simeon bar Yohai (on the slope of the mountain, above the spring): It is here that Simeon and his son are supposed to have found refuge while fleeing from the Romans.

Greek Orthodox Church: This is a simple 19C village church, containing, however, many beautiful *icons*.

Environs: Fassuta (13 km. NW): Arab Christian settlement. *Greek Orthodox church:* The modern church was built in the present century and looks something like a fortress.
Gadin (13 km. NW): The ruins of the *Crusader castle of Judin* (Qal'at Jiddin) are situated near the Yehi'am

Peqi'in, synagogue, menora

Gadin (Peqi'in), Crusader castle

kibbutz (founded in 1946). It occupied two storeys, with an inner courtyard on each storey, each enclosed by strong walls. In the 18C it was converted into a manor house by Daher el-'Amr.

Hosen/Suhmata (3 km. NW): 5 km. to the SE can be seen a 6C *church* which has been excavated. It measures 74 ft. 4 in. × 41 ft. 4 in. and comprises a nave and two aisles, which are separated from each other by two rows of four columns each. The various mosaics depict: geometrical patterns (in the narthex, which measures 8 ft. 4 in. × 33 ft.); garlands (in the N. part of the nave); circles and ellipses, with an amphora between two peacocks which are facing each other (in the N. aisle); and, between the columns, birds and pomegranates.

Mi'ilya (11 km. NW): This Arab village stands on the ruins of Chastiau dou Rei, of which two corner towers have been preserved. *Church:* This is built of stone blocks and has a fortified appearance. The doors are decorated with crosses which are surrounded by circles. There are some

beautiful 19C icons. On the way out, two capitals with acanthus leaves can be seen by the door; these belonged to the Byzantine church which originally occupied this site.

(Er)Rama (6 km. SE): Arab settlement at the foot of HarHa'ari hill. The *Franciscan church* (1959) has a Latin cross made of oblong ashlars above the entrance.

Petah Tiqvah
Central District/Israel   p.320□C 6

This was the first agricultural settlement in what is now Israel and was founded in 1878 by devout Jews from Jerusalem, who called it 'the gate of hope'.

Beit Yad LaBanim Museum (Rehov Arlozoroff 30): Well-documented collection illuminating the history of the town; archaeological discoveries from the area; and contemporary art.

Environs: Maqam an-Nabi Yehya

Peqi'in, cave of Simeon bar Yohai

(3 km. SE): This is a free-standing rectangular building, made of ashlars, which dates from the 2/3C AD and is the only Roman building in Palestine to have retained its roof. The portico has angular corner pillars flanking two Corinthian columns which support the architrave. There are two burial chambers. The Muslims built a mihrab into the S. wall (or qibla), and used this place to venerate St.John the Baptist (Nabi Yahya).

Mirabel (7 km. E.): To the E. of the Afeq Pass can be seen the ruins of the *Crusader castle of Mirabel* (Migdal Afeq), dating from the 12C, whose NW tower, central courtyard, and keep have survived. Next to the doorway leading into the keep there is a Byzantine stone with a Greek inscription (commemorating the martyrdom of St.Kerkyos), which has been reused in the present building.

Tel Afeq (4 km. NE): This site has been occupied, over the centuries, by a Canaanite town, then by the Biblical *Aphek*, later by the Hellenistic town of *Pegai*, later again by the Roman *Arethusa*, and then by the Herodian town of *Antipatris*.

Tel Afeq (Petah Tiqvah), Antipatris

Qazrin
Golan   p.318□F 3

This is the Jewish Qisrin or Qesareyon of Roman and Byzantine times. It is situated 8 km. to the SE of the Benot Ya'akov Bridge.

Synagogue: The synagogue (51 ft. × 60 ft.) is aligned from N. to S. and was discovered during excavation and restoration work in 1971. The W. wall has been preserved to a height of 10 ft.

There is a frieze above the jamb and the lintel. In the middle of the lintel a garland is depicted with a pomegranate and amphora on either side. There is another entrance through the E. wall. The interior contains the remains of two rows of stone benches, which were set along the walls. Remains of a floor mosaic. There are several capitals lying on the ground in front of the main entrance. An adjoining room contains a lintel with a rosette pattern in a tabula ansata. A door-jamb has been decorated with a five-armed menora and a peacock(?), and a three-armed menora can be seen depicted on a capital. On a cornerstone on the outside of the S. wall there is a one-line inscription. The synagogue was built in the 4C AD.

Environs: Dabbura (5 km. NE of the Benot Ya'akov Bridge): This is an abandoned Arab village in which many *individual objects* have been discovered which indicate the existence here at one time of one or more synagogues. Two large lintels can still be seen where they were found. The first one is decorated in its centre with a garland in the middle of which there is a flower (?) with four leaves. On each side stands an eagle with outstretched wings and its head turned outward. Each holds a snake in its beak. Of the other lintel, only the left part is preserved.

Gamla(10 km. SE of Q.): On Tell el-Ahdab stand the ruins of the city of *Gamalah*, which was destroyed by Vespasian in AD 68. It was rediscovered in 1970. The ruined city contains the remains of an old *castle*. The identity of the 'Masada of the North' has not yet finally been clarified, but it contained one of the oldest synagogues in the country.

Khan el-Jukhadar/Givat Orha (10 km. to the E. of Gamla): Remains of an 18C Ottoman *caravanserai*. Buildings dating from the Roman, Byzantine and Mameluke periods have been excavated on the tel (2,323 ft.). *Finds:* Gravestone with a Greek inscription (AD 27).

Khasfin (5 km. SE. of Gamla): Abandoned Syrian village which was built on the ruins of the Jewish town of Hisfiyya/Hizpiyya. Mentioned in the Old Testament by the name of Kas-

Maqam en-Nabi Yehya (Petah Tiqvah), Roman ashlar structure

pin (1 Maccabees 5, 26). *Church:* Basilica with three outside apses (5C AD). Mosaic: The mosaic is framed by intertwining rhombi. It was intersected by rows of red and blue fleurets which themselves form rhomboid patterns.

Umm el-Qanatir (15 km. SE of Q.): A 3C *synagogue* (46 × 63 ft.) was discovered here, on the site of the Qamattirya of the Talmud. Its longitudinal axis runs from N. to S. It has the form of a basilica, with a wide nave and two narrow aisles, which are separated from each other by two rows of five columns each. Opposite the N. wall there is another row of two extra columns. Unlike the other synagogues in Golan, which are West-facing, this one is aligned towards the N. *Finds:* Relief with lion. Part of a window lintel decorated with vine tendrils and grapes. Eagle with outstretched wings. Stone depicting an eagle; frieze, rosettes, and palmette.

Qubeiba/El-Qubeibeh

West Bank   p.320☐D 7

Qubeiba stands on a hill a few km. to the W. of Jerusalem, and is identified by many historians with the Emmaus of the New Testament (Mark 16, 12; Luke 24, 13-32). However, no scientific proof has been found for this hypothesis.

A church, monastery, fortress, and small village were established here in the 12C by the Canons of the Holy Spirit. They were driven out in 1187, but were able to return to their by then dilapidated village following a treaty concluded in 1244 which accorded the area between Beit Hanina in the E. and Latrun in the W. to the Crusaders. After the Crusaders had been expelled from Jerusalem and the mountains of Judaea, pilgrims to the Holy City followed a route through Beit Nuba, Qubeiba, and Nabi Samwil. Jerusalem was captured by the Turks in 1517; and in the ensu-

ing years the stones were removed from Qubeiba's ruined medieval church to be used in the building of the Holy City's town wall. Only the foundations were left. The site of the ruins was bought by the Marquise Paolina de Nicolay in 1861, and in 1901–2 a new church was built there by the Franciscans on top of the foundations of the old Crusader church.

Franciscan church: The *Crusader church* which originally stood on this site had the shape of a trapezium, so that the S. end measured 107 ft., the N. end 103 ft. 2 in., the W. end 70 ft. 6 in., and the E. end 66 ft. It consisted of a nave and two aisles, comprising four bays, which ended with three apses at the E. end. The groined vault had pointed arches and was supported by compound pillars. The N. row of pillars consisted of just one pillar, and the W. part of the roof was born by a wall 60 ft. long which divided the interior of the church in two. The traces of a half-faded fresco were discovered near the side apses.

The design of the *modern church* was copied from the plans of the architects Fra Vendelino di Menden and P. Barnaba and built in the style of the 12C. This modern building in fact incorporates the apses, pilasters, and parts of the masonry, of the old Crusader church. It was consecrated by Cardinal A. Ferrari on 12 October 1902.

W. façade: The façade is divided into segments by simple ornamental lines. There are Gothic-type arches beneath the cornice; in the middle is a window framed by columns; while the beautiful door has columns and a tympanum. The plinth of the W. wall is made of old stones from the Crusader church.

The *interior* has been built of large stones; the sanctuary alone is made of polychrome Carrara marble which forms a geometrical pattern. Especially worth seeing are the four altars in the nave, aisles and sanctu-

Qazrin, synagogue ▷

ary. *Main altar* (in the nave): The altar table (mensa) is supported by four columns and pilasters of a pinkish-red local stone and has an antependium decorated with three paintings in tempera (representing the Saviour and St.Kleopas and St.Simon). The altarpiece is of white marble and contains six bronze statues. These represent, from left to right: the Immaculate Virgin Mary, St.Francis and St.Joseph, the Apostle Peter, and St.Antony of Padua and St.Luke. *Side altars:* Each of these incorporates four small columns and an antependium of coloured marble with bronze decorations (depicting lilies and crosses). There is a kind of ciborium on each altarpiece. Both altars have capitals decorated with a cross in the middle of acanthus leaves. Sanctuary altar: This is made of white marble and takes the form of a grooved sarcophagus, with an altarpiece made of classical mouldings.

Windows: All the windows in the church are of stained glass (painted by F.X. Zeller of Munich). The window in the central apse shows Jesus breaking the bread. Those in the side apses

depict the symbols of the two disciples, the mitre (left), and the cross (right). Wall above the main arcades: the Immaculate Virgin Mary; St.Luke; St.Clare; St.Frediano; St.Joseph; St.Mary Cleopas; St.Paschal Babylon; St. Paula, and a martyred woman.

Lamps: There are two lamps in the Gothic style, representing the Trinity, which hang in the central apse by the main altar. Three kneeling angels in high relief form the corners of a triangle, and between them are the three silver bas-reliefs which constitute the main body of each lamp.

Statues: There are two large wooden statues of St.Francis of Assisi and Francesco Solano in front of the pillars near the sanctuary. Above the altar in the central apse can be seen a baldacchino, resembling a triptych, which incorporates a wooden carving of the figures of Jesus and his two disciples at the supper.

Memorial to the Marquise Paolina de Nicolay: This small memorial consists of a marble slab framed by a tympanum with two small columns. The inscription refers to the Mar-

Qazrin, synagogue

quise's reburial (for, after her death in 1868, she had originally been laid to rest in the Latin Cemetery on Mount Zion in Jerusalem).

Bell tower and monastery: These were built in 1911. The four large bells are dedicated to the supper at Emmaus, the Immaculate Virgin, St.Cleopas, and to St.Antony, who is the patron saint of the Franciscans in the Holy Land. The clock (made in Paris) was placed in the bell tower in 1913.

Environs: Abud (35 km. NW): Small village (pop. 1100) inhabited by Christians and Muslims. *Sitti-Mariam:* Greek Orthodox church built in the 5C and rebuilt in the 11C. In and around the village can be seen the ruins of: *Mar Abadiah church* (which measured 50×23 ft. and includes the remains of a white floor mosaic); the *Church of St.Barbara* (dating from the 6C; there is a large stone with a Greek inscription by the entrance); the *Church of St.Theodore* (7/8C); and the *Church of St.Anastasia* (7/8C).

Beitin (18 km. NE): This is the Bethel of the Old Testament, which marked the border of the lands belonging to the tribe of Ephraim (Joshua 16, 1–4) and several excavations were carried out between 1927 and 1961. It was here that Jacob had his dream of the ladder reaching up to heaven and set up a cult stone there as a memorial (Genesis 28, 11–19). King Jeroboam (926–907 BC) put up a golden calf in Beth-el and established it as the holy place of the Northern Kingdom (1 Kings 12, 28), but this was later destroyed by King Josiah of Judah (2 Kings 23, 15). Some members of the tribe of Benjamin returned to Beth-el after the exile in Babylon (Nehemiah 11, 31). The town was fortified by the Seleucid general Bacchides (1 Maccabees 9, 50) and later destroyed by Vespasian during the course of the First Jewish War against Rome. There are remains of houses, a Canaanite cave sanctuary with an altar, and a town wall including a striking gateway, all dating from the *middle of the Bronze Age. Burj Beitin* (865 yards behind the village): Ruins of a square Frankish fortified tower (33 ft. wide), the stones of which were probably taken from the remains of an earlier Byzantine church. There is a *mosque* (1892) now standing on top of the ruins of a Byzantine church which again commemorated Jacob's dream. The minaret is built of massive blocks of stone which may perhaps have been taken from a medieval monastery near the church.

Jifnah (22 km. NE): The present Arab village stands on the site of the Biblical Ophni (Joshua 18, 24) and the Roman Gophna. It contains two *churches*, next to which there stands a small *Crusader castle* built in 1182 by Raymond de Jafenia. This is square and includes an inner courtyard (with cistern). The monumental entrance gate is set in the E. wall. The erection of walls next to it has meant that the gate with the arcade supported by columns is today part of a dwelling.

Nabi Samwil (5 km. SE): Christian tradition marks this as the burial place of the Prophet Samuel. The Byzan-

Qubeiba, Franciscan church

tines, Arabs, and Franks built in turn on the Mons Gaudii (2,980 ft.; also known as Montjoie, or the 'Mountain of Joy'), so called because it afforded the Crusaders their first view of Jerusalem. Nabi Samwil was identified by Greek travellers with the Biblical Rama (1 Samuel 25, 1). The Crusaders built a Premonstratensian church here in 1157 on the ruins of an earlier Byzantine church. This took the form of a basilica (120 × 27 ft.) which was built in the shape of a Latin cross, above the grave of the Prophet Samuel. To the E. of the nave (120 × 27 ft.) is the transept (77 ft. long), and to its N. a section has been added which comprises three bays and has a groined vault. The prominent transept made this a unique example of Frankish church architecture in the Holy Land. It was destroyed in the 18C by an earthquake, after which the Turks erected a *mosque* on top of its foundations. They also sealed the Prophet's tomb and built a crypt above it which contains a massive cenotaph decorated with carpets. Muslim tradition relates that the mosque contains the graves of Elkana and Hanna, the Prophet Samuel's parents. The mosque was destroyed during the Second World War, but was later restored.

Ramallah (15 km. NE): This was founded in the 14C by Christians who had been expelled from Shobak in Jordan, and is now inhabited by Christians and Muslims. To the NW of the town centre, on the road to En Quinya, can be found the ruins of a *church* and *monastery* dating from Byzantine times.

Qumran/Khirbet Qumran
West Bank   p.320☐E 8

Qumran is situated on the NW edge of the Dead Sea, on the West Bank,

◁ *Nabi Samwil (Qubeiba), mosque, minaret*

Qumran, monks' cells

which Israel occupies. It is the site of archaeological ruins which were only systematically investigated in the 1950s and include numerous caves where, since 1947, texts of priceless value for Biblical scholarship have been discovered. Most experts believe that the members of the religious community which lived here from about 150 BC until the destruction of Qumran by the Romans in AD68, were in fact Essenes.

History: From about 150 BC, a monastic-type community had established itself here on the site of the ruins of an earlier settlement dating from the 9–6C BC (sometimes identified with the Ir-Melach mentioned in Joshua 15, 62). Its quarters included a main room with a tower, a writing-room (or scriptorium), and, next to that, an assembly room and refectory; there were also cisterns, a

pottery, and an aqueduct. The cemetery had about 1,200 graves, most containing the bodies of men. Most of the members of the settlement (about 200 in all) probably lived in the surrounding caves. The settlement was destroyed, probably in 31 BC, by a combination of earthquake and fire, and was then largely abandoned; by the turn of the millennium it had been restored, only to be once more destroyed, this time for good, by the Romans during the First Jewish War (in AD 68). After that, what had once been the main room of the community was used as the living quarters attached to a sentry post which was kept here until the end of the 1C BC. During the Second Jewish War, the ruins were used by Jewish resistance fighters as a place of refuge; after that, the place was laid waste.

Finds: The texts which have been

discovered comprise more than 500 Hebrew, Aramaic, and Greek manuscripts, most of which were written on leather scrolls and some on papyrus; one text was chiselled on copper. Each manuscript has been classified, firstly by the number of the cave (from 1–11) in which it was found, and secondly by an abbreviation designating its text: for example, 1QIs signifies a text of the Book of Isaiah found in cave 1 in Qumran. The texts can be divided, in terms of content, into: a) Biblical texts and apocrypha; b) commentaries on Biblical texts; and c) liturgical or legal texts, including the rules of various sects, and astrological, juridical, and other texts. The so-called Damascus manuscript is addressed to the members of the community who were scattered across the country. Its name is allegorical, referring to the fact that the community designated itself as 'the community of the new covenant in the region of Damascus'.

The origins of the community go back to Maccabean times, when its members not only set themselves against the efforts then being made to Hellenize the region, but also came out in opposition to the Maccabean high priest. They were led by their 'Teacher of Righteousness' (otherwise not named), who first became the rival of the high priest of the Maccabeans (dubbed by the Essenes 'the sacrilegious priest'), and then, after they had broken publicly, 'went into the desert to prepare the path for the Lord' and founded Qumran. He was ascribed prophetic powers and even after his death was regarded as the supreme authority on the interpretation of Scripture. He was probably the author of the rules of the community as well. According to his exegesis, the aim of the community was to wait out the last days in a state of religious purity and of complete obedience to the Law. Its members, being the 'sons of light', possessed the true knowledge of the meaning of the Old Testament, and their purpose was to turn this knowledge into practice within the framework of the strict rules of their order.

The excavations can be seen on a rugged marl terrace at the bottom of a steep slope down from the Judah desert. A large complex of buildings (267 × 333 ft.) was uncovered here during the course of five seasons from 1951–6.

Monastery: The *main building* is square, measures 125 × 125 ft., and has a massive fortified tower in the NW corner which dominates the other ruins.

The inner couryard is rectangular and had various rooms going off it, including the conference room, which had benches and niches, the scriptorium (on the upper storey), which was also furnished with benches (now in the museum in Amman) as well as two inkwells, one terracotta and one bronze, and a kitchen and storage rooms. It was in the scriptorium that fair copies were written out of Biblical texts and of the sects' manuscripts. A refectory (80 x 15 ft.) and a pottery containing two kilns were built on to the S. side of the complex.

Aqueduct: The entire complex was supplied with water from the nearby mountains by means of an aqueduct. This was elaborate and traversed the site from N. to S. Eight ponds have been discovered among the ruins, most of them rectangular and equipped with steps.

Caves: Some 40 caves have been discovered in the area around Q., and finds were made in 11 of these. Cave 1 was accidentally discovered in the spring of 1947 by Bedouins belonging to the Ta'amora tribe. It was found to contain the scroll with the Book of Isaiah A and B, the commentary on the Book of Habakkuk, the rules of the sects, the War Scroll, the Hymn Scroll, and the Genesis Apocrypha (now in the possession of the Hebrew University of Jerusalem).

Environs: En-Feshcha (3 km. N.):

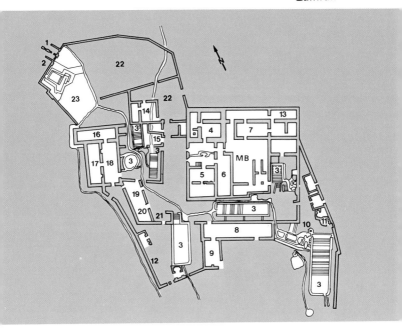

Qumran, monastery 1-3 Basins of irrigation system 4 Tower with reinforcements 5 Common room 6 Scriptorium (writing room) 7 Kitchen 8 Assembly hall and refectory 9 Plate-room 10 Pottery 11-21 Storerooms and stables 22 Courtyard 23 Filter bed **MB** Main building

The remains of a large *group of buildings* were excavated here in 1958, 110 yards from the spring. In the centre is a large building (80 × 60 ft.) containing various rooms and an inner courtyard from whose SE. corner a staircase led up to the second storey. Next to the vestibule and two rooms used as living quarters there were two fairly small storage rooms and a warehouse. There was an enclosure 13 × 13 ft. in which animals could be kept. Next to the N. wall there were a detached room and some shelters. To the N. of the enclosure are some water basins.

Khirbet Mird (7 km. W.): The Empress Eudokia built a tower here in

AD 455 on Jebel el-Muntar ('the mountain with the view'; 1,713 ft.). Out of this grew, around AD 508, a *monastery*, which was headed for 34 years by John Scholarius. Some remains of the walls have been preserved, together with some fragments of mosaics. If one follows the curves of the mountain on its S. side and heads in a SE direction for the rock fort of Hyrkania (Khirbet Mird), one comes across the *Spelaion Monastery*, which is in a cave, and was founded by St. Sabas in AD 508. The *rock fort of Hyrcania* is situated on an E. foothill, running down from the Judah desert, which is conical in shape and only approachable from the W. The fort was built by John Hyrcanus (died 104 BC) and later used as a treasury by the Hasmonaean queen Alexandra (76–67 BC). It was razed by Gabinius in 57 BC but later rebuilt in 31 BC by Herod, who used it as a prison. Herod's fort was rediscovered in the 4C AD, and in AD 492 St.Sabas founded the Monastery of Mardes on top of it. This was inhabited by monks until the 9C. In 1925 some monks from Mar Saba tried once more to establish a presence here, but were prevented by the resistance of the Bedouins. **Dead Sea/Yam HaMelach:** This salt lake, 80 km. long and up to 18 km. wide, is situated in the Jordan rift-valley in what is the deepest depression on earth: the level of its surface is actually almost 1,300 ft. below that of the sea, and its floor is roughly 2,700 ft. below sea-level. It is surrounded by a high plateau which falls abruptly down to the lake from a height of up to 2,700 ft. The surrounding countryside is largely infertile, and only in the ravines (or wadis) which descend from the mountains of the plateau, is there some sign of vegetation. According to geologists, the lake is still sinking by about 0.4 in. every thousand years.

Name: The Dead Sea was also known in the Old Testament as the 'Salt Sea' (Numbers 34, 3) because of its extremely high salt content (up to about 30 per cent on the surface, and over 32 per cent at a depth of 330 ft.), which is due to intense evaporation. The Greeks and Romans called it the 'asphalt lake' ('asphaltitis limne'). The substance which they called 'bitumen judaicum' or 'Jewish pitch', which broke off from the floor of the Dead Sea and could be collected from its surface, was then the most prized form of asphalt. The Arabs knew the Dead Sea as 'Bahr Lut', meaning 'The sea of Lot'. (Lot was the nephew of Abraham who lived in Sodom).

Shape and peculiar features: The Dead Sea is divided into two basins by the peninsula of Lisan ('tongue' in Arabic) which juts out from the E. coast. It is fed by the River Jordan, as well as various streams, most of which run down from the plateau to the E. There are no streams running out of it. Yet, despite this, the water-level always remains relatively constant, a fact which must be explained by the intense rate of evaporation produced here by the extraordinarily high temperature (which averages 30C in summer and not less than 10C in winter) in what is, after all, the deepest spot

Qumran, stairs in monastery complex

By the Dead Sea (Qumran)

on earth. During summer, up to one inch evaporates every 24 hours. At the beginning of the 19C the water-level was 10 ft. lower than it is today, though by the turn of this century it was 23 ft. higher than its present level. The difference is to be explained by varying levels of precipitation. The many pumping stations now drawing water from the Jordan are also contributing to the constant fall of the Dead Sea's water-level, to the extent that there is a possibility of the S. basin drying up. To prevent this happening, the construction of a channel to the Dead Sea from the Mediterranean is being contemplated. Atmospheric pressure at the Dead Sea reaches the highest levels anywhere on the planet. The air here is, equally, the driest and purest on earth, and contains the highest amount of oxygen (10 per cent more oxygen than at sea-level). The mineral content of the water is also higher than that of any of the seas, so high, however, that it cannot support flora and fauna, and only microscopic organisms such as sulphur bacteria, among others, can survive here.

Ramat Rahel

West Bank   p.320☐D 8

This kibbutz was founded in 1926 by the Gedud Ha'Avoda movement and is situated 4 km. to the S. of Jerusalem, on the SE and NW slopes of a 2,727 ft. mountain. From 1948–67, it formed the tip of a peninsula of Israeli territory extending into Jordan. The excavated site of Khirbet Salih is on the SW slope of the mountain, and Rachel's tomb is 4 km. from there.

Qumran, caves

Khirbet Salih (excavated hill): Three archaeological expeditions were mounted here from 1954–62 which unearthed sites dating from the Second Iron Age. The oldest layer dates from the 8/7C BC and consisted of a small fort which was replaced, at the end of the 7C, by a spacious royal country residence. The place was uninhabited during the Hellenistic period, and then, in Roman times, an agricultural settlement was established here.

Church of the kathisma: The remains can still be seen of a large complex of Byzantine buildings probably dating from the second half of the 5C. The church's storehouse consisted of two halls, each 50 ft. long and aligned from E. to W., which had pairs of columns along their walls. The ruins of the church itself (53 × 45 ft.) can be found to the E. of the N. casemate wall. Its interior is divided into a nave and two aisles by two rows of five columns each, one on the N. and the other on the S. side. The apse occupies the entire width of the nave (21 ft.). The aisles are considerably narrower (8 ft.). There are two extra columns at the W. end, which thus would have an enclosed what may have been a sort of 'inner' narthex, between this W. colonnade and the W. wall and within the area of the nave. Three doors led inside the church from the outer narthex. Mosaics: Originally the entire floor of the church was covered with a mosaic, whose remains can still be seen in the S. aisle. It depicts simple geometrical patterns in white, blue and red. The only church furnishings consisted of a stone plaque (2 ft. 10 in. × 2 ft. 9 in.) with a large cross in the middle, the arms of which extended 4–6 in. beyond the plaque. It was found in front of the W. end and was perhaps the base of an altar standing in the apse. There was a well-paved street, or perhaps a courtyard (?), along the outside of the S. side of the church, with three rooms (sacristies or pastophoria) running off it to the S. The apse is polygonal, and there is a tribelon on the W. side. Only the foundation walls of the church now survive. It was excavated in 1954.

Citadel: The upper citadel (167 × 200 ft.) was surrounded by a casemate wall. A gate on the E. side led into a rectangular courtyard which gave access to a palace, administration buildings, and storehouses. Finds: Four proto-Aeolic capitals and small columns which may have belonged to a window balustrade (?). They are decorated with scrolls and have an oval shield in the centre, and their shafts are edged with bosses. Statuette of the goddess Astarte. Of the entire upper citadel, only some parts of the foundation walls survive.

Environs: Rachel's tomb/Qever Rahel (4 km. S.): Rachel was the favourite wife of the Patriarch Jacob and is revered by Jew, Christian and Arab. The whitewashed domed building in which her remains are supposed to be buried, dates from Crusader times.

Mahmud Pasha extended the walls upwards and added the dome in 1623. In 1841, the English philanthropist Sir Moses Montefiori had the structure rebuilt and built another section on to it on the E. side. One enters the tomb through Montefiori's two porches. The S. wall of the first porch contains the mihrab placed there by Ta'ami Bedouins in 1967.

Ramla
Central District/Israel   p.320□C 7

Ramla was the only new city established by the Arabs in Palestine. It was founded in AD 716 by the Umayyad Caliph Suleiman ibn Abd el-Malik and became the capital of the new province of Filistin (Palestine), with splendid palaces and mosques. After the advent of the Abbasid

Ramla, El Jami'a el-Abyad ▷

Caliphs, who were strict in their religion, Ramla in the 8C drew immigrants from Sunni and Shi'ite Muslims and Karaite and Rabbinical Jews. It was destroyed by severe earthquakes in 1033 and 1067. The Crusaders found it to be ruined when they arrived in 1099. As they confused it with the town of Rama, they built a Church of St.John here (now the Great Mosque), as well as the Monastery of Nicodemus. During the Third Crusade, Ramla was divided into two sectors, one Christian and one Muslim, by the terms of a treaty concluded between Saladin and Richard the Lionheart. It was ruled by the Franks from 1205 until 1268, when it was captured by Baibars. The Mamelukes built a mosque with a minaret which could be seen from afar (the 'White Tower', completed in 1318) on the site of the Caliph Suleiman's old palace. Christian monks established a presence here during the 14C. In the 17C the town fell into decay.

Ramla 1 Entrance **2** Mosque (El Jami'a el-Abyad **3** Portico **4** N. wall **5** Minaret (White Tower) **6** Underground cisterns **7** Qabr en Nebi Saleh

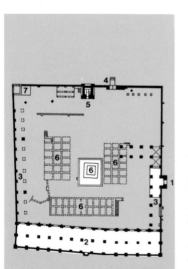

El Jami'a el-Abyad (White Mosque): The mosque is built around a rectangular courtyard (310 × 280 ft.) which is lined on the E. and W. sides by colonnades. It was excavated in 1948, and had three phases of construction. In the first phase, the Umayyads built the mosque, which was aligned E.-W., the E. wall and colonnade, the N. wall (without the minaret), and three underground cisterns. Saladin's construction of the right side of the mosque, as well as the W. wall and the fountain in the middle of the courtyard (where the believers can purify themselves), comprised the second phase. During the last stage, the Mamelukes built the White Tower, the colonnade to the E. of the minaret, and two halls outside the courtyard adjoining the E. wall. *Mosque:* The room where worship is conducted is long and narrow (273 × 41 ft.) and was divided into two sections by a row of 12 pillars, of which four have been preserved. These support a groined vault. The mihrab is situated in the middle of the S. wall. Beneath the mosque are the burial vaults containing, according to Muslim tradition, the remains of the 40 Companions of the Prophet. *White Tower:*(on the N. side of the walled courtyard): This was built in 1318 by the Mameluke Sultan Muhammad ibn Qalaun (as is stated by the inscription above the lintel of the door, which has a pointed arch). The platform is 90 ft. high and is approached by a flight of 128 steps. The minaret is rectangular (27 × 23 ft.) and has six floors, whose arched windows derive from medieval European architecture. Its corner supports are provided by elegant columns. It was converted into a minaret in the 16C, having been originally designed as a defensive tower.

El Jami'a el-Kabir (Great Mosque): This was originally built by the Crusaders in the 13C as a Romanesque Cathedral (the Cathedral of St.John), and is still one of the best preserved medieval buildings in Palestine. It comprises a nave and two aisles, composed of seven bays, and measures 130 × 61 ft. The nave is higher than the two aisles, from which it is separated by a row of columns on each side. The three apses are rectangular. The nave's pointed barrel vaulting and arcades, as well as the groin vaulting of the aisles, make this one of the most beautiful of Frankish interiors. The small columns supporting the relieving arch above the main apse do not descend all the way to the floor, but disappear in the wall (an architectural feature which was common in southern France and northern Spain). There is a round window in the front wall above the apse. The pillars extend upwards as pilasters to the level of the clerestory and support the wall-arches. A cornice, in which are set the windows of the clerestory, runs along the level of the springing line of the tunnel vault and above the arcades. There are lunettes above the windows. A minaret stands above the W. door, which has been walled in.

Bir al-Unaiziyya (St.Helen's pools):

These underground pools are called 'the goats' pools' by the Arabs, known to the Jews as the 'lake of the arcades' (Brekhat Hakeshatot), and were named by Christian pilgrims during the Middle Ages after St.Helena, the mother of the Emperor Constantine. They measure 5,500 sq. ft. by 30 ft. deep, and were begun by Suleiman and completed in AD 789 by a later Caliph, Harun ar-Rashid (786-809). The whole constitutes an irregular rectangle measuring 80 × 68 ft. Inside, there are three rows of pillars supporting six groin vaults, each of which is divided into four parts. Each of these 24 sections had an aperture. A stairway leads down to the reservoir from this structure, which is roofed over and suppported by medieval columns.

Also worth seeing: *Church of St.Joseph* (rebuilt by the Franciscans). *Hospice of St.Nicodemus*. A *mosaic* dating from the 8C was discovered in 1973 in the courtyard of a private house in the SE part of the town. It is in three parts and consists of geometrical patterns together with an (early)

Gezer (Ramla), row of stele

text in Kufic script, thus providing the only example known to us so far of an Islamic mosaic having an inscription.

Environs: Gezer (8 km. SE): Gezer is now ruined but its hill-top site, together with a number of springs, made it strategically important. It was continuously occupied, under the same name, from the 15C BC until Roman times. In fact, it was settled during the early Bronze Age and is mentioned, by the name of *Gazru*, as a Canaanite city-state in the list of towns drawn up by the Egyptian Pharaoh Thutmosis III (1490–1436 BC), who belonged to the 18th Dynasty. Joshua conquered King Horam of Gezer (Joshua 10, 33 and 12, 12), but the Canaanites of Gezer could not be driven out by the Israelites, but 'dwell among the Ephraimites to this day and serve under tribute' (Joshua 16, 10). During the 12C BC, Gezer fell to the Philistines, but later passed to the Israelites as a result of the marriage of King Solomon (964–926 BC): 'For Pharaoh King of Egypt had gone up, and taken Gezer, and burnt it with fire, and slain the Canaanites that dwelt in the city, and given it for a present unto his daughter, Solomon's wife. And Solomon built Gezer, and Beth-horon the nether'. In 734 BC, the town was captured by Tiglat-Pileser III, King of Assyria, and lost its importance from then until its capture by Simon Maccabaeus in 142 BC. Simon fortified it and built a residence there. In 141 BC he made his son John Hyrcanus commander of all the forces, with his headquarters in Gezer (1 Maccabees 13, 53). After the Maccabees, or Hasmonaeans, had consolidated their power, Gezer became their personal possession.
Tel el-Jazari: The excavations have unearthed various layers indicating Canaanite, Israelite, Roman, Christian, and Arab periods of settlement.
Canaanite temple: Between the two hills of the Tel, and within the inner

fortifications, is a site which is aligned N.-S. and consists of 10 monoliths (masseboth) up to 10 ft. high. It dates from the middle of the Bronze Age, around 1600 BC, and may have been built as a memorial to the dead. The block of stone which has a hollow in the middle may have been a basin or the base of another monolith. There are two rotundas, one to the N. of this stone and one to the S., each with a diameter of 14 ft. (second half of the second millennium BC). *Solomon's Gate:* The gateway dates from the 10C BC and incorporates three rooms, each of which has a bench along three of its walls. A paved gutter by the W. corner chanelled the rain from the roof to the drain beneath the street. There are traces of a casemate on either side of the gate. The gateway's measurements are very similar to those in Megiddo and Hazor. It is 63 ft. long (Megiddo, 67 ft.; Hazor, 67 ft.) and 54 ft. wide (Megiddo, 58 ft.; Hazor, 60 ft.), and the walls are 5 ft. 4 in. thick (Megiddo 5 ft. 4 in.; Hazor 5 ft. 4 in.).

Safed/Zefat
Northern District/Israel　　　　　p.318☐E 3

Safed (Zefat in Hebrew) is one of the four holy cities of the Talmud (together with Hebron, Tiberias and Jerusalem), and is situated to the NW of the Sea of Galilee the W. slope of Har Kanaan, at an elevation of 3,330 ft. Little is known of this town, which is not mentioned in the Bible.

Nothing is known of Safed from the Talmudic to the Frankish period. Around 1100, when it was a Frankish possession, Safed and Galilee belonged to the dominions of the Norman prince Tancred. In 1102/3 Hugo of St.-Omer built a small castle, later enlarged in 1140 by King Foulques of Anjou, on HaMetzuda hill (2,780 ft.). This was donated to the Templars by King Amalric I in 1168. Safed, Belvoir and La Fève defended the eastern border of the Kingdom of Jerusalem.

The castle was captured by Saladin in 1188 and demolished in 1220 by al-Mu'azzam, only to be rebuilt in 1240 as the strongest Frankish fortress in the Holy Land. After being captured by Baibars in 1266, Safed became the headquarters of a 'mamlakah', or province, which extended to Galilee and the Lebanon. During the 14&15C, it possessed a Jewish community which, after the expulsion of the Jews from Spain in 1492, became, during the 16C, a Jewish spiritual centre. Joseph Caro (author of the 'Shulkhan Arukh'), Moses Trani, Isaac Luria, and Hayyim Vital all lived in Safed and made it the centre of the Kabbalist movement. The Ashkenazi brothers established the first printing-press in the Orient in 1563.

In the 17C Safed possessed 18 schools, 21 synagogues, and a large yeshiva with 20 teachers. Its population consisted of four groups: Ashkenazis, Sephardim, and Provençal and Italian Jews. The community was destroyed by a combination of earthquake and epidemic in 1759, and five years later there were only 60 families living there. In 1778 over 300 Hassidim who were pupils of the Rabbi Israel Eliezer Ba'al Shem Tov came to Safed, led by the Rabbi Menahem Mendel from Vitebsk. They were followed in 1810 by the disciples of Elijah, the gaon of Vilnius. The town's fortunes rose once more during the reign of Ibrahim Pasha (1831–40), but in 1836 some 4,000 Jews were killed in an earthquake, and

Safed, synagogue of Rabbi Joseph Caro, detail

many others abandoned the town and settled in Hebron. The Hebrew printing press of Israel Bak was moved to Kefar Yemaq in 1831 and later again to Jerusalem. In 1913 there were about 11,000 Jews living in Safed (comprising half the population). During the war of 1948, members of the Palmah group captured the town (in May), and it has since remained an orthodox Jewish community. The new town was built in 1948 around the nucleus of the old one. Artists moved into the old Arab quarters.

Synagogues: *Ashkenazi synagogue of HaAri:* This was built a few years after the death of the important Rabbi Isaac Luria (1534–72) and displays simple and austere arches and vaulting. The windows above the main entrance are highly decorated. There are Cabbalist frescos on the walls, some including Hebrew writing which over and again declares the name of God. Naïve wall paintings can be seen depicting the symbols of the 12 tribes, as well as various musical instruments (a lyre, viola, zither, and flute) and fruit (dates, grapes, etc.). The graceful sofas by the walls invite one to meditate. Next to the S. wall of the prayer-hall there is a precious Thora shrine, made by a wood engraver from Kolomea in the Ukraine, which is decorated with a pattern of intricate open spirals. Ribbons resembling flame emerge from the mouth of a mythical fish (or dragon), ending in ornamental leaves. Above the lintel is a Hebrew inscription which reads: 'How unutterably holy is the Synagogue of the great Master HaAri, blessed be His Name.' The synagogue was destroyed by an earthquake in 1837 and later reconstructed. It possesses an extensive library devoted to the Cabbala. *Sephardi synagogue of HaAri:* To enter the synagogue, one takes a staircase leading into an open courtyard surrounded by high walls. An ornamented wall contains a door leading into the porch, which in turn gives access to the small main hall. This faces S. and abuts on a small grotto. The hall is lit by three windows and painted blue. Allegorical paintings adorn the walls. The precious furnishings made of wrought iron and carved wood date from a later period. To the left of the prayer-room is a small chamber to which the wise retreated for meditation. The main hall has two vaults, beneath one of which stands the almenor, or pulpit. The synagogue dates originally from the 17C, since when it has been altered on several occasions, and is one of the best preserved in S. During recent years it has been thoroughly restored. *Issac Aboab Synagogue:* This dates from the time of the important Rabbi Issac Aboab (1433–93) and was completely rebuilt, except for the S. wall, after the earthquake of 1837. The interior contains a richly furnished room with a raised pulpit. The central dome is decorated with Judaic symbols, palms, fig-trees, and inscriptions. The synagogue possesses two manuscripts written by HaAri in calligraphy in his own hand.

Jewish cemetery: (W. of the synagogue quarter): This is an old cemetery containing, among others, the graves of the learned Rabbis Isaac Luria (d. 1572), Moshe Cordovero (d. 1570), Ya'akov Beirav (d. 1546), Joseph Caro (d. 1575), Shelomo Alkavets (d. 1584), Moshe Alsheikh (d. 1600), and Hayyim Vital (d. 1620).

Beit ha-midrash shel Shem va' Ever (in the S. part of Safed): It was on the slope of the mountain where the castle stands that, according to Jewish tradition, Noah's son, Sem, and grandson, Ever, studied the Tora.

Kiryat ha-Omanim (an artists' quarter, formerly an Arab quarter): Exhibitions by Israeli, Polish, American, and German artists and sculptors can be seen in the many galleries and in the Milo House.

Museums: *Glicenstein Municipal Museum:* This is housed in the old residence of the Turkish Kaimakam and was established in 1953 by the family of the painter, sculptor and printer Enrico (Henoch) Glicenstein (1870–1942) and by the town. It contains Glicenstein's sculptures and paintings by European artists. *Museum of the Art of Printing:* This throws light on the development of the Jewish art of printing in the Middle East in the 16C. The exhibition shows the history and development of the various Hebrew alphabets and scripts; the history of the art of printing in Hebrew; book-plates and ornamental printing; collector's editions; and the history of printing.

Also worth seeing: *El-Jami'a el-Ahmar* (Red Mosque): This was built by Baibars in 1275, during the Mameluke period. *Zawiyat Banat Hamid:* Tomb of the Emir Muzaffer ed-Din Musa, dating from 1372. *Hametzuda* (citadel): The former Crusader castle stands 3,530 ft. above the Sea of Galilee. A park containing cypresses,

pine-trees and cedars now looks down on the old fortifications.

Environs: Kefar Hananya(22 km. SW): This was an important Jewish settlement in Roman and Byzantine times, famous for its pottery.

Samaria/Shomron/Sabastiya
West Bank   p.320☐D 5

Samaria was founded by King Omri around 880 BC (1 Kings 16, 24) and became the capital of the Northern Kingdom of Israel. It was a centre of the cult of Baal (1 Kings 16, 32) and as such attracted the denunciations of the prophets. It was besieged in 724 BC for three years by Salmanassar V, King of Assyria, and captured in 722 by his successor, Sargon II, an event which marked the end of the Northern Kingdom (2 Kings 17). In the period following the Exile, the town was the capital of the Samaritans, to whom the Jews were hostile. After being captured by Alexander the

Safed, synagogue of Rabbi Joseph Caro, Torah niche (left), Jewish cemetery (right)

Great towards the end of the 4C BC, it was settled by Macedonians and, being a Hellenistic town, was subject to attack from the Maccabees. Herod the Great had the town (which he called *Sebaste*) magnificently fortified and expanded. In Jesus' time, Samaria was the capital of a Roman administrative district (which was also called Samaria: John 4, 4 ff.; Acts 9, 31). The town was destroyed during the First Jewish War (AD 66–70), and later rebuilt during the 2C AD by the Emperor Septimius Severus, who accorded it the rights and status of a Roman colonia around the year 200. During the fourth century it became an episcopal city, possessing many churches. At this same time it acquired the reputation of a holy place, since it was believed to to contain the grave of John the Baptist. After the Arab conquest in the 7C and, later, the brief period of Frankish rule in the 11&12C, the town fell into decay. All that is left of it now is the Arab village of Sabastiya.

Excavations: The various excavations conducted by British and American archaeologists principally uncovered the palace of the Israelite kings and parts of the outer walls of the acropolis (dating from the second Iron Age). The years 1931–5 saw the excavation of the Hellenistic fort, the colonnaded street, the forum, the stadium, the Temple of Kore, a theatre, some Roman graves, the Roman waterworks, and a Byzantine church.
Israelite period. Period of Omri and Ahab (880–852 BC): The *residence* on the acropolis was built in the Assyrian style and given massive *fortifications* by Omri. It is rectangular, and its interior is divided into chambers with thick walls, resembling cells. The inner wall was 5 ft. thick and measured 59 ft. from E. to W. and 30 ft. from N. to S. To the NE of the N. wall was the so-called 'deeper terrace' which was later expanded by 55 ft. to the N. and 100 ft. to the W. and surrounded with a casemate wall. This consisted of two parallel walls, the outer one 6 ft. thick and the inner 3 ft. 3 in. thick, which were linked by transverse walls in such a way as to form numerous cells.
Hellenistic period: The Israelite fortifications were now reinforced by a number of round towers. To the NE can be seen a *tower* (28 ft. high; diameter 43 ft.) which is considered the most beautiful Hellenistic building in Palestine. 19 sites are preserved.
Roman period: Roman Samaria was about 1 km. across from E. to W. *Colonnaded street:* This was 870 yards long and 41 ft. wide and was lined by more than 600 monolithic columns, 18 ft. high, which were mounted with Corinthian capitals. The colonnade was roofed over, providing shelter for the shops beneath it. Between the acropolis hill and what is now the Arab village of Sabastiya was the *forum* (427 × 242 ft.). There were originally four colonnades, but of these only the W. one has survived.

Jesus and the Samaritan woman by the fountain, 15C book illustration

Samaria, church of St.John the Baptist ▷

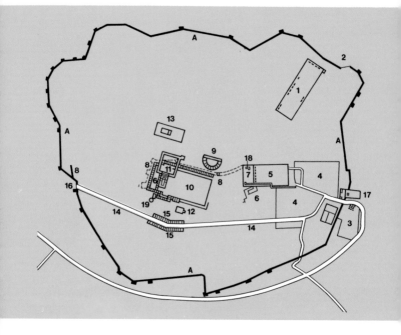

Of its 27 columns, only four are still standing; all that is left of the others are their bases, which are supported by a stylobate. A door in the W. wall led to the adjoining *basilica* (227 × 109 ft.), whose interior was divided by two rows of columns into a nave and two aisles. Some of these monolithic columns are still standing (they are 20 ft. high, and two of them have Corinthian capitals). To the NE of the nave was the bema, with a semicircular niche and two benches. The forum and basilica perhaps performed the

function of an agora in Samaria. *Augusteum:* This temple (117 × 80 ft.) was built by Herod in 25 BC in honour of the Emperor Augustus. It has a stairway 83 ft. wide as well as a forecourt. The interior comprised a wide main aisle and two narrow side aisles. The wide steps and the altar date from the reconstruction of the temple by the Emperor Septimius Severus in the 2C AD. A huge statue was found near the altar which probably represents the Emperor Augustus. To the N. of the Augusteum was the *Temple of Kore* (120 × 52 ft.), standing within a temenos measuring 280 × 150 ft. which may once have been lined with columns. The temple was probably built by John Hyrcanus. The *stadium* (770 × 200 ft.) to the NE was also connected to the cult of Kore. It was surrounded by four halls of columns containing Doric and Corinthian columns, which dated respec-

Samaria, theatre

tively from the reigns of Herod and Septimius Severus. A statue of Kore and a Greek inscription dedicated to the same goddess were discovered in a cistern in the stadium. At the bottom of the NE end of the acropolis are the ruins of a *theatre* (diameter 22 ft.). The façade of the stage was decorated with alternating round and rectangular niches. A *Roman mausoleum* was excavated in 1937 in the SE area of Sabastiya. It is a square structure (18 × 18 ft.) of hewn blocks of stone, and is decorated on the outside by pilasters. The tomb consists of a chamber 10 × 10 ft., with three vaulted niches on three sides. Stone sarcophagi were discovered in two of these niches, and five more were found lying on the ground. *Finds:* Ivories discovered in the Ivory Room of King Ahab. The high reliefs have evidently been inspired, both in motif and style, by Syria and Egypt. They show winged sphynxes (cherubims), lions fighting oxen, and human figures. The bas reliefs depict Egyptian themes, including Horus on a lotus and Isis and Nephthys flanking a column.

Church of St.John the Baptist (E. of the town): This is supposed, by Christian and Muslim tradition, to contain the grave of St.John the Baptist. A Byzantine church was erected here in the 5/6C above the crypt, but it was destroyed in the 9C, and all that has remained of it are a few layers of stone at the level of the bottom layers of the N. wall. Between 1150 and 1160, the Crusaders built, on top of its remains, one of the finest Frankish churches, which was in the Burgundian style, with a nave and two aisles. Its outlines, except for the apse, have been preserved. The entrance to the church is now considerably below the level of the village. After the Arab conquest, it was converted into a mosque. In 1893, the triple apse was demolished and replaced by a straight wall. The buttresses and the vaulted arches on the S. wall can still be clearly seen. A mosque was built in the former transept. The church measures 170 × 83 ft., and is now open to the sky. 20 steps lead down to the crypt from a small domed structure in the middle of the nave. At the entrance to the crypt there is a Roman basalt door dating from the 2/3C AD which once closed off the burial chamber itself. The six burial niches were blocked off by panels containing six circular holes.

Church of the Discovery of John the Baptist's Head (between the Augusteum and the colonnaded street): This Byzantine church was built in the 6C in commemoration of John the Baptist (for, at that time, the Augusteum was mistaken for the palace of Herod Antipas, in which the Baptist's head was delivered to Herodias). It was reconstructed in the 11C, the apse being left in place, while the

other three walls and the narthex were built afresh. During the second half of the 12C the Greeks restored the W. door and extended the four columns upwards to support the heavy dome. They also erected a chapel dedicated to John the Baptist on the spot where his head was thought to have been found in 1185. The foundations of the four columns can still be seen outside the main entrance and inside the walls. The S. aisle contains a polychrome *mosaic* with geometrical patterns and a Greek inscription. To the left of the altar are eight steps leading to a vaulted chamber in which can be seen the countless crosses carved by pilgrims in the stone. At the E. end, above the niche, there is a fresco which, though extensively destroyed, can still be recognized as showing the Baptist's execution and the discovery of his head.

Shekhem (Shechem)/Nablus
West Bank   p. 320□E 6

Shechem (which means 'neck' in

Samaria, colonnaded road

Hebrew) was situated near the modern Shekhem, on the ridge (or 'neck') between Mts. Ebal and Gerizim (Judges 9, 7). It was mentioned in Egyptian texts of the second millennium BC as a Canaanite centre, and later became the first capital of the Northern Kingdom of Israel. It is first mentioned in the Old Testament in the context of Abraham's journey to Canaan.

During the course of the Israelite conquest of Canaan, Joshua built an altar on Mt. Ebal, from which he read out the Law of Moses (Joshua 8, 30–5). At the end of his life he gathered all the tribes of Israel together once more at Shechem (known as the Great Assembly at Shechem) and made his last address (Joshua 24, 1–28).

After the death of Solomon, the ten Northern tribes of Israel held an assembly at Shechem at which they renounced their allegiance to Judah and the House of David. Their new King, Jeroboam, then fortified Shechem and made it his capital. Samaria replaced it as capital of the Northern Kingdom during the reign of King Omri (1 Kings 16, 24).

When the Jews returned from their Babylonian Exile, they built the Temple at Jerusalem. The Samaritans were not allowed to take part in its construction, so they erected their own sanctuary on Mt. Garizim, at the same time making Shechem their capital.

In AD 72, Vespasian founded the settlement of Flavia Neapolis in the mountains of Samaria, 2 km. to the NW of the remains of the town of Shechem (Tel Balata). It acquired the status of a colonia in AD 244. In AD 636, it was conquered by the Arabs, who called it Nablus. It was captured by Tancred in 1099, and between 1152 and 1161 belonged to the Frankish Queen Melisande, later being conquered by Saladin in 1187. During the 16C it was one of four administrative capitals of Ottoman Palestine. Between 1918–48 it formed part of the British mandated territory, from 1948–67 it belonged to Jordan, and since 1967 has been held by Israel. The town was destroyed by an earthquake in 1927.

Tel Balata (site of the excavations of

Samaria, basilica by forum

the Biblical Shechem): Shechem was settled as early as the chalcolithic period. *Cyclopean wall* (between 1650 and 1550 BC): This was sloped, filled from the inside, and made of unhewn blocks of stone (7 ft. 4 in. × 1 ft. 8 in) which rose 33–50 ft. above the surrounding country. To the NW is a gateway incorporating four chambers. The E. gate consisted of two rectangular towers at each side of the entrance. *Temple:* This is a rectangular structure (69 ft. 6 in. × 86 ft. 4 in.), with walls 17 ft. thick, which was used both as a fortress and as a place of worship (migdal). A tower stood on each side of the entrance. The reception hall (23 × 17 ft.) had a large, carefully hewn rock in the centre which supported the upper storey. The migdal (which was used as a model for the Temple in Jerusalem later built by Solomon) contained three rooms, namely a front room, a square room with pillars to the ceiling standing on square foundations, and a small rectangular room. There was an altar in front of the entrance to the square room. The migdal faced SE. and stood on the site of a temenos. On the inside of the fortress rampart are the remains of Israelite houses dating from the 7C BC and a Samaritan house dating from the 3C BC.

Jami' el-Kebir: Large mosque built in 1168 on top of the foundations of a Frankish church. During its construction, the apse belonging to the church was demolished, and the entrance transferred to the E. side. Until the earthquake in 1927, there was a Gothic portal by the outer door of the mosque, as well as three Frankish bays inside (on the W. side). After the earthquake, it was reconstructed, this time without those elements of the Frankish church.

Also worth seeing: *Haret es-Samira*, which was the Samaritan quarter. Its *synagogue* displays an old Thora scroll dating from the 1C AD.

Environs: Har Gerizim (Garizim)/Jebel et-Tur (altitude 2,737 ft.): When the Israelites entered the Promised Land, the blessings were

Shekhem, excavation hill of Tell Balata

spoken from Mt. Gerizim, and the curses from Mt. Ebal opposite (Deuteronomy 11, 29 and 27, 12; Joshua 8, 33). It was also on the summit of Mt. Gerizim that Jotham related the parable of the king of the trees (Judges 9, 7–21). Later, the mountain became the principal holy place of the Samaritans after they had split off from the Jews. During the Byzantine period a church and fortress were built here, but, after these had been destroyed, the Samaritans once more took possession of the mountain.

Various archaeological expeditions have unearthed a temple of Zeus, parts of a Samaritan temple, and a Byzantine church dating from the 6C AD.

Tell er-Ras (excavations): *Temple of Zeus:* This was built by the Emperor Hadrian (AD 117–38) on top of an artificial platform 27–33 ft. high (and measuring 216 × 147 ft.) which had been constructed of rubble and mortar. The temple was probably destroyed in an earthquake in the 4C AD. It measured 72 × 47 ft. The remains of a three-stepped crepi-

doma, which was made of half-hewn blocks of limestone one-fifth of an inch high, can be seen by the E., W., and S. sides. The crepidoma was originally covered with white marble and rested on a three-sided podium. A stairway led up from the bottom of the valley to the *small temple* (pronaos 27 × 11 ft.; naos 27 × 34 ft.). *Church of the Virgin Mary* (Church of the Theotokos): This is an octagonal structure which was built by the Emperor Zeno in AD 486 and rebuilt in the 6C by the Emperor Justinian. It is situated within the castrum (245 × 207 ft.) which Justinian built around the church and ramparts. There is a rectangular tower at each of the corners and another in the middle of the N. wall. Four sides of the octagon (diameter 71 ft.) have chapels adjoining, and there are entrances in the N., W., and S. sides. The apse, at the E. end, is flanked by two pastophories. The roof above the middle of the church was supported by an octagon of eight pillars and 12 columns, which also separated the space beneath the dome (43 ft. wide) from

Shekhem, Samaritan synagogue, Torah scroll (left), Sychar (Shekhem), Jacob's fountain (right)

the barrel-vaulted ambulatory. There are two columns between every two pillars (except in front of the apse). The columns had Corinthian capitals. The floor of the church was covered with a colourful mosaic decorated with geometrical patterns. The church was destroyed by the Muslims in the 10C AD. Only the foundation walls of the castrum and the Church of the Theotokos have been preserved.

Shillo (Shilo)/Shiloh (30 km. SE): Shiloh in mentioned in the Bible as a town situated in the highlands of Ephraim, N. of Beth-el, on the road from Beth-el to Shechem (Judges 21, 19). After their conquest of Canaan, the Israelites made Shiloh their principal sanctuary, setting up the Ark of the Covenant (Joshua 18, 1) and celebrating their holy days there (1 Samuel, 1, 3). The young Samuel conducted worship at the altar in Shiloh under the supervision of Eli, the chief priest (1 Samuel 2). God told Samuel that, because of the sins of Eli's sons Phinehas and Hophni, he would let Shiloh and the house of Eli be destroyed. Hophni (the name means 'young frog' or 'tadpole') and his brother Phinehas unscrupulously abused their priestly status to their own advantage (1 Samuel 1, 3), stealing the sacrificial meat from those offering a sacrifice (1 Samuel 2, 12–17) and sleeping with the women staying 'at the door of the tabernacle of the congregation' (1 Samuel 2, 22), while their aged father was unable to put a stop to their behaviour. God then spoke through the young prophet Samuel and another man of God to tell Eli of the coming downfall of his family: 'And this shall be a sign to thee, that shall come upon thy two sons, Hophni and Phinehas; in one day they shall die both of them'. They were duly killed during the course of the battle in which the Philistines also made off with the Ark of the Covenant (1 Samuel 4, 11). When he heard the news of the loss of the Ark and the death of both his sons, the 98-year-old Eli fell backwards off his chair and broke his neck.

Basilica (end of the 5C/beginning of the 6C): This consists of two aisles, with no apse. Remains of a polychrome mosaic with geometrical patterns. *Pilgrims' church* (end of the 5C/beginning of the 6C): This measures 45 × 18 ft. and includes an atrium and narthex. It contains the remains of three mosaics. These are as follows: the first (in the apse) depicts vine-leaves and grapes and the second (in the nave) geometrical figures. The third is in the prothesis and shows two hinds with a pomegranate in the centre. Behind each hind is a fish. There are also two mosaic inscriptions in Greek. The first, in the prothesis, is a funeral inscription which is set inside a circle and occupies five lines. The second takes up two lines and is in the narthex. *Jami' Settin* (Mosque of the Sixty): This abandoned building may once have been a synagogue. Its open wall measures 29 × 29 ft. The four columns with Corinthian capitals probably belonged originally to a Byzantine basilica. The W. wall contains the lintel of a small window. The mihrab is set in the S. wall and flanked by two windows. There are three entrances in the N. wall. Above the lintel of the middle entrance can be seen a painting which depicts an amphora together with two garlands and two horned altars. The two side entrances were later covered over by the strong walls which were built outside the N., W., and W. walls in order to give the building the appearance of a tent.

Sychar (1 km. E.): As early as around AD 380 a cross-shaped church stood here above the well (Beer Ya'akov, or *Jacob's well*) which is supposed to have been sunk by Jacob and was later the site of Jesus' conversation with the Samaritan woman (John 4, 1–26). That early church was destroyed during the Samaritan uprising of AD 529. Later, in the second half of the 12C, the Crusaders built a new church on the same site; this had a nave and two aisles, and, beneath the choir, a crypt containing the well. On the right and left sides of the nave there was a staircase leading down to the crypt and the well itself, which was situated directly beneath the apse. The altar stood behind the well. This church was destroyed in the 15C. In 1885 it came into the possession of the Greek community of Balata, who began to rebuild it in 1903 with the financial support of the Russian church. All that can be seen today are the crypt and the lower layers of the outer walls. Jacob's well is 170 ft. deep. Its top is edged right around by a single stone 1 ft. 7 in. wide (through which a hole has been made in the middle). Many icons have been hung around the well. The stone which used to edge the top of the well was taken to Constantinople in the 4C.

Joseph's grave: According to Samaritan, Christian, and Arab tradition (the 12th sura of the Koran, which has 111 verses, is entirely devoted to Joseph), the remains of Joseph, the son of Jacob and Rachel, are buried 220 yards to the S. of Jacob's well, on the plot of land which belonged to Joseph's sons (Joshua 24, 32). 'A lovelier place of rest is no longer to be found, and in any case the son was more fortunate in this respect than his lovely mother, buried between Jerusalem and Bethlehem' (L. A. Frankl) (see Ramat Rahel: Environs). At the beginning of the 5C, a Byzantine church was erected over Joseph's grave, but it fell down and was never rebuilt. A small rectangular domed church, built of quarry-stone, was erected here in 1868 inside an enclosure. Its interior is whitewashed, and in the centre lies Joseph's sarcophagus, covered with a dark blue cloth. The low truncated columns at either end of the tomb are similarly covered in cloth, for, according to the Samaritan tradition, these mark the graves of Manasseh (Genesis 41, 50–1) and Ephraim (Genesis 41, 50–2), from whose families the Samaritans considered themselves to be descended. On the wall opposite the entrance there are two niches, each containing a marble tablet with an inscription. The tablet in the upper niche has been engraved, while the inscription on the other tablet has

Shillo (Shekhem), town wall

been made in raised script. Both quote the passages in the Bible which refer to Joseph's death and burial.

Shivta/Subeita
Southern District/Israel   p.322☐B 11

Roughly 50 km. to the SW of Beer Sheva, in the Negev, is the ruined site of Shivta, a city founded by the Nabataeans in the 1C BC which at its height had a population of up to 7,000 and was the largest town in the Negev, but was abandoned in the 10C AD. Numerous *Nabataean houses* have been preserved and partially restored, as have a double *water reservoir* and other archaeological remains. Two *early Christian churches* dating from the 4C, and the *main church*, dating from the 6C, are notably important.

Sodom
Southern District/Israel   p.322☐E 10

The city of Sodom no longer exists,

though it is marked on every map of Israel. At the time of the patriarch Abraham, Sodom was a city near the Dead Sea which was one of a confederation of five cities (the others being Gomorrah, Admah, Zeboiim, and Bela : Genesis 14, 2–3, and 10, 19). Together with the other cities in the confederation, King Bera of Sodom was defeated in the battle in the Valley of Siddim (i.e. the Salt Sea, meaning the Dead Sea) by a coalition grouped around King Chedor-laomer of Elam and Amraphel, King of Shinar, who proceeded to plunder the defeated towns (Genesis 14, 1–11). Abraham's nephew Lot, who had settled in Sodom, was also taken away with them as a prisoner. When Abraham heard the news, he attacked Chedor-laomer, seized the entire booty, and returned it all to the King of Sodom, goods, animals, and people (Genesis 14, 12–24).

Sinfulness: The inhabitants of Sodom were considered 'wicked and sinners before the Lord exceedingly' (Genesis 13, 13). The names of Sodom and Gomorrah are often linked because of their proverbial sinfulness: 'They

Shivta, Byzantine church (S. church)

commit adultery, and walk in lies: they strengthen the hand of the evildoers, that none doth return from his wickedness: they are all of them unto me as Sodom, and the inhabitants thereof as Gomorrah' (Jeremiah 23, 14). Again, 'For their vine is of the vine of Sodom, and of the fields of Gomorrah: their grapes are grapes of gall, their clusters are bitter: Their wine is the poison of dragons, and the cruel venom of asps.'(Deuteronomy 32, 32–3). Ezekiel 16, 48–50 also mentions social injustice as a reason for Sodom's destruction.

Sodomy: This word signifies sexual relations between persons of the male sex. Its use as a synonym for homosexuality derives from the passage in Genesis 19, 1 ff., which describes how two angels accepted Lot's hospitality and stayed the night at his house in Sodom in the guise of men. During the evening, the inhabitants surrounded the house and asked Lot to send the men out to them, calling out 'Bring them out unto us that we may know them.' In his despair (for the law of hospitality was inviolable), Lot offered them his two daughters, saying that they were virgins and the men could do as they pleased with them. Then the angels struck the men blind. The word has also been used in the past to denote bestiality. This meaning can be taken from the passage in Jude, 7 : 'Even as Sodom and Gomorrah, and the cities about them in like manner, giving themselves over to fornication, and going after strange flesh, are set forth an example, suffering the vengeance of eternal fire.' This states that they ran after 'strange flesh', in other words, creatures of a different species.

Destruction: The two angels told Lot that Sodom was going to be destroyed and advised him to leave the town as soon as possible (Genesis 19, 12 ff.). This he did, together with his wife and his two daughters, but without his prospective sons-in-law, who stayed behind, thinking he was joking. His wife disobeyed the angels'

injunction not to look back, and was turned into a pillar of salt. Sodom and Gomorrah perished in a rain of 'fire and brimstone'.

Their fate is seen in the Bible as a classic example of divine punishment, while at the same time the rescue of Lot is taken as a model for the deliverance of good people from an ordeal: 'And turning the cities of Sodom and Gomorrah into ashes condemned them with an overthrow, making them an example unto those that after should live ungodly; and delivered just Lot, vexed with the filthy conversation of the wicked: (For that righteous man dwelling among them, seeing and hearing, vexed his righteous soul from day to day with their unlawful deeds); The Lord knoweth how to deliver the godly out of temptations, and to reserve the unjust unto the day of judgement to be punished: But chiefly them that walk after the flesh in the lust of uncleanness, and despise government' (2 Peter 2, 6–10).

The two angels outside Sodom, 14C book illustration

Tabgha/En Sheva
Northern District/Israel   p.318□F 3

The town of Tabgha, which Christian tradition identifies as the site of the miracle of the loaves and fishes (the Feeding of the Four Thousand; Matthew 15, 32–9) is situated on the NW bank of the Sea of Galilee (3 km. S. of Kafarnaum/Kefar Nahum). The name means 'place of the seven springs' (the Arabic 'Tabgha' is a corruption of the Greek 'heptapegon',

translated into Hebrew as 'En Sheva'). Many churches have been excavated here, and during this century two new ones have been built.

Church of the Miracle of the Loaves and Fishes: This was built in 1982 in the Byzantine style by the German Society of the Holy Land, on the site where two earlier churches had once stood. *First church on this site:* This was built in the 4C and consisted of a single aisle (58 × 27 ft.). *Second church on this site* (5C): This formed part of a monastery measuring 190 × 80 × 110 ft. which also included a courtyard and hospice. The church was 1 ft. 8 in. above the level of the atrium and the walls survive up to a height of 48 ft. The church was built of local basalt, and only the doorstone and stylobate are of limestone. It was a cruciform basilica (99 × 50–67 ft.) whose interior was divided by two rows of five columns each into a nave and two aisles (the nave being 26 ft. wide and each of the aisles 12 ft. wide). This compact section was traversed by a wide transept which extended 6 ft. from the body of the

Tabgha, church of the Feeding of the Five Thousand

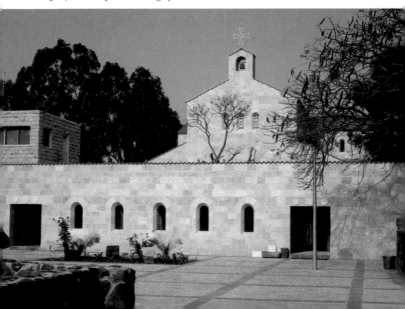

church and had a series of columns along the W. side. The semicircular apse was flanked by the prothesis (17 × 15–17 ft.) and diaconicon (17 × 17 ft.), which were connected through another room behind the apse. The church was built of rough-hewn basalt; the interior walls were plastered. The altar, whose base has been preserved, was placed in front of the apse and was surrounded by transennae in early Christian times. This second church was the only known example in Palestine of a basilica with a transept. The sanctuary (23 × 20 ft.) stood in front of the apse and was divided from the transept and the nave by the railing of the choir. It contains a block of unhewn limestone (taken from the first church on this site) which was believed by Christians as late as the 5C to have been the Lord's table (mensa Christi).
Floor mosaics: These have geometrical patterns (in the atrium, narthex, and side aisles, in the space between the columns in the W. aisle of the transept, the sanctuary, and the side rooms), and depict plants and figures (in the transept and behind the altar).

The mosaics are made of local limestone. The transept contains rectangular mosaics measuring 83 × 17 ft. which are edged with ornamental ribbons of lotus flowers twining in and out.

Church of the Sermon on the Mount: This was designed by A. Barluzzi and built in 1938 on the 'Mount of the Beatitudes' (Monte delle Beatitudine) as a replacement for the chapel there which had been abandoned in the 7C. It is octagonal and is made of local black basalt, except for the arches, which are of white stone from Nazareth, and the columns, built of Roman travertine. It stands in a beautiful garden setting, together with the Franciscan hospice. Its octagonal shape is meant to symbolize the eight Beatitudes (Matthew 5, 3–10). The interior is simple, the walls devoid of ornament. The dome, however, is decorated with mosaics set against a gold background. The eight windows and the dome depict the nine Beatitudes. In the apse can be seen a massive, ostentatious *altar* made of Carrara marble, on which stands a

Tabgha, church of the Feeding of the Five Thousand, mosaic

ciborium used both as a tabernacle and as the base for the monstrance.

Chapel of the Primacy (Chiesa del Primato): This is a simple structure, comprising a single aisle, which was built by the Franciscans in 1933. It commemorates the appearance of the resurrected Christ to His Apostles at the lakeside here, during which He thrice gave Peter a last commandment (John 21, 15–16). The rock (known as the mensa domini) in the E. part of the chapel is supposed to be the table at which Jesus and His disciples ate. The walls of the structure which formerly stood on this site can still be clearly seen by the foundations of three of the sides of the modern chapel, at the end furthest from the altar. By the side of the church facing the lakeside there are steps cut out of the rock, and beneath these are six heart-shaped stones (which are sometimes under water). These were bases for double columns which stood at the end of a colonnade. They are called the '12 thrones' or the 'chairs of the 12 Apostles', and were first mentioned in AD 808. The ruins of a Frankish building can be seen immediately to their side.

Monastery of the Sermon on the Mount (325 yards from the Church of the Miracle of the Loaves and Fishes): This was built in the 4C. The rooms of the monastery were on the S. side, while the church (24×15 ft.), which consisted of a single aisle and had a white altar, was to the N. The East-facing apse extended beyond the monastery walls and had pews for the priests inside. The whole of the square sacristy, on the N. side, was hewn out of the rock. The church was destroyed in the 9C. The narthex and the nave contained mosaics with geometrical and floral patterns (now in the garden at Kafarnaum/Kefar Nahum). Beneath the church there is a rectangular grotto which measures 14×7 ft. and is 12 ft. deep.

Environs: Khirbet el-Minya (2 km. W.): The Palace of the Umayyad Caliph Walid I (AD 705–15) was partially excavated from 1932–58. *Palace:* This was a nearly square fortress with round towers (each with a

Tabgha, church of the Sermon on the Mount

diameter of 17 ft.) at the corners and in the middle of each side. The limestone outer walls were 5 ft. thick and still stand up to a height of 10 layers of stone blocks. The merlons were trapezoid. On the E. side, between two semicircular towers there is a gatehouse 55 ft. wide. The porch of the gate-house is set forward and has niches on both sides, and is vaulted by a pendentive dome which is decorated with reliefs and glass mosaics. A second archway leads into a square inner courtyard which is surrounded on all four sides by colonnades. At the SE corner is the *mosque* (64 × 44 ft.), which excavations have shown to be one of the earliest mosques in existence. Its shape is long and narrow. The mihrab was set in the S. wall (one of the narrow sides) and has been preserved up to a height of two layers of stone above the basalt foundations (5 ft. 5 in. wide and 3 ft. 8 in. deep). On each side of the mihrab there are niches in which small columns were intended to be set. The boundary walls to the E. and S. are still 7 ft. high, while the W. wall is 4 ft. high, and the N. wall has been destroyed.

There is a group of three rooms on the S. side, of which the middle room is itself divided into three sections and richly ornamented. The floor was decorated with a mosaic which looks like a carpet, thanks to the fringes at the edges and the suggestion of having been woven. The *S. palace* (140 × 67 ft.) incorporates the throne hall (in the centre), a room (to the E.) which is divided by the row of supports, and, at the W. end, a group of five rooms. It is bordered to the E. by the mosque and by a group of offices to the W. Throne hall (known as the throne room or marble room): This is divided by two rows of supports into a wide central paasage and two narrow passages at each side. The main part of the throne room is 67 ft. long. Every fragment of the outer walls, down to the lowest level, has been robbed. Of the six supports, only the middle one in the E. row is still standing on its original site.

Tell el-'Oreme (on the W. bank of the Sea of Galilee): Tell el-'Oreme is thought to have been founded during the middle Bronze Age II B, and was still extant in the late Bronze Age. It

Khirbet el-Minya (Tabgha), palace ruins

was resettled in the early Iron Age by the nomadic Naftali tribe. After its destruction by the Assyrians towards the end of the Northern Kingdom (of Israel), it seems not to have been rebuilt, though there is evidence of an occasional human presence here during the Persian, Hellenistic, and Roman periods. The period of Roman rule saw the foundation of Ginossar on the plain. The excavations of Tell el-'Oreme are on a mountain, whose W. peak, being the highest part of the mountain, was in fact the site of the settlement. The S. peak of the mountain is a rectangular tell whose plateau measures 200×100 ft. To its NE. is an almost rectangular area measuring 200×300 ft. which would have been the lower town; this rises to the N. and up to the N. summit. The tell was presumably the acropolis. There are some traces of cultivation in ancient times on the E. slope, which falls towards the lake. The whole area measures 680×500 ft. The traces of settlement remaining on it were excavated by three archaeological expeditions in 1932, 1939, and 1967. *Finds:* Early Bronze Age ceramics; Roman

pottery; and Roman waterworks. The finds from the middle Bronze Age II include round vessels with flat bottoms and vessels dating from the Persian and Hellenistic periods.

Tabor, Mount/Har Tavor
Northern District/Israel   p.318☐E 4

This mountain, which looks like a flat cone, stands on the edge of the Plain of Yezreel, to the SE of Nazareth. It has been asserted by Christian tradition ever since the 4C to have been the mountain on which Christ's Transfiguration took place (Matthew 17, 1–2; Mark 9, 2; Luke 9, 28), and which St.Peter therefore called the 'holy mountain' (2 Peter 1, 18). Before that, Psalms 89, 13 mentioned it and Mt. Hermon as the most important mountains in Palestine (see also Jeremiah 46, 18).
Mt. Tabor stood on the border dividing the lands of the tribes of Zebulun and Issachar (Joshua 19, 22), and was seen from the most ancient times as a sacred mountain; sacrifices were

Tabgha, Chapel of the Primacy

Mount Tabor, Transfiguration basilica

offered here (Deuteronomy 33, 19), and unorthodox cults are also mentioned (Hosea 5, 1) as having been practised on Mt. Tabor.

Three churches were built on the mountain in the 6C AD, and there are supposed to have been four churches standing here by the 9C. Some Benedictine monks were settled on the mountain by Tancred in 1099, but they lost their lives during an Arab attack in 1113. The Crusaders built a wall around the oval of the summit, parts of which are still visible today. The Benedictine monastery, which included chapels to Moses, Elijah and Jesus, was destroyed by Sultan Baibars in 1263. In 1867 the Greek Orthodox monks began to build the Church of Elijah. They were followed here by the Franciscans in 1873. The summit is divided into two parts by a wall running from W. to E., with the S. part belonging to the Franciscans and the N. half being the property of the Greek Orthodox.

Basilica of the Transfiguration:
The Transfiguration, reported in Mark 9, 2–10, Matthew 17, 1–9, and Luke 9, 28–36, consisted of the revelation of Jesus' Messianic status, on a mountain not mentioned by name and in the presence of the Apostles Peter, James and John. As it took place, Jesus was transformed before the eyes of His apostles, His face shining like the sun and His clothes taking on the blinding radiance of pure light. Moses and Elijah appeared and spoke to Jesus; then, from behind a shining cloud which covered them with shadow, a voice said: 'This is my beloved Son, in whom I am well pleased; hear ye him.' (Compare Matthew 3, 17; Isaiah 42, 1; Deuteronomy 18, 15; Psalms 2, 7).

This Franciscan church was built in 1924 in a bizarre style which combines East and West. It is surrounded by a walled cloister. The garden of the convent contains a tablet commemorating the architect A.Barluzzi, as well as a memorial to Pope Paul VI's visit to Mt. Tabor in 1964.

The basilica is built of a light-coloured limestone. The façade is divided into three sections by two symmetrical bell towers which bear carved ornament and project

Mount Tabor

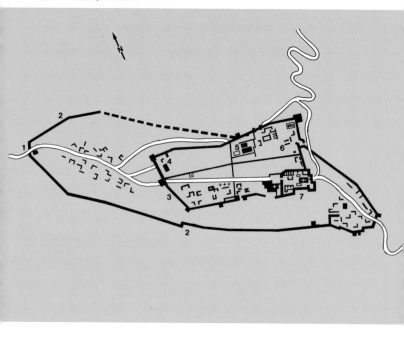

forwards; between them is an archway which leads into the porch and stands beneath a pediment. The windows are framed with scrolls. Three triangles can be seen, symbolizing the three tents which Peter suggested building at the Transfiguration (Matthew 17, 1–9). The large rectangular door is set back from the parvis.

The basilica itself is divided by columns into a nave and two aisles. The nave, which is slightly higher, ends in a semicircular apse which is lit by windows and decorated with a mosaic depicting the Transfiguration against a gold background. The central *mosaic* above the altar shows Jesus in the middle, flanked by Moses (left) and Elijah (right); beneath them are the Apostles Peter (left) and James and John (right). The nave is separated by broad arches from the aisles. The timber roof is supported by small columns in the clerestory. The side chapels are dedicated to the Holy Sacrament and the Immaculate Conception. The heavy towers in the façade have been built on top of the foundations of the Frankish Chapel of Moses and Elijah.

Church of Elijah: The Crusaders built a church here over the remains of an earlier Byzantine church dating from the 4/5C AD, but it was destroyed in 1183 by Sultan Saladin. In 1511 a small chapel dedicated to Elijah was built here by monks, above the cave of Melchizedek. The present church dates from 1911. The courtyard contains some cisterns, and its N. and E. sides are adjoined by rows of cells. The two apses and the floor

Mount Tabor, Transfiguration basilica, mosaic above altar

mosaic have been preserved from the Frankish church.

Cave of Melchizedek: Inside the medieval Arab wall there is a small iron door, flanked by two windows, which leads into the cave of Melchizedek. Melchizedek is described as king of Salem and 'priest of the most high God' (Genesis 14, 18). He blessed Abraham from 'the most high God, possessor of heaven and earth' (Genesis 14, 19), after which Abraham gave him a tithe of everything (Genesis 14, 20). As can be seen from Psalms 76, 2, ('In Salem also is his tabernacle, and his dwelling place in Zion'), the Jewish tradition, as well as many of the Fathers of the Church, identified Salem with Jerusalem, so that Melchizedek, the priest-king of (Jeru)Salem, was seen not just as the archetype of an absolute monarch, but as prefiguring the Messiah (Psalms

110, 4: 'Thou art a priest for ever after the order of Melchizedek').

Al-'Adil: This is an *Arab fortress*, built in 1211–12, which was once one of the largest and strongest fortifications in the Holy Land. It spans the entire hill. It is 5,830 ft. long on the N. side, 1,930 ft. on the S. side, 1,500 ft. long on the E. side, and 830 ft. on the W. side. It used to have a massive square tower and ten rectangular towers. The modern entrance to the monastery stands above the ruins of the old W. gate, which was known as the Damascus Gate. The walls and towers are built of rough-hewn blocks of stone in the Ayyubid style.

Tel Aviv-Jaffa (Yafo)
Tel Aviv District   p.320□C 6

Tel Aviv-Jaffa is Israel's biggest city

and its economic centre, containing 30 per cent of its population.

History: Jaffa ('Japho' in the Bible) has been inhabited since the fifth millennium before Christ. According to Jewish tradition, it was founded by Noah's son Japheth forty years after the end of the Flood and is supposed to be one of the oldest towns on earth and certainly the oldest port. The name is said to derive from that of Japheth. The Roman historian Pliny the Elder connected it with Jopa, who was the daughter of Aeolus, the god of wind. *Period of Egyptian rule:* The first mention of Jaffa in an inscription was made during the reign of the Egyptian Pharaoh Thutmosis III, who captured the town in 1486 BC.
Phoenician harbour: During or after the reign of Ramses II (1290–1224 BC), Jaffa fell to the Philistines. According to Joshua 19, 46, the 'territory facing' Japho belonged to the tribe of Dan, though the town itself seems not to have been captured by the Israelites. The wood for the construction of Solomon's temple was brought to Jerusalem from the Lebanon via Jaffa (2 Chronicles 2, 16). Jaffa still seems to have belonged to the Philistines during the reign of King Jeroboam II. of Israel (787–747 BC), for the prophet Jonah, who lived then, is related to have boarded a Phoenician ship in Jaffa in order to escape to Tarshish (Jonah 1, 3 ff.).
The myth of Andromeda: During the second half of the 8C BC Jaffa once more came under Egyptian rule. The governor of Jaffa at this time is supposed to have been Kepheus, an Ethiopian; and it is this which links Jaffa, the only town in Israel with a background of ancient myth, to the myth of Andromeda. According to that legend, Cassiopeia, the wife of Kepheus, had boasted that she was more beautiful than the Nereids, the lovely sea-nymphs who formed Poseidon's retinue. To punish her, Poseidon flooded the land and sent a sea-monster, Ketos, to infest it. Kepheus

was told by an oracle that his country would be freed from these afflictions if he fed his daughter Andromeda to the monster. So he fastened her to the rock of Jaffa on the sea-shore, from which however she was released by the hero Perseus, who wedded her and killed the monster. Today, a rock near the old harbour is pointed out as the so-called Andromeda Rock. The legend also has it that, for the love of his wife, Cassiopeia, Kepheus named the town 'Iopeia', from which the Hellenistic name Ioppe was supposedly derived.
After the Exile: After the period of Assyrian rule (following the Assyrian conquest in 702 BC), Jaffa once again became a Phoenician city in the 6C. When the Second Temple was being built (after the Exile), cedarwood for its construction was brought to Jerusalem from the Lebanon via Jaffa (Ezra 3, 7), just as it had been when Solomon's Temple had been built.
The Hellenistic period: In 332 BC, Jaffa became part of the empire forged by Alexander the Great; after his death, it came under the Egyptian empire of the Ptolemeys. At this time, it was engaged mainly in the transhipment of wheat. An outbreak of Jewish persecution is described by 2 Maccabees, 12, 3 ff. The Jewish inhabitants of the town, including women and children, were persuaded to board ships which were then sunk in the open sea. 200 Jews perished in this way. When Judas Maccabaeus heard the news, he set fire to the harbour and burned the boats there, though he was unable to capture the town itself. It fell to his brother Jonathan to effect its capture in 144 BC (1 Maccabees 10, 76), after which Jonathan's brother Simon fortified it (in 142 BC) and settled Jews there (1 Maccabees 14, 34).
The period of Roman rule: Jaffa was captured in 63 BC by Pompey, the Roman general and triumvir. After his defeat of Pompey in the Roman civil war, Julius Caesar placed Jaffa under the direct rule of the Jewish high priest. Its importance declined,

however, when King Herod the Great built the port of Caesarea, and in AD 6 it became part of the Roman province of Judaea.

St.Peter spent some time in Jaffa. It was here that he raised from the dead a female disciple named Tabitha (Acts 9, 36–43), and here too that he had a vision enabling him to recognize that his missionary work should not be restricted to Jews but should be directed no less towards the Gentiles (Acts 10, 9–23/34–5). The town was destroyed by the Romans during the First Jewish War (AD 66–70) but was later rebuilt, and the Jewish community there also managed to survive the Second Jewish War (132–5) and the Bar Kochba uprising. In the 4C it had a resident bishop, and during the same period a number of Babylonian Jews settled here.

Middle Ages: Jaffa was conquered by the Arabs in 636. Its importance grew once more after their foundation of Ramla in 711 as the provincial capital, and during the Crusades it was the principal port used by pilgrims; but, after it had been finally recaptured by the Muslims in 1268, its significance declined to that of an unimportant fishing village.

Tel Aviv-Jaffa: The Jewish settlements of Tel Aviv, Petah Tiqvah, Neve Zedek, and Neve Shalom were established in the 19C. The town of Tel Aviv, whose name means 'the hill of spring', was founded in 1908. (The name also recalls Tel-Abib, which was a town in Babylon where deported Jews lived during the Exile). The population rose to 75,000 in 1934 and 230,000 by 1948 (of whom 100,000 lived in Jaffa). The State of Israel was proclaimed on 15 May 1948 by the Jewish National Council in Tel Aviv, and the town of Jaffa, which according to the line of demarcation proposed by the UN in 1947 should have remained in Arab hands, was captured by the Israelis during the First Arab-Jewish War later in 1948. In 1950 Tel Aviv and Jaffa were combined into a single city.

Museums:
Museum of Antiquities of Tel Aviv-Yafo (Jaffa): Finds from Tel Aviv-Jaffa; the Venus of Yafo (fifth millennium BC).

Tel Aviv, panorama

Bet Dizengoff (Tel Aviv: Sderot Rothschild 16): *Museum of the Bible*. It was in this house that David Ben Gurion proclaimed the State of Israel on 15 May 1948.

HaAretz Museum (Ramat Aviv): This incorporates nine separate collections and museums covering the history of writing, ethnography, and popular art, and including also a Glass Museum, Museum of Ceramics, Numismatic Museum (which displays coinage), and a Museum of Science and Technology.

Haganah Museum (Tel Aviv: Museum of the Israel Defence Forces: Sderot Rothschild 23): History of the Israeli armed forces in Palestine.

Helena Rubinstein Museum (Tel Aviv: Sderot Tarsat): Exhibitions of art.

Historical Museum of Tel Aviv (Rehov Bialik 17): Museum describing the history of the city.

Nahum Goldmann Museum of the Jewish Diaspora (Bet HaTefutsot): Museum describing the history of the Jews after the destruction of the Second Temple in AD 70.

Tel Aviv Museum (Sderot Shaul Hamelekh 27): Art of the last four centuries and of the modern period. The works of leading painters and sculptors (Picasso, Degas, Moore and others) are displayed.

Also worth seeing: *Old harbour* (Jaffa): This is used as a harbour for yachts and fishing boats and is the setting of the so-called Andromeda Rock. What used to be the slums around the old harbour is now an *artists' quarter* with studios and galleries. Archaeological zone of *Gan HaPisga. Habimah* ('the stage': Tel Aviv: Sderot Tarsat): Israeli National Theatre and cultural centre. *Main synagogue* (Tel Aviv: Allenby Road): Built in 1923–6. *HaYargon* (Tel Aviv): Promenade along the shore. *Karmel market* (Tel Aviv: Shuq HaKarmel): Oriental market. *Migdal Shalom* (Tel Aviv: The name means 'tower of peace'): This is 470 ft. high and the tallest building in the Middle East, incorporating a department store, offices, a hotel, and an observation platform. *Tel Qasile* (Ramat Aviv): Philistine site under excava-

Tel Dan, stairs on S. side

tion. *Second-hand market* (Shuq HaPishpeshim: Jaffa: S. of the Great Mosque, also called the Mahmudiya Mosque): Flea market.

Tel Dan/Tell el-Qadi
Northern District/Israel   p.318□F 2

This is situated to the E. of Kiryat Shemona, in the region settled by the Israelite tribe of Dan after it had abandoned its old tribal lands to the W. of Jerusalem at the beginning of the 11C BC. During this migration, the Danites destroyed the town of Laish and rebuilt it as their own capital, to be known as Dan (Judges 18, 27–9). After the division of Israel into two states, Jeroboam I (*c.* 930–08 BC) became king of the Northern Kingdom, and he set up two golden calves in the sanctuaries of Dan and Beth-el. The settlement came to an end with the Assyrian invasion in 732 BC. The hill of Tel Dan (in Arabic, Tell el-Qadi, meaning 'hill of the judge'), which stands above the ancient settlement, has been under excavation by Israeli architects since 1965. The discoveries so far made include masonry dating from the early and middle Bronze Age and, in the S. part of the site, the remains of a massive S. gate dating from the 10C BC. The *S. gate* (also called the Gate of Jeroboam) was a monumental structure measuring 80 ft. across and built of brown basalt. It incorporated two watch towers.

A platform measuring 62 ft. 4 in. × 60 ft. 8 in. may have been used as the supporting stand for Jeroboam's golden calf. The sanctuary was surrounded by a wall which was open to the S. A stairway (27 ft. wide) on the S. side led up the hill. The wall, whose masonry incorporated stretchers and headers, was expanded by King Ahab and Jeroboam II.

Tiberias/Teverya
Northern District/Israel   p.318□F 3

Tiberias, on the W. bank of the Sea of Galilee (John 6, 23), was built by Herod Antipas around 26 BC as capital

Tiberias, tomb of Moshe Chaim Luzzatto

of the tetrarchy of Galilee, in honour of the Roman Emperor Tiberius, after whom it was also named. The Sea of Galilee was also called Lake Tiberias after this town. Like most Jews, Jesus avoided this Hellenistic town, which was considered to be unclean because Jewish graves had been destroyed during its construction (according to the Talmud, the site on which it was built had once been occupied by the Old Testament city of Hammar-Rakath; see also Joshua 19, 35). However, since the nearby town of Ammathus contained warm springs which were considered therapeutic, Tiberias was later declared ritually clean. In the 3/4C AD it was the seat of the rabbinical Patriarch, and the Mishna and the Jerusalem Talmud were edited here.

From 1099 to 1187, Tiberias was part of the Frankish kingdom and capital of the principality of Galilee. After being destroyed by Sultan Baibars in 1247, it was not resettled until 1517. In 1562 the Spanish Jewish adventurer Don Joseph Naxi and his aunt, Gracia Mendes, acquired Tiberias from the Sultan, their intention being

to establish a Jewish town under Ottoman sovereignty; but the experiment failed, and during the 17C the town fell into decay. It was rebuilt in 1738 by the Druze Emir Daher el-' Amr. 1765 saw the immigration here of some Jews from Poland. In 1837 Tiberias was destroyed by an earthquake. During the 19C there were some 5,000 Jews living here, and by 1940 their numbers had reached 12,000. The last Arabs left Tiberias on 19 April 1948.

Excavations: The Roman city extended over an area of $4,000 \times 830$ ft. to Hammat Tiberias, S. of the modern town. Systematic excavations in 1973 and 1974 revealed a Byzantine bath-house with superb mosaics (see Hammat Tiberias), a market-place dating from soon after the Arab conquest, a colonnaded street (Cardo) in the W. part of the site, and, in the E. part, a large building from late Roman times, perhaps a church.

Cardo: The basalt gate was flanked by two round towers with a diameter of 23 ft. Between the round towers and the jambs of the gate there were two plinths supporting columns with rhomboid patterns in relief. The street was paved with square basalt stones. The Cardo probably dates from the foundation of the city.

Graves: 260 yards NW of the post office on Rehov Hatanaim is the old Jewish cemetery, which contains, among others, the graves of the Spanish philosopher *Maimonides* (1135–1204; known as Rambam) and the famous legal scholars *Rabbi Johanan ben Zakkai* (1C AD) and *Eliezer ben Hyrcanus* (end of the 1C and beginning of the 2C AD). Maimonides (Moses Ben Maimon) left his native Cordoba for Fez in 1148, then in 1165 moved on to Cairo, where he died in 1204. Apart from being Saladin's physician, he is considered to have been the greatest Jewish religious philosopher of the Middle Ages. His

Tiberias, Franciscan church of St.Peter

main work, written in Arabic, is the 'Guide for the Irresolute'; and he is revered as much by Muslims as he is by Jews. Johanan ben Zakkai was the leading scholar during the period of the Second Temple. He is supposed to have lived 120 years, like Moses and Hillel before him. Eliezer ben Hyrcanus taught at the famous school of Yavneh after the destruction of the Second Temple; he lived in Lydda (Lod), where he founded an academy. To the W. of the old cemetery, set on a slope, is the white *mausoleum* of the great *Rabbi ben Akiba* (AD 50–137), who led the Bar Kochba uprising against the Romans. He was condemned to death in Tiberias and skinned alive in AD 137 in Caesarea.

Franciscan church of St.Peter: This was built on top of the foundations of an earlier Crusader church. The Franciscans bought its ruins in 1847 and restored it extensively in 1870 and 1944. The present church has a beautiful *cloister*. The triangular apse recalls the prow of Peter's fishing-boat. The courtyard contains

a memorial for the Polish soldiers in the Second World War.

Al-Jami'a el-Bahri: This mosque was built in 1948 and incorporates fragments of an earlier Jewish Christian church. The basalt lintel of the door is decorated by crosses which are set around a vase containing flowers.

Magen David Museum (S. of the Rambam Synagogue): The town museum was founded in 1952 by Tirzah Ravani and is housed in a former mosque. The exhibits consist of objects discovered in Tiberias and its environs, including an archway and stone reliefs from the Roman and Byzantine periods, inscriptions, a seven-armed candelabra dating from the 3/4C (found in Tiberias), coins, Hittite reliefs, and finds made in old synagogues and tombs.

Also worth seeing: *Grave of Abu Huria* (died 677), the Companion of the Prophet Muhammad. (Situated between the old town and Hammat). *Kasr el-Bint:* The remains of the

Deganya (Tiberias), baptism site

Migdal (Tiberias), Roman sarcophagi

acropolis of Herod Antipas can be seen on the spur of the mountain. *Crusader fort:* This was restored by Daher el-'Amr in the 17C and is now a cultural centre.

Environs: Deganya (10 km. S.): This is the oldest kibbutz in Israel, having been established in 1909. The cemetery contains the graves of Otto Warburg, Joseph Bussel, A.D. Gordon, and Arthur Ruppin.*Bet Gordon Museum* (museum of natural science). **Hammat Tiberias:** See entry. **Khirbet Ha'Amudim** (19 km. W.): At the E. edge of the Bet Netopha Valley can be seen the ruins of an old village, together with the remains of a *synagogue* dating from the 3/4C AD. Its interior measures 47 × 75 ft. and is divided into three aisles by two rows of seven columns each. The columns have Ionic capitals. The main aisle is 20 ft. 8 in. wide, and each of the side

aisles 10 ft. 6 in. wide. There is another row, with two extra columns, in front of the back wall. The wall facing Jerusalem contains the main entrance as well as two side entrances. *Finds:* Three door lintels. The first of these, the main lintel, is broken in two. On each side is a lion, seen in profile, with one paw upraised and the other resting on the head of a bull. In the middle are the remains of an amphora. The second lintel comes from a side-entrance and is also broken in two. It has three sections, of which that on the right depicts a flower, the middle one represents half of a garland, and that on the left another flower. The third lintel also has three sections, of which that on the right depicts a flower and the one in the centre the head of the Medusa. **Me'arat Amira** (13 km. NW): Two prehistoric caves were excavated in Nahal 'Ammud. *Cave of the column*

(430 yards N. of the bridge, on the W. side of the wadi). Finds: the complete skeleton of a young man who was buried lying on his left side with his knees drawn up (about 6 ft. tall and 25 years old). Also the skeletons of two children aged three to four. *Cave of the gipsy woman* (430 yards S. of the bridge). Finds: Remains of the skull of the 'Galilean man'; also the bones of bears and hippopotami. The caves were inhabited during the middle Stone Age (80,000–35,000 BC).

Migdal (5 km. NW): Birthplace of Mary Magdalene. Migdal (known as Magdala in the Bible) was a large town in ancient times. *Excavations:* Parts of a paved street, remains of a Roman villa with bath, and a synagogue (?) dating from the 1C BC.

Sea of Galilee (Genezareth)/Yam Kinneret: This freshwater lake, with its abundant population of fish, is situated 700 ft. below sea-level in the basin of the River Jordan (which flows into and out of it), between the mountains of Galilee and the Golan Heights. It is 21 km. long and up to 13 km. wide.

The fertile Plain of Gennesaret which during Jesus' lifetime was quite densely populated, extends to the NW of the lake. It was in the nearby towns (Kafarnaum, Betsaida, Gadara) and on the lake shore itself that Jesus performed much of His public ministry.

It is referred to by the name of Lake Gennesaret in 1 Maccabees 47, 67 and Luke 5, 1. Apart from that, the Old Testament knows it as the 'sea of Chinnereth' (Numbers 34, 11; Joshua 12, 3 and 13, 27), and also refers to the plain to its NW as 'Cinneroth' (1 Kings 15, 20). The New Testament calls it the 'Sea of Galilee' (Matthew 4, 18) and, elsewhere, 'the sea of Tiberias'(John 6, 1), after the city of Tiberias which had been founded on its SW shore by Herod Antipas. The outstanding events around the Sea of Galilee during Jesus' ministry were: His call to the first four Apostles (Matthew 4, 18–22); Mark 1, 16–20; Luke 5, 1–11); the storm on the lake (Matthew 8, 23–7; Mark 4, 35–41; Luke 8, 22–5); the raising of Jairus' daughter from the dead (Mark 5, 21 ff.; Luke 8, 40–56); the feeding of the five thousand (Matthew 14, 13–21); the miraculous feeding of a crowd of people by Lake Tiberias (John 6, 1–15); Jesus' walking on the water (Matthew 14, 22; Mark 6, 45–52; John 6, 16–21); healings of the sick (Matthew 14, 34–6; Mark 6, 53–6); the healing of a deaf man (Mark 7, 31–7); the feeding of the four thousand (Matthew 15, 32–9; Mark 8, 1–13); and the appearance of the resurrected Christ by the lakeside (John 21).

Yesreel plain/Emeq Yizre'el
Northern District/District of Haifa/Israel

The Yesreel plain forms a triangle. Its base at the foot of Mount Carmel, extending from Yokne'am to Jenin, is some 30 km. long, and its apex in the N. lies below Nazareth. It is 365 sq.km. in area. Afula (q.v.) is the main town.

The Yesreel plain has frequently been the scene of military conflict. It was here that Deborah's battle was fought (Judges 4), Gideon the judge defeated the Midianites (Judges 6, 33), and the Egyptian king Nechoh vanquished king Josiah of Judah (2 Kings 23, 29).

Glossary

Acanthus: Decorative element found especially on → Corinthian capitals; it developed from the stylized representation of a sharply serrated, thistle-like leaf.

Aedicule: Wall niche housing a bust or statue; usually with a → gable, → pillars or → columns.

Altar: Sacrificial table of Greeks and Romans. The Lord's table in the Christian faith. Catholic churches often have several side altars as well as the high altar.

Ambo: Stand or lectern by the choir screen in early Christian and medieval churches; predecessor of the → pulpit.

Ambulatory: A corridor created by continuing the side aisles around the choir; often used for processions.

Annunciation: Annunciation by the angel to Mary of the birth of Christ.

Antependium: Covering for the front of the altar.

Apodyterium: Changing room in ancient Roman baths.

Apse: Large recess at end of the → choir, usually semicircular or polygonal. As a rule it contains the → altar.

Apsidiole: A small apsidal chapel.

Aquamanile: Pouring-vessel or bowl for ritual washing in the Catholic liturgy.

Aqueduct: Water pipe or channel across an arched bridge; frequently built as monumental structures by the Romans.

Arabesque: Stylized foliage used as a decorative motif.

Arcade: A series of arches borne by columns or pillars. When the arcade is attached to a wall (and is purely decorative), it is called a blind arcade.

Architrave: Main stone member on top of the columns; lowest part of the → entablature.

Archivolt: The face of an arch in Romanesque and Gothic portals; often more than one.

Ashlar: Hewn block of stone (as opposed to that straight from the quarry).

Atrium: In Roman houses a central hall with an opening in the roof. In Christian architecture, a forecourt usually surrounded by columns; also known as a → paradise.

Attic: A (usually richly decorated) storey above the main → entablature; intended to conceal the roof.

Baldacchino: Canopy above altars, tombs, statues, portals, etc.

Baluster: Short squat or shaped column.

Balustrade: Rail formed of → balusters.

Baptistery: Place of baptism; may be a separate building.

Baroque: Architectural style from *c.* 1600–*c.* 1750. Distinguished by powerfully agitated, interlocking forms.

Bartizan: A small corner turret projecting from the top of a building.

Basket arch: A flattened round arch.

Basilica: Greek hall of kings. In church architecture, a type of church with nave and two or more aisles, the roof of the nave being higher than the roofs above the aisles.

Bay: Vertical division of a building between pillars, columns, windows, wall arches, etc.

Bosquet: Clumps of trees and bushes, particularly common in French gardens and parks.

Bracket: A projection from the wall used as a support—for a bust, statue, arch, etc.

Calidarium: Warm bath in ancient Roman bath house.

Calotte: Half dome with no drum.

Calvary: Sculpture of the Crucifixion and Mount Calvary.

Campanile: Bell tower; usually free standing.

Capital: Topmost part of a column. The shape of the capital determines the style or → order.

Cartouche: Decorative frame or panel imitating a scrolled piece of paper, usually with an inscription, coat-of-arms, etc.

Caryatid: A carved figure supporting the entablature.

Cella: Main room of ancient temple containing divine image.

Chapterhouse: Assembly room in which monks or nuns discuss the community's business.

Charnel house: House or vault in which bones are placed.

Choir: That part of the church in which divine service is sung. Shorter and often narrower than the nave, it is usually raised and at the E. end. In the Middle Ages the choir was often separated from the rest of the church by a screen.

Ciborium: Canopy over high altar; usually in the form of a dome supported on columns.

Classicism: Revival of Greek and Roman architectural principles.

Clerestory: Upper part of the main walls of the nave, above the roofs of the aisles and pierced by windows.

Cloister: Four sided covered walk (often vaulted) and opening inwards by arcades.

Coffered ceiling: A ceiling divided into square or polygonal panels, which are painted or otherwise decorated.

Column: Support with circular cross-section, narrowing somewhat towards the top; the type of column is determined by the → order. → Pillar.

Compound pillar: Often found in Gothic buildings. A central shaft has attached or detached shafts or half-shafts clustered around it.

Conch: Semicircular recess with a half-dome.

Confessio: Chamber or recess for a relic near the altar.

Corinthian order: → Order with richly decorated → capitals; the base has two or more tiers and is similar to that of the → Ionic order.

Cornice: Projecting upper limit of a wall; topmost member of the → entablature of an → order.

Cosmati work: Decorative technique involving the use of marble inlay, mosaics etc.; many Roman marble workers had the family name Cosma.

Crocket: Gothic leaf-like decoration projecting from the sides of pinnacles, gables etc.

Crypt: Burial place, usually under the → choir. Churches were often built above an old crypt.

Curtain wall: Outer wall of castle.

Cyclops wall: Ancient wall made of large rough bocks of stone of irregular shape.

Diaconicon: Room in or attached to a church, used in Early Christian times for the reception of the congregation's offerings and serving as archive, vestry and library, later used only for the latter functions.

Dipteros: Temple in which porticoes are connected by a double row of lateral columns.

Diptych: A painted hinged double (altar) panel.

Directoire style: French style under the Directoire (1795–9), influenced by Antiquity.

Dolmen: Chamber tomb lined and roofed with megaliths.

Doric order: → Order in which the columns lack a base and bear flat, pad-shaped → capitals.

Dormer window: Window in sloping roof which projects and has its own gabled roof.

Drum: Substructure of a dome; as a rule either cylindrical or polygonal.

Dwarf Gallery: Romanesque feature; wall passage of small arches on the outside of a building.

Empire style: Classical style in France at the beginning of the 19C, with Graeco-Roman and Egyptian models.

Enclos Paroissal: Enclosed churchyard in France, often with a → Calvary.

Entablature: Upper part of an → order; made up of → architrave, → frieze and → cornice.

Eremitage: Pavilion in park or garden, lonely castle or palace.

Exedra: Apse, vaulted with a half-dome; may have raised seats.

Facade: Main front of a building, often decoratively treated.

Facing: Panelling in front of structural components not intended to be visible.

Faience: Glazed pottery named after the Italian town of Faenza.

Fan vault: Looks like a highly decorated rib vault; Concave-sided cone-like sections meet or nearly meet at the apex of the vault.

Fascia: Raised horizontal band in an architrave.

Filigree work: Originally goldsmith's work in which gold and silver wire were ornamentally soldered on to a metal base. Also used in a more general sense for intricately perforated carvings and stucco.

Finial: Small decorative pinnacle.

Flying buttress: Very large Gothic windows made it necessary to buttress or strengthen the outer walls by half-arches and arches. This support transmitted the thrust of the vault to the buttress.

Foliate capital: Gothic capital in which the basic form is covered with delicate leaf ornaments.

Fosse: Artificially created ditch; often separated castles from the surrounding land with access by a drawbridge.

Fresco: Pigments dispersed in water are appplied without a bonding agent to the still-damp lime plaster. While the mortar dries, the pigments become adsorbed into the plaster.

Frieze: Decorative strips for the borders of a wall.

The frieze can be two- or three-dimensional and can consist of figures or ornaments.

Frigidarium: Cold bath in Roman bath house

Gable: The triangular upper section of a wall. Normally at one end of a pitched roof but it may be purely decorative.

Gallery: Intermediate storey; in a church it is usually for singers and the organ. Arcaded walkway.

Gobelin: Pictorial tapestry woven in the Gobelins factory in Paris.

Gothic: Period in European art and architecture stretching from the mid 12C to the 16C.

Grisaille: Painting in various shades of grey.

Groin vault: Vault in which two → barrel vaults intersect at right angles. The simple groin vault is to be distinguished from the rib vault, in which the intersecting edges are reinforced with ribs.

Half-timbering: Beams are used as supporting parts with an infill of loam or brick.

Hall church: In contrast to the → basilica, nave and aisles are of equal height; no → transept.

Hermitage: Pavilion in parks and gardens; originally the residence of a hermit.

Holy Sepulchre: Structure representing Christ's tomb as discovered by Constantine, who later encased it in a miniature temple.

Iconostasis: In the Eastern church, a screen of paintings between the sanctuary and the nave.

Immaculata: The unblemished one, name for the Virgin Mary.

Intarsia: Inlaid work in wood, plaster, stone etc.

Ionic order: → Order in which the columns stand on a base of two or more tiers; the → capital has two lateral → volutes.

Keep: Main tower of a castle; last refuge in time of siege.

Lantern: Small windowed turret on top of roof or dome.

Loggia: Pillared gallery, open on one or more sides; often on an upper storey.

Lunette: Semicircular panel above doors and windows, often with paintings or sculptures.

Mandorla: Almond shaped niche containing a figure of Christ enthroned.

Mannerism: Artistic style between → Renaissance and → baroque (*c*. 1530–1630). Mannerism neglects natural and classical forms in favour of an intended artificiality of manner.

Mansard: An angled roof in which the lower slope is steeper than the upper. The area gained is also called a mansard and can be used to live in. Named after the French architect F.Mansart.

Mausoleum: A splendid tomb, usually in the form of a small house or temple; from the tomb of Mausolus at Halicarnassus.

Menhir: Rough-hewn prehistoric standing stone.

Mensa: Flat surface of the altar.

Mezzanine: Intermediate storey.

Miniature: Small picture, hand illumination in old manuscripts.

Monks' choir: That section of the choir reserved for the monks, frequently closed off.

Monstrance: Ornamented receptacle in which the consecrated Host is shown (usually behind glass).

Mullion: Vertical division of a window into two or more lights.

Narthex: Vestibule of basilica or church.

Nave: Central aisle of church, intended for the congregation; excludes choir and apse.

Neo-baroque: Reaction to the cool restraint of → classicism. Re-uses baroque forms; developed in the last part of the 19C as a historicizing, sumptuous style with exaggerated three-dimensional ornamentation and conspicuous colours.

Neo-Gothic: Historicizing 19C style, which was intended to revive Gothic structural forms and decorative elements.

Net vault: Vault in which the ribs cross one another repeatedly.

Nuns' choir: Gallery from which nuns attended divine service.

Nymphaeum: Roman pleasure house, often with statues and fountains.

Obelisk: Free-standing pillar with square ground plan and pyramidal peak.

Odeum: Building, usually round, in which musical or other artistic performances were given.

Onion dome: Bulbous dome with a point, common in Russia and E.Europe; not a true dome, i.e. without a vault.

Opisthodomos: Rear section of Greek temple; behind the cella.

Orangery: Part of baroque castles and parks originally intended to shelter orange trees and other southern plants in winter. However, orangeries often had halls for large court assemblies.

Oratory: Small private chapel.

Order: Classical architectural system prescribing decorations and proportions according to one of the accepted forms: → Corinthian, → Doric, → Ionic, etc. An order consists of a column, which usually has a base, shaft and capital, and the entablature, which itself consists of architrave, frieze and cornice.

Oriel: Projecting window on an upper floor; it is often a decorative feature.

Pallium: A cloak worn by the Romans; in the Middle Ages, a coronation cloak for kings and emperors, later also for archbishops.

Pantheon: Temple dedicated to all gods; often modelled on that in Rome, which is a rotunda. Building in which distinguished people are buried or have memorials.

Paradise: → Atrium.

Pastophory: Room in an Early Christian or Byzantine church serving as a → diaconicon or → prothesis.

Pavilion: Polygonal or round building in parks or pleasure grounds. The main structure of baroque castles is very often linked by corner pavilions to the galleries branching off from the castle.

Pendentive: The means by which a circular dome is supported on a square base; concave area or spandrel between two walls and the base of a dome.

Peripteros: Greek temple in which the porticoes are connected laterally by single rows of columns.

Peristyle: Continuous colonnade surrounding a temple or open court.

Pilaster: Pier projecting from a wall; conforms to one of the → orders.

Pilaster strip: Pilaster without base and capital; feature of Anglo-Saxon and early Romanesque buildings.

Pillar: Supporting member, like a → column but with a square or polygonal cross section; does not conform to any order.

Plinth: Projecting lower part of wall or column.

Polyptych: An (altar) painting composed of several panels or wings.

Portico: Porch supported by columns and often with a pediment; may be the centre-piece of facade.

Predella: Substructure of the altar. Paintings along lower edge of large altarpiece.

Pronaos: Area in front of ancient temple (also of churches); sides enclosed and columns in front.

Propylaeum: Entrance gateway, usually to temple precincts. The Propylaeum on the Acropolis at Athens, 437–432 BC, was the model for later buildings.

Prothesis: Room used for the preparation of the Eucharist before the mass.

Prothyra: Railing before door of Roman house.

Pseudoperipteros: Temple in which porticoes are connected laterally by → pilasters and not → columns.

Putto: Figure of naked angelic child in → Renaissance, → baroque and → rococo art and architecture.

Pylon: Entrance gate of Egyptian temple; more generally used as isolated structure to mark a boundary.

Quadriga: Chariot drawn by four horses harnessed abreast.

Refectory: Dining hall of a monastery.

Régence style: French style transitional between the → baroque and the → rococo.

Relief: Carved or moulded work in which the design stands out. The different depths of relief are, in ascending order, rilievo stiacciato, bas-relief and high relief or alto-rilievo.

Reliquary: Receptacle in which a saint's relics are preserved.

Renaissance Italian art and architecture from the early 15C to the mid 16C. It marks the end of the medieval conception of the world and the beginning of a new view based on classical antiquity (Ital. rinascimento = rebirth).

Retable: Shrine-like structure above and behind the altar.

Rib vault: → Groin vault.

Rocaille: Decorative ornaments adapted from the shell motif; chiefly late → Renaissance and → Rococo.

Rococo: Style towards the end of the → baroque (1720–70); elegant, often dainty, tendency to oval forms.

Romanesque: Comprehensive name for architecture from 1000–*c.* 1300. Buildings are distinguished by round arches, calm ornament and a heavy general appearance.
Rood screen: Screen between → choir and → nave, which bears a rood or crucifix.
Rose-window: A much divided round window with rich → tracery; found especially in Gothic buildings, often above the portal.
Rotunda: Round building.
Rustication: Massive blocks of stone separated by deep joints.

Sanctuary: Area around the high altar in a church.
Sarcophagus: Stone coffin, usually richly decorated.
Secularization: Transfer of ecclesiastical possessions to secular use, especially in the Napoleonic period (1803).
Sedilia: Seats for clergy; usually in the wall of the S. side of the choir.
Sgraffito: Scratched-on decoration.
Spandrel: The triangular space between the curve of an arch, the horizontal drawn from its apex, and the vertical drawn from the point of its springing; also the area between two arches in an arcade, and that part of a vault between two adjacent ribs.
Springer: The first stone in which the curve of an arch or vault begins.
Squinch: An arch or system of arches at the internal angles of towers to form the base of a round drum or dome above a square structure. → Pendentive.
Stela: Standing block.
Strapwork: Renaissance carved work modelled on fretwork or cut leather.
Stucco: Plasterwork, made of gypsum, lime, sand and water. Used chiefly in the 17&18C for three-dimensional interior decoration.
Synagogue: Jewish place of worship.

Tabernacle: Receptacle for the consecrated host.
Tabula ansata: Frame for an inscription, with two triangles attached to the narrow sides.
Talus: Earth embankment compacted by stamping.
Tambour: Lower section, or 'drum' of a dome, usually cylindrical or polygonal.
Telamon: Support in the form of a male figure (male caryatid).
Tepidarium: Lukewarm bath in Roman bath house.
Terra sigillata: Roman crockery of the Imperial period, with distinctive red colouring.
Tesserae: Small, usually square, stones used to build up a mosaic.
Tracery: Geometrically conceived decorative stonework, particularly used to decorate windows, screens, etc. If it embellishes a wall, it is known as blind tracery.
Transenna: Screen or lattice in openwork found in early Christian churches.
Transept: That part of a church at right angles to the nave; → basilica.
Triforium: Arcaded wall passage looking on to the nave; between the arcade and the clerestory.
Triptych: Tripartite altar painting.
Triumphal arch: Free-standing gateway based on a Roman original.
Trompe l'oeil: Special kind of image which the eye is deceived into viewing as three dimensional.
Tunnel vault: Simplest vault; continuous structure with semicircular or pointed cross section uninterrupted by cross vaults.
Tympanum: The often semicircular panel contained within the lintel of a doorway and the arch above it.

Volute: Spiral scroll on an Ionic capital; smaller volutes on Composite and Corinthian capitals.

Winged altar: Triptych or polyptych with hinged, usually richly carved or painted, wings.

Important Hebrew and Arabic terms

Ayyubids: Egyptian-Syrian dynasty (1171–1263).
Almenor: Pulpit.
Aron ha-kodesh: Shrine for the Torah.
Ashkenazis: Jews from Central and Eastern Europe.
Bema: Podium in a synagogue from which the Torah (a scroll containing the Mosaic Law) is read out.
Dikkah: Podium in large mosques.
Etrog: Fragrant citrus tree which is one of the 'bunch of the four species' at the Feast of Tabernacles.
Hadas: Myrtle.
Hammam: Public bath.
Hanukka candelabrum: Lamp or candelabrum containing from one to eight candles which are lit at the Festival of Hanukka.
Khan: Caravanserai.
Kibbutz: Israeli collective farm.

Kokhim: Tombs with sliding lids; family tombs dating from the period between the 2C BC and the 2C AD.
Lag be-Omer: 33rd day of Omer, a day of celebration between Passover and the Pentecost.
Lulav: Palm branch which has given its name to the bunch made up on the Feast of Tabernacles.
Mahta: Shovel used for throwing incense on to the fire during morning and evening worship at the Temple.
Maqam: Holy place.
Menora: Candelabrum with seven arms, based on the candelabrum in the Temple at Jerusalem.
Mihrab: Niche set in the wall (of a mosque) which faces Mecca, in front of which Muslims pray. It is made to stand out by various architectural features and/or mosaics.
Minbar: High pulpit, made of stone or wood, which stands to the right of the mihrab.

Miqveh: Ritual bath.
Mishna: 'Teaching by Repetition'; a code of law arranged by subject and compiled in the 2C AD by Rabbi Juda Ha-Nassi.
Moshav: Rural settlement in Israel whose members independently farm state-owned land.
Nefesh: Column or stela by a grave which represents the dead person.
Ner Tamid: 'Eternal light'; chandelier in a synagogue.
Paskha (Passah): Passover, the Jewish festival commemorating the Exodus from Egypt.
Qibla: The direction in which Muslims must turn when praying.
Qubba: Arab sanctuary.
Sanhedrin (Synedrium): Jewish high council.

Sephardis: Jews from the Iberian peninsula and elsewhere in the Mediterranean.
Shofar: Ram's horn which is blown on New Year's Day and on the Day of Atonement.
Sohar: 'Shining light'; the book which expounds the basis of the Kabbala.
Soreq: Lattice.
Suq: Market.
Tel (Hebrew), **Tell** (Arabic): Hill on which a settlement has been established.
Thora (Tora): 'Teaching'; the five Books of Moses.
Umayyads: Dynasty established by the Caliphs of Damascus (661–750).
Wali: Family and friends of the Prophet; there are often small chapels above their tombs.

Towns with a separate entry in the text are indicated by △. Other sites are referred to the entry in which they are listed by the → symbol.

B

34° 45'

C

35°

D

1

33° 15'

⊙ Soûr

MEDITERRANEAN SEA

2

33°

Rosh HaNiqra

Han

Tel Akhziv
Gesher
HaZiv

Montf

Nahariya /
Nahariyya

Evron

Shave Ziyyon

Gi

Lohame HaGeta'ot

Akko / Acre

3

Qiryat Yam

HAIFA

Qiryat Bialik

Shefa
Shafa

Qiryat Motzkin

Qiryat Ata

Nesher

32° 45'

Tirat Karmel

Allone Abba

4

Atlit

Daliyat
HaKarmel

Isfiye

Qiryat Tiv'on

En Hod /
Ein Hawd

Bet Shearim

M

Nahal ha-Me'arot /
Wadi el-Mughara /
Valley of the Tombs

Khirbet
Summaq

Muhraqa

Yoqne'am

Kerem
Maharal

HaZorea

Dor

Mishmar
HaEmeq

Y

Megiddo

Zikhron Ya'akov

Map Key

●●● ● Town listed as a
separate entry

● ● ● ● Town listed in
environs section

Main road

Secondary road

Railway

⊕ Airport

Bet Hananya

Caesarea

Pardes
Hanna-
Karkur

Kefar Glickson

Sedot Yam

Scale 1:650,000

0   10 km

5

Barqai

Contd.
p. 320

C

Hadera

35°

D

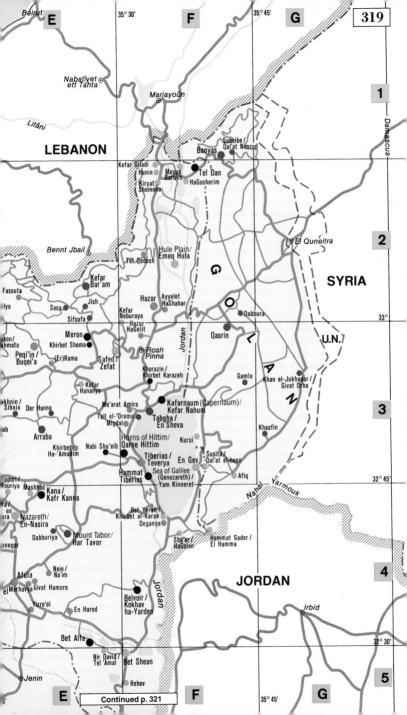

Beirut

35° 30' E   F   35° 45' G

1

Nabatîyet
ett Tahta

Marjayoûn

Litâni

Damascus

LEBANON

Banyas

Subeibe /
Qal'at Nimrud

Kefar Bilâdi

Hunin   Mayan
         Barukh   Tel Dan
Kiryat
Shemona   HaGosherim

Bennt Jbail

2

El Quneitra

Hule Plain /
Emeq Hula

Tel Qedesh

SYRIA

Fassuta

Kefar
Bar'am

Ilya

Sasa   Jish

Hazor   Ayyelet
        HaShahar

G

Kefar
Neburaya

O

Dabbura   33°

Hazor
HaGelit

L

ahmata

Meron

Khirbet Shema

Qasrin

U.N.

Peqi'in /
Buqei'a

(Er)Rama

Rosh
Pinna

A

Safed /
Zefat

Khorazin /
Khirbet Karazeh

Gamla

N

Khan el-Jukhadar /
Givat Orha

Kefar
Hananya

akhnin /
Sihnin

Der Hanna

Me'arat Amira

Kafarnaum (Capernaum) /
Kefar Nahum

ab

Arraba

Tell el-'Oreme
Migdal

Tabgha /
En Sheva

Khasfin

3

Khirbet
Ha-'Amudim

Nabi Shu'eib

Horns of Hittim /
Qarne Hittim

Kursi

ppori /
Touriya

Mashhad

Tiberias /
Teverya

En Gev

Susita /
Qal'at el-husn

fa /
sra

Kana /
Kafr Kanna

Hammat
Tiberias

Sea of Galilee
(Genezareth) /
Yam Kinneret

Afiq

32° 45'

Nazareth /
En-Nasira

Nahal Yarmouk

Dabburiya

Mount Tabor /
Har Tavor

Bet Yerah /
Khirbet al-Karak

Deganya

nnegar

Sha'ar /
HaGolan

Hammat Gader /
El Hamma

Afula

Nein /
Na'im

el Merhavya Givat Hamore

JORDAN

4

Yizre'el

En Harod

Belvoir /
Kokhav
ha-Yarden

Jordan

Irbid

Bet Alfa

32° 30'

Jenin

Nir David /
Tel 'Amal

Bet Shean

Rehov

E   Continued p. 321   F   35° 45'   G   5

Parc
Hann
Kark

Hader

5

Hefer Plain
Emeq Hefer /
Wadi el-Hawarith   Mabaro

Avihayil   Kefar Monas

Netanya

32° 15'

Ra'ananna   Kefar
Sava
Herzliyya   Qalq

Ramat
Ha Sharon

6   *MEDITERRANEAN SEA*   Tel A

Bene   Petah Tiq
Beraq

TEL AVIV –
JAFFA (YAFO)   Mi

Bat Yam

32°   Holon

Rishon le Zion   Lod /
Lydda

Nes Ziyyona   Mo

7   Ramla

Rehovot   Gezer

Yavne

Ashdod

31° 45'

Ashqelon

8

Bet Guvrin
(Bet Jibrin)

Qiryat Gat

Lachish /
Lakhish

31° 30'   Gaza

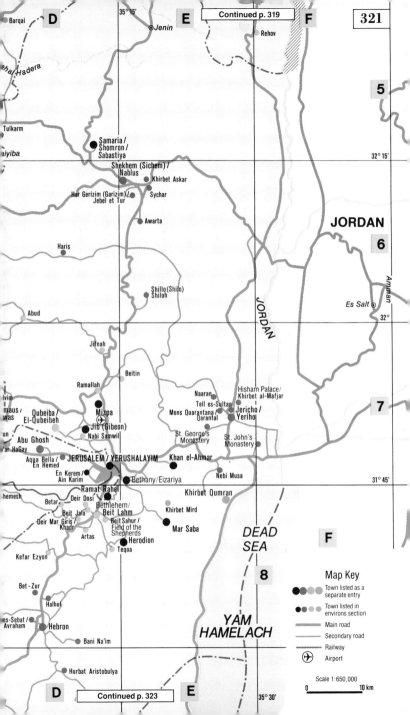

Barqai

D

35° 15'

E

Continued p. 319

F

⊙ Jenin

Rehov

5

aha/Hadera

Tulkarm

aiyiba

Samaria /
Shomron /
Sabastiya

32° 15'

Shekhem (Sichem) /
Nablus

Khirbet Askar

Har Gerizim (Garizim) /
Jebel et Tur

Sychar

JORDAN

Awarta

6

Haris

Amman

Shillo (Shilo)
Shiloh

Es Salt ⊙

Abud

32°

Jifnah

J
O
R
D
A
N

Beitin

Ramallah

7

ivim
maus /
was

Mizpa

Qubeiba /
El-Qubeibeh

Naaran

Hisham Palace /
Khirbet al-Mafjar

Jib (Gibeon)

Tell es-Sultan

Mons Quarantana /
Qarantal

Jericho /
Yeriho

un

Nabi Samwil

Abu Ghosh

ar HaGay

St. George's
Monastery

St. John's
Monastery

Aqua Bella /
En Hemed

JERUSALEM / YERUSHALAYIM

Khan el-Ahmar

En Kerem /
Ain Karim

Bethany/Eizariya

Nebi Musa

31° 45'

Ramat Rahel

hemesh

Betar

Deir Dosi

Khirbet Qumran

Beit Jala

Bethlehem /
Beit Lahm

Khirbet Mird

Deir Mar Giris /
Khadr

Beit Sahur /
Field of the
Shepherds

Mar Saba

Artas

Herodion

DEAD
SEA

F

Kefar Ezyon

Teqoa

Bet - Zur

8

Halhul

es-Sebat /
Avraham

Hebron

YAM
HAMELACH

Bani Na'im

Hurbat Aristobulya

D

Continued p. 323

E

35° 30'

Map Key

● ● ● ● ● Town listed as a
separate entry

● ● ● ● ● Town listed in
environs section

▨▨▨ Main road

Secondary road

Railway

✈ Airport

Scale 1:650,000

0   10 km

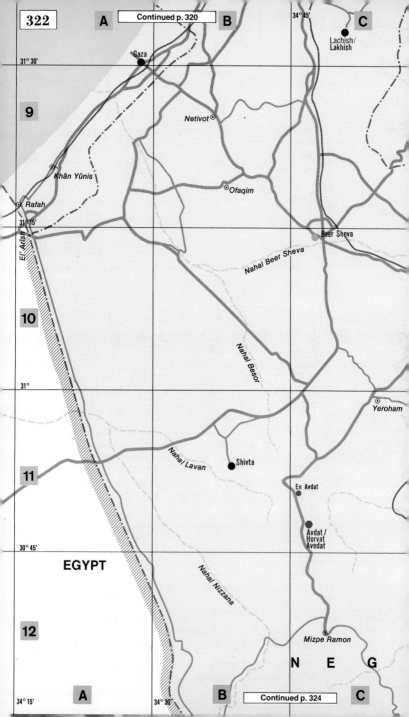

A

Continued p. 320

B

34° 45'

C

Lachish/
Lakhish

31° 30'

Gaza

9

Netivot ⊙

Khân Yûnis ⊚

Ofaqim ⊙

Rafah ⊚

31° 15'

Beer Sheva

El 'Arîsh

Nahal Beer Sheva

10

Nahal Besor

31°

Yeroham ⊙

11

Nahal Lavan

Shivta ●

En Avdat

Avdat /
Horvat
Avedat

30° 45'

EGYPT

Nahal Nizzana

12

N   E   G

Mizpe Ramon ⊚

34° 15'

A

34° 30'

B

Continued p. 324

C

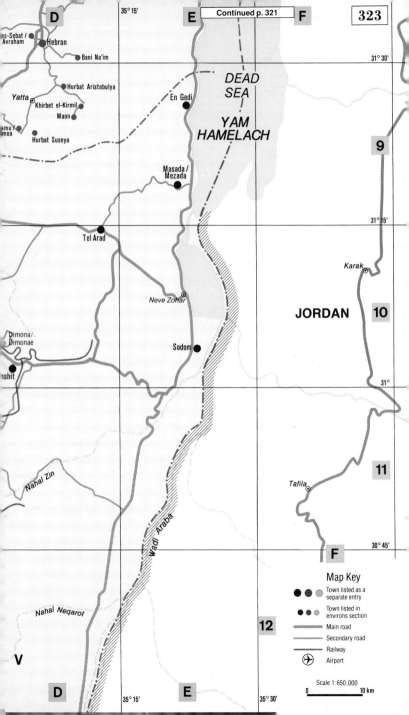

Continued p. 321

D

E

F

35° 15'

31° 30'

es-Sebat /
Avraham

Hebron

Bani Na'im

DEAD
SEA

Hurbat Aristobulya

Yatta

En Gedi

YAM
HAMELACH

Khirbet el-Kirmil

Maon

9

mu /
moa

Hurbat Suseya

31° 15'

Masada /
Mezada

Tel Arad

Karak

Neve Zohar

JORDAN

10

Dimona /
Dimonae

Sodom

31°

nshit

Nahal Zin

11

Tafila

Wadi Araba

30° 45'

F

Nahal Neqarot

12

V

Map Key

- Town listed as a separate entry
- Town listed in environs section
- Main road
- Secondary road
- Railway
- ✈ Airport

D

E

35° 15'

35° 30'

Scale 1:650,000

0   10 km

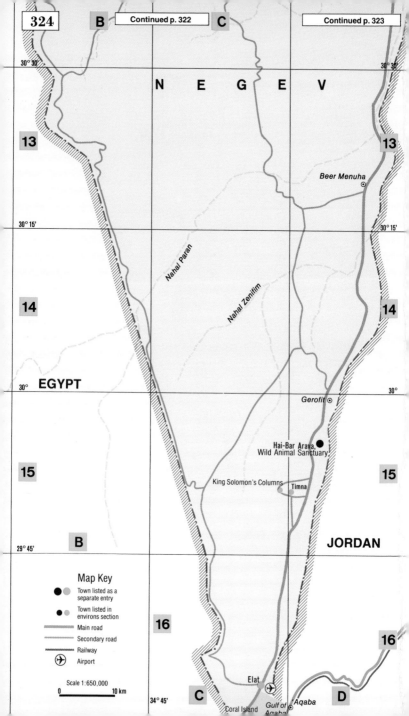

B Continued p. 322 C Continued p. 323

30° 30'
30° 30'

N E G E V

13
13

Beer Menuha ⊙

30° 15'
30° 15'

14
14

Nahal Paran

Nahal Zenifim

30° EGYPT
30°

Gerofit ⊙

15
Hai-Bar Arava ●
Wild Animal Sanctuary
15

King Solomon's Columns Timna

29° 45'
B

JORDAN

Map Key

● ● Town listed as a separate entry

• • Town listed in environs section

—— Main road

—— Secondary road

—— Railway

⊕ Airport

16
16

Scale 1:650,000
0   10 km

34° 45'
C
Elat ⊕
D
Coral Island Gulf of Aqaba
Aqaba